Modern European History

OTHER BOOKS IN THE HARPERCOLLINS COLLEGE OUTLINE SERIES

ART
History of Art 0-06-467131-3
Introduction to Art 0-06-467122-4

BUSINESS
Business Calculus 0-06-467136-4
Business Communications 0-06-467155-0
Introduction to Business 0-06-467104-6
Introduction to Management 0-06-467127-5
Introduction to Marketing 0-06-467130-5

CHEMISTRY
College Chemistry 0-06-467120-8
Organic Chemistry 0-06-467126-7

COMPUTERS
Computers and Information Processing 0-06-467176-3
Introduction to Computer Science and Programming
    0-06-467145-3
Understanding Computers 0-06-467163-1

ECONOMICS
Introduction to Economics 0-06-467113-5
Managerial Economics 0-06-467172-0

ENGLISH LANGUAGE AND LITERATURE
English Grammar 0-06-467109-7
English Literature From 1785 0-06-467150-X
English Literature To 1785 0-06-467114-3
Persuasive Writing 0-06-467175-5

FOREIGN LANGUAGE
French Grammar 0-06-467128-3
German Grammar 0-06-467159-3
Spanish Grammar 0-06-467129-1
Wheelock's Latin Grammar 0-06-467177-1
Workbook for Wheelock's Latin Grammar
    0-06-467171-2

HISTORY
Ancient History 0-06-467119-4
British History 0-06-467110-0
Modern European History 0-06-467112-7
Russian History 0-06-467117-8
20th Century United States History 0-06-467132-1
United States History From 1865 0-06-467100-3
United States History to 1877 0-06-467111-9
Western Civilization From 1500 0-06-467102-X

Western Civilization To 1500 0-06-467101-1
World History From 1500 0-06-467138-0
World History to 1648 0-06-467123-2

MATHEMATICS
Advanced Calculus 0-06-467139-9
Advanced Math for Engineers and Scientists
    0-06-467151-8
Applied Complex Variables 0-06-467152-6
Basic Mathematics 0-06-467143-7
Calculus with Analytic Geometry 0-06-467161-5
College Algebra 0-06-467140-2
Elementary Algebra 0-06-467118-6
Finite Mathematics with Calculus 0-06-467164-X
Intermediate Algebra 0-06-467137-2
Introduction to Calculus 0-06-467125-9
Introduction to Statistics 0-06-467134-8
Ordinary Differential Equations 0-06-467133-X
Precalculus Mathematics: Functions & Graphs
    0-06-467165-8
Survey of Mathematics 0-06-467135-6

MUSIC
Harmony and Voice Leading 0-06-467148-8
History of Western Music 0-06-467107-7
Introduction to Music 0-06-467108-9
Music Theory 0-06-467168-2

PHILOSOPHY
Ethics 0-06-467166-6
History of Philosophy 0-06-467142-9
Introduction to Philosophy 0-06-467124-0

POLITICAL SCIENCE
The Constitution of the United States 0-06-467105-4
Introduction to Government 0-06-467156-9

PSYCHOLOGY
Abnormal Psychology 0-06-467121-6
Child Development 0-06-467149-6
Introduction to Psychology 0-06-467103-8
Personality: Theories and Processes 0-06-467115-1
Social Psychology 0-06-467157-7

SOCIOLOGY
Introduction to Sociology 0-06-467106-2
Marriage and the Family 0-06-467147-X

Available at your local bookstore or directly from HarperCollins at 1-800-331-3761.

HARPERCOLLINS COLLEGE OUTLINE

Modern European History

John R. Barber, Ph.D.
Ball State University

 HarperPerennial
A Division of HarperCollins*Publishers*

An American BookWorks Corporation Production
Project Manager: Jonathon E. Brodman
Editor: Robert A. Weinstein

Library of Congress Cataloging-in-Publication Data

Barber, John R. 1937–
    Modern European history / John R. Barber
        p.   cm. — (HarperCollins college outline)
    Includes bibliographical references and index.
    ISBN: 0-06-467112-7
    1. Europe—History—1789–1900.   2. Europe—History—20th century.
I. Title.   II. Series.
D299.B25   1993
940.2—dc20   90-56009

98   ABW/RRD   10 9 8 7

Contents

Preface

A powerful surge of change has swept over Europe since 1985. One especially significant transformation is the replacement of the Soviet Union and its East European empire by a multitude of independent states, most of them self-governing. A rapidly accelerating movement toward European unity constitutes a less dramatic but perhaps ultimately more important alteration of life in the region.

Such upheavals indicate that these are exceptional times in Europe. The potentially far-reaching effects of trends since the mid-1980s greatly magnify the importance for students and the general public to gain an understanding of present-day circumstances in Europe. Ironically, an adequate grasp of these current conditions requires a knowledge of the region's past.

This text is meant to provide the information about European history that is most essential to students and others who need to understand Europe in the 1990s. The volume is designed for use as a core text studied in conjunction with documents, monographs, and other more narrowly focused sources. *Modern European History* also should well serve beginning students who need a short text to help them master the contents of a longer one. Advanced students who want a review of modern European events in preparation for an upper-division course or graduate-placement examination should also find this text very beneficial.

Modern European History depicts concisely the main events of the era from the 1700s to the present, emphasizing the material common to the leading texts in the field. This volume, therefore, is above all an outline history. It differs, however, from typical review texts in that it devotes somewhat more attention to often neglected topics and regions. Topically, this text highlights socioeconomic and technological history for the era during which European industry emerged and matured (mid-1700s to mid-1900s). The volume also focuses more on Scandinavia, Iberia, and the smaller states of Europe than does the usual brief history.

This text differs in another important way from most introductory histories. Books of this kind often leave the meaning of critically important words unclear. *Modern European History* does not. The vocabulary and writing style should make this volume comprehensible and pleasantly readable to people with widely differing levels of verbal ability. Chapter introductions, summaries, chronologies, and the structure provided by headings and subheadings should further increase the ease with which readers can grasp and retain this information. (An additional chronological aid is the inclusion of the life-span years for many important people and the years of monarchs' reigns, indicated by "r.")

The many students with whom I have worked during the past thirty-two years have taught me much about what and how to communicate in an introductory text. I sincerely appreciate their contribution. In the immediate task of composing this volume, however, I am most indebted to David Kamens and Robert Weinstein for their invaluable critiques of both the content and the writing.

It is a measure of Fred Grayson's and Jonathon Brodman's exceptional personal and professional traits that after two years of increasingly intense effort to produce this book, I am still glad that they were in charge of the project. Jonathon, the person with whom I worked most directly, helped so much and so often that he became a friend, although we have never met. Above all, I want to acknowledge the contribution of my dearest friends— my wife, Nan, and our children, Christie, Jeff, Brian, and Alison.

John R. Barber

1

The Age of Modern Europe, 1790s–1990s

300s A.D.	A distinctly European civilization emerges
500s	Conventional interpretations view this as the first century of the European Middle Ages
800s to 1000s	The feudal phase of the Middle Ages
1000s	Kings become more powerful than feudal nobles
	Trade revives and cities multiply after centuries with very little commerce and urbanization
1100s	The foundations of Modern European life begin to become evident during this century and after
1400s	During the middle years of this century, European kings begin about 200 years of exceptional royal power
	Insurance for commercial shipping and joint-stock companies becomes common in this era
1500s	Traditional opinion marks the end of the Middle Ages and the beginning of the Modern period of European history at this juncture
	The Europeans begin to force non-European regions under their control

*E*uropean *nations and the culturally related United States had advantages in power that gave them dominance over the globe from the 1790s to the 1990s. In a sense, therefore, these last two centuries of the second* *millennium comprise "the age of Modern Europe," a period when people in any part of the world might find themselves under the control of one or more nations of European culture.*

By the mid-1900s, all but two of these countries rapidly began to lose their military and political grip on the world, but cultural influence diminished little, if any. The decline in power, furthermore, did not mean an end to European supremacy. The Union of Soviet Socialist Republics (USSR) and the United States continued to dominate global affairs until the 1980s, despite their own hostile relationship. In the 1990s, however, the global political and military supremacy of Europe appeared to be ending.

This chapter begins with a depiction of Europe today, at the end of the second millennium. It concludes with a review of conditions within Europe during the Early Modern era, the years from about 1500 to the mid-1700s, when Europeans completed the foundations for 200 years of world power. Subsequent chapters will review the history of Europe from the end of the Early Modern period to the present, the two centuries that comprise the age of Modern Europe.

EUROPE TODAY

Europe and Asia form a single land mass ("Eurasia") that includes much of the earth's dry surface and contains the majority of its people. Eurasia extends toward the west ending in a triangle, often called the "continent" of Europe. The Ural mountains in central Russia extend south to north as the broad eastern base of the European triangle. The tip of Europe lies to the west in Spain and Portugal.

Since no oceans or other bodies of water set it apart from Asia, Europe is not technically a continent. But the way of life (culture) of the people who live west of the Ural mountains is common enough to distinguish them from those who live in eastern Russia and Asia, and so Europe is a culturally defined territory.

The Region

As a cultural region rather than a geographically distinct land, Europe has somewhat vague borders that have varied over the centuries. A traveler in late twentieth-century Europe flying west from Ufa near the Ural mountains to Lisbon in Portugal would see the vast Atlantic off Europe's west coast after a 3,000-mile trip. An east-to-west flight across the United States would be 400 to 500 miles shorter.

Transits north to south compare in a somewhat similar way. At its widest, Europe stretches about 2,000 miles from Odessa, Ukraine, on the Black Sea coast to Seroya, Norway, on the cold waters of the Barents Sea north of the

Arctic Circle. Odessa, Texas, lies about 150 miles above the southern U.S. border. An Odessa resident going north would cross the North Dakota line into Canada after a trip of about 1,400 miles. So the greatest distance north to south across the United States is about 450 miles less than for Europe.

The Topography and Climate

The Europeans have altered the surface and atmosphere of the region over the centuries, but these features probably have remained more stable than has the culturally defined outline.

PLAINS AND MOUNTAINS

A vast plain stretches from Russia across Poland, northern Germany, the Netherlands (Holland), Belgium, northern France, and the southern British Isles. Other sizable but much smaller plains sections lie in Romania, Hungary, Italy, Spain, and Portugal. Hills and mountains rise over much of southern Europe. The most imposing are the Alps, a chain that decorates parts of France, Switzerland, Italy, and Austria and which has one peak almost 16,000 feet high. Other groups of mountains frequently mentioned in European history are the Pyrenees between Spain and France, the Carpathians situated mostly in Romania, and the Apennines that stretch through central Italy.

CLIMATIC CONDITIONS

Europe generally enjoys a hospitable climate. Compared to many global regions, extremes of temperature and precipitation have not troubled the lives of Europeans.

The Mediterranean Region. Nations such as Spain and Italy with extended borders along the Mediterranean Sea have very warm, dry summers and more moisture-laden but mild winters. Snow seldom falls in these Mediterranean areas except in higher elevations.

Eastern Europe. From central Germany eastward, the climate is more humid and colder than in the Mediterranean area, with markedly lower winter temperatures in the heartland of Russia. The summers in the Russian interior, however, are as warm as those of West Europe, even though considerably shorter. This pattern means that in East Europe temperatures change more drastically with the seasons than in West Europe.

Northwestern Europe. The people of the region from central Germany westward through France and to the north of Italy and Spain seldom face cold winters, hot summers, or drought; but they also do not often bask in the sun. Clouds, fog, and gentle rains frequently enshroud them instead. (Londoners once encountered rain every day for over ten weeks.) Such conditions might not strike twentieth-century vacationers as ideal, but they have favored West European society by making it relatively easy to develop thriving modern states in the region.

GEOGRAPHY AND THE COURSE OF EVENTS IN EUROPE

The topography, climate, and other geographic traits of Europe have an important bearing on the modern history of the region. Conditions have made productive agriculture easier in much of Europe than in many other parts of the world. Similarly, European climate and topography favored the growth of commerce and industry, especially in the west. Yet geography also presented barriers to the ambitions of modern Europeans, as when Peter the Great of Russia (r. 1682–1725) began the struggle to found his country's navy without access to warm-water ports. Furthermore, at several historic moments, geography became especially important in either a harmful or helpful way, depending on the perspective of the observer. The island-influenced security of Britain from attack by Napoleon's and Hitler's forces (early 1800s and early 1940s, respectively) illustrates this latter circumstance.

The People

The borders of Europe encircled about one-sixth of the world's people, a population of about 800 million by the 1990s. All these Europeans share enough characteristics to justify speaking of Europe as a cultural region or continent, but at the same time they exhibit in certain respects a great diversity. In fact, in the Modern period the tendency of Europeans to emphasize these differences among themselves has been an important and influential historical trend.

THE STATES

Historians and social scientists apply the term "state" to a territory organized under a government that recognizes no higher political authority over it. More than fifty units of this kind form a patch-work European political map. It contains such very small pieces as the Republic of San Marino, a tiny state of less than twenty-four square miles perched in the scenic highlands of north-central Italy. Many others are relatively little, but the borders of Russia encompass enough of the earth's land surface (about one-eighth) to make it one of the largest countries in the world.

The Most Noted Countries. More than size determines which states attract the most attention from observers of Europe, even though several of the nations that gain such notice are the larger ones. The list of most prominent states includes France, Germany, Italy, Russia, and the United Kingdom (Britain).

Other Prominent States. Both the most noted countries and others that are very prominent receive special attention in part because of the effects of their more urban-industrial socioeconomic order. Other "developed" states in addition to the five mentioned above are countries such as Austria, Belgium, Czechoslovakia (Czech lands and Slovakia divided in 1992), Denmark, the Netherlands, Norway, Sweden, Switzerland, and Ukraine.

Although less industrialized, several other countries often highlighted in accounts of recent events are Greece, Hungary, Ireland, Poland, Portugal, Romania, and Spain.

States in Flux. The political map of Europe has been unusually fluid recently. Within three years after the collapse of the East European Communist governments during the autumn of 1989, East and West Germany reunited, the USSR divided into fifteen states, Yugoslavia began to fragment under the clouds of civil war, and Slovakia voted to separate from the Czech lands. Other states, including several of the new ones, show signs of splintering along ethnic lines. Since the mid-1980s, there also has been a countertrend toward greater unity among states, a development noticeable above all among the twelve West European members of the European Community. (See chapter 18.)

EUROPEAN CULTURES

The people in these numerous European states have certain ways and traits (cultural characteristics) that especially distinguish them. Most inhabitants of this continent, for example, speak an Indo-European language and live in societies in which Christianity has long been the dominant religion. Machine technology also pervades life in much of Europe to a greater extent than in other regions. Despite these and other common bonds, the multiplicity of states suggests the numerous subgroup identities typical of the continent.

Ethnic Divisions. When aspects of culture such as language, religion, rituals, and clothing and adornment identify a collection of people, they comprise an ethnic group. Such cultural circumstances tend to encourage divisions within Europe. Although most Europeans speak a language that falls within the larger Indo-European linguistic family, the languages within that group vary considerably. English and Russian, for example, differ greatly. Furthermore, certain of the languages such as Hungarian belong to language families other than Indo-European. Similarly, the predominant Christian religion exhibits subdivisions, and sizable numbers of people adhere to other faiths, such as Judaism. The people within ethnic groups have much more in common than do Europeans as a whole and, therefore, tend to have a greater sense of identity. These ethnic divisions exist within all European states and are especially evident in several, such as Belgium and Switzerland. Even though diverse cultural groups exist today within various countries, by the late 1800s it became especially typical of Europeans to organize states based on ethnic identity.

Nations and the Nation-State. Nations are ethnic groups that have become acutely aware of their identity. They usually are also relatively large cultural groups and make up a high percentage of the people within a territory. When an ethnic group of this kind organizes as a sovereign political unit, it becomes a nation-state. Europeans invented this kind of state early in their history, and made it characteristic of their cultural region during the last two centuries. Nationalism, a strongly held system of beliefs about the nation, also gripped Europe by this time. This commitment of Europeans to the nation-state strongly influences the unity and power of their countries, increasing or decreasing the cohesion and strength within each one depending on the presence or absence of alienated ethnic minorities. Throughout the twentieth century, devotion to the nation-state principle has affected even more drastically the relations *among* countries both at the European and global levels.

EARLY MODERN EUROPEAN GOVERNMENT

Among themselves and in their relations with other peoples, the Europeans for the past 200 years have made three traits especially evident—their genius in machine technology, military strength, and governing prowess. The formation of these characteristics began long before the centuries of European supremacy. From about the twelfth century onward, the Europeans took noticeably different directions than had their predecessors in the era of the 300s to 1100s A.D. They changed in government, economy, social relationships, and outlook so much by the 1500s that historians generally consider that century to be the first of the Modern period. But a few of the most important traits implied by the term "modern" did not appear until the latter 1700s. The era from 1500 to the mid-1700s, therefore, often is called "*Early* Modern." In this period the governmental machinery that helped empower Europeans matured.

The Emergence of the Centralized State

During much of the European Middle Ages (traditionally dated 500–1500 A.D.), central government remained weak, at times almost nonexistent. Countries did not always even have clearly defined borders in the feudal phase of the Middle Ages (late 800s to 1000s). Gradually, rulers with titles such as king or emperor gained authority within their relatively large territories and exercised supremacy over local figures, many of whom were descendants of the feudal military nobility. The kings of Spain, France, and England reached exceptional levels of power during the years from the mid-1400s to mid-1600s.

THE BASES OF STATE POWER IN THE KINGDOM OF FRANCE

The French state under Louis XIV (r. 1643–1715) illustrates the institutions and practices that intensified the strength of European governments. Louis built a huge and lavish palace at Versailles near Paris and used it to awe French nobles and foreign rulers. He worked energetically as the leader of an increasingly professional group of governing officials, the bureaucracy, to extend his control over the affairs of the French state. The wide-ranging jurisdiction of royal courts, built up over many generations, and the expansive authority of the king to tax proved his strength and added to it. Above all, the monarch could demonstrate his power with his large military force. He had a massive and permanently organized army and navy. Rulers in the Middle Ages had used small temporary collections of troops.

WAR AND EMPIRE BUILDING

Louis XIV and the other Early Modern European rulers kept their military forces busy. They used them against threats to their rule within their kingdoms or in sometimes vicious and extended wars of rivalry with other monarchs of Europe. Beginning in the late 1400s, several of these countries also ventured beyond Europe. They seized lands around the fringes of Africa, in portions of India, and then throughout the Americas. The troop strength and political organization typical of these European states made effective resistance by those they attacked very difficult. The military technology of the gun-wielding Europeans made their conquests virtually impossible to stop. By the 1600s Europeans thus dominated large portions of the globe.

Mercantilism

Rulers who were engaged in building central authority, fighting rival European states, and taking colonies had to devote special attention to the economy of their government and country. Under these circumstances, a typical pattern of attitudes and policies emerged. Many government leaders in the 1500s and 1600s believed that the amount of trade possible for Europeans had fixed limits. They assumed also that the power of their country depended on trade-produced wealth, especially in the form of precious metals. European rulers wanted to surpass rival governments in wealth and power, which meant that they must win control of more of the markets for trade.

Government involvement in economic development made great sense for people with such attitudes. Governments thus tried to lessen tax barriers to trade inside their countries and erect tax blocks to commerce from the outside. They improved roads and waterways and set up industries and trading companies. In general, that is, these commercially oriented governments tried to spur trade with the intention of enriching the state and increasing its power. Later observers named these attitudes and practices "mercantilism," a policy characteristic of this era, and one that helped cause trade expansion to hold an especially important place in Early Modern economic growth.

EARLY MODERN EUROPEAN ECONOMY AND SOCIETY

The Europeans made their power felt over much of the world by the 1700s. Their highly effective political and military organization, productive economies, advanced technology, and social unity enabled these states to extend European control into other regions. By the dawn of the age of Modern Europe in the 1700s, economic developments became central to the transformation that gave Europeans globe-controlling power, a transformation usually called "modernization."

Agriculture

Few Europeans in the Early Modern period lived and worked in ways now viewed as "modern." Almost everyone survived on the fruits of farm labor, as they had since European society emerged in the 300s to 400s A.D. The workers who tended the fields of Europe from about 1500 to 1800 plowed with animal-drawn equipment, but did almost everything else with simple tools or with just their hands.

Typically, peasants of each rural village labored in teams on schedules set by the sun, weather, and tradition. They worked under the dictates of nature and community. Through much of the Early Modern era, European agricultural laborers thus supplied almost all of their own needs and, to a great extent, also supported the non-farm workers and the nonlaborers of their locale. In most respects, then, peasant agricultural life continued as it had for generations.

The Peasants

England, the most urban European country, was about four-fifths rural in the late 1700s. Across Europe at that time, farming peasants made up two-thirds or more of the population of the rural areas. They lived in villages that rarely included more than 500 people and had little contact with the world beyond their settlements. A relatively small number of people who did not do farm work resided in these settlements too. The latter included mainly artisans, who were craft workers producing tools, utensils, and other articles that required special skills. Nonlaborers who served other community needs—a priest, for example—also lived in many agricultural villages.

PEASANT SOCIAL STRUCTURE

A portion of the peasants near the bottom of rural society worked for other people and had no land of their own. People with small amounts of land stood above them, and still higher in the social order were the few with comparatively large holdings.

ADULTHOOD AND MARRIAGE

Adulthood came late for peasants in this era because poor nutrition delayed sexual maturity. About two-thirds of the peasantry married and enjoyed adult independence once they reached reproductive age. The one-third or more who remained single held a very inferior position in society. These unmarrieds included males who inherited no land, females too poor to provide an enticing dowry, or people (usually women) rejected for marriage because of appearance.

The Aristocrats

The Early Modern European aristocracy enjoyed special legal privileges and exercised power over their society even though they comprised only one to two percent of the population.

ARISTOCRATIC PRIVILEGES

Aristocrats enjoyed many exclusive rights. These nobles usually depended on agriculture to supply their needs, as did the peasants, but very few members of the aristocracy farmed or worked physically in any way. In most places, they alone could arm themselves with swords or hunt for game. Legal disputes among aristocrats brought them into their own noble courts, but the aristocracy ordinarily conducted the trials of peasants.

THE RULING POWER OF THE ARISTOCRACY

Nobles exercised control not only through the courts but also as leaders in government, the churches, and the military. Aristocrats sometimes held their top social position as descendants of the feudal nobility. Others gained the distinction by government service in Early Modern times. Most nobles exercised authority at the local level. They all tended to oppose strong central government. But from the 1000s onward, aristocrats gradually lost authority as kings increased central political power, especially in West Europe. By the 1700s, the nobility faced still more serious challenges. Aristocratic supremacy came to an end during the 1800s and early 1900s.

Business

Money-making business became one of the important forces that eventually ended aristocratic power. The nobles' leadership depended especially on their place in an agricultural economy that shunned change. A more innovative and expansive economic system developed from the influence of trends that began as early as the 1000s but especially from changes after the mid-1600s. Aristocratic supremacy would last many more generations, but signs of a new economic climate that eventually favored other social groups became increasingly clear in the century before the 1750s.

NEW FINANCIAL PROCEDURES

The emergence of modern business required many changes in economic operations. Credit letters and other such banking devices to pay debts, although used for centuries, took on a more advanced form and became more widespread in Early Modern times. These banking instruments made the exchange of money more efficient and safe. Merchants could not so easily reduce the risks involved in the transport of goods, but insurance for shipping ventures became common by the 1400s and provided the necessary protection.

Reduced chances for business losses also resulted from the practice of shared investment, an arrangement achieved through joint-stock companies. Europeans first established such companies on a significant scale in the 1500s. These investor groups also served another important purpose. They made possible the accumulation of much larger sums of money for business operations on a grander scale. The circumstances of the period virtually demanded these different business practices.

THE PRICE REVOLUTION

In the 1500s a price rise greater than Europe had ever experienced strongly influenced the changes that produced the new economic climate of the late 1600s and early 1700s. Annual inflation rates of three percent, extreme for that era, drastically elevated prices, especially for bread, the mainstay of almost everyone's diet. A sudden surge in population since the mid-1400s and the flow of precious metal wealth into Europe from the newly discovered Americas probably caused this price revolution.

FARMING FOR MONEY

The great inflation prompted action by a portion of the farmers who saw a chance for huge profits. Landowners in northwestern Europe and England led all others in the expenditure of energy and funds on farming innovations such as crop rotation and animal breeding. They sometimes reaped tremendous returns on such investments.

Because these ventures required the alteration of very old and widely revered rural customs, the changes did not come quickly or over a wide area. Much of Europe experienced almost no alteration in its agricultural ways until the mid-1700s. But during the 100 years before that, a few rural nobles had begun commercial agricultural practices that foreshadowed a modern economic world which aristocrats would not control.

TRADE

The unusual climb in population and prices stimulated trade as well as commercial farming. The booming demand for food and other goods meant that the merchants who transported and sold these products had the opportunity for exceptional profits, just as the farmers did. Early Modern governments often promoted the expansion of trade in the belief that the inflow of wealth from commerce heightened state power. With growing bureaucracies, armies, and navies, these governments also spent heavily. In many ways, therefore, government helped drive trade forward. Population, prices, and governmental action also affected industry.

MANUFACTURING

To manufacture literally means "make by hand." Most Early Modern European industry still depended on human or animal effort instead of the less frequently applied wind or water power. Furthermore, new processes and devices seldom appeared during this era. In these respects manufacturing showed no signs of a coming "modern age." But certain important changes did take place.

Luxury Industry Improvements. Many workers in these years produced luxury items. With increasing skill, craft workers made furniture and products of silk, lace, china, and glass in a style to suit the tastes and pocketbooks of the rich. These luxury industries appeared in new regions and exhibited an increasing tendency to operate in the capitalist spirit of profit making and growth.

The Cottage System of Production. Much of the manufacturing in Early Modern Europe took place in the cottages of workers. Merchants delivered raw materials, perhaps wool or some other fiber, and later picked up finished products, such as cloth. This "putting-out" or "cottage" system of production enabled merchants to evade the rigid craft organization controls on production in the towns. At the same time, it indicated a further movement away from the much more thoroughly agricultural socio-economic order of pre-Modern Europe. The laboring population was slowly shifting from farming to manufacturing.

A Changing Work Ethic. Hard necessity led agricultural peasants to burden their children with farm work throughout European history. In the 1500s and 1600s, families that engaged in cottage manufacturing usually included their children in the work because they needed everyone to produce income. As the Early Modern period drew to a close, the leaders of European society for the first time spread the message that hard labor was not only necessary for children but *benefited* them. This changed ethic foreshadowed new times.

Secularism

The changing attitude of businesspeople was part of a more general transformation of outlook associated with modernization. Educated Europeans in the Middle Ages, most of whom belonged to the Catholic clergy, had a very religious worldview. They urged everyone to devote their lives to the fulfillment of God's will as revealed by the church. These intellectuals contended, furthermore, that people could gain an understanding of the conditions, forces, and occurrences of the natural world only by turning to God.

By the 1200s, a few prominent intellectuals argued that humanity could discover the truth about the makeup and operation of the earthly environment by scientific means. They insisted, that is, on explaining the world around them by careful observation and a systematic study of facts. This tendency to view life in a secular rather than a spiritual way strengthened during the late Middle Ages and after. By the 1500s and 1600s, most leading scientists had accepted this modern view of nature.

Intellectuals in the late 1600s and 1700s began to contend that human affairs could also be studied and understood scientifically. Religion remained important to Europeans in the 1700s and after. But following this Early Modern era transition to secularism among intellectuals, the masses too turned away more and more from a religious approach to life.

Urban Life

Urban Europe exerted a powerful influence on the change to modern ways. Beginning around 1000, trade and cities revived rapidly, after a long period in which commerce and town life diminished to very low levels. The settlements that sprang up and grew with a surge in this period differed from those in ancient times; commercial people dominated these towns instead of the landowning nobles who set the tone of life in ancient population centers.

THE CITIES

The many new cities organized by Europeans after 1000 and the older towns that revived and grew before 1500 usually contained closely packed commercial, religious, administrative, and residential structures with a security wall surrounding all. The necessity of a fortified urban border placed a premium on space. Thus the buildings stood close along narrow streets with upper floors jutting out over lower ones. This arrangement darkened the cities, but they still blossomed as socioeconomic centers through much of the Middle Ages.

The establishment of new cities occurred much less frequently by the 1500s than in the previous five centuries. But they grew more rapidly in size, creating or adding to the ring of dwellings (the suburb) gathered around the older urban center. By the 1600s, these trends gave Europe an urban population that varied from somewhat less than five percent in some areas to just over ten percent in others. Urbanization before the mid-1700s also spawned a few large cities, with London, for example, growing to about three-fourths of a million.

THE BOURGEOISIE

The commercial populations that reigned supreme in the cities of the Middle Ages and Early Modern period comprised a "middle class" between the aristocrats and peasants. In addition to their description as a middle class, these city dwellers acquired labels derived from the words for "town" in the various languages. People knew them in Germany as burghers, in England as burgesses, and in France and eventually everywhere as the bourgeoisie. Accounts of life in Early Modern Europe apply the term "bourgeoisie" to merchants, bankers, lawyers, doctors, skilled craft workers, and various urban residents of similar status. Servants, unskilled laborers, and others also lived in cities but did not belong to the middle class. The word "bourgeoisie" does not refer to these unskilled urban workers.

The Bourgeois Hierarchy. With their widely different occupations and incomes, middle-class people formed a hierarchy, a pyramidlike social structure. The few with the most prestige and wealth held the upper positions, places that rich merchants or lawyers, for example, might achieve. They tended to imitate the aristocracy's life-style and sometimes became titled nobles. People such as artisans filled the more numerous lower ranks of the bourgeoisie.

Middle-Class Attitudes. The acceptance of hierarchy and longing for aristocratic titles indicate that bourgeois attitudes in certain ways differed little from the outlook of others in the Middle Ages and Early Modern period. The middle class distinguished itself, however, by its powerful devotion to work. This trait set the bourgeois apart from the typical aristocrat who avoided labor and from the working poor who honored their work less. The particular labor that the middle classes loved marked them as unique too. Unlike most aristocrats and farm workers, the life of the bourgeoisie centered on moneymaking enterprise rather than the land. Their attitudes and activities, therefore, contrasted with those of the social leaders and working masses of the Middle Ages and Early Modern era.

The Influence of the Commercial Classes. The business-minded bourgeoisie remained a minority in numbers and influence before the Modern period. Even in pre-Modern times, however, they strongly affected society and influenced the movement toward a very different way of life. In the mid-1700s, the European bourgeoisie stood on the threshold of a modern world that they would come to dominate during the next century.

Trends that began in the Middle Ages and became especially evident after 1500 not only brought the bourgeoisie into power after 1750 but also changed the overall nature of European life. These tendencies of the years before 1750 also carried Europeans to world supremacy in the Modern era. In short, before 1750, Europeans began an internal transformation that also affected the world structure of power. The term "modernization" summarizes this process of change that occurred before the 1750s.

This modernization of Europe entailed changes in the structure, attitudes, and material culture of society. The modern direction in social organization involved a shift from the dominance of local structures (such as family, clan, or tribe) over government, economy, and culture to the centralization of power over these aspects of life.

One change in outlook especially associated with becoming modern was increased secularism, at least in the sense of a subordination of religion to or a separation of religion from government and economy. A closely associated transformation of attitudes was the turn away from reverence for tradition toward a glorification of change, particularly in technology.

This favorable attitude toward new products has strong links to the transition in material culture that is the essence of modernization—the application of inanimate power to the machines of production, transportation, and communication. This technological change had weaker force than the other new trends before the 1750s, but Europeans devised new machines rapidly beginning in the 1760s.

The drive for business profits provided much of the force behind modernization. Bourgeois groups led this enterprising movement and soon reaped rewards in wealth. Later they would achieve benefits in power. Middle-class commercial activity, as well as the other behaviors and developments associated with modernization, grew with and also stimulated city life.

This process of modernization first occurred in Europe with origins especially apparent in the social and economic history of the years after 1000 A.D. European modernity originated as an undercurrent in the Middle Ages, gained strength and breadth in the Early Modern period, and achieved full force after the 1750s. Parts of Europe became socially and economically modern during the industrial revolution that occurred between the 1760s and 1850s. In these years, northwestern Europeans began on a significant scale to produce goods and move materials and passengers with machines driven by inanimate power. The age of Modern Europe thus began with the emergence of this industrial revolution.

**Selected
Readings**

Cipolla, Carlo M. *Before the Industrial Revolution: European Society and Economy, 1000–1700.* 2nd ed. New York: W. W. Norton and Company, 1980.

Hay, Denys. *Europe: The Emergence of an Idea.* New York: Harper & Row, 1966.

Jordan, Terry G. *The European Culture Area: A Systematic Geography.* New York: Harper & Row, 1973.

Koenigsberger, H. G., and Asa Briggs. *Early Modern Europe, 1500–1789.* New York: Longman, 1987.

Stettner, Edward A., ed. *Perspectives on Europe.* Cambridge, MA: Schenkman Publishing Company, Inc., 1970.

2

The Industrial Revolution, 1760s–1850

1712 Thomas Newcomen builds the first modern steam-powered pumping engine

1717 One of the first true factories begins operation

1721 The first Newcomen pump in Belgium is placed in service

1733 John Kay devises the flying shuttle for cloth-weaving

1764 James Hargreaves produces the spinning jenny for rapid hand-operated thread manufacturing

1767 Richard Reynolds builds the first cast-iron railway

1768 Richard Arkwright devises the water frame for powered thread production

1769 James Watt patents an improved version of the steam engine

1779 Samuel Compton constructs his spinning mule

1793 Eli Whitney develops the cotton gin

1784 Henry Cort patents an improved iron-processing method described as "puddling"

1807 Robert Fulton's steamboat, the *Clermont*, first plies river waters in the United States

1825 The British Parliament legalizes the incorporation of businesses

1829 George Stephenson's *Rocket*, a steam locomotive for railroads, completes a successful trial

1834 The *Zollverein*, a customs union under Prussian leadership, is formed among several German states

1844 In the United States, the first telegraph message is sent over a line between Baltimore and Washington, D.C.

1856 Henry Bessemer improves steel processing

A number of the new technological, economic, and social changes that remained subordinant in Early Modern Europe became very prominent and drastic in effect in England and northwestern Europe between 1760 and 1850. As a result, people of that time and since have described this occurrence as an "industrial revolution."

Many of the technological instruments fashioned during this industrial revolution differed from the machines of the previous era in that inanimate power drove them. This transition from a predominantly human- and animal-powered agricultural life to an economy of machine production was an outstanding trait of the industrial revolution. A multitude of sometimes hulking and noisy inventions thus appeared as typical elements of the new economic order.

The economic revolution became evident in many other striking ways. Commercial innovators in this era for the first time in history established factories. This system of productive organization dramatically increased the manufacturing capability of societies that used it. The tendency toward new thinking about economic methods and organization led not only to a restructuring of production but also to similarly sweeping changes in systems of finance.

Europeans made this industrial transformation even more complete by the application of their new technology to the means of transportation and communication. Steamboats began to stir through the waters of Europe in the early 1800s. In the same period, railroads began to mark the surfaces of the lands dominated by the machine-driven Europeans. In the 1840s, they began to stretch wires and cables across terrain and under water so that they could flash messages around their European realm at electric speed.

The business revolutionaries of England led the way to a new economic order throughout the late 1700s and the first half of the 1800s, but Belgium, France, and the German states joined the march to modernity before 1850. East Europe and Russia by that time had scarcely taken the first steps in that direction.

In the areas that the revolution began to transform, smoke-enshrouded cities grew to sizes that were huge by all previous standards. Industrialists and other members of the business-oriented middle classes rose rapidly in wealth and influence in this emerging urban world. At the same time, the

numbers of factory workers increased at a faster rate than any group and began the transformation of the working class.

These wide-ranging and swift changes heightened the differences between the economy of Modern Europe and that of earlier European society. The revolution in economic and social life also increased the contrast between Europe and other world regions during the years after 1760. With this new technology and economy, Europe could gather the materials and fashion the devices to ensure their global supremacy until the end of the millennium. The age of Modern Europe had begun.

THE POPULATION EXPLOSION

Humans have distinguished themselves among living creatures in part by a phenomenal growth in their numbers throughout history. Despite periods during which no multiplication occurred or the numbers even declined, this increase in population ordinarily has continued at varying rates around the world. Europe, however, experienced especially high levels of growth from the latter 900s to the early 1900s, compared to other regions and its own earlier history. An explosive advancement in numbers that began in the mid-1700s helped to foment the industrial revolution. The new economy then boosted the population growth rate still further for several decades.

Population of Europe, 1760 to 1850

Europeans probably numbered fewer than fifty million in 1000 A.D. It took almost 650 years for this population to increase to 100 million. Then, in only 100 years (1650–1750), Europe grew by another fifty million. In the following century, the first of the industrial era, Europeans multiplied to an additional 100 million. This surge from 150 to 250 million between the mid-1700s and the mid-1800s was a remarkably fast increase.

CAUSES FOR THE INCREASE

The population explosion that began in the 1750s might have resulted from an increasing birth rate, a declining death rate, or the combined effect of both trends. Expert opinion on the reasons for the pattern remain in conflict.

EFFECTS OF THE POPULATION EXPLOSION

An industrial revolution requires a rapid expansion of the labor supply and the market for goods. The sudden leap in European population provided the workers and buyers necessary for the new economy. At the same time, the surge in numbers changed the age-group proportions. Europe became younger with many more children, youths, and young adults. This development expanded the market for the goods needed by this segment of society. The sudden increase in numbers of people and the enlarged percentage of youths spawned problems as well as benefits for European society. The older generation could not, for example, expand and adjust educational facilities and practices rapidly enough to meet the needs of this changing population. Other institutions experienced similar strains.

THE MODERNIZATION OF AGRICULTURE

Europe's population surge could have caused famine. A revolutionary improvement in agriculture prevented this consequence, however, and also contributed to the preparation of Europe for industrialization. The agricultural modernization that brought these benefits involved changes in farming methods, in the organization of the agricultural economy, and in the devices used to exploit the land.

New Farming Methods

The Early Modern turn toward commercial agriculture became even sharper after the mid-1700s as growing populations raised the demand for farm products and increased the opportunities for profit. The circumstances encouraged much greater expenditures of money to increase yields. These conditions also spurred farmers to find ways to use their land more efficiently. Agricultural entrepreneurs in the Netherlands and England in particular took such modernizing steps.

NEW DEVELOPMENTS IN CROPPING

Europeans before this period overcame the depletion of soil that resulted from cropping by allowing a portion of their land to lie fallow (unused). Farmers in the Netherlands by the 1700s made more efficient use of their fields by rotating crops. After harvesting grains that reduced soil nutrients, they planted crops such as clover that increased the fertility of the land.

Charles Townsend and Thomas Coke. Two Englishmen thereafter enhanced rotation practices. Charles Townsend (1725–1767) popularized the practice of sowing turnips as the restorative crop. Turnips both replenished the fields and added the soil-loosening effects of a large root plant. Thomas Coke further improved the method by a four-crop rotation plan that multiplied the productivity of his land about 1,000 percent.

New Crops. Tomatoes, potatoes, and sugar beets grew in Europe for the first time beginning in the Modern era. The first two of these foods improved the vitamin content and increased the calorie level of the Europeans' diets. Sugar beets provided the sweets that they had come to crave since the opening of the New World and ended their dependence on sugar cane imported from the Americas. In 1784, Arthur Young published a journal, *Annals for Agriculture*, that increased the probability that a widening circle of farmers would learn of these new farm practices and crops and thereby raise the productivity of their land.

IMPROVEMENTS IN THE USE AND BREEDING OF STOCK

Certain of the crops introduced for rotation served as valuable food for farm stock. Farmers could plant crops on more of the land as they used less for pastures to feed the animals. Enclosing the stock in pens or stalls increased the supply of manure and thus also provided more fertilizer for the croplands. At the same time that these changes in stock use raised the yields of the fields, more advanced breeding practices improved the quality and increased the supply of meat.

New Means of Land Organization

European farmers during the Middle Ages organized their land in various "open field" patterns. They divided the village crop area into strips with each farmer's share scattered among everyone else's. Cattle grazed over common pastures, and villagers similarly shared other resources, such as the use of the woods. These traditions presented problems to the commercially inclined modern farmers. The strip division system stood in the way of new rotation and field preparation methods. Unfenced common pastures made controlled animal breeding impossible. Thus innovations in cropping, cultivation methods, and stock breeding required new approaches to land organization.

THE ENGLISH ENCLOSURE MOVEMENT

A movement by landlords to take land from tenants and enclose it, usually for commercial sheep farming, began in England more than 200 years before the industrial revolution. The more rapid conversion to a capitalist form of agriculture after the mid-1700s sped this shift away from the open-field system. Within less than fifty years, agricultural entrepreneurs enclosed more than two million acres of farmland along with additional previously uncultivated common plots.

THE CONSEQUENCES OF REORGANIZATION

The landlords and the more well-to-do tenants who had the means to adopt the new farm methods, the wealth to purchase land, and, the influence to arrange enclosures reaped the rewards of the agricultural revolution in England. This change, furthermore, expanded the yields of the English countryside; it also brought into the cities many former small-time farmers who lost their plots. The food and work force for industrialization thus became more readily available. Many displaced tenants, however, suffered extreme hardship from this reorganization of the farm economy. A part of society realized profits from the emergence of modern commercial agriculture, but another segment paid a price.

New Implements

The machinery for farming changed along with cropping methods and land organization. New equipment for field preparation and harvesting increased productivity, thus magnifying the effects of rotation and the use of new plants. This increasingly mechanized agriculture, moreover, was well suited to the arrangement of fields on enclosed farms. The compatibility of these changes ensured the multiplication of machines on the rural landscape, a clear sign of the industrial times.

THE BRITISH INDUSTRIAL REVOLUTION

The industrial revolution from the 1760s to the 1850s mainly took place in portions of the British Isles (comprising England, Scotland, Wales, and Ireland). The quick advancement of the British into the agricultural revolution provided part of the momentum for the broader process of change to an industrial economy in Britain. From the countryside there came part of the supply of material and laborers vital to a more far-reaching modernization. Several other circumstances made it possible for Britain to industrialize before any other country.

Population Growth and the Labor Supply

Another trend of the times expanded the number of potential workers in the nation. The population explosion in England, Scotland, and Wales increased the total of inhabitants from about 8 million to more than 25 million in the ninety years after 1760. This multiplication of people added to the forces that enabled Britain to rush into the industrial revolution ahead of all other nations.

Geographic Advantages

For the early industrial giants to rise, they had to have an abundance of coal and iron. Relatively large and accessible stores of both raw materials were available to industry in several parts of Britain. New enterprises sprang to life especially in these areas or at points where industrialists could profitably move iron and coal by canal, river, or sea transport. The island geography that facilitated the shipping of these and other raw materials also gave the British an edge in the distribution of manufactured goods.

Favorable Sociopolitical Conditions

Early Modern European governments did much to drive and guide economic developments as the region turned toward industrialization. The British political system of the latter 1700s affected the change to a modern economy in a somewhat different way. Since the government did not establish legal monopolies or taxes on domestic trade, people who turned to the new business pursuits encountered relatively few obstacles to their ambitions. At the same time, tariffs on certain goods from abroad presented barriers to potential foreign competitors; they thus gave English business advantages by both freeing and restraining enterprise. English society in these years also prized inventiveness and opened the way to the social advancement of successful industrialists. Such attitudes and conditions further encouraged a transformation of the economy.

Markets and Capital

Another attitude helped to turn the British toward economic revolution. An urge to buy grew in the part of this society made increasingly rich by the fortunes of commercial agriculture and the wealth extracted from colonies and trade. This mood created market conditions that enticed producers. Other factors also affected demand. The population boom of the latter 1700s influenced industrialization not only by its enlargement of the labor force, but also by expansion of the market for goods. The rising wealth of the English had a dual effect as well. It both increased the market for products and provided capital for industrial expansion. England's rapidly expanding banking system yielded additional investment funds.

THE MACHINES OF INDUSTRY

Tools, machines . . . the multitude of contraptions by which people magnify their power to build, produce, travel, communicate, and carry on all the other activities that strike their fancy: such implements abound among modern Europeans. Even more than their tendency to multiply as a species, this mechanical bent sets humans apart from the other inhabitants of the planet. Most societies in Europe and North America have carried this tendency to an extreme. They are more machine-driven than any in previous history.

In Europe, devices powered by animals, water, or wind served the needs and whims of people for many generations before the 1700s. With industrialization, people in Europe turned increasingly to machines that operated with the special force of energy sources such as steam. When Europeans brought these inventions into their lives, they unleashed a revolution of awesome proportions; they unwittingly manufactured the instruments for global supremacy. Inventors in several nations on both sides of the Atlantic Ocean fashioned these machines of the industrial revolution, even though the technological transformation during the first industrial decades centered on Britain.

Coal and Iron—Raw Materials of the Machine Age

The use of coal and iron began long before the industrial revolution. At the dawn of the Modern age, however, these minerals became much more important factors in the economy. Europeans turned increasingly to coal as the source for heat to warm structures, produce glass and metals, and drive the engines of industry. A worsening shortage of wood in the 1600s had encouraged this change, but the advantages of coal in industrial applications sped the transition still more.

IRON-PROCESSING IMPROVEMENTS

One of the special values of coal was its usefulness in iron production. Coke, which is coal in a heat-altered form, enabled Abraham Darby to smelt iron in a way that greatly improved its quality. This processing advancement in the first decade of the 1700s soon led growing numbers of builders to erect structures of iron. In the latter 1700s, Englishman Henry Cort found a way to make even higher quality iron, an advancement important to the production of machines for a factory age. He began with a furnace of French design and added the idea of stirring or "puddling" the melted iron in order to speed the processing and yield purer metal. The puddling process heightened the demand for iron and thus also for coal.

ADVANCEMENTS IN MINE-PUMPING DEVICES

The greater need for coal throughout the 1700s drove miners deeper underground and into wetter strata. Although vacuum and steam pressure pumps had served to keep underground workers' heads above water during the 1600s, the mines of the next century required more advanced machines. The technology of early German, French, and English pressure pumps, one of which involved a piston-cylinder interaction, provided the fundamentals for a pump of improved design first constructed in England in the early 1700s. Thomas Newcomen and an associate devised a machine in which steam from a boiler forced a piston through a cylinder in one direction after which the entry of cold water condensed the steam and reversed the action. This motion powered a suction mechanism that lifted the water from the mine. The Newcomen pump was more than a pump. It was a steam engine as well.

James Watt and the Steam Engine

Faced with the task of providing a working Newcomen steam engine for the university at Glasgow, Scotland, where he was employed as a technician in the 1760s, James Watt made a better one instead. The original machine operated by heating and cooling the entire cylinder in which the piston moved. Watt crafted an engine with two connected chambers, one always hot for the steam drive, the other cold for condensation and the counterdrive. The change increased both the efficiency and force of the machine. In the 1800s, the improved steam engine became one of the most profound influences in shaping the industrial socioeconomic system.

The Mechanization of the Cotton Textile Industry

When economies leave the agricultural stage, they typically move into the manufacture of textiles. In Early Modern Britain, the woolen industry as a factor in trade was second only to agriculture. Modernization brought another cloth-making business to the commercial forefront, and simultaneously industry strode toward dominance over agriculture. Cotton textile producers formed the vanguard that marched ahead of the ranks of other industrialists into this economic revolution. They went armed with an array of relatively simple yet market-conquering inventions.

JOHN KAY'S FLYING SHUTTLE

Before 1733, in order to weave cloth of any but very narrow widths, two people had to work the shuttle that carried the thread across the loom. John Kay, a craftsman in British Lancashire, in that year invented a shuttle that would fly across the loom under the control of a single worker. This wheeled device driven by string-tripped hammers not only raised the operator's output by 100 percent but soon also increased by similar proportions the pressure for faster thread production.

SPINNING JENNIES, WATER FRAMES, AND SPINNING MULES

Kay's invention did not appear in many factories until the 1760s when James Hargreaves eased the thread-shortage problem. In 1768 this British inventor finished his improvements on the spinning jenny, a human-powered mechanism that enabled one worker to produce thread on multiple spindles. Soon thereafter, Richard Arkwright brought out his water frame, an invention that harnessed the power of either water or animals to the spinning of thread. Within eleven years from the appearance of the jenny, Samuel Compton conceived another multiple-spindled machine, the spinning mule, that further advanced the operator's capacity to produce with human power. Thread production increased yet again when industrialists used the energy of animals and water to drive the spinning mules.

LOOMS AND GINS AT THE ENDS OF THE PRODUCTION LOOP

This cascade of thread presented a problem for the weavers. They worked at the end of the production process and finished the work at their looms. The shuttles of old no longer flew across looms fast enough to convert the abundance of thread to cloth. Edmund Cartwright found a solution. His power loom appeared in 1787, and with it the final stage of textile manufacturing once more could keep pace with the spinning, until another advancement in thread making occurred. The productive escalation continued.

If the suppliers of raw fiber for this booming textile industry had continued to remove the seeds from the cotton by hand, a difficult and thus labor-intensive process, the production of cloth could not have grown so rapidly. But the producers in the United States sent the bales of fiber across the ocean in adequate numbers, for they could extract the seed with remarkable speed after 1793 by using Eli Whitney's relatively simple device, the cotton gin.

Trains, Steamboats, and Bicycles

The presence or absence of roads and waterways adequate to the needs of industry helped to determine when and where economic modernization began. Once advantages in transportation and in other respects launched Britain toward industrial leadership, the expansion of manufacturing placed increasingly heavy demands on the facilities for moving goods. At the same time, certain of the products of the industrial revolution became the means for remarkable advancements in transportation. The revolution in mobility at first came in forms such as canals and hard-surfaced or "macadamized" roads. During the 1800s, however, railroads became the most important means of industrial-age transportation.

RAILROADS

Rails of wood had eased the job of hauling a small part of Europe's commerce throughout the Early Modern period. For the most part, in pre-industrial rail transport, vehicles pulled by horses had taken coal from mines to ships. By the 1700s, wagons on rails also profitably served the needs of the iron industry. The latter industry, in turn, made improvements in rails possible, as metal plate was added to sections of the wood rail lines that were subjected to the greatest wear.

This partial plating technique used in the early 1700s foreshadowed the most important rail improvements, most of which occurred in the 1760s and after. These advancements began with Richard Reynolds's building of the first all-cast-iron line in southwest England in 1767. Other enhancements followed. By the early 1800s railways started to meet the needs of society more generally. The steam engine was critical to this advancement of railroading.

THE LOCOMOTIVE

The locomotive, a steam engine on wheels built especially for railroad use, carried this form of transportation to its place of supremacy among industrial conveyances, a position that it kept from the mid-1800s into the twentieth century. Inventors first tried a locomotive on the roads of England as early as 1803, but its size, noise, and sooty plume of smoke made it an unwelcome companion to other vehicles. It suited iron railways quite well, however. After George Stephenson's locomotive, the *Rocket*, plummeted across twelve miles of track at about ten miles an hour in 1829, the special roads for steam-powered trains rapidly multiplied. At the time of the *Rocket*'s miracle trip, all of Britain had less than 500 miles of track. By midcentury the rail net extended nearly 7,000 miles. Canals and roads were becoming subsidiary parts of industrial Europe's transportation system.

STEAM-POWERED WATER TRANSPORTATION

Despite the importance of serviceable water transportation to the early emergence of industrialization in England, relatively few steamboats churned through British or other European rivers. Robert Fulton's successful trial of his steam-driven *Clermont* on the Hudson River in the northeastern United States in 1807 did not affect river transportation in Europe as the *Rocket* influenced railways. This slower change in water travel probably resulted from the scarcity of waterways suited to steamboat travel in the regions of Europe that industrialized before the 1850s.

At sea, the sailing ship remained more efficient and profitable than the steamship until the advent of new engine and propeller designs in the latter 1800s. Even so, Samuel Cunard of Scotland began to offer steamship transportation across the Atlantic in 1840. Passengers and mail began to move over oceans under industrial power. The ships could carry little freight in their holds so long as their engines required the huge quantities of coal typical in the years before the 1860s.

BICYCLES

Before the 1700s, a French artisan built a four-wheeled, human-powered vehicle. The industrial revolution made it possible to produce more effective types of self-propelled vehicles and to mass-produce them. A Scottish craftsman constructed a two-wheeled device that outran a horse-drawn mail coach in 1842. This handmade bicycle differed a great deal from the modern vehicle. It also was less truly a product of the industrial revolution than the types manufactured a few years later.

In the 1860s, a French bicycle firm began operation and reached an annual production rate of 400 vehicles in 1865. This bicycle, and others made in France during the decade, had components much more like the ones familiar to present-day riders. Bicycle builders of the mid-1800s thus had barely begun an enterprise that would mature later. But these early developments indicated the broad scope of the influence of industry on society, from work to play and beyond.

Machinery for a Still Greater Revolution

The devices and related economic changes that propelled Britain ahead in the industrial revolution during the century after 1760 did not provide the means for unchallenged leadership after the 1850s. Machine-age technology began to drive nearby nations toward industrial power; then Britain and other European countries surged into a more advanced stage of the economic revolution. The force behind this further rush toward industrialization came in part from new technologies of the mid-1800s. Other innovations would speed the economic transformation in the latter decades of the century.

ELECTRICAL COMMUNICATION

One of the important new inventions, the telegraph, conveyed the first speed-of-light message over approximately thirty miles of wire from Baltimore to Washington D.C. in 1844. An underwater telegraph cable across the English Channel linked Britain to the European mainland by 1851. Such lines of electrical communication signaled the opening of a new era in the transmission of messages, a change of special significance to government and business.

STEEL

Iron with a high carbon content is very hard but also brittle. These are valuable qualities for certain metal products. Ironworks of the early industrial era, however, made more extensive use of the metal in a low carbon and thus much more malleable form. The workers needed this purified iron so that they could pound and bend it into desired shapes. When the carbon content of iron is partly restored by a special heating process, the resultant alloy, steel, has a combination of properties of strength, flexibility, and malleability that makes it a superior metal for most tool-making and building purposes. Until 1856, the technology did not exist for the production of large quantities of reasonably priced steel. Henry Bessemer at that juncture discovered a processing method that was an important step toward ensuring that the industrial age would rely on the strength of steel.

THE FACTORY SYSTEM

Industrialists intended to mold, bend, and control workers as well as machines. Thus they ushered in more genuinely revolutionary changes than if they had concentrated mainly on technology. Gigantic economic opportunities and risks loomed before these investors. They needed maximum productivity from their employees. The factory system emerged as the organizational embodiment of these business purposes and attitudes.

The First Factories

Modern European industrialists developed a mostly new system of labor organization when they established the first factories. They built central work sites to which their employees came for the supervision of their activities. Often the workers labored under a single roof; at times one power system drove all the machines in the factory. Conditions in these workplaces—ventilation, lighting, temperature, noise level—often left much to be desired. The first place to combine all these productive advantages and disadvantages, a silk factory built in Britain in 1717, did not inspire the erection of many others during the next fifty years. Craft shops and cottage producers still manufactured most goods.

The Spread of the Factory System

A shortage of cheap labor in Britain during the 1760s and 1770s made cottage production less profitable than before and, therefore, became an incentive to set up factories. This development coincided with the appearance of new labor-saving devices for cotton textile production. As a result, the new form of work organization became especially attractive to the manufacturers of cotton fabric. Thereafter, many more factories appeared in England, although they continued to be mainly a phenomenon in the cotton textile industry until the 1820s. From that decade onward, the factory system expanded more rapidly. It became increasingly typical in additional British industries, and began to become a more significant feature of industrialization in other European countries as well.

Factory Work

Commentaries on the modern economy sometimes refer to owners of manufacturing enterprises as "captains of industry." The label is appropriate. Systems with powerful authority had a strong appeal to Europeans in the 1700s. A portion of the early factory operators, in fact, explicitly compared their labor organizational tasks to the work of military commanders, prison wardens, or even slave owners. The outlook of the age encouraged the perception of workers as lazy creatures in need of a hard discipline that would meet the economic requirements of employers and also benefit the employee morally. Employers viewed their employees as troops or inmates in need of regimentation.

These workers had descended from generations of farmers and cottage producers who were accustomed to hard but loosely scheduled labor and extended periods of leisure. They did not readily conform to the demands of the industrialists that they arrive on time, at hours precisely marked by clock, bell, or whistle. Laborers also tended to resist the pressure to exert maximum effort throughout a long day. Thus, given the mood of the times and the conflict between employer and employee attitudes, factories became places in which bosses minutely organized labor and gave orders. Workers performed specified tasks and obeyed the rules or suffered the consequences. The factory emerged as an austere reflection of a prison or military establishment.

HIGHLY STRUCTURED AND LESS SKILLED WORK

Workers during the Middle Ages or Early Modern period produced their goods in small craft shops or in cottages. In the shops, a master of the craft supervised a small skilled group. In the cottage system, "putters out" gave some direction to individual or family members. These cottage workers even experienced the division of a production process into a series of simple steps, each to be performed by a different laborer.

The factory, however, intensified this tendency toward fragmentation into a multitude of routine rather than skilled tasks; bosses arranged employees in a machine-like setup. In the early years of the industrial revolution, employers established these highly structured procedures in relatively unmechanized factories. Increasingly, however, people labored in plants at machines that exercised greater power over factory conditions than did the workers. The demands of the equipment and the orders of the industrialist reigned supreme.

RULES AND REGULATIONS

The employers' commands took generalized form as lists of obligations for the laborers. These rules specified work schedules and other behaviors on the job. They might, for example, ban talking, singing, and eating. The regulations could apply also to life outside the factory with stipulations about acceptable marriage age and numbers of offspring.

PUNISHMENT

Workers paid for failure to adhere to the rules. Employers levied fines, fired offenders, and at times resorted to physical punishment. A report to the British Parliament on conditions in factories during the early decades of the 1800s contained descriptions of the injurious means of control. For example, witnesses told government investigators that children sometimes returned to the textile mills after only four hours in bed, fell asleep on the job, and then suffered blows from supervisors wielding rollers from the machines.

BENEFITS AND REFORMS

Despite the prevalence of bad physical conditions and harsh discipline in the plants, not all factory workers encountered these hardships. A minority of industrialists considered it their responsibility to provide a good work environment, comfortable housing, or, for young laborers, education. Reformers also emerged very early to begin campaigns to improve working conditions in factories and mines. They showed a special interest in the protection of groups that they considered to be the most vulnerable—children and women. In this quest for change, reformers usually pressed for public or private action that would ensure survival necessities for the very poor, establish limitations on work hours, and in other ways better the lives of those detrimentally affected by industrialization. (See chapter 8.)

THE EVOLUTION OF INDUSTRIAL FINANCE

Economic leaders more often exhibited concern for the costs of their business pursuits than for the social costs of the economic transformation. Early in the industrial revolution, the acquisition of money to cover the expenses of manufacturing ventures posed no serious problems. But as industrialization accelerated in England and began on the continent, it became more difficult to secure enough investment funds.

Other developments made the capital supply problem still worse. The increased mechanization of industry caused the price of establishing and operating a company to rise sharply. Furthermore, the founding of new types of enterprises, such as railroads, involved costs of astronomical proportions and heightened the demand for capital funds still more. Both government and private interests responded to this need by developing the financial institutions and practices for the further growth of European industry.

Funds from Individuals and Banks

People with wealth from trade or land ownership continued to provide capital for industry, as they had before the mid-1700s. Britain in particular remained a dependable source of such funding; entrepreneurs in other European countries turned to the British for loans to build industry. Additional capital funds came from banks as in the past, but the burgeoning industrial economy required changes in the system. In Britain the government promoted bank mergers and thus the growth of larger and stronger institutions suited to the times. Alterations in British law improved the system in another way. The government allowed banks to issue paper currency, a response to the sometimes critical shortage of cash caused by rapidly expanding business. The banks themselves acted on this problem by supporting the wider use of checks and other paper transactions.

Incorporation— the Company as Person

The practice of pooling funds through investment in a joint-stock company facilitated the rapid growth of trade during the Early Modern period, but this business arrangement entailed great risks. Each investor took on full responsibility to pay a company's creditors. Industrial Europe found ways to make investment more appealing. In Britain in 1825, for example, lawmakers reduced this financial threat by opening the way to the establishment of a special type of business organization. Investors could arrange for an important degree of protection by incorporation, an act that made a company into a legal "individual." Once incorporated, the creditors of a company could pursue funds from shareholders only to the extent of their ownership percentage. This protective arrangement drew investment money into many companies. By the 1840s, over 200 incorporated firms operated in France, and Britain had almost five times that number.

THE ONSET OF INDUSTRIALIZATION ON "THE CONTINENT"

Compared to Britain, France and other European countries had very few industrial enterprises by the 1840s. Across the English Channel from the British Isles on the mainland of Europe, the region that commentators usually call "the Continent," conditions in the late 1700s and early 1800s favored industrialization but less so than in Britain. Nevertheless, the transformation came. Once begun, it moved in some regions with the same revolutionary force as it had in England. The surge of change advanced first in the areas of northwest Europe adjacent to Britain. This region included northern France, Belgium, and the northern part of the Germanic Confederation which contained such countries as Prussia.

France— Millions of Farms, Thousands of Steam Engines

Social revolution struck France in 1789. By the 1790s the nation plunged into a war against most of Europe that lasted until 1815. (See chapters 5 and 6.) Among continental nations, France stood in the forefront of the march toward industrialization by the end of the war. This transition had begun before 1789; it accelerated during the years of international conflict. Even as a leader in industry on the mainland, however, France had not moved very far from its agrarian economic heritage by 1815.

A SMALL FARM ECONOMY

Most of the nearly thirty million French citizens worked on small farms in the early 1800s; they exhibited a strong commitment to agriculture on this scale rather than to consolidation for commercial purposes. Many farmers also remained unaffected by the efforts of the advocates of scientific agriculture who wanted to promote the new methods of cropping and stock breeding. The French countryside produced abundantly and profitably most of the time in this era, but without a revolution in land organization, in farm practices, or in the use of contraptions.

INFANT INDUSTRY

During the first half of the 1800s, as the British cotton textile industry began to clothe people in many parts of the globe, the younger and smaller system in France prospered with sales in its own protected market at home. French linen textile manufacturing thrived as well in the years after 1815; it benefited from the government tax on competitive imports as did the cotton cloth business. Another fabric enterprise boomed, however, without the tariff-sheltered market. French silks flowed from the most mechanized textile industry in the country, at a time when cotton and linen cloth still came largely from cottage production. Other similar signs of youthful, growing industry appeared before midcentury with the establishment of new iron and machinist enterprises, the improvement and expansion of canals and roads, and the construction of the first miles of a rail net (about 3,000 miles completed or under way by the 1840s). Above all, the sounds of the more than 5,000 steam engines in operation before 1850 signaled the industrial revolution that had begun.

Belgium— Continental Machine Shop

French textile production far exceeded Belgium's during the first decades of industrialization. But even with the impressive multiplication of steam engines into the thousands in France, Belgium surpassed all other continental countries in machine technology. The central place of mining in the economy of this country encouraged this early advancement in engineering; it accounted for Belgian interest in the particular kind of steam engine developed by Newcomen.

THE PROMOTION OF STEAM POWER

The Belgians had a Newcomen engine, a device well suited to pumping water from mines, in operation by 1721. Within thirty years, they established a factory to produce them. Thereafter, the machines at work in the country rapidly increased in number. Belgian engineers began to influence the mechanization of other European states, especially the Germanic ones.

THE SECOND MOST INDUSTRIALIZED NATION

Measured by industrial output per person, Belgium and Britain led all other European states by 1850. In that year, Belgian iron use per person was ninety pounds, about sixty percent of the British average, but more than twice the French rate and three times the German usage.

Industry in Germany

In the mid-1700s, Germans did not live in a united country. Central Europe then contained more than 300 Germanic states; the French Emperor, Napoleon, consolidated them into fewer than fifty when he conquered the region a few decades later. European leaders redrew the map of the continent after Napoleon's defeat in 1815. They combined the German territories into the thirty-eight independent states of the very loose German Confederation. (See chapter 7.) Although the Austrian Empire was a multiethnic state, Germans led its society and government, and Austria joined the confederation. Prussia and Austria dominated within this complex mosaic of thirty-eight German or German-ruled states.

PRUSSIA—LAND AND A LITTLE IRON

A Prussian leader in the 1860s contended that "blood and iron" rather than parliamentary discussions would decide the issues of the times. Even though iron did pour from Prussian furnaces at that time at an incredible rate compared to 1850, none of the German states of the 1860s had moved very far from the old land-based economy into the new age of iron. For the most part, Prussia remained a society in which a relatively few powerful agrarian nobles (the *Junkers*) held sway over the masses of farm workers, many of whom had no land of their own.

Industrialists, financiers, and government leaders, however, put the first pieces of an economy of iron in place beginning in about the 1820s. They established machine and engineering enterprises, produced steam-powered riverboats, and began their rail net. Iron had much to do with the strength of the emerging economic order, but the economy already included other important components. Soon after 1815, entrepreneurs labored to raise the first parts of a textile industry designed on the British model. Workers in this growing business at first used the old productive technology. By 1850, machines made their noisy entry into these cloth-making facilities of northern Germany. The Prussians still had a mostly agricultural economy; but they made more and more iron and a little industrial-age cloth.

THE *ZOLLVEREIN*—A PRUSSIAN CUSTOMS ASSOCIATION

Customs duties, which are taxes on trade, formed a serious barrier to commerce within Prussia in the late 1700s and early 1800s. The government nullified all such tariffs on domestic trade in 1818. This change helped to speed the transition to an industrial economy in the decades thereafter. The environment became even more conducive to this transformation with the establishment of a customs association, the *Zollverein*, in 1834. This organization brought most of the German states into a Prussian-led commercial union and resulted in greatly increased trade for this dominant member of the *Zollverein*.

THE AUSTRIAN EMPIRE—ENOUGH FACTORY WORKERS FOR A FIGHT

Austria remained outside the *Zollverein*, kept the tariff barriers to internal trade in place, and made only weak efforts to stimulate the development of railroads. Not surprisingly then, the country turned toward industrialization even more slowly than Prussia. The economic adventurers who established a few enterprises in the first decades of the 1800s concentrated mostly on textiles and usually set up operations in the northwestern third of the empire. When economic hard times struck in the 1840s, the factory workers in one of the industrializing cities of that area rioted.

Russian Industry—a Few Giant Factories

Russia experienced rebellions during the first century of the European industrial revolution. Violence erupted hundreds of times. But, unlike the outbreaks in Austria in the 1840s, in Russia farmers rampaged, not factory workers. Russian outbreaks differed in part because almost no one worked in industry. When British population became over fifty percent urban in the 1850s, about five percent of the seventy million Russians lived in cities.

Within this vast East European empire, fewer than 3,000 factories with sixteen or more employees operated by 1850. The number of industrial workers had not reached one million by that date, and they turned out only ten percent of Russia's total economic production.

These figures although indicating a low level of industrialization, also reveal that economic modernization at least had begun. As in Britain, the advancements were most noticeable in the cotton textile industry. A few totally new enterprises, such as beet sugar manufacturing, also appeared in the first half of the 1800s. The factories that Russians put into operation in these decades tended to be very large, sometimes employing hundreds of workers. This pattern of industrialization on a gigantic scale became characteristic of Russia.

EARLY INDUSTRIAL SOCIETY

A multitude of changes in European society before the mid-1700s exercised a powerful influence on the emergence of the mostly economic and technological developments that historians describe as an industrial revolution. The multiplication of cities and the growth of urban populations from 1000 onward had an especially strong effect on the beginning of industrialization. This economic revolution from the 1760s on then brought further dramatic changes in European society. The most striking and important of these social effects, perhaps, was accelerated urbanization.

Urbanization and City Life

As Europe industrialized, a growing percentage of people worked in factories, shops, and offices rather than on farms. The concentration of these economic institutions in urban centers made good business sense. Technology influenced this process of centralization. The steam engine, for example, provided great flexibility in the location of factories by virtually ending the dependence on waterways a relatively fixed power source. Urbanization came quickly. Whereas nine-tenths of all Europeans lived in rural areas during the latter 1700s, by the 1850s more than half the British, over one-third of the Germans, and about one-fourth of the French resided in cities.

THE BIG-CITY PHENOMENON

At the same time that new economic and technological influences encouraged the movement from countryside to city, the population of Europe rapidly expanded. Since the founding of new towns became rare in the age of the industrial revolution, Europeans migrated to and expanded their numbers mostly in previously established centers. The combined effect of these trends was a remarkable growth in the size of European cities.

London led the way with an increase from about 700,000 in the early 1700s to 1,000,000 before 1810 and 2,000,000 by the 1850s. By the latter date the population of Paris reached 1,000,000. No other European cities were so large by 1850, but many others experienced phenomenal growth. The age of the European metropolis had dawned with the industrial revolution.

PHYSICAL TRAITS OF THE INDUSTRIAL CITY

Earlier cities functioned mainly as centers of government, religious administration, and commerce. Europeans designed buildings, monuments, and other structures to serve these purposes and honor important people or agencies. Therefore, the Europeans sometimes consciously developed cities or portions thereof with a widely recognized beauty. Still, the cities tended to be crowded; they contained many sections, such as the residential areas for the less wealthy, that were dark and dirty.

The industrial revolution caused these cities to take on a new function as manufacturing centers. This change brought very rapid growth and the construction of factories and housing for industrial workers. The appearance of the urban landscape declined a great deal as a result.

The Industrial District. Factories often stood near the center of the city. The inadequacy of urban transportation at the dawn of the industrial age encouraged the growth of laborers' housing areas very near the workplace. Factory workers and their families crowded into dwellings built as "rowhouses" with shared walls in structures several floors high. Residents typically would find their water supply at a common well in a dirt or stone-covered yard between sections of houses. A gutter in the middle of the street drained away whatever waste they produced to the extent that its consistency and the terrain permitted.

The "Better" Neighborhoods. Craft workers usually lived better than factory laborers. The housing of these more skilled artisans varied in type from rowhouses to single-family residences on separate lots. In cities with industry and worker housing at the center, the artisans' houses usually stood in the circle just beyond the center. People with still greater wealth enjoyed the finer and more spacious homes that they often built in the suburbs at the edge of the industrial city. Most of these urban dwellers, from rich suburbanite to poor laborer, to some degree struggled with the problems of inadequate city lighting, poor transportation, and polluted air and water. These blights marred the appearance of the early industrial cities and threatened the well-being of virtually all urban citizens.

Social Classes in the Early Industrial Age

The varied elements that made up the bourgeoisie usually inhabited the most pleasant districts of the growing industrial cities. These "middle classes" had led the way into the industrial revolution. The economic transformation that got under way between the 1760s and 1850s quickly accelerated their march toward greater wealth and power. Industrialization had a similarly drastic effect on the social position of the European upper and lower classes, but the movement in their case was not toward supremacy.

THE RISING MIDDLE CLASSES

The bourgeoisie advanced in numbers and wealth in the first century of industrialization (1750s to 1850s). Despite this expansion in class size and riches, the social supremacy of the aristocracy usually did not come to an abrupt end. In most of Europe, the bourgeoisie climbed gradually. The change involved the conversion of a few aristocrats to middle-class ways, the acquisition of noble status by some members of the bourgeoisie, and the spreading belief that aristocracy in the old sense was wrong. The French social conversion differed. It climaxed abruptly. Within a single year (1789), revolution broke out and a bourgeois legislature decreed an end to noble privilege.

This process of social change created a diverse middle class. They were industrialists, bankers, merchants, small business owners, doctors, and lawyers, and usually the wealthiest if they were one of the first three. Despite the identity of these groups as a "middle" class in certain senses, the bourgeoisie became supreme, at least economically, in most regions of Europe as industry came to predominate.

THE URBAN WORKING CLASSES

The growth of bourgeois wealth and power reduced, even if it did not end, the social distance between middle and upper classes. As they climbed, however, the gap widened between the bourgeoisie and those people who worked in their factories, made their clothes and other articles, and served them in their homes. The middle classes, that is, moved further above the urban workers—the factory laborers, artisans, and domestic servants.

The Industrial Laborers. Industrialization encouraged the development of a virtually new social class, the factory workers or *"proletariat."* Like the bourgeoisie, these proletarians' lives were closely tied to the industrial revolution, but the new economic age by 1850 improved conditions for only a small portion of these workers. Most factory workers during the first century of industrialization suffered the pain of losing close village social relationships, the discomfort of sweatshops, the disadvantages of illiteracy and poverty, and the bleakness of life in rowhouse or slum neighborhoods. They soothed the effects of lower-class city life to a degree by the pleasures of working-class pubs. Many also enjoyed sports either as participants or spectators.

By the 1850s, these inhabitants of factories, slums, and pubs were a class growing faster than any; but at that time the proletariat remained a minority everywhere in Europe. Lack of organization as well as minority status ensured the weakness of this group. Only a relative handful of factory workers had joined unions, even in the few places where such associations were legal. For most of these laborers in industry, the benefits of the industrial revolution lay in the future.

Artisans. Another segment of the working class, most of whom lived in urban areas, were the artisans. Their special skills in carpentry, clothes making, luxury crafts, and similar pursuits gave most members of this group a better income and a higher status than the factory workers. Artisans also outnumbered other urban working-class groups throughout the first half of the 1800s. These craft workers enjoyed the benefits of being the best educated urban laborers. They maintained a degree of organizational strength through their guilds, except in Britain and France where the influence of these groups had withered by the 1800s. In places where such advantages left them with sufficient power, artisans fought the threats posed to them economically by industrial mass production and socially by the growth of the proletariat.

Domestic Servants. The largely female force that worked in the wealthier city homes increased in number as the industrial revolution progressed, but not so rapidly as did the proletariat. These servants typically lived in their employers' homes; they seem to have accepted quietly the extensive control that their masters exercised over their lives. Their functions and attitudes thus ensured the presence of much social distance between them and the other members of the urban working class.

THE ARISTOCRACY

Industrialization hastened the economic displacement of the hereditary upper class. Aristocratic political power diminished more slowly, however, leaving the nobles still superior to the bourgeoisie in governing influence in nearly all of Europe in the mid-1800s. The aristocracy in most European countries held even more securely to their social privileges and prestige. Nobles sometimes even avoided the relative economic decline by turning to trade or industrial pursuits to protect or increase their wealth.

The economic tide of an industrial age, however, ran against the continued supremacy of the aristocracy as a whole. Furthermore, soon after the onset of industrialization, the forces of sociopolitical revolution began to surge across France and then through much of Europe. Aristocratic privilege and political influence virtually disappeared wherever this new and broader revolution spread.

The pounding and fuming machines of industry dramatically revealed the obvious and drastic reconstitution of European technology and economy between 1760 and 1850. Machines produced goods and carried material and people in quantities and at speeds that amazed contemporary observers.

The landscape in many areas showed equally striking signs of the new order as industry swelled the limits and raised the skylines of Europe's cities.

A great degree of change in the work, social relationships, and life-styles of Europeans accompanied the economic transformation. Many business people and professionals, the dynamic leaders of this leap toward modernity, enjoyed a great advancement in wealth and soon reached for the levers of political power. Except in France where a social and political revolution occurred, these gains by the middle classes did not yet displace the aristocracy from their heights of privilege and influence.

Similarly, artisans continued as the top echelon of laborers, even though they, like the aristocrats, suffered a relative decline in society. Other workers, who lacked the skills and tradition-based eminence of the artisans, found their lives altered drastically, as had the industrial middle classes. These laborers converged on industrial towns to work in the booming factory system. At a remarkable rate, the ranks of this urban "proletariat" multiplied; it became an industrial-age social force that would seriously challenge the established order beginning in the latter years of the 1800s.

By 1850 industrialization had spawned a new technological and economic order in Europe. But during the middle decades of the industrial revolution, still another vital force had helped to reshape Europe. In 1789, a second modernizing revolution, different in character from the first, erupted in France, and within months it destroyed the old social and political system of that country. Adherents of the new order for the next twenty-five years fought violently to develop it within France and spread it throughout the continent. The French Revolution changed Europe profoundly by 1815; it virtually ensured that as European civilization industrialized it would use the power of its machines and technology to complete a drive to global domination.

Selected Readings

Blackwell, William L. *The Beginnings of Russian Industrialization, 1800–1860.* Princeton, NJ: Princeton University, 1968.

Briggs, Asa. *The Age of Improvement.* New York: Longman S. Green, 1965.

Burke, James. *Connections.* Boston: Little, Brown and Company, 1978.

Cipolla, Carlo M. *Guns, Sails, and Empires: Technological Innovation and the Early Phases of European Expansion, 1400–1700.* New York: Pantheon Books, 1966.

Deane, Phyllis. *The First Industrial Revolution, 1750–1850.* Cambridge, England: University Press, 1965.

Gerschenkron, Alexander. *Economic Backwardness in Historical Perspective.* Cambridge, MA: Belknap Press, 1962.

Gillis, John R. *The Development of European Society, 1770–1870.* Boston: Houghton Mifflin Co., 1977.

Hamerow, Theodore S. *The Birth of a New Europe: State and Society in the Nineteenth Century.* Chapel Hill: University of North Carolina Press, 1983.

Henderson, W. O. *The Industrialization of Europe, 1780–1914.* New York: Harcourt, Bruce, & World, 1969.

Himmelfarb, Gertrude. *The Idea of Poverty: England in the Early Industrial Age.* New York: Knopf, 1984.

Landes, David S. *The Unbound Prometheus: Technological Change and Industrial Development in Western Europe from 1750 to the Present.* London: Cambridge University Press, 1969.

McKeown, Thomas. *The Modern Rise of Population.* New York: Academic Press, 1976.

Pollard, Sidney. *Peaceful Conquest: The Industrialization of Europe, 1760–1970.* New York: Oxford University Press, 1981.

Thompson, E. P. *Making of the English Working Class.* New York: Pantheon Books, 1964.

3

The Ancien Régime and Its Critics, Late 1600s to Mid-1700s

A.D. 1000s The rise of strong centralized monarchies begins

1614 The French Estates General convenes for the last time until 1789

1642 The birth of Sir Isaac Newton (1642–1727)

Mid-1600s The English Enlightenment begins

1651 Thomas Hobbes publishes *Leviathan*

1690 John Locke publishes *Two Treatises of Government* and *Essay Concerning Human Understanding*

1694 The birth of Voltaire (1694–1778)

1721 Montesquieu publishes his *Persian Letters*

1748 David Hume publishes *Inquiry Concerning Human Understanding* and Montesquieu's *The Spirit of the Laws*

*E*conomic and technological change in Europe over many centuries led to the emergence of the first industrial economies in history, beginning in the mid-1700s. This revolution fostered a strengthening of the economic forces that had made industrialization possible. Thus the historic trends that produced the industrial revolution intensified after 1760; by the latter 1700s *they ushered in modern life at the most fundamental level, powerfully affecting the technology of communication and the way Europeans nourished, housed, clothed, and transported themselves.*

From the 1680s to the 1750s, as Europe moved toward its industrial revolution, the already noticeable contrast between an emerging new economy and an aging social structure became a glaring difference. In France, this divergence between the old social order (Ancien Régime in French) and the changing economic system was especially sharp. A small and privileged French aristocracy looked down on the masses of commoners, a group that included not only the poorest peasants but also rich businesspeople whose lack of noble status hindered their economic activity and angered them. All of Europe chafed under a similarly restraining Ancien Régime.

The people who shaped European thought from the late 1600s to the 1750s fashioned it into a frame of mind that was much more modern than the social system of the era, an outlook more nearly consistent with a modernizing economic order. Knowledge of the universe advanced so rapidly beginning in the 1500s that theorists by the late 1600s thought they had entered an era of special intellectual brilliance. This period became known as the "Enlightenment" or "Age of Reason."

During the Enlightenment (1680s–1780s), intellectuals expected to gain the same complete understanding of humanity that they believed they recently had acquired of physical forces and objects. They placed almost absolute faith in reason and science to reveal the path to a perfect society. Enlightenment intellectuals concentrated their attention on the imperfections of the Ancien Régime. To the critics, the superstitious ways of the Middle Ages appeared to prevent the progress in which these theorists so profoundly believed.

Even though the intellectuals of the early Enlightenment despised much about the existing social system, they revered monarchy. They did so in part because they believed royal institutions to be potential instruments of progressive reform. By the 1750s, however, the expressions of high esteem for monarchical government began to disappear from the works of Enlightenment theorists. Soon, both the social and political systems of the Ancien Régime would come under sharp attack.

THE ANCIEN RÉGIME

Although the contrast between social conditions and the expectations of intellectuals gave France the most vivid image as an *Ancien Régime*, many sources suggest that the problem of antiquated social systems went far beyond France. They apply the label *Ancien Régime* to European society as a whole or even to all the region's social and political institutions during the two centuries before 1789. Early Modern European society had changed more since the Middle Ages than this image as an "old regime" indicated, but very old institutions did remain. They became increasingly ill-suited to modern needs.

Aristocratic Privilege and Irresponsibility

The European aristocracy originated during the feudal phase of the Middle Ages (late 800s to early 1000s A.D.). In that era, the members of this upper-class minority enjoyed special rights and held grants of land in return for which many owed military and other services to a higher noble. All were obligated to govern their region and protect it from invasion.

THE LAPSE IN NOBLE SERVICE

The rise of centralized government, beginning in the 1000s, eventually ended the aristocracy's protective activities and made their efforts to control local affairs an unwanted burden to many nonaristocrats. This governing warrior nobility thus no longer served society. It kept its privileges and continued, as always, to shun productive labor. Furthermore, aristocrats in some areas paid no taxes to the state, and many more resisted taxation on the basis of hereditary right. They also could force nonnobles to provide personal services to them. Circumstances varied widely across Europe, but these and an array of other special aristocratic rights persisted. Hostility toward the nobility grew. Even a few intellectual aristocrats joined the chorus of complaint against noble privilege.

SOCIAL STRATIFICATION—THE FRENCH ESTATES AS AN EXAMPLE

The *Ancien Régime* included not only a heritage of special aristocratic rights but also a legacy of theories that justified a pyramidlike structure of classes. These beliefs about social hierarchy communicated the same social message conveyed by noble privilege—the superiority of the people at the top.

European systems of social stratification varied, but most were similar to the one in France. It divided the nation into three "estates." Church leaders and nobles comprised the First and Second Estates, respectively. Each of these groups numbered about 200,000 in a nation of 25,000,000. This small fraction of the population enjoyed the privileges typical of the European aristocracy, including ownership of one-third of the land. With few exceptions, members of the upper clergy and nobility meant to perpetuate their social supremacy. Even though they belonged to the First Estate, the local priests who made up the lower clergy identified with the millions of "commoners" in the Third Estate. Most priests came from that class.

Since industry had advanced very little in France by the latter 1700s, almost everyone still farmed for a living. Peasants, therefore, greatly outnumbered all other social groups in the Third Estate. Rural commoners in France lived better than peasants elsewhere in Europe. Still, they had a dismal existence compared to the circumstances of the aristocracy.

The other people who shared Third Estate status with the peasants were the urban working classes and the bourgeoisie. Laborers in the cities held jobs at varied skill and income levels. Living conditions thus also differed considerably among them. All faced the danger of starvation whenever hard times struck. Owners of small shops, merchants, bankers, lawyers, and others in similar pursuits who made up the bourgeoisie disliked the disadvantages of their low social estate, but hunger did not haunt these middle-class members of the Third Estate.

THE ESTATES GENERAL IN FRANCE

During the Middle Ages, rulers in central and western Europe began to meet periodically with members of the various social classes. In France, kings gathered representatives of the three estates in meetings called the "Estates General." Each estate had one vote when the monarch asked these assemblies to express approval of his actions. The aristocratic upper estates thus won on any issue if they so desired. The masses of people in the Third Estate carried little weight.

For 175 years after 1614, none of the classes in France exercised power through the Estates General. The kings did not convene an assembly between 1614 and 1789. In these years, the independent authority of the monarchy greatly increased. Noble privileges and the theories that honored them remained. But the authority of the aristocracy virtually disappeared. The Third Estate continued without the dignities of nobility and lost the small influence it had exercised in the assemblies.

Special Interest Groups

Noble privileges had angered nonaristocrats during the Late Middle Ages and Early Modern period. By the 1700s, many other *ancien* traditions and institutions burdened and enraged social critics.

CRAFT GUILDS

Skilled workers in the towns of the Middle Ages established craft guilds to protect their special interests. In Early Modern times, these organizations in many locales still fixed prices on goods or monopolized production of specified items. The guilds thus frustrated the dynamic bourgeois entrepreneurs.

CORPORATIONS—THE ROMAN CATHOLIC CHURCH

Guilds were not the only interest groups that remained as remnants of the Middle Ages in the late 1700s. Social "bodies" or "corporations" with special rights and powers had emerged also in earlier European history. In the Modern period, businesses became the most typical corporations, but in the late 1700s people more often felt the power of the oldest corporate institution, the Roman Catholic Church. This organization possessed great wealth, mainly enjoyed by the upper clergy. The church exercised several exceptional traditional powers too. For example, church agencies, such as "The Inquisition," severely punished variations from approved belief, especially in Spain and parts of Italy. In France, bishops could have people imprisoned for making their confessions to priests who were considered unorthodox.

The Catholic Church's use of its inherited corporate rights made it a very forceful counter to the drive toward new ways and freer thought in Europe in the 1700s. People in other interest groups, such as judicial officials, used corporate authority to similar effect.

During the Middle Ages, aristocrats, church leaders, judicial figures, and royal officials formed the upper class. These groups remained securely in place for centuries. Many of the less privileged Europeans of the 1700s who became devoted to their own climb to greater eminence and power decided to bring down this *Ancien Régime*.

THE ENLIGHTENMENT—IDEAS AGAINST THE OLD REGIME

Early Modern European intellectuals strongly influenced the emergence of hostile attitudes toward the old social system. Advances in science since the 1500s inspired these brilliant social critics to lead the attack on the *Ancien Régime*. Scientists, such as Sir Isaac Newton (1642–1727), had made startling discoveries about the physical laws underlying the organization and operation of the solar system. These discoveries about the natural world encouraged many thinkers in the 1600s and 1700s to have great optimism about their ability to understand any kind of problem, social as well as scientific, and solve it. Ignorance, rather than fate or other supernatural forces, appeared to account for the misery in which many people lived under the old regime.

In the 1500s and early 1600s, only a few intellectuals accepted this idea of progress through the application of scientific knowledge. By the late 1600s, however, many educated Europeans had concluded that reason could produce the good society, perhaps a flawless system. They exuded supreme confidence that virtually eternal progress was possible. If natural laws had produced a universe that operated with mechanical precision, then living in keeping with natural laws could bring "a more nearly perfect" social system.

This "enlightened" thinking that emerged in every European state was at first most prevalent in England.

The Early Enlightenment in England

The new intellectual movement in its English form originated in the mid-1600s. At that time, cultural trends and the turmoil produced by the struggle between kings and the legislature encouraged theorists to shift attention from scientific to social issues.

THOMAS HOBBES (1588–1679)

In 1651, on the eve of the Enlightenment, Thomas Hobbes published *Leviathan.* In it he discussed the origins and nature of government in a strictly secular way, a unique approach for these times. Early Modern thinkers had displayed more secular attitudes than had theorists in the Middle Ages. But until the Enlightenment, intellectuals still justified monarchical authority with religious arguments. *Leviathan* reflected the Modern contempt for the use of appeals to the supernatural to gain acceptance of human institutions.

Hobbes formulated his views in England in the era when a civil war raged between the supporters of royal absolutism and the advocates of legislative authority. He reasoned that earthly conditions, not divine will, warranted the awesome power of kings. Self-interest drove human behavior in his view, and chaos could result. The strong hand of the monarch, the "leviathan," was necessary to control the selfish masses. Over the course of human history, societies had recognized the wisdom of royal authority. In effect, a contract had evolved between the monarch and the people. This contract justified the sovereignty of kings, and it stood for eternity.

JOHN LOCKE (1632–1704)

John Locke, and other Enlightenment theorists, warmly approved of Hobbes's secular perspective on government. The idea of a political contract appealed to them also. Locke, however, gave the latter notion a very different twist. Kings ruled, he agreed, because the people of the realm granted them that power, but this political contract was not necessarily permanent. The citizenry might determine that royal behavior had dissolved the agreement that gave the government the right to exercise authority.

Locke advanced another startling belief. He contended that the people possessed absolute rights that rulers could not violate. Natural laws controlled the motions of the planets. They also guaranteed to all people their rights to life, liberty, and property. Societies should inscribe these and other fundamental principles of government in a constitution, a body of law to which even rulers must submit.

Whenever government negated fundamental rights, Locke asserted, the people had the right to rebel. Rulers who infringed on property rights, encroached on personal liberty, and unjustly took lives nullified the political contract. No law protected the reign of such despots. Their tyranny justified violent revolution.

Locke expressed his political views in *Two Treatises of Government*, a work published in 1690 but composed before the battle between the legislature and the king climaxed in 1688–1689. A second important publication by Locke in 1690, *Essay Concerning Human Understanding*, presented his views on the learning process, a conception of psychology that further justified his preferred form of government.

In his essay, Locke concluded that the human mind at birth was a *tabula rasa* ("blank slate"). He believed that people learned as experience, acting on the five senses, "wrote" on this slate. No one, therefore, entered the world innately superior as a thinking creature. Nature prepared everyone for equality, but flawed systems denied certain members of society the experiences needed for advancement.

Pantheism. Locke believed that natural laws had created a flawlessly operating universe. In his opinion, humans could discover these codes of nature and use them to judge existing societies. Any practice or institution that contradicted Natural Law had to come to an end. The reverence for "nature" reflected in these views was typical of Enlightenment theorists. In a sense, they had turned to pantheism, the belief that God is found in nature. The dedication to science and reason that led them to this faith also resulted in a materialist outlook.

Materialism. The psychological theories that Locke presented exemplify the Enlightenment tendency to think of everything in the world as being composed of and explained by matter. This philosophical materialism precludes the idea of supernatural forces operating in human affairs or the physical world. Materialism is the essence of the Enlightenment version of secularism.

DAVID HUME (1711–1776)—SKEPTIC

Many Enlightenment figures, such as David Hume, are remembered for their skepticism, the rejection of all dogmas. Such an attitude led Hume to explain aspects of life in a secular and materialist way, as had Locke. Hume, however, carried materialism even further and advanced theories about religion itself. He denied the validity of a religion founded on divinely inspired truths and advocated the use of reason to establish a system of worship for all humanity.

In one of Hume's most important publications, *Inquiry Concerning Human Understanding* (1748), he expressed the ultimate skeptical attitude with his denial that supernatural powers of any kind controlled history. He argued that the idea of cause and effect in human affairs was simply a figment of the imagination. Hume and others in his day had reached the conclusion that human events developed at random.

The Enlightenment in France

Eventually, France became an important center in the whirls of enlightened expressions. One indication of the special importance of French theorists is that commentaries on Enlightenment intellectuals usually refer to them by the French word *philosophes*.

THE *PHILOSOPHES* AND THE *SALONS*

The French *philosophes* attacked many of the same issues and expressed many of the same attitudes as the English Enlightenment writers. The social critics in France distinguished themselves, however, in a variety of important ways. For example, they developed the practice of gathering for discussions, *"salons,"* that enabled them to spread their ideas among intellectuals and test their views before publication. Women, moreover, moderated most of these *salons* and, thus, exercised an important influence on the French Enlightenment. This female contribution made the movement in France still more distinctive.

An especially important *philosophe* technique was the communication of social criticisms to the broadest possible public. French critics used styles of communication that would appeal to individuals who might care little for very formal scholarly works. The *philosophes* intended to arouse enough people to change the world.

The *philosophes* presented specific plans for a new order. They spoke out for their kind of enlightened and tolerant world, often demanding a reform of the existing systems. The religious establishment in particular became the target for much of their criticism of the old regime. Certain of the *philosophes* launched especially vicious attacks on Christianity.

DEISM

Many social critics who rejected traditional religion turned to deism. Enlightenment deists thought of God as the great force that had fashioned the universe, a clocklike mechanism that continued after creation to operate according to its own inner principles—a typical Natural Law idea. The deity did not intervene once the "clock" began to tick. Deists saw no way in which religion and science could disagree, and so anything seen as scientifically proved had to be accepted. Contradictory religious notions had to be rejected.

PIERRE BAYLE (1647–1706)—ANTIRELIGIOUS SKEPTIC

Pierre Bayle viewed human affairs in the analytical fashion urged by the deists. In writings done from this perspective before the Enlightenment, he attacked the flaws of the old system in works that foreshadowed those of the later critics. His skeptical assault struck with special severity at the

Christian churches. Bayle probably saw them as the sources of the intolerance and superstition that he so hated.

VOLTAIRE (1694–1778)

Voltaire, whose real name was François Marie Arouet, shared Bayle's view of Christianity. The theology of this faith struck Voltaire as an example of human "madness." This essayist and poet was an especially prominent member of the French salons. As a master of French-language expression, he communicated his views with especially great effect in discussions among intellectuals and in print as well.

Newton's conception of a mechanistic universe and Locke's belief in the mind as a "blank slate" strongly influenced Voltaire's ideas. On such intellectual foundations he went on to elaborate his criticisms of clerical intolerance and other social errors of the day. It seemed wrong to him for the clergy to resist the views of people who used their experience and reason to come to conclusions.

A universe so ordered, according to Voltaire, suggested the necessity of systematic and effective government. He further reasoned that law rather than the arbitrary whims of rulers should prevail. Under a lawful and just system, people should enjoy greater freedom to practice a religion of their own choice and present their views in print. In this reformed state, the cruel punishment of criminals also would end. Justice naturally required such changes.

MONTESQUIEU (1689–1755)

The Baron de Montesquieu's *Persian Letters* (1721) reflected an attitude toward established religious institutions much like Voltaire's. In Montesquieu's opinion, the churches of the day offered virtually nothing of value to society. Religion interested people mostly when sickness struck, he observed.

Persian Letters also indicated that much about European civilization other than its religious practices bothered this enlightened noble. He disapprovingly surveyed the many contradictions in European life and listed highly varied observations, some of which revealed his foreboding. The use of gunpowder weapons worried him, for example, and he pondered the horrors of forces that might be developed to kill on an even more massive scale.

At about age forty, Montesquieu began work on his most important publication. He was almost sixty when this volume, *The Spirit of the Laws*, appeared in print in 1748. Whereas *Persian Letters* had presented a critique of diverse aspects of society, his monumental production systematically described the fundamental types of political systems, explained how such different forms of state emerged, and evaluated a number of their sociopolitical practices.

Montesquieu proposed that states are always one of three types—despotic, monarchical, or republican. In the first two of these, a single person rules but a despot exercises much more complete and unshared power than does a monarch. A king might, for example, possess ultimate authority but govern in association with social entities such as the nobility, urbanites, or the church. The greatest division of authority occurs in republics, a system that lacks any central figure with the power of despot or king.

A complex interaction of influences produces a particular form of state in Montesquieu's view. He contended that common historical experiences, religious institutions, climate, and other factors combine to shape a society and incline it toward one of the three state forms. In the case of England, a state Montesquieu much admired, he proposed that the climate of the country prevented the public from having the submissive attitudes necessary for a despot to rule.

Apparently Montesquieu thought that human action as well as the forces of nature affect the degree of despotism or freedom in a society, for he argued that personal liberty requires the separation and balancing of powers among the branches of government—legislative, executive, and judicial. This latter idea directly influenced the plan for government in the United States.

In his analysis of state systems, Montesquieu expressed or implied several judgments. He concluded that the size of a society determines the extent of freedom needed by the population. Large states need a despot, small states function better as republics, and states of medium proportions fare best as monarchies. Montesquieu also recommended certain state policies, including the toleration of religious diversity and the promotion of a commercial economy. His concern about a state's business conditions surfaced also in his comments on slavery; he preferred to keep this labor system so that the price of sugar would remain low. In several respects, the Baron de Montesquieu loved the *Ancien Régime*.

Enlightened Despotism or Democracy?

Montesquieu admired certain forms of monarchy. Voltaire did not believe that the people as a whole possessed the competency to develop and operate the ideal society that he envisioned. In short, these two *philosophes* did not trust democracy. This attitude was typical of Enlightenment thinkers who until the latter 1700s directed their arguments for reform to the great monarchs. Many of the *philosophes* longed for a despot who could absorb light from critical intellectuals and then lead everyone out of the darkness of the *Ancien Régime*.

The faith of the *philosophes* in enlightened despotism was not wholly misplaced. Several monarchs in the 1700s made a conscious effort to learn from the Enlightenment. With varying degrees of success, these rulers applied their knowledge within their realms.

When leading members of European society, such as Montesquieu, saw the system as seriously flawed and in need of extensive reform, it meant that the prevalent social mechanisms had definitely outlived their usefulness. Aristocratic privilege and institutions that perpetuated both these special rights and many other old social practices appeared to be undeniably wrong to a growing proportion of the best-educated people. These brilliant critics also thought that the structures of the Ancien Régime *blocked the way to a new and eminently better life.*

The intellectuals who challenged the Ancien Régime, *the* philosophes, *shared much more than their contempt for the centuries-old social structure. They also expressed very similar ideas about the characteristics of the universe. The science of the 1500s and 1600s, to the minds of the* philosophes, *conclusively demonstrated that humanity lived in a world governed by changeless and mathematically precise natural laws. Theirs was a universe of material substances and forces that the reasoning mind could grasp and use, to great human advantage.*

The philosophes, *furthermore, held a common notion about the stage of intellectual development that humanity had entered. They thought of their times (1680s to 1780s) as an age of "Enlightenment." It seemed an enlightened era in part because of the great Natural Law discoveries of the previous generation of scientists. For the first time in history, they began life, it seemed to them, with a full knowledge of the forces that controlled the material world. Their times struck the* philosophes *as brilliant even more because they expected to use the amazing powers of the reasoning mind to discover the laws of human relationships. They anticipated this latter achievement as the next logical step for their enlightened generation.*

In an array of publications, many of unusual clarity and exceptionally broad appeal, the intellectuals of the Enlightenment shed a glaringly harsh light on the evils and inadequacies of the Ancien Régime. *They presented in equally dazzling brilliance their images of a reformed society. The* philosophes *vividly portrayed their vision of a human order ruled by reason rather than superstition, marked by tolerance rather than oppression, and structured by merit rather than traditional privilege. They continued until the latter 1700s to expect the great monarchs to respond to these well-reasoned complaints and plans and become enlightened despots who would lead the states of Europe into the modern age. As the* philosophes *wished, monarchs and emperors who appeared dedicated to the reign of reason did become typical figures from the 1750s to 1790s.*

Selected Readings

Anchor, Robert. *The Enlightenment Tradition.* New York: Harper & Row, 1967.

Becker, Carl. *The Heavenly City of the Eighteenth-Century Philosophers.* New Haven: Yale University Press, 1932.

Cragg, Gerald R. *The Church and the Age of Reason, 1648–1789.* New York: Atheneum, 1961.

Gay, Peter. *Age of Enlightenment.* New York: Time, 1966.

Goubert, Pierre. *The Ancien Régime: French Society, 1600–1750.* London: Weidenfeld and Nicolson, 1973.

Hufton, Olwen H. *The Poor of Eighteenth-Century France, 1750–1789.* Oxford, England: Clarendon Press, 1974.

Jacob, Margaret C. *The Radical Enlightenment: Pantheists, Freemasons, and Republicans.* Boston: Allen and Unwin, 1981.

Ogg, David. *Europe of the Ancien Regime, 1715–1783.* New York: Harper & Row, 1965.

Quennell, Peter, ed. *Affairs of the Mind: The Salon in Europe and America from the 18th to the 20th Century.* Washington, DC: New Republic Books, 1980.

Rudé, George F. E. *Europe in the Eighteenth Century: Aristocracy and the Bourgeois Challenge.* London: Weidenfeld and Nicholson, 1972.

4

The Despots and the High Enlightenment, 1750–1789

1643 Louis XIV becomes king of France (1643–1715)

1649 The English Parliament carries out the execution of Charles I

1682 Peter I, the Great, begins his reign as Tsar of Russia (1682–1725)

1740 Maria Theresa of Austria (1740–1780) and Frederick II, the Great, of Prussia (1740–1786) begin their reigns

1750s The High Enlightenment begins

1751 Diderot publishes the first volume of the *Encyclopedia*

1756 The Seven Years' War breaks out

1760 The reign of George III of England begins (1760–1820)

1762 Catherine II, the Great, becomes Tsarina Empress of Russia (1762–1796)
Rousseau publishes *Émile* and *The Social Contract*

1776 Adam Smith publishes *Wealth of Nations*

1780 Joseph II begins his reign in Austria (1780–1790)

1781 Immanuel Kant publishes *Critique of Pure Reason*

1788 Kant publishes *Critique of Practical Reason*

1792 Mary Wollstonecraft publishes *Vindication of the Rights of Woman*

The European political system in the latter 1700s was less modern than the outlook of the intellectuals, but it also had a less "ancient" tarnish than did the social order, the Ancien Régime. Government in Europe had taken on its somewhat modern gleam during the late Middle Ages and Early Modern period. Rulers had built up central authority and streamlined administration. Most of the kings of the latter 1700s used their partly updated political systems to promote economic and social modernization. For a time, it seemed that forward-looking intellectuals were right to praise and support their extremely powerful rulers. After all, the monarchs based their reforms on the ideas of the intellectuals.

Despite the improvements initiated by various governments, Europe had not achieved political modernity by the mid-1700s. Almost all European states remained monarchical, as they had been in the Middle Ages. Furthermore, they still depended on old institutions, including the churches, to provide additional support for royal authority. Kings in the early 1700s began to justify their power with "enlightened" arguments instead of divine-right theories, but monarchy still remained attached to institutions and ideas that the leading intellectuals rejected as completely outmoded.

An especially active phase of social criticism occurred from 1750 to 1789 in France. In these years of the "High Enlightenment," theorists denounced much more than social privileges, superstition, and divine-right theories. Most critics condemned the Ancien Régime in its entirety. Eminent Enlightenment commentators advocated extremely violent actions against the leaders of the old regime in France. The idea of a murderous rebellion appealed to growing numbers of people by the 1780s.

THE EUROPEAN STATE SYSTEM IN THE LATTER 1700s

In the 1780s, kings or emperors reigned over all the large European countries. Only a few states described themselves as "republics," indicating government by representatives of some portion of the citizens. Most republics were small entities, such as the Netherlands, Switzerland, and the Italian principalities of Venice and Genoa. At that time, even republics did not necessarily allow more than a very small percentage of people to exercise power. Among the four listed above, a tinge of democracy existed only in parts of one, Switzerland.

Near the end of the 1700s, therefore, monarchs sat securely on their thrones nearly everywhere in Europe, and many enjoyed virtually unrestrained power within their realms. The European form of monarchical state had originated in the Middle Ages. In the 1500s and 1600s, European kings acquired much greater authority as they modernized their governments. The steps these rulers took toward political modernity included the subordination of their nobles, the establishment of ruler supremacy over religious institutions, the propagation of theories of "divine-right" monarchy, the growth of central bureaucracy, and the expansion of royal armies. Historians call this early modern form of kingship "absolute monarchy." It reached its zenith in the reign of Louis XIV in France (1643–1715).

The States of East and Central Europe

Sweden, Denmark, Poland, and the various states of the Italian peninsula exercised much less influence in the affairs of East and Central Europe than did the other countries in that region. Swedish power had declined from the great heights it reached in the 1600s in part as a result of costly wars with Russia.

The weakening of Sweden's monarchy that came with a resurgence of noble strength both contributed to the lessened influence of this state and reduced the effectiveness of the government in domestic affairs. King Gustavus III (r. 1771–1792) took advantage of the nobles' factional strife and reversed the declining fortunes of the government at least within Swedish borders.

The Danes and the Italians experienced even less success than did the Swedes. In Denmark as in Sweden, the monarchy took action against the nobility. But the Danish government failed in its attempt to overcome aristocratic power and reform the state. The Italian states experienced a continuing decline in international standing. This weakened position resulted from the domination of Italy by Austrian and Spanish rulers.

Most of the vast expanse of land from the eastern border of France to the Siberian coastline of Russia on the Pacific Ocean fell within the borders of three empires—Russia, the Holy Roman Empire, and the empire of the Ottoman Turks. Most of the Turkish Empire was non-European including territories that extended from Asia across the Middle East to Egypt. The Ottoman rulers held European principalities in the Balkan peninsula, but these concerned them much less than their other holdings. The Holy Roman Empire had emerged during the Middle Ages. By the latter 1700s, it existed as little more than an almost meaningless border that surrounded important German states such as Prussia and Austria and other smaller states, most of them also Germanic. Russia, Prussia, and Austria dominated affairs within East and Central Europe.

THE RUSSIAN EMPIRE

In the mid-1400s, the rulers of a small Russian state centering on Moscow began to use the title "tsar," the Russian word for Caesar. The title implied that these leaders were emperors carrying forward the traditions of

Fig. 4.1 Central Europe, 1740

ancient Rome. In the 1500s, Russian tsars also began to call themselves "autocrat." They added this title to suggest that they were godlike rulers in the tradition of the Byzantine Empire (an eastern Mediterranean state with Greek culture that lasted from the 300s to 1400s A.D.).

The tsars acted on their imperial ambitions and eventually created a state that truly was an empire since these rulers conquered not only relatively open lands in the east but also previously independent states to the west. (A ruler over a collection of states is an emperor.)

Peter I, the Great (r. 1682–1725), was a member of the Romanov family that began to rule in the 1600s. He emphasized the vision of imperial grandeur in 1721 by adopting an additional title, Emperor, and by annexing still more territory. His forces had defeated Sweden, and the Treaty of Nystadt, 1721, added holdings in the northwest on the Baltic Sea coast (the location of present-day Estonia and Latvia). Russian rulers during the rest of the 1700s continued their march into new lands to the east and west, with especially important acquisitions from Finland in the north, Poland and Lithuania to the west, and Turkey in the southwest. Catherine II, the Great (r. 1762–1796), led the state through most of these imperial ventures. She also supported new intellectual movements and reforms strongly enough to become known as an enlightened despot.

By the end of Catherine's reign, the tsars had thoroughly subdued the gentry, the small but highly privileged class of landowning nobles that comprised the top of Russian society. Almost everyone else in Russia lived as impoverished peasants who in local matters owed full obedience to the nobility. About half of the peasantry held the lowest status of all, belonging to the special peasant category of serf. Although technically not slaves, serfs became virtual possessions of the gentry, due in no small part to the actions of Catherine the Great. Serfs often had no choice but to do the aristocracy's bidding in everything from manual labor to sexual favors. But all of society, whether noble or peasant, was expected to look to the tsar-emperor as the all-powerful ruler who "spoke as the most high God" when issuing governing decrees. By the latter 1700s, European states to the west of Russia also had to recognize the great, if not divine, power of the Romanov empire.

THE AUSTRIAN EMPIRE

Rudolf, a member of the Hapsburg family, established a realm in East Central Europe in the late 1200s, and the dynasty ruled states with varying borders in that region until 1918. Compared to the Romanovs, the Hapsburgs of the 1700s ruled over a small collection of territories. Furthermore, the scattered and ethnically diverse nature of Hapsburg holdings made effective rule difficult. Their possessions centered on Germanic Austria but also included Hungary (Magyar culture), Bohemia (ethnically Czech), Belgian lands, and several Italian territories. This lack of geographic and cultural unity probably lessened the state's power in international affairs and weakened the government at home.

Still, no other state controlled as much of Central Europe as did the Hapsburg dynasty. Their holdings comprised an empire with considerable influence in Europe, unlike the Holy Roman Empire, the almost meaningless title to which the Hapsburgs also usually held. Inside the Hapsburg state, the territorial and ethnic divisions hampered but did not nullify government authority. At home and abroad, therefore, these Austrian rulers stood as a very significant political force.

The character of the imperial bureaucracy enhanced the governing potential of the Hapsburgs in this period. Over the years administrators had pitted themselves against the class privileges of the aristocrats and the obligations of the serfs. Officials also promoted population growth and a more just and effective tax system. The two rulers who led the Austrian state from 1740 to 1790 attempted an even more vigorous reform program than had the imperial administrators of previous years.

Empress Queen Maria Theresa (r. 1740–1780). Maria Theresa was another of the monarchs of the Early Modern period who gained a reputation as an enlightened despot. She attempted reforms designed to move the state toward modernity. She tried, that is, to encourage industry, develop a more rational and effective central governing system, promote a primary commitment of all the people to central authority rather than to the local community, reduce the privileges of the upper classes, and lessen the obligations of the peasants to the nobility.

Even though Maria took all these steps toward a modern society, she moved with great caution. Joseph II, her son who ruled jointly with her in the last years of the Empress's reign, wanted to overcome such hesitancy about reform and even advocated the revolutionary step of ending the division of society into hereditary upper and lower classes.

Joseph II (r. 1780–1790). Joseph believed that a monarch should rule with unrestrained power, and once he took exclusive possession of the throne in 1780, he commanded drastic innovation. This enlightened despot took action against the old social system by freeing the serfs on his royal estates. He failed, however, to abolish the aristocratic structure of the realm.

Joseph attacked Catholic Church traditions even more forcefully. He ended the power of the church to censor the press, converted a number of its properties into funds for the advancement of education, and declared greater freedom for the practice of varied religions. His other efforts to improve the imperial system included steps to reduce wasteful spending and streamline government operations. These innovations provoked a very hostile reaction within some of Joseph's territories. Most of his reforms did not last very long after his reign.

THE KINGDOM OF PRUSSIA

Prussia, the other leading state of Central Europe, lay to the north of Austria. This kingdom also had scattered territory, but less so than in the case of the Austrian Empire's lands; furthermore, the Prussian population was mostly German rather than ethnically diverse. The Hohenzollern family of kings who ruled Prussia also had developed a government financial system that further solidified the state. More ominously, the strength of Prussia's military and a social tradition of strict obedience to ruling authority gave the state a special potential for control at home and influence abroad.

Frederick II (r. 1740–1786)—King as Public Servant. Frederick II, another enlightened despot, inherited the throne of a rising German kingdom in 1740. He proclaimed that a ruler was the "first servant of the state" and became a model of diligence for his society. Frederick read widely, wrote profusely, and worked energetically at the tasks of government. His political actions suggested that he cared for the welfare of the Prussian people, even though he thought their interests were best served by freezing them in their social positions—the peasants in rural servitude, the middle class barred from buying noble lands, the aristocrats secure in their special rights. In several respects, however, Frederick showed that he could flout tradition. For example, he ignored the customary ceremony and grand style associated with monarchy. More significantly, he instituted the most open policy toward the practice of religion of any ruler in his century.

Frederick II, the Great—a Warrior King. Europeans ordinarily add the descriptive "Great" to a ruler's name when he or she energetically pursues conquests. Frederick II acquired this label. Through much of his reign, the king led Prussia into costly battles, usually involving competing coalitions but with Austria as the chief adversary. The human cost of these wars for his own country, according to Frederick himself, was 300,000 soldiers and possibly more than thirty percent of noncombatant Prussians. Once victorious, this king believed in dictating a severe settlement to the defeated state, a traditional Prussian practice that Frederick probably intensified.

The French Monarchy— Absolute and Bankrupt

The Europeans had well established the traditions of a warrior state and despotic rule long before the rise of a militant Prussia under Frederick the Great. France epitomized this combination of military aggressiveness and royal absolutism throughout the reign of Louis XIV (1643–1715). This "Sun King" left to his heirs an extremely powerful monarchy but also a government deeply in debt from nearly constant warfare.

LOUIS XV—AN UNCONCERNED KING

Louis XV took the throne but not real authority at the age of five when his great-grandfather died in 1715. In the first years of the new king's reign, officials reduced the tendency of the government to overspend. Louis personally controlled the French state from the late 1730s until his death in 1774. During his years in charge, the country plunged into war again and by 1763 lost its North American empire to Britain. Taxes and government debts spiraled upward once more. The king took the desires of his female acquaintances into account as he formulated government policies in these years. He ignored, however, the worsening economic condition of the masses.

LOUIS XVI—AN INADEQUATE RULER

When the nineteen-year-old Louis XVI claimed the throne from his grandfather in 1774, he launched a promising reform program. The young king exhibited much more concern about the mounting problems of France than had Louis XV. The monarch's progressive goals included public debt reduction, fewer regulations on commerce, a lighter tax burden for peasants, and a degree of public participation in government.

The privileged classes stopped this reform effort when it had succeeded only in raising the expectations of the nonnobles without bringing satisfaction. Then, in the 1780s, the aristocrats launched an attack on the king's power. They meant to restore the authority they had lost to monarchy in the Early Modern period. Unknowingly, the nobles had taken a step that led to the destruction of both the French monarchy and aristocracy by the early 1790s.

In this last reign before the revolution, the king continued traditional courtly practices even as he worked for reform. For example, Louis sometimes spent nearly an hour going through the ritual of preparing for bed, in the presence of all the royal guests of the moment. As a final part of this ceremony called *coucher*, the king walked to each of the visitors who encircled him, moving awkwardly in a night robe with breeches dropped to his ankles.

The queen, Marie Antoinette, influenced royal policies and participated in monarchical ceremony, but also found a less courtly activity that she enjoyed. Louis and his wife had a model peasant hut constructed on the royal estates so that the queen could have the pleasure of playing the role of commoner. But neither the king's ritual associations with the nobility nor the queen's peasant games adequately prepared them to bridge the gulf that separated the monarchy from both the aristocracy and the commoners by 1789. That year, the crisis of society and government reached cataclysmic proportions. A king who could not carry out a program of moderate reform now faced a much more difficult challenge.

The Iberian States

The two countries on the Iberian Peninsula, Spain and Portugal, had passed their days of greatest glory by the 1700s. Both states, however, enjoyed improved fortunes for a time after the early years of this century.

SPAIN

Charles III (r. 1759–1788) inherited a more highly centralized and effective state as a result of the reforms enacted by the previous king, Philip V (r. 1700–1746). The loss of holdings in Italy and North Central Europe during Philip's reign also benefited Charles by leaving him a more compact and less expensive state. The new king advanced the fortunes of his monarchy still further by his subordination of the Catholic Church. The gains helped future monarchs very little, however. The greatest menace to the kings remained unchanged. At the end of Charles's reign, the aristocracy still had the same formidable power to challenge royal authority that they had enjoyed when he took the throne.

PORTUGAL

The resurgence of the Portuguese state came under the guidance of the Marquis of Pombol, the head of the government bureaucracy from 1751 to 1777 during the reign of Joseph I. Reforms that Pombol instituted reflected the attitudes of the *philosophes* as much as did those of any of the enlightened despots. As chief royal minister, Pombol reduced the power of the nobles and the Catholic Church, adopted a policy of free trade within Portuguese territories, improved governmental operations and financial procedures, and made political leadership positions accessible to nonaristocrats. These changes made Portugal more politically modern. So too did Pombol's establishment of a secret police agency.

Typical of the despotic reform efforts, the vigor that Pombol brought to the Portuguese system did not last. The Iberian states remained in the shadow of the greater powers to the east and north.

Parliament and Monarchy in England

Across the English Channel, the kings of Britain struggled to achieve total monarchical supremacy, but they encountered a formidable foe. Early Modern English kings, as well as many others in Europe at the time, had greatly expanded royal power. Then, during the 1600s, the rulers attempted to establish a truly "absolute" monarch. The legislature ("Parliament") stopped them by using laws and force, however. The necessity of extreme measures gave the Parliamentarians no pause. They beheaded King Charles I in 1649.

THE ENGLISH PARLIAMENT

In the Middle Ages, the English Parliament began as a conference of royal officials and others, such as leading members of the warrior aristocracy, summoned by the king. Monarchs convened these assemblies especially when they needed a group to serve as a high court, but they typically used the sessions to present royal policies, seek advice, or conduct other business of government.

Eventually, it became the practice to call to Parliament members of the lower nobility and representatives of the towns. Centuries of development in this way produced the Parliament of the 1600s, a law-making body with a House of Lords for the aristocracy and a House of Commons for nonnobles. The English viewed Parliament in this form as an agency empowered to act for all the people of the kingdom, even against the monarch, if he or she overstepped the proper limits of authority. Despite the image of Parliament as an institution that spoke for everyone, this early modern legislature actually represented the interests of the aristocrats, other well-to-do country landowners, prosperous merchants, and others of similar socioeconomic standing.

GEORGE III (1760–1820) AND HIS QUEST FOR GREATER POWER

George III, the king who ruled Britain at the time of the American Revolution, launched into a struggle to wrest from Parliament certain of the powers lost by the monarchy since the mid-1600s. He intended neither to subdue Parliament nor regain absolute power. The king meant, however, to have the heads of the divisions of government report to him instead of to the House of Commons, a change that would restore monarchical control over administration. George achieved his dream of power during the 1770s, but the results seemed a nightmare to many critics, especially to his opponents in Parliament: With the king fully in charge of policies, Britain lost the American colonies and then continued to suffer from the financial costs of the conflict.

WILLIAM PITT THE YOUNGER

King George's selection of William Pitt the Younger as prime minister in 1783 opened the way to much improved governmental and economic conditions. Pitt, whose father had been prime minister twenty years earlier, took the top administrative office at the age of twenty-four. Parliament as well as the king viewed this young but politically experienced leader favorably. He lived up to their expectations. Pitt dealt effectively with the problems of excessive government debt and financial mismanagement. He also arranged a trade agreement with France that benefited both nations. For Britain, the treaty provided the especially important advantage of an expanded market for products of the new and growing industrial system.

Diplomacy and Warfare in the Age of Reason

Even though rival states such as Britain and France reached accord on certain issues, and despite the image of this era as an age of reason and enlightenment, it was also a time of persistent warfare. Standing armies with the ranks filled by nonnoble soldiers had become a fact of life by the 1600s, but an aristocratic military and political leadership still guided European armies and governments as they interacted and made war.

"THE DIPLOMATIC REVOLUTION"

One of the main conflicts of the era was between France and England. They fought over dominance in North Europe, North America, and India. (Both countries were building colonial empires.) In another area of continuing conflict, Austria and Prussia struggled for supremacy in Central Europe. France and England sometimes became entangled in these battles.

At first Austria had the support of England, largely because of Austria's historic rivalry with France. But after a serious loss in a war with Prussia in the 1740s, Austria turned to France for support. At this juncture, England dropped Austria and sided with Prussia. This reversal of relationships became known as "The Diplomatic Revolution."

THE SEVEN YEARS' WAR

This new alignment of powers fought in the Seven Years' War (1756–1763), but the arrangement of forces and territories changed little as a result. Still, Prussia's ability to fight so well without a major ally on the continent showed that this country had become a leading force among the European states. During the Seven Years' War, France and England fought in North America as well as in Europe, a conflict called the French and Indian War in the New World. This war on two fronts was typical of struggles between these two nations in this period.

England won the upper hand in North America by 1763, and, as a result, became more actively involved in the affairs of the British New World. The Americans soon turned rebellious, often expressing their discontents and dreams in a manner typical of Enlightenment reformists and rebels.

THE PARTITIONS OF POLAND

Poland ranks among the leading states of its region in most eras of European history. Contrary to that pattern, this country vanished as a political entity during the latter 1700s to reappear only in 1918. A weakened state in the early 1700s as a result of aristocratic actions against the central government, Poland fell prey to its grasping neighbors beginning in the 1770s.

Three power-hungry states—Russia, Prussia, and Austria—struggled for dominance in East Europe during the 1700s. Not only did they threaten one another, the three also competed to take the lands of lesser states. With relatively weak governments and armies, the Ottoman Turkish Empire and Poland became favored targets of their aggression. The forces of Catherine II of Russia struck the Ottomans in 1768. Soon disaster loomed over the Turks.

An impending Russian land grab north and west of the Black Sea at the expense of the Ottomans meant a defeat of sorts also for Austria and Prussia. Catherine's strategic gain would leave her two rivals relatively weaker. Russia and Austria moved toward war. Prussia feared an Austro-Russian conflict might end with these two countries taking Turkish land and growing in power. In the political calculus of the age, such an outcome would constitute a loss for Prussia.

The three greater powers of the region found a solution to the conflict generated among them by the Russo-Turkish war. They decided to take land from Poland. In 1772, the aggressors each seized a piece of Poland—a sector from the north for Prussia, from the south for Austria, and from the east for Russia. Poland lost control of half its people and one-third of its land. The diminished state suffered two similar dismemberments in 1793 and 1795. It disappeared, absorbed in a process begun by three enlightened despots.

THE HIGH ENLIGHTENMENT— AN INTELLECTUAL ASSAULT ON MONARCHY

By the mid-1700s, the *philosophes* had largely completed the intellectual framework begun by early Enlightenment theorists. They also had devised elaborate structures of ideas that fit within this larger system. This refinement of thought climaxed during the years from 1750 to 1790, the era of the "High Enlightenment."

In these decades, several critics used Enlightenment principles in their descriptions of specific evils of the *Ancien Régime*. The demand for reform and the resistance to change both intensified. Other intellectuals continued the more comprehensive work of criticizing entire social systems and describing the ideal or "just" society as a guide to the complete revision of the human order. These *philosophes* of the High Enlightenment thought, wrote, and felt passionately about reform. Their ideas bred revolution.

Diderot (1713–1784) and the Encyclopedia

Critics could not freely launch their verbal barrage against the Old Regime in France. Censors stood ready to counterattack. Efforts to stop the assault backfired, however, and condemned works sold better than others. A very active effort to publish the views of Enlightenment critics of the established order flooded France with pantheist and materialist writings supporting the new outlook.

The *Encyclopedia* became a large and important stream in this deluge of material. This publication appeared as a series of encyclopedic volumes produced during two decades beginning in 1751. Denis Diderot wrote articles for and edited the *Encyclopedia*. It contained compositions by virtually all the other leading French thinkers of the period on a great variety of current topics. They wrote about government, the social system, and religion, attacking traditions in all these areas from a scientific materialist perspective. Contributors to the *Encyclopedia* summarized and praised the advances in biology and chemistry. They used the premises of these sciences to support their scorn for the essentials of Christianity.

Most of the early *philosophes* had stayed closely associated with the rich and powerful members of society and favored a moderate reform program. The educated public had viewed these relatively tame reformers of the early Enlightenment as a dangerous fringe element of the literate world. After 1750, this same public revered Diderot and the rest of the new generation of *philosophes*, even though they posed a real threat to the Old Regime. The mood of discontent had grown broader and deeper, especially in France.

Quesnay (1694–1774) and the Physiocrats

The Physiocrats, a group of bourgeois reformers in France, advocated the establishment of a capitalist agricultural system free of all controls except nature. They denounced mercantilism because, as a policy of state manipulation of the economy, it prevented the operation of natural laws that could ensure material prosperity. Physiocrats also condemned the usual nonagricultural commercial pursuits of the bourgeoisie. In the opinion of these reformers, only farming generated wealth because agriculture actually expanded the invested substance.

François Quesnay produced the most noted work by a member of this group. *The Economic Table*, which he published in 1758, advanced the physiocratic idea of an uncontrolled capitalist agricultural system. Despite the Physiocrats' use of these *laissez-faire* theories to argue against industrial capitalism, urban bourgeois entrepreneurs adopted these principles and transformed them into their own articles of faith supporting capitalist industrial enterprise.

Jean Jacques Rousseau (1712–1778)

Enlightenment critics thought alike in many respects. Yet they also expressed divergent ideas. Locke represented one of the strongest intellectual tendencies. He brought science and reason to the support of a social cause dear to the hearts of the rising bourgeois industrialists. The Physiocrats, however, illustrate a weaker but important theoretical crosscurrent. Despite their advocacy of reform and the typical appeal to nature, these critics wanted adjustments that would reinvigorate an agricultural society.

Rousseau's ideas differed in a special way. His theories agreed with many fundamental Enlightenment tenets, but his perception of their logical implications was radically new. To Rousseau, the principles of the Enlightenment brought a vision of a society led by neither a revived rural elite nor a recently advancing industrial class. He looked forward to a society of equals.

ROUSSEAU'S CRITIQUE OF THE *ANCIEN RÉGIME*

Up to a point, Rousseau approached his task, a comprehensive critique of society and culture, like a secular, reasoning *philosophe*. He differed from most of his contemporaries, however, in his strong emphasis on the idea that the discovery of truth involved reason *and* emotion. He believed that without the good feeling that a logical quest brought, no worthwhile intellectual trek would begin.

Rousseau asserted that humans, as beings governed by both passion and reason, needed to live in a truly free society. In agreement with High Enlightenment thought, he condemned despotic government for its denial of this necessary liberty. Yet Rousseau also blamed the literature, arts, and science of his era for the enslavement of humanity. Thus he damned the culture that the *philosophes* revered as the way to human perfection.

Rousseau concluded that the fundamental cause of the disharmony between society and human nature was private property. Originally, he reasoned, the land on which people lived belonged to no single person. When individuals first took property for themselves, greed became a dominant influence in human relationships. A struggle for material superiority began. The dedication to the truly inherent needs for love and friendship weakened. By the 1700s, this pattern of human development produced a society constructed by the wealthy to preserve and justify their status. Such a civic order made fulfillment of the need for caring relationships difficult to realize. Rich and poor alike suffered from the denial of love and friendship in this unnatural state. The impoverished masses felt the additional pain of oppression—a life without freedom.

ÉMILE—LEARNING BY HEART

The formation of a society that provided the freedom to satisfy natural inclinations of heart and mind required, in Rousseau's view, a new form of education. In *Émile* (1762), he presented the then revolutionary idea that children were not miniature adults who needed an authority to stuff information into them. Rousseau insisted that children had to explore the world and discover its truths under the guidance of an intelligent and sensitive adult in order to develop their unique young minds to full potential. Learning in this way would prepare people for citizenship in a civic order best suited to common human needs.

THE SOCIAL CONTRACT—FREE ASSOCIATION

Rousseau did not think that education alone could produce the transformed society that he so desired. People had to found a new political order as well. In *The Social Contract* (1762) Rousseau presented his views on the voluntary association of equal citizens that he believed should replace the oppressive *Ancien Régime*.

Rousseau rejected the widely held Enlightenment idea of liberation achieved by the establishment of a body of constitutional law to protect natural rights to life, liberty, and property. Rather, he advocated the formation of a society in harmony with universal human traits. These characteristics, he affirmed, included an urge to self-preservation, an ability to care about the suffering of others, and a natural sense of how to achieve the common good.

Given these qualities, humanity needed and had the potential to establish a system in which the power of the collective citizenry would provide the freedom to act on universal natural impulses. Such a civic order also would protect the person and possessions of all individuals. A society of this kind could exist when its members willingly surrendered certain individual prerogatives and gained a commensurate share in social authority. People would enter, that is, a *social* contract among equal citizens rather than a political contract between ruler and citizens.

Despite this submission to the collective, individuals would not lose their freedom, Rousseau argued. Indeed, the liberty natural to humans could exist beyond primitive times only by membership in a society governed by laws that agreed with the natural traits of people. Codes in harmony with this universal human nature would all meet the single standard of contributing to the common good.

When citizens maintain conditions and support actions beneficial to all members of society, they are expressing the "general will," according to Rousseau. The prevalence of private interests that favor certain individuals or factions, to the detriment of others, perpetuates a corrupt civic system. The operation of the general will brings the good society to life. This beneficial state, moved by the general will, can exist only when all members of society enjoy equality and every citizen participates in government through a representative.

Rousseau presented *The Social Contract* as his plan for the thorough reform of society. It did become a rich source of inspiration for generations of political thinkers. Not all of them, however, saw the treatise as a directive for reform. Even before the end of the century, it became for certain leaders a blueprint for violent revolution.

Beccaria (1738–1794) on Crime and Punishment

Cesare Beccaria, an Italian contributor to High Enlightenment thought, offered a less comprehensive analysis of society than did Rousseau. He presented, however, a provocative commentary on the causes of and solutions for crime. Beccaria's ideas about this issue had radical implications for the same reason that portions of Rousseau's thought did. Like Rousseau, Beccaria saw private property as an evil influence. He blamed the acquisitiveness of "the haves" for the tendency of "the have-nots" to violate social codes. According to Beccaria's argument, the rich made the laws and in so doing favored themselves, thus creating injustices that provoked others to crime.

Because of his views on the evil of property ownership, opponents called him a "socialist," and thus coined a new word. They believed that chaos would result from acting on his ideas. Supporters, however, saw his work as aimed at going beyond simple reform of the legal system and removing the fundamental causes of crime.

Adam Smith (1732–1790) and the Wealth of Capitalists

Most Enlightenment theorists held a very different view of property than did Rousseau and Beccaria. Among the "natural rights" that seemed so important to most of these thinkers, property rights usually were the most honored. No one wrote more effectively in behalf of the Enlightenment idea of property rights than did Adam Smith.

In Smith's *Wealth of Nations* (1776), this English theorist spoke out for the operation of natural laws in the economic world. He believed that government should leave business alone (a *laissez-faire* economic policy) since the free operation of economic laws would lead to the best of all possible worlds. Like many in his era, Smith not only had a powerful faith in natural laws, but also a strong conviction that living in harmony with nature ensured progress.

Smith anticipated that this process would produce a society blessed with small competing businesses, each making what it made best at a fair price. Nations also would make and trade the goods that they were most suited to manufacture and buy from other countries the specialties each turned out. The resultant societies should have no great disparity between rich and poor, and there should be no impoverished masses. Although it is contrary to this vision of Smith's, his ideas acquired an image as the doctrine of rich, large-scale, inhumane capitalism.

Wollstonecraft (1759–1797) and Women's Rights

Most intellectuals during the Enlightenment believed that they were the heirs of two centuries of intellectual and cultural progress. In their view, this advancement enabled them to recognize the flaws in society and discover how to correct them. These theorists did see injustices scarcely recognized earlier; but despite their "progress," they largely ignored the fate of the enslaved and many of the unprivileged, including women.

In the case of women, it appears that their lives had worsened in these Early Modern centuries. Hobbes and Locke did not find any reasons in the natural world for women to live as social inferiors, but they gave little attention to this issue. Rousseau thought that women had no place in the governance of the political order, and Immanuel Kant (1724–1804), a leading German philosopher, seemed to think that they hardly deserved to be educated.

Mary Wollstonecraft, however, took a quite different view of the situation for women. This English advocate of female rights contended that Enlightenment conceptions applied to women as well as men, and that women should bring about a reformation in their social circumstances. They had to end the male-imposed oppression, she argued, and claim their natural human rights. The ideas she presented in *Vindication of the Rights of Woman* (1792) became very important influences in the 1800s and thereafter.

THE WANING OF THE ENLIGHTENMENT

Enlightenment intellectuals usually exhibited a supreme confidence in the existence of changeless natural laws. They also generally championed the values of the bourgeoisie. Rousseau and Beccaria displayed many typical Enlightenment attitudes. To Rousseau, however, the idea of natural laws was an invention that the bourgeoisie used to justify their wealth and the poverty and oppression of the poor. Both men condemned the principle of private property so sacred to the industrial middle class. The works of Rousseau and Beccaria thus indicate a shift away from central Enlightenment beliefs.

The Marquis de Sade (1740–1814)

For the Marquis de Sade, not only was nature unworthy of faith, it deserved contempt. Humanity, he believed, could find no guide to correct behavior in either divine or natural law. Therefore, Sade considered moral codes and laws to be devices used by the rich and powerful to exploit and abuse the poor and weak.

The proper response to such a miserable circumstance, Sade proclaimed, was to violate all social principles whether they pertained to property rights, sexual behavior, or other aspects of conduct. The horrible injustices of society made any attack on it appropriate. Above all, he sanctioned an assault on the established order through sexual offenses, for then the rebel struck at the evil social system and at nature itself, the sire and deserter of a hopeless humanity. Few of the attributes of the Enlightenment *philosophe* remained in Sade's ideas. Because of his views and behavior, the word "sadism" eventually entered many languages.

Immanuel Kant

Like the Marquis de Sade, Immanuel Kant believed that no natural laws existed to guide the course of human affairs. For Kant, however, a humanity orphaned by nature was mentally equipped to take charge of its own destiny and move toward the most highly moral social order. Kant thus denied the central Enlightenment tenet that nature provided laws for life, but he kept the faith in reason and progress. Indeed, Kant presumed that humanity could struggle *against* impulses instilled by nature and discover a way to approach individual and social perfection. The knowledge and moral insight that *all* rational beings possessed made such a quest possible, according to Kant.

KANT'S THEORY OF KNOWLEDGE

This German philosopher presented his epistemology, or theory of knowledge, in *The Critique of Pure Reason* (1781). In this work, he explained his conception of the great potential of the mind, its power to formulate plans for human betterment. The thinking person, he affirmed, could gain knowledge not only by experience in the natural world, but also by the recognition of universal rational truths. People acquired certain aspects of knowledge, that is, simply because of the traits of the human mind. For example, the mind could draw conclusions about how events occurred without encountering their causes. It also could envision a new social order that had never existed. Such mental capacities gave humanity much of what it needed for a life of progress.

KANTIAN ETHICS

Kant based his epistemology on an assertion. He proclaimed that there was knowledge which always held true for everyone. In *The Critique of Practical Reason* (1788), Kant announced the existence of a similarly universal ethics, or system of morality. All rational beings, he assured, could recognize and accept these globally valid moral principles, just as they could the knowledge that accorded with reason.

Kant further declared that the possession of an inherent morality (sense of right and wrong) necessarily meant that humanity also had free will. Since universal truths and morality existed, since the reasoning mind had the power to ascertain these universals, and since people had the ability to choose the good, humanity was endowed with everything necessary to develop the more nearly perfect society of which the Enlightenment dreamed.

The new social order that Kant preferred would be one in which people were free and self-governing. The universal characteristics of humankind made such a system appropriate for them. Kant anticipated that this rational and emancipated humanity could even establish global peace.

In many respects, the great works of Kant represent the ultimate achievement of Enlightenment thought. This philosopher demonstrated his profound understanding of the ideas and methods of the Age of Reason. He displayed with exceptional brilliance the special value that he saw in many of them. Kant's writing also paradoxically contained evidence of the weakening hold of Enlightenment thought on the minds of leading European intellectuals. For even though he gave powerful support to the idea of human reason, he blasphemed nature, a virtual god for many philosophes. Furthermore, Kant pointed toward a new way of thinking that the next generation of theorists, ironically, would use to deny the intellectual supremacy of reason.

This waning of the Enlightenment at the end of the 1700s is significant in part because the movement had lasted so long (about 100 years) and had affected European life so deeply. Even in its last phase, the High Enlightenment (1750–1789), this mentality of the Age of Reason entered the throne rooms of Europe and inspired rulers such as Catherine II of Russia, Frederick II of Prussia, and Joseph II of Austria to carry out remarkable programs of reform. Even if they might have done so mainly to enhance monarchical power, these "enlightened despots" consciously tried to modernize the Ancien Régimes *they had inherited.*

The weakening of the intellectuals' faith in the dogmas of the Enlightenment in no way indicated that the principles of the movement would no longer influence Europe. The Enlightenment outlook became a very prominent, if not always dominant, feature of Western intellectual life throughout the coming years. These ideas, moreover, continued to affect the attitudes and behavior of societies both within and beyond Europe.

In addition to these persistent direct effects of the Enlightenment, this movement profoundly influenced modern history in a number of indirect ways. The French Revolution (1789–1815) was a medium of special importance through which the Enlightenment permeated European history. This great political upheaval began to a great extent as the result of the modernizing forces of the industrial revolution and the Age of Reason. Industrialization changed the way Europeans lived. The Enlightenment transformed the way they thought. The French Revolution ushered in a new social and political system that still functions today.

Selected Readings

Artz, Frederick B. *The Enlightenment in France*. Kent, OH: Kent State University Press, 1968.

Dukes, Paul. *Catherine the Great and the Russian Nobility: A Study Based on the Materials of the Legislative Commission of 1767*. Cambridge, England: University Press, 1967.

Goldberg, Rita, ed. *Sex and Enlightenment: Women in Richardson and Diderot*. New York: Cambridge University Press, 1984.

Rousseau, G. S., and Roy Porter, eds. *Sexual Underworlds of the Enlightenment*. Chapel Hill, NC: University of North Carolina Press, 1988.

Spencer, Samia I., ed. *French Women and the Age of the Enlightenment*. Bloomington, IN: Indiana University Press, 1984.

Treasure, Geoffrey R. R. *The Making of Modern Europe, 1648–1780*. New York: Methuen, 1985.

Wangermann, Ernst. *The Austrian Achievement, 1700–1800*. New York: Harcourt, Brace, and Jovanovich, 1973.

Williams, E. Neville. *The Ancien Régime in Europe: Government and Society in the Major States, 1648–1789*. London: Bodley Head, 1970.

5

The French Revolution and the Reign of Terror, 1789–1795

1774	The reign of Louis XVI begins (1774–1792)
May 5, 1789	The Estates General convenes—first meeting since 1614
June 17, 1789	The National Assembly forms
June 20, 1789	The Assembly issues the Tennis Court Oath
July 14, 1789	The fall of the Bastille
Mid-1789	The Great Fear begins, continues three weeks
August 4, 1789	The National Assembly decrees an end to aristocratic privilege
August 26, 1789	The Declaration of the Rights of Man and of the Citizen
October 5, 1789	The Women's March on Versailles
1790	The Civil Constitution of the Clergy
June 20, 1791	The flight of the king
October 1791	The Legislative Assembly replaces the National Assembly
April 20, 1792	France declares war on Austria
September 1792	The September Massacres
September 20, 1792	The National Convention replaces the Legislative Assembly

January 21, 1793	Execution of Louis XVI
September 1793	Robespierre and the Jacobin-dominated Committee of Public Safety in control
October 1793	The Reign of Terror begins
July 1794	Thermidorean Reaction and execution of Robespierre end the Terror
1795	The Constitution of 1795 establishes a new government, the Directory

Europeans became economically and intellectually modern as the changes engendered by the industrial revolution and the Enlightenment spread over the continent in the 1700s and after. New political currents joined those that brought industry into European civilization. As these political, economic, and intellectual forces converged, they swept the people of the region along even more tumultuously after the 1780s.

In France, these movements brought about a modernizing political revolution that burst to the surface in 1789. Within that nation, rebels quickly completed the destruction of the old social and governing system.

France soon became the only large European state ruled by representative citizens rather than a king. The French citizenry, moreover, won constitutionally guaranteed individual rights and thereby escaped their former status as subjects of an absolute government. The special privileges of the aristocracy and the church also ended with this revolution. This latter social change, in combination with the political shift toward citizen power, produced the form of state that many historians now define as "modern."

Monarchs in surrounding states moved rapidly to end the dangerous rise of modernizing sociopolitical movements both within their own territories and in France. French revolutionaries responded to the challenge. They raised massive citizen armies and aroused the country with a sense of nationalism new to Europe. Amazingly, this infant modern state fought off the host of foreign enemies, but the dire threat to the new French system led its rulers to resort to bloody terror in order to defeat real and imagined domestic foes.

The Reign of Terror (1793–1794) brought France to its most extreme point of change away from the Ancien Régime. *Leaders in these years favored the extension of power to more of the populace than had any in the past. In the crisis atmosphere, however, government practice became increasingly dictatorial rather than living up to the pledge of democracy. The French had realized many of their revolutionary dreams, but the accompanying violence and tyranny became intolerable. Opposition forces overthrew the terrorist leaders and by 1795 established a less radical republic. Even though the new government set stricter limits on popular influence, the revolution had broken the power of the traditional rulers forever. The modern state had fully emerged.*

THE ORIGINS OF THE FRENCH REVOLUTION

Circumstances conducive to the French Revolution emerged throughout the Early Modern period. Economic modernization caused the middle class to grow increasingly rich and ambitious without equivalent gains in political influence or social privilege. The bourgeoisie thus felt more and more frustrated and hostile toward the *Ancien Régime*. When they began their overt political attack, the specific target at first was the monarchy. The government faced a dangerous foe.

Revolutionary Trends

Intellectual trends that began in the 1600s also helped to foster a rebellious mood by the latter 1700s. As the years of the Enlightenment progressed, theorists poured out increasingly hostile commentaries on the *Ancien Régime*. The *philosophes* always despised the established Christian church, a central pillar of the old order. Most of their writing flashed with the contempt they felt for the aristocracy, whatever the progressive attitudes of a few nobles. Ultimately, Age of Reason theorists who hated despotism, whether enlightened or not, became the leading voices of the modernizing intellectual movement. Their weapons against aristocracy and monarchy were verbal barbs and broadsides. By the 1790s, revolutionaries used these Enlightenment ideas, but they also wielded the executioner's blade in their assault on the *Ancien Régime*.

Long-term political trends combined with socioeconomic and intellectual developments and brought about a crisis of gigantic proportions in France by 1789. The campaigns that Louis XIV began in order to expand royal wealth and military power continued under his successors. The negative effects of these practices became increasingly apparent. The Sun King's victories abroad had left huge debts by 1715. Wars thereafter consumed additional funds, and the kings had to borrow still more. Despite the heavy price paid, mid-century war led to stalemate in Europe instead of glorious victory. The French also experienced severe losses in the imperial struggles with Britain in North America. (See chapter 4.)

Challenges to Royal Authority

Even a successful adventure could prove harmful. When France provided money and troops to help the American colonists in their revolt against the British mother country (1775 to 1783), the expenditures pushed the French government to the brink of financial disaster. The effort to cope with the problem by a further expansion of monarchical taxing power prompted the aristocrats to lead a drive against the king's authority. In this way, the royal warfare, empire building, and tax policies that helped make France dominant in Europe also directly fostered the crisis of the late 1780s that doomed the French system.

The huge war debt and tax problems of the king gave the long-subdued nobility its chance to challenge royal authority. Aristocrats in French judicial bodies blocked tax increases in order to force convocation of a policy-making assembly that they intended to dominate. Their goal was power for the nobles. Ironically, this upper-class action opened the way for a middle-class revolutionary triumph over both monarchy and aristocracy.

French Society on the Eve of Revolution

The formal structure of French society as revolution neared in the late 1780s remained unchanged from the shape it had taken in the Middle Ages and the Early Modern period. According to long-held tradition, the 400,000 members of the First Estate (clergy) and the Second Estate (nobles) deserved an honored and privileged place at the top of the social order. Regardless of wealth, education, or other distinctions, the other 24,000,000 to 25,000,000 people who belonged to the Third Estate held an inferior position in the social order, at least in theory.

Although actual conditions in the 1780s varied from this theoretical view of society, the first two estates did have privileges, such as exemption from certain taxes and legal restrictions, that no members of the Third Estate enjoyed. Privileges without power over the king left the aristocrats deeply dissatisfied. With neither special rights nor a share in political control, members of the Third Estate had strong grievances against both the monarch and the aristocrats.

Was the *Ancien Régime* now surely doomed? The aristocratic drive to reduce the ruler's power and restore the nobles authority did not indicate that this upper class wanted revolution. The conditions under which the other classes lived and their attitudes toward them also did not suggest the inevitability of a sweeping social upheaval. Still, the circumstances in French society in the 1780s made the potential for rebellion unusually high.

THE CLERGY AND THE ARISTOCRACY

The eminence and power of the aristocracy significantly increased after the death of Louis XIV in 1715. Since the upper clergy usually came from noble families, they too shared in the advance of this class. Parish priests who made up the lower clergy had privileges because they were members of the First Estate. Yet they lived and thought more like the commoners whose social backgrounds were the same as most of theirs.

By the latter 1700s the aristocracy had made all the top church and state offices their exclusive preserve, thus shutting out the bourgeoisie who before had successfully competed for these positions. Despite the privileged place of nobles in society and their increased influence during the 1700s, they were very discontented. They wanted to bring the monarchy under their permanent control. The social position and gains of the first two estates in the 1700s, therefore, gave the Third Estate additional reasons for complaint without bringing satisfaction to the aristocracy.

THE BOURGEOISIE

More than 2,000,000 financiers, industrialists, merchants, and professional people made up the bourgeoisie in the 1780s. By that decade, any of them who wanted top positions in government, the military, or the church faced new and virtually insurmountable barriers to such careers, thanks to the efforts of the nobles since 1715. This condition encouraged the aspirants to such posts to place blame on the aristocracy. Most of the bourgeoisie, however, found satisfactory careers at somewhat lower levels, or they could purchase noble titles and open the way to privileged jobs. Moreover, virtually all bourgeois elements shared the benefits of an economic advance that began in the 1730s. Thus the middle classes had many reasons to remain content.

Nevertheless, a rebellious mood grew. In addition to the members of the bourgeoisie who continued to feel hostile toward the aristocracy, others became increasingly disturbed by the way both monarchical government and the traditional estate structure prevented the realization of their social, economic, and political ambitions. The explosive potential of this attitude was all the greater because certain aristocrats had the same progressive outlook. Even the less reform-minded nobles could find common ground with these malcontents in their opposition to monarchical power.

THE PEASANTS

About fifty percent of the 20,000,000 French farmers owned land in the 1780s. Collectively, these peasants held more than one-third of the nation's territory. The other 10,000,000 farmers worked either as sharecroppers or hired laborers. Landowners or not, the French peasants lived better than those of any other nation on the continent. Even so, they too harbored many resentments and felt extremely dismayed by their circumstances in the latter decades of the 1700s.

The relatively good life of the French peasantry resulted in part from having good farmland and a favorable climate. Nearly all the farmers also had won freedom from serfdom. In the nations to the east, a much higher percentage remained enserfed. These comparative advantages, however, could not induce contentment in a rural population aggravated by nobles who still had the right to hunt on their farms, demand fees for such vital services as the use of a mill, and raise the rents on land. A series of bad crop years, persistent inflation, and an unfair burden of taxes intensified the bitterness of the peasantry. No passion for political revolution gripped the rural masses, but their temper could move them to use force to reverse hated social and economic conditions.

THE URBAN WORKERS

The artisans, unskilled laborers, and servants who worked in French cities also became a highly volatile social force by the 1780s. Economic trends of the mid to late 1700s that enriched the middle classes oppressed these poorer groups. The mounting prices that brought rising incomes for businesspeople and landlords confronted urban workers with economic disaster. Rents more than doubled in Paris, for example, and the bread which provided most of their calories also took as much as half their income. Wages rose much more slowly than living costs. Then a depression struck in the late 1780s.

Under these conditions, segments of the working population faced starvation. They expected a government remedy quickly. If relief did not come, the 2,000,000 common laborers of France's cities could pose an extreme threat to the system. Despite their relatively small numbers, these workers lived in the larger cities, such as Paris. If they turned violent, the people at the centers of power were near at hand.

The Financial Crisis, 1786–1789

The leaders of France, including King Louis XVI (r. 1774–1792), knew that the country was in serious trouble, and they worked vigorously, if not effectively, to find solutions. For the central government, though, a massive debt rather than the price or availability of bread was the most critical problem. The amount owed by the monarchy had surged upward from less than 2,000,000,000 livres at the beginning of Louis XVI's reign to more than 4,000,000,000 by the late 1780s. As always, the government's military spending accounted for most of the debt. Specifically, in this case, the cost of aid to the American revolutionaries brought on most of the increase in the deficit.

The king could have paid the price of imperial adventures by establishing a more equitable tax system that tapped the wealth of the first two estates and the bourgeoisie. Instead he avoided a confrontation with the now more assertive privileged classes and borrowed heavily at high interest rates. Then, in 1786, the banks stopped the loans. The king's credit had run out. Charles de Calonne, the royal controller-general or treasurer, decided that an extensive revision of government finance was unavoidable. He formulated a plan that included provisions for increased taxes on the first two estates and the bourgeois business community. Powerful social interests would surely resist such reform.

THE ASSEMBLY OF NOTABLES, 1787

The government decided to arrange a meeting of leading aristocrats, clergymen, and judicial officials to court the support of such notable people. The agreement of these social leaders to new taxes might sway the upper estates toward the financial reform demanded by the debt crisis. But when the Assembly of Notables gathered in February 1787, they opposed Calonne's plan. The controller-general responded with a call for support from the population at large. Louis dismissed Calonne for this unusual action. A replacement for Calonne, selected for his compatibility with the notables, still could not end their resistance. The government dissolved the Assembly in May.

CONFRONTATION WITH THE ARISTOCRATIC *PARLEMENTS*

By long tradition, French kings could establish new policies by presenting decrees to the *Parlement* of Paris and the twelve *parlements* of the subdistricts (provinces) of the kingdom. These French *parlements* acted as judicial bodies rather than as legislatures. The officials who comprised them were aristocrats, often wealthy bourgeois with purchased noble titles. When the king presented a decree, they could accept it as valid or declare it illegal because it violated precedent. The government had chosen to convene the Assembly of Notables in 1787 in order to avoid turning to the *parlements* where, according to recent experience, defeat seemed likely. When the Assembly denied the royal plan, the king had only one remaining avenue— the *parlements*.

The Parisian *Parlement* accepted parts of the financial proposal but rejected the critical element, taxes on the rich and privileged. Louis ordered the establishment of his policies against the will of the *Parlement*, as tradition allowed, and disbanded the Parisian group. He then presented his financial decree to the provincial *parlements*, but they proved to be more hostile to the reform than the *Parlement* of Paris.

Even though the king had the right to override the decision of the *parlements*, members of these judicial bodies launched a public campaign of opposition to royal despotism and presented themselves as champions of liberties, by which they meant the privileges of the upper classes.

The rebellious aristocrats called for a convocation of the Estates General (see chapter 3), which had not met since 1614. When it convened, they intended to dominate it and establish changes that would place the king under their control. The appeal against despotism and for a gathering of the Estates won powerful public support. Facing financial collapse and a possible rebellion at every level of society, the king yielded. In August 1788, Louis appointed a new controller-general, Jacques Necker, and charged him with the task of arranging for the Estates General to meet.

THE MODERATE REVOLUTION

The aristocracy welcomed the calling of the Estates as an opportunity to restore the supremacy over monarchy that they had enjoyed in the Middle Ages. Louis accepted the convocation of this assembly as a way to stifle revolt and end the financial crisis. Unknowingly, the nobles and the king had launched a moderate revolution that would give the upper bourgeoisie control over France. After that, a more radical transformation would come.

The Estates General

The perception of royal despotism that had closed the ranks of all three estates against the king could not keep them together once elections to the assembly got under way. The Third Estate and a significant minority of reformist clergy and nobles demanded a break from traditional procedures for the Estates General. In earlier assemblies, each estate had an equal number of delegates, they met as three separate units, and each group arrived at a single vote on an issue. One clergyman, Abbé Emmanuel Sieyès, wrote a pamphlet titled "What Is the Third Estate?" in which he argued that the nonnobles were the nation and should decide every question. Most members of the two upper estates held a very different view. They insisted on the old system that ensured their victory on every vote. The privileged and unprivileged classes were at odds.

THE ELECTION OF DELEGATES

Louis agreed to double representation for the Third Estate (about 300 delegates for each of the upper estates, approximately 600 for the third). He did not, however, respond to the reformers' call for votes in the assembly by head rather than by estate, a method that would enable the Third Estate delegates and their progressive aristocratic supporters to control the Estates General.

In the ensuing elections, all the adult male nobles and most of the clergy had the right to vote and directly selected their representatives. The government restricted the vote of the Third Estate not only by gender but also by economic status—only taxpayers could cast a ballot. The lower estate also influenced the selection of representatives through several layers of electors rather than directly voting for estate delegates. Urban businesspeople and lawyers won a disproportionate share of the Third Estate seats as a result of these procedures.

THE *CAHIERS*

The plans for the gathering of the Estates not only provided for the selection of delegates but also called for the electors to compose *cahiers de doleances*, grievance statements. The representatives were to bring these to the assembly scheduled for May 1789. These *cahiers* indicated a strong consensus among all estates favoring an end to careless government spending and the abuse of power. Furthermore, the statements revealed wide agreement on the need to have a constitution that maintained royal authority but gave the estates influence over laws and guaranteed certain liberties, such as freedom of the press.

The *cahiers* reflected very important social conflicts too. The upper estates spoke out for a continuation of their historic privileges. Contrary to this attitude, the Third Estate grievance statements attacked these special rights and demanded their total abolition.

The Formation of the National Assembly

Conditions in France rapidly worsened in the months before the Estates General met. Many businesses failed, masses of urban workers lost their jobs, prices shot upward, and riots erupted. In an atmosphere thus charged, the representatives of the estates convened on May 5, 1789.

A deadlock immediately developed. Third Estate delegates refused to conduct business unless each member of the assembly had equal voting power. The monarchy, clergy, and nobility demanded adherence to traditional procedures. The Third Estate responded with a truly revolutionary step. On June 17, 1789, it acted in the spirit of Abbé Sieyès's tract and declared that the Third Estate was the "National Assembly." Members of this new body, which had no basis in current law, urged clerical and noble representatives to unite with them. A few days later, the clergy voted to join this National Assembly.

THE TENNIS COURT OATH, JUNE 20, 1789

When the Third Estate gathered on June 20, 1789, their hall was locked. They mistakenly assumed that the government had closed the chamber as an act of opposition. The delegates of the lower estate withdrew to a convenient indoor tennis court and formulated a pledge not to disband until they completed a constitution for the nation. Only a single Third Estate delegate refused to support this declaration.

Three days after the Third Estate's Tennis Court Oath, Louis decreed that the formation of this self-proclaimed National Assembly was invalid. The king also ordered the estates to gather in their separate chambers as before. The privileged estates complied. A rebellious Third Estate spurned the decree, and one of its delegates declared that bayonets alone could make them yield. Louis did not order his military to force submission; instead, as rumors of mob action against the king in his palace began to spread, he issued a new decree. On June 27, Louis told the three estates to merge. France now had a National Assembly dominated by the mostly bourgeois Third Estate delegation.

THE FALL OF THE BASTILLE, JULY 14, 1789

The king's tacit acceptance of the National Assembly signified a revolutionary triumph for the middle class. Yet the royal government and the aristocrats, most of whom now forgot their opposition to monarchy and sided with the king, still had the resources to turn the rebels back.

Royal troops with weaponry superior to that of any domestic opposition posed an especially terrifying threat to the opponents of monarchy and aristocracy. The Bastille, a fort built to protect Paris in the Middle Ages, housed a few of these forces. Parisians believed it held stores of guns and ammunition as well. They knew that the king imprisoned his enemies there, and that its cannon could blast one of the most rebellious working-class city districts. Even though the citizens of Paris had these reasons to consider the Bastille a practical danger, they despised it more just as a symbol of monarchical and aristocratic power.

Soon after Louis's concessions to the National Assembly on June 27, it appeared that he was ready to use force and other actions to reverse the trend of events. This impression resulted in part from the multiplication of royal troops in the vicinity of the king's palace in the Parisian suburb of Versailles. Then, on July 11, Louis heightened fears by his dismissal of Necker, the reform-oriented controller-general.

Parisians responded forcefully to circumstances too. A year earlier they had spent half their income on bread. Now it took more than three-fourths of their money to purchase this essential food. Mobs raided bakeries and stole bread. Seized by fear of an attack by royal troops, they also invaded shops and government centers in a quest for weapons. On July 14, one such venture by a crowd of almost 8,000 brought about 30,000 muskets into their hands. Members of this group then called for an attack on the Bastille.

Several hundred citizens, mostly skilled craft workers and other laborers rather than the dregs of society as antirevolutionaries later charged, converged on the fortress with its forbidding double ring of high walls. They called for gunpowder and the redirection of the threatening cannon. De Launay, the commander of the Bastille, agreed not to initiate an attack on the crowd, which now stood within the outer circle of walls. When the citizen force began to lower a drawbridge that would open the way through the inner wall, de Launay called for his troops to shoot. Nearly 100 besiegers fell dead. Over seventy others suffered wounds.

A small contingent of French Guards which had turned against the king then arrived with cannon. They blasted a way into the fort, and the Bastille fell to the Parisians. Six hundred of the defending troops and de Launay died in the slaughter that ensued. The invaders subsequently decapitated the commander and several dead troops and displayed the heads, impaled on pikes, as a sign of their victory over despotism. This great symbolic triumph caused July 14, 1789, to become celebrated as the first day of French liberty.

Parisian violence had affected the course of the revolution. In the wake of this mob action, Louis stopped his movement toward dissolution of the National Assembly. The king visually expressed his acceptance of the Assembly and its revolution. He entered Paris and wore a hat decorated with the three colors associated with the city's revolt—the red and blue that symbolized Paris and the white of the royal family's flag. Royalist nobles made their feelings about this turn of events clear. They began to leave the country.

Parisian crowd violence had helped the cause of the upper middle class, but such action still troubled bourgeois leaders. The business and professional elements intended to have governing decisions made through their deliberations and not in the streets. They organized for the political and military control of the city by selecting a mayor, Jean Bailly, and placing the marquis de Lafayette in charge of a new Parisian security force, the French Guard. Lafayette, as a moderately reformist aristocrat who had joined the American revolutionaries in their struggle for liberty, made an ideal leader for a bourgeois revolutionary guard. The National Assembly leaders thus hoped to control both royalists and radical lower-class revolutionaries.

THE GREAT FEAR

Events in other French cities somewhat paralleled developments in Paris. Related actions occurred outside the towns, especially from mid-July to early August 1789. Peasants began to dismantle the old system of aristocratic control and privilege. In some areas, when the peasants demanded it, the clergy simply surrendered their right to collect tithes, and the nobles gave up their power to take fees. More radical action sometimes took place, as when the peasants seized and burned the records of their obligations to the lords.

These conditions bred hysteria. Those who attacked the old regime heard rumors of violent royalist counteraction. Reports circulated that Louis's royal forces or foreign monarchical armies were gathering to slaughter rebels. Stories also persisted that the nobility would incite bands of thugs to make vicious attacks on their Third Estate enemies. The extreme anxiety that gripped the French people for three weeks in late July and early August 1789 became known as the Great Fear.

THE AUGUST DECREES

As the peasant revolt and the Great Fear climaxed during the first days of August, the National Assembly passed resolutions and decrees indicative of their acceptance of the spontaneous revolution sweeping the country. In a single night, August 4, 1789, the delegates declared an end to all noble privileges and special corporate rights, such as those exercised by church and guilds since the Middle Ages. Days later, formal decrees from the Assembly specified this abolition of the *Ancien Regime*'s social system.

THE DECLARATION OF THE RIGHTS OF MAN AND OF THE CITIZEN

As yet, the new French leadership had no fundamental laws under which to operate. Thus, the responsibilities that the National Assembly assumed included the production of a constitution. As a result of this work, this body of representatives also became known as the "Constituent Assembly."

The members adopted a broad statement of political principles on August 26, 1789, as one step in the development of a constitution. This Declaration of the Rights of Man and of the Citizen affirmed that government belonged to the people rather than the king. It further declared that all citizens had natural and irrevocable rights to liberty, equality, property ownership, and security. The Declaration specified that no person could be denied freedom of thought and expression. This document consciously embodied Enlightenment ideals and, consequently, somewhat parallels the American Declaration of Independence. It also completed the process begun in the August Decrees of formally ending the *Ancien Régime*.

THE WOMEN'S MARCH ON VERSAıLLES

Whatever the Assembly might decree, Louis XVI again turned resistant. He gave no indication of approval of the measures it passed in August. Popular fear of repression rose. So did the price of bread, to even more prohibitive levels than before. A group of Parisian women responded on October 5, 1789, with a mass march to the king's palace twelve miles away in the suburb of Versailles. A smaller contingent of men went along. Within hours, Lafayette and several thousand troops of his French Guard followed to maintain control in the interest of the bourgeoisie.

Once at Versailles, the protesters demanded reduced bread prices, to which the king agreed. His verbal submission failed to satisfy them, and they forcibly entered the palace, killing several guards in the process. Lafayette helped convince the king to comply with the wishes of the crowd and relocate in Paris. On October 6, the royal family and the commoners of Paris went together to the more revolutionary environment of the capital city. The king soon accepted the August Decrees and the Declaration of the Rights of Man.

THE CIVIL CONSTITUTION OF THE CLERGY

The August Decrees took away clerical privileges. The church kept much wealth and power over religious affairs, however, at least until further action by the National Assembly. The law makers soon took additional steps.

In November 1789, political leaders seized church lands and began to sell government notes, *assignats*, with this property as collateral. Thereafter, they drew up a Civil Constitution of the Clergy, which, when proclaimed in

July 1790, thoroughly subordinated the church to the state. Under this document's provisions, the government reorganized the church, gave the election of its leaders over to the citizens, and placed the clergy on the state salary rolls.

Assignats backed by church property temporarily eased the financial crisis that had sparked the revolution. With the passage of the Civil Constitution, the French Catholic Church lost its organizational and economic independence. The rebel bourgeois leaders also suffered an unexpected loss, however. Most of the clergy accepted the will of the pope and refused to uphold the religious constitution. A portion of their parishioners who had favored the revolution then turned against it.

THE CONSTITUTION OF 1791

The National Assembly presented the primary laws of a new regime in a constitution adopted in September 1791. It formally nullified the absolute authority exercised by French kings for generations. A one-house (unicameral) legislature, the Legislative Assembly, would decide all matters of taxation and government spending. The monarch could temporarily veto assembly actions, but votes against the king in three subsequent legislatures could override his will. The ruler remained in charge of foreign policy and the military.

Limited Democracy. The constitution gave the vote to all males who paid taxes equivalent to three days' wages. But the law did not permit citizens to elect representatives directly. Instead, they cast ballots for electors who then selected the 745 members of the Legislative Assembly. Furthermore, the constitution allowed only the richest men to become electors or legislators. The level of wealth stipulated was so high that only about 50,000 could qualify. Even with restrictions that guaranteed power to the upper bourgeoisie, the constitution promised France the most democratic system in Europe.

A Bourgeois Economic System. The new system granted economic as well as political power to the business and professional interests who comprised the upper middle class. The tariffs, tolls, and organizations, such as guilds, that might restrict trade within France were nullified, allowing the business community to trade more freely and profitably. Taxes on foreign goods to reduce competition from abroad and laws against labor unions further ensured the success of French producers and merchants. Bourgeois lawmakers thus benefited themselves by placing certain restraints on Third Estate workers. The constitution, however, did extend to laborers, and all citizens, the freedom to choose their jobs.

Administrative and Judicial Modernization. As in the economic legislation, the provisions for the new government bureaucracy and court system also reflected the attitudes of the businesspeople and professionals who dominated the National Assembly. They streamlined the administrative structure of France, establishing eighty-three uniform territorial divisions. These "departments" contained smaller units—districts, cantons, and communes. Citizens elected the officials who governed these local political divisions. The constitution provided for a similarly rational reorganization of the courts. It also called for jury trials in criminal cases and outlawed the use of torture.

LIBERALISM

Between 1789 and 1791, the National Assembly codified many of the principles that the Enlightenment intellectuals had held most dear. The bourgeois leaders of the moderate revolution believed, as had the *philosophes*, that reason could guide them in the construction of a new regime in harmony with Natural Law. In the Constitution of 1791, the Assembly wrote into law the High Enlightenment vision of such an ideal system. It guaranteed freedom of thought and expression, individual liberty, legal equality, property rights, and government by the people, or at least by the bourgeois-defined citizenry. In the 1800s, this new creed became known as liberalism, a modern political ideology that would well suit European states as they industrialized.

THE POLITICAL LEFT AND RIGHT

Although liberals controlled the mostly bourgeois National Assembly and wrote a constitution nearly ideal for the rising middle class, factions developed among Assembly members. Identifiable groups first began to appear as the Assembly debated the constitutional issue of a royal veto. The radicals, those in favor of the most drastic change, wanted the king to have no veto power at all. In keeping with European practice, the radical faction sat on the left side of the hall, viewed from the platform at the front. The most conservative group sat on the right, and on this issue took a stand for a royal veto that the legislature could not override. Members seated in the center advocated a veto by which the king could suspend a law until legislators repeatedly reversed it. The Center had its way.

In this and subsequent debates, the Left distinguished itself by its stand for popular sovereignty—the sharing of political power by all the people. The effort to deny the king a veto of any sort coincided with this belief. Leftists showed their commitment to this principle even more clearly in the arguments over voting rights. They advocated that every adult should have the vote. The Center opposed popular sovereignty, but favored the extension of political power to more of the people than did the Right. The Constitution of 1791 completed a moderate revolution that the bourgeois liberal Center had led. The Left lost on most issues but had not suffered a permanent defeat.

THE ORIGINS OF THE
RADICAL REVOLUTION

The administrative and judicial reforms, the Constitution of 1791 as a whole, and much else accomplished or accepted by the National Assembly promised a better life for most French people, regardless of social class. The revolution of 1789–1791 embodied above all, however, the values of the upper bourgeoisie and opened the way for this predominantly business class to pursue its dreams. Before the National Assembly adjourned, September 30, 1791, the delegates voted to bar themselves from the new Legislative Assembly. They expected other men of their outlook to preserve the bourgeois regime established by their moderate revolution. But many people did not share this vision of the new order. They wanted more drastic change.

The Sans-Culottes

Male French aristocrats in the 1700s wore knee-length breeches. Wealthy members of the bourgeoisie tended to copy the styles of the nobles. Poorer male commoners, however, donned full-length trousers, and thus became known as the people "without breeches" (*sans-culottes* in French). In the cities, and especially in Paris, the *sans-culottes* provided vital support for the revolution of 1789–1791.

Even so, the new regime severely limited their political role and remained unresponsive to the poor's insistent demand for economic relief, especially affordable bread. The lower bourgeoisie, craft workers, unskilled laborers, and servants who comprised the *sans-culottes* became a force for a radical revolution. This left-wing contingent wanted an equal voice in government and an increase in their relative wealth. Members of the aristocracy and upper bourgeoisie who sympathized with the cause of the lower classes greatly strengthened the drive for drastic change.

The Legislative Assembly

When the Legislative Assembly mandated by the new constitution convened in October 1791, the prospect of war as well as radical revolution loomed on the horizon. King Louis had tried to escape from France in June 1791, supposedly with the intention of organizing a counterrevolutionary invasion. Legislators decried the treachery of *émigré* French nobles. They believed the aristocrats who took flight were concentrated in Austria and plotting to join France's foreign enemies in such an attack. The Assembly had heard warnings that Austria intended to launch this assault on the new regime. As the legislature confronted critical issues, especially the consideration of war, several factions and political clubs struggled to carry the vote their way.

THE POLITICAL CLUBS

In 1789 groups of political activists had formed associations in order to influence the course of events. These political clubs gradually increased in power as the National and Legislative Assemblies proceeded with their work.

The Jacobins. The most radical of the leading clubs met in Paris in a monastery located in the Rue St. Jacques. Because of the street name, club members became known as Jacobins. Maximilien Robespierre led this group as it developed a network of clubs across France. Even though as advocates of popular sovereignty the Jacobins belonged to the Left, this mostly bourgeois club wanted to maintain control over the more radical *sans-culottes*, with whom they sympathized. Jacobins also struggled for central government supremacy over local political authority.

The Girondins. The delegates to the Legislative Assembly included a contingent from the department of the Gironde, a district in the Bordeaux region. These Girondins shared the Jacobin hostility toward aristocratic and monarchical power but opposed popular sovereignty. Girondin federalism—a belief in strong local government—also clashed with Jacobin ideals.

On the question of war, the Girondins favored an offensive response to the danger. They urged a war against Austria both to defeat this chief enemy and encourage popular revolutions against monarchy in other countries. The Assembly declared war on Austria on April 20, 1792. Both Austrian and Prussian troops thereupon invaded France and drove back the defending armies.

THE BRUNSWICK MANIFESTO

The Duke of Brunswick, who led the Austro-Prussian invasion, proclaimed on July 25, 1792, that any injury to Louis and his family would result in harsh reprisals when his forces reached Paris. In early August, the Parisians responded to this "Brunswick Manifesto" by setting up a more radical city government, the "Paris Commune," and invading the king's residence. The royal family rushed to the Legislative Assembly to escape this threat. They gained momentary security, but the legislature revoked all the constitutional powers of the king. Soon, the Legislative Assembly voted to call a convention to write a new constitution. Then it disbanded.

THE SEPTEMBER MASSACRES

The Brunswick Manifesto provoked widespread fear of counterrevolutionary violence. The hysteria focused on nobles and clergymen imprisoned for offenses against the new regime. In the first days of September 1792, groups broke into jails in Paris, hastily tried the people they seized, and immediately executed them. More than 1,000 victims died in these "September Massacres."

THE NATIONAL CONVENTION

Civil violence and the revolutionary war created a crisis atmosphere during the elections to the constitutional assembly, or "National Convention," as it came to be called. Fear and coercion kept the more moderate citizens from casting ballots. Representatives opposed to monarchy in any form won decisively. Now they would carry out a radical revolution.

The Execution of Louis XVI

Delegates to the National Convention gathered on September 20, 1792, to the heartening news of a great victory against the Prussians at Valmy. Soon, the French reoccupied the lands lost to the invaders. The Convention turned its attention to the fate of its imprisoned king.

In Convention sessions, the Jacobins filled the seats on the left in a section of chairs positioned above all others. These most radical delegates thus became known as the *"Montagnards"* or "men of the Mountain." Girondins occupied the right side of the chamber, a position indicative of their relative conservatism. Delegates of less extreme left or right opinion sat in the center of the hall in the lowest seats, the "Plain" or "Marsh."

These factions united to abolish monarchy and establish a republic, a representative government with no king. They clashed, however, over what to do with Louis XVI, whom they now called Citizen Capet. (The name referred to the first French royal family that began its reign in the Middle Ages.) From the Mountain, the Jacobins poured down their arguments for execution—a living king would continue to inspire counterrevolution, they insisted. The deputies knew that the mobs of *sans-culottes* cried for Louis's blood too. Girondins resisted and pled for the king's life. The center delegates yielded to the Jacobins and the Parisian radicals. The king would die.

On January 21, 1793, rows of troops stood in the cold, shrouded in mist. They formed a pathway to the guillotine, a recently invented device designed to accomplish more humane beheadings. Clad in plain clothes rather than royal trappings, Louis walked through the lines of soldiers to the block.

The Reign of Terror

The Jacobin-dominated republic faced serious threats from internal opponents of the revolution, foreign invasion, and a reeling economy. After the execution of the king, hostility toward the revolution intensified within France, especially in the *Vendée* region where peasants felt a strong attachment to royal government and Catholicism. Monarchists outside France also reacted to the king's death. The enemy force abroad grew to gigantic proportions as Britain, Spain, the Netherlands, Sardinia, Austria, and Prussia formed an anti-French coalition. Stricken by reversals on the war front, French leaders resorted to a military draft. Resistance in the *Vendée* turned violent. At the same time, rampant inflation and food shortages sparked revolts against the government in cities across the nation. The Jacobins determined to save the new system by whatever means necessary.

THE COMMITTEE OF PUBLIC SAFETY

By April 1793, a Committee of Public Safety emerged in the Convention and began to exercise executive authority. Georges Jacques Danton, a *Montagnard,* led the nine-member Committee at first. The *Montagnards* soon not only dominated the Convention's executive committee but also took complete control of the assembly. With the backing of the Parisian masses, the predominantly Jacobin forces of the Mountain purged the Girondins from the Convention in June.

THE CONSTITUTION OF 1793

With the deputies from the Right out of the way, the Convention wrote the supreme principle of the Left, popular sovereignty, into a new constitution. Previously, only people with a specified minimum of property could vote. The Constitution of 1793 extended the vote to all adult males.

CRISIS LEGISLATION

By July 1793, Danton shared control in the Committee of Public Safety with three of the more radical *Montagnard* deputies. The new leaders were Robespierre, Louis de Saint-Just, and Georges Couthon. Under the direction of this more revolutionary executive group, the government reacted to the crisis of war and civil unrest. It decreed a Levy-in-Mass, a draft of all males capable of fighting, and issued a plea for the entire nation to support the war by helping with supplies and inspiring the troops. Since chaotic wage and price fluctuations heightened the economic crisis, the government also began to issue regulatory decrees. The draft proved more effective than the economic controls.

ROBESPIERRE AND THE REPUBLIC OF VIRTUE

During the crisis-ridden summer, Robespierre established his supremacy within the Committee of Public Safety. This executive group now included twelve people. In September 1793, this mostly Jacobin leadership began to exercise dictatorial authority over France. Their Law of the Maximum, for example, fixed wages and determined prices on virtually all necessities, thus expanding earlier controls. Robespierre also turned the Committee and the Convention toward the achievement of his great cause, the establishment of a "Republic of Virtue." He proclaimed that popular sovereignty or democracy could not exist without "public virtue," by which he meant absolute dedication to the revolutionary nation and its new laws. Robespierre resorted to terror against all enemies of the revolutionary republic in order to create that spirit of total loyalty.

JACOBIN TERROR

Robespierre and the Jacobins intended to form an emergency dictatorship and launch a campaign of state terror in order to establish a completely democratic political system. The leaders insisted that they exercised absolute power in keeping with the will of the sovereign people. Anyone who opposed the revolutionary government thus threatened popular sovereignty and deserved no mercy.

This paradoxical dictatorial-democracy began to cut down its assumed enemies in October 1793. During a ten-month reign of terror, the former queen, Marie Antoinette, and other nobles died on the guillotine. Most Terror victims, however, were not aristocrats. Advocates of federalism, such as the Girondins, and proponents of a more extreme democracy than the Jacobins could tolerate also suffered the same fate. No one was safe. The revolutionary courts even condemned Danton and Jacques Hébert, a leader of the *sans-culottes*. The wave of violence swept across France. Victims of the Jacobin Terror died not only on guillotines but also in mass drownings, before firing squads, and, sometimes, by cannon shot. The revolutionaries slaughtered 30,000 to 40,000 before the Terror ended in July 1794.

The Jacobin Republic

The Convention never implemented the Constitution of 1793. Confronted with crises from the outset, the delegates to the constitutional assembly began to act as a representative legislature. It evolved into a Jacobin republic as the assembly passed acts, such as the Law of the Maximum, to solve specific problems. When the crisis worsened, the Convention established special judicial agencies to conduct the terror.

At the same time that the government killed assumed traitors, it proceeded to enact more of its revolutionary program. Legislation ended imprisonment for debt, abolished slavery in French colonies, and outlawed the granting of noble titles. The Convention also established the metric system, introduced a new calendar with ten-day weeks and a ten-month year, and organized a state "Religion of Reason." Metric weights and measurements became popular and permanent. The new calendar and religion did not.

CARNOT, THE "ORGANIZER OF VICTORY"

The Jacobin republic achieved its most unqualified success on the battlefield against the European coalition. In mid-1793, the Convention selected Lazare Carnot as its "Organizer of Victory." With the help of a corps of able assistants, he lived up to his title. The Levy-in-Mass gave France an army of nearly 1,200,000 by the early months of 1794. With this largest army in European history, Carnot's generals rolled back the forces of the many nations aligned against them. The march toward victory abroad reduced the crisis atmosphere in France enough to make the dictatorship of the Jacobins and their reign of terror intolerable to the nation.

THE THERMIDOREAN REACTION

The ten months of the new calendar had vividly descriptive names. On the ninth day of Thermidor ("heat") of revolutionary year II (July 27, 1794), Convention delegates reacted against the terror and Robespierre. They clamored so loudly that he could not speak to the assembly, then voted for his arrest. Within a day, this "Thermidorean Reaction" brought Robespierre's death on the guillotine.

The Demise of the Jacobin Republic. Radical revolution ended with the execution of Robespierre. The Convention stopped the operation of the Committee of Public Safety, dismantled other organizations of the dictatorial republic, and closed the Paris Jacobin Club. Girondin deputies who had escaped death in the terror returned to the Convention. A much more moderate republican spirit prevailed thereafter, as the Thermidoreans eased restrictions that the radicals had placed on the press, the economy, theater productions, and Catholic worship.

Reactionary Terror and Public Protest. Reactionaries, people who want to reverse the process of social change, took more drastic counter-revolutionary steps in the southwestern districts of France. They launched a campaign of terror against Jacobin sympathizers and people who had bought lands taken from the church and aristocracy. Friends of the Jacobin Left did not disappear, however, and they contributed to the disorder that spread across the land. Inflation returned with a vengeance after the Thermidoreans removed economic regulations. The masses of Paris poured into the streets to protest their plight. Some of these demonstrators campaigned for the implementation of the Jacobin Constitution of 1793.

The Constitution of 1795. The Convention did not institute the Constitution of 1793. Instead, it wrote a very different one. After the Thermidorean Reaction, the assembly remained committed to republican government but not to popular sovereignty. The Constitution of 1795 denied the vote to the twenty-five percent of the people at the bottom of the economic scale. It also called for a two-house legislature, a structure less susceptible to the influence of the masses than a unicameral assembly. As a further guarantee of political moderation, the Convention stipulated that upper- house (Council of Elders) members be at least forty years old and married or widowed. Finally, Thermidoreans arranged for a weak and restrained executive by planning a five-member Directory to be nominated by the lower house (Council of 500) and elected by the Elders. France still had its modern state, but a very different one than the Jacobin democrats had intended. The government of the Directory that now began operation would look less to the masses and more to the military for its support—a fateful redirection.

The European monarchies, especially in France and Britain, modernized in many ways beginning in the latter 1400s. Yet these governments failed to develop fully modern states. Even though queens and kings centralized and bureaucratized government, established large standing armies, extended royal law to most of the nation, subordinated religious institutions, and promoted commercial development, they left intact the traditional structure of class, church, and guild privilege. Above all, royal despots never drew the masses into affairs of state. An essential feature of the modern state was lacking.

Rather than achieving political modernization through mass involvement in government, by 1789 the Bourbons had alienated every social segment, even the privileged aristocracy and clergy. These traditionally favored classes struck the first blows against the French monarchy. They expected to reestablish their own supremacy over the realm. Commoners, especially the rich bourgeoisie, joined the attack on royal government. All classes wanted an end to the abuse of monarchical power and the achievement of other, sometimes contradictory, ambitions.

Once the revolution began, the upper middle class quickly took charge. This dynamic bourgeois leadership placed strict limits on the king within a year. At the same time, the peasantry ended aristocratic privileges and control of the land. Middle-class leaders sanctioned this peasant action and proceeded to more drastic steps against the government. In 1792, the bourgeois revolutionaries overthrew monarchy altogether. They executed the king early in 1793.

Once the bourgeoisie created the revolutionary modern state in France, European royalists prepared to defend the monarchical tradition. In 1792, France struck first and attacked Austria, the presumed leader of European monarchical reaction. Twenty-three years of brutal warfare followed, with France usually pitted against a coalition of nations.

The war generated a mood of extreme intolerance toward anyone suspected of disloyalty. The ruling Jacobin faction, dominated by Robespierre, established a dictatorship and launched a reign of terror to force conformity to their democratic conception of the revolution. After almost a year, the Terror ended in the month of Thermidor (July) 1794.

This Thermidorean Reaction brought a more moderate group of republicans to power. They at once wrote a constitution that embodied the particular liberal principles favored by most of the upper bourgeoisie. Dire threats from internal and foreign enemies led this new government, the Directory, to turn to the military for salvation. General Napoleon Bonaparte stood ready to act, but not always in defense of the Directory.

Selected Readings

Doyle, William. *Origins of the French Revolution*. New York: Oxford University Press, 1988.

Hampson, Norman. *The Life and Opinions of Maximilien Robespierre*. London: Duckworth, 1974.

Jordan, David P. *The Revolutionary Career of Maximilien Robespierre*. New York: Free Press, 1985.

Lefebvre, Georges. *The Coming of the French Revolution*. Princeton, NJ: Princeton University Press, 1947.

Levy, Darline, Harriet B. Applewhite, and Marlene D. Johnson, eds. *Women in Revolutionary Paris, 1789–1795*. Urbana: University of Illinois Press, 1979.

Rudé, George F. E. *The Crowd in the French Revolution*. Oxford: Clarendon Press, 1959.

Sutherland, Donald M. G. *France, 1789–1815: Revolution and Counterrevolution*. New York: Oxford University Press, 1986.

6

The French Revolution and the Napoleonic Empire, 1795–1815

August 1795	The Constitution of 1795 establishes the Directory
November 9, 1799	Napoleon's "18 Brumaire" coup abolishes the Directory
December 1799	Government under the Consulate begins, with Napoleon as dictator
July 16, 1801	Napoleon signs the Concordat of 1801 to improve state relations with the Catholic Church
March 21, 1804	France establishes the first part of the Code Napoléon
December 2, 1804	Napoleon crowns himself Emperor
October 1805	France defeats Austria at Ulm; Britain wins control of the seas by victory over France at Trafalgar
December 1805	France triumphs at Austerlitz, and the Treaty of Pressburg indicates the subordination of Austria
November 21, 1806	The Continental System begins with the issuance of the Berlin Decree
July 1807	Treaties with Russia and Prussia at Tilsit mark Napoleon's triumph on the Continent
March 1808	The French invasion of Spain begins the Peninsular War (1808–1813)

June 1812	Napoleon opens his campaign to conquer Russia. The French Emperor loses most of his army by the end of its withdrawal in December 1812
March 1814	Napoleon abdicates after a European monarchical coalition takes over Paris
March 1815	Napoleon escapes from exile on Elba and during the "One Hundred Days" rules France and resumes war
June 18, 1815	British and Prussian forces achieve final triumph over Napoleon at Waterloo

The reaction against the Terror brought a more moderate but still repressive republican government to power in France during the last five years of the 1790s. War and serious domestic problems persisted. Discontent with the government grew again. In 1799 General Napoleon Bonaparte had sufficient support among citizens and the ruling elite to take control of France.

The century ended with this new leader gathering more power into his own hands than the king had possessed before the revolution. But Napoleon kept and extended the administrative, judicial, socioeconomic, educational, and other reforms spawned by the revolution. He thus built a modern dictatorial state.

As a new century dawned, an intense patriotic fervor gripped the French. Mobilized for war, and guided by Napoleon's military genius, France was invincible for more than a decade and took control of almost all the continent.

Great Britain remained supreme at sea, however, and Napoleon defeated the Russian tsar's armies without taking that country. When the French invaded Russia in 1812, they suffered disastrous losses and withdrew. Thereafter, a coalition of European powers defeated Napoleon, banished him from Europe, and redrew the map of the continent. Even though France lost decisively by 1815, the revolution that had begun there in 1789 would continue to transform the states of Europe. Political modernization was under way.

THE DIRECTORY

After the Thermidorean Reaction ended the Reign of Terror in 1794 and purged the Convention of its more radical members, the deputies legislated a new system in the Constitution of 1795. The new government, known as the Directory, emphasized order and control rather than revolutionary change. At the outset, however, this law-and-order government faced turmoil. The requirement that two-thirds of the members of the new legislature be people who had served in the National Convention sparked outbursts in Paris. General Napoleon Bonaparte commanded a revolutionary army force that suppressed the Parisians with a "whiff of grapeshot," a form of cannon fire. More disorder followed.

Babeuf and the Conspiracy of Equals

The new republic especially represented the interests of a rich minority—the bourgeois business classes. The Directory forcefully displayed its intolerance for expressions and actions by or for the masses when Jacques Babeuf, a journalist, attempted to carry out his "Conspiracy of Equals." Babeuf intended to overthrow the infant capitalist regime, outlaw private property, and distribute wealth equally among the people. The Directory discovered this plot to establish socialism and thwarted it in May 1796. The next year, Babeuf went to his death.

Suppression of a Monarchist Resurgence

Opponents of the moderate republic who struck from the Right used different methods than had Babeuf on the Left. Monarchists campaigned for election to the legislature and the Directory in 1797. Enough royalists won to shock the Directory into drastic action. Once more the government turned to the army. Backed by military force, the Directory excluded the royalists from the legislature and expelled some of them from the country.

The Militarization of the Revolution

After 1795, the military became an increasingly important force in domestic affairs, as the Directory used the army against enemies on the Left and Right. The long duration of a revolutionary war purposely organized to involve the entire population also made the military become more and more central to the life of republican France. The heroes of the revolutionary army, especially the young generals, won a popular following that no figure in the faltering government of the Directory could match.

THE RISE OF NAPOLEON BONAPARTE (1769–1821)

Although a native of the culturally Italian island of Corsica, Napoleon began military training in the schools of France before he was ten. The French had annexed the island in 1768, and the prospect of a career in the army of the new mother country attracted this son of lower-level Corsican nobility. The revolution brought a phenomenal growth of the military and drove away French noble officers, opening the way for the rise of many young commanders.

Early in the revolutionary wars, Napoleon displayed exceptional talent as an artillery lieutenant and advanced in rank with remarkable speed. He became a brigadier general at age twenty-six. The young general took command of the French armies in Italy two years later (1796) and led them to victory over the Austrian forces there by 1797. After a triumphal visit to France, Napoleon opened a campaign in Egypt in July 1798. He planned to strike a devastating blow against Britain by seizing the route to that enemy's imperial riches in India. Instead, the British navy blocked Napoleon's access to supplies from France. In August 1799, the general deserted his men and fled home. But he suffered no loss of reputation and soon thereafter took over the government.

THE EIGHTEENTH BRUMAIRE

In late 1799, more than seven years after the revolutionary French republic launched its war to transform monarchical Europe, the Directory gave the nation little hope for success in that venture. The economy continued to languish too. Unscrupulous people found ways to use government policies to amass great wealth. For most people, however, life grew more miserable. Revolutionary fervor waned.

With support for the moderate republic virtually gone, Napoleon arrived from Egypt. Two members of the Directory, Roger Ducos and Abbé Sieyès, plotted with the thirty-year-old general to overthrow the government. Their coup succeeded, and on November 9, 1799 (18 Brumaire on the revolutionary calendar), the rule of the Directory ended. Republican government ended as well. Thereafter, Napoleon established a military dictatorship and took charge of the revolution.

THE NAPOLEONIC DICTATORSHIP

General Napoleon issued a new fundamental law for France, the "Constitution of the Year VIII" (1799). He incorporated many of Abbé Sieyès's ideas and a few of his own into this plan for the new government. The constitution appeared to create a representative republic. All males over twenty years of age with established residency of at least one year could vote in the election of a local body of commune "notables." The winners at this level then selected one-tenth of their group to serve as notables of a larger district, the department. This latter body chose one-tenth of its members to become notables of France. From this group, the Senate, a judicial body of eighty, picked the members of the two-house legislature. The voters had no real power.

The constitution further limited popular influence by having one house, the Tribunate, discuss laws without voting while the Legislative Chamber had to vote on them without debate. Napoleon organized the executive branch and arranged legislative procedures in a way that ensured his personal authority over the entire government. A three-member Consulate, led by Napoleon as First Consul, held directive authority. In that position,

Napoleon appointed and controlled the Council of State, the agency empowered to formulate all laws for consideration by the legislative houses.

When this government of the Consulate began its rule in December 1799, France came under the dictatorial authority of Napoleon. In February 1800, the people of France voted by a margin of 3,011,107 to 1,562 to accept the new constitution. Two years later another plebiscite (a yes-no vote on an issue) approved by an even larger margin the extension of Napoleon's term as First Consul from ten years to life and allowed him to choose his successor.

The Consulate

Napoleon achieved broad popular support for the Consulate by his quick and effective response to the problems of France and to the needs of most segments of society. He began by restoring order in the land. The First Consul dispatched forces to end a siege of banditry in southern France and the royalist rebellion that had continued for years in the Vendée. As the pacification proceeded, Napoleon initiated reforms that within four years made him almost universally popular.

ADMINISTRATIVE AND JUDICIAL REFORMS

The restoration of order by military force both enhanced Napoleon's appeal and increased his personal power over France. His political reforms had the same dual effect. Revolutionaries had combined the reorganization of France's administrative system with election procedures that enabled the citizens to select local officials. A law of February 1800 left this bureaucratic structure unchanged but gave Napoleon the power to appoint all the system's leaders.

Early the next year, Napoleon revised the court system and took the responsibility for selecting most judges. His expansion of the educational system in 1802 brought more students into the schools, but central control over their learning also greatly increased. With loyal subordinates in charge of an efficiently organized governmental, judicial, and educational machine, Napoleon could control the nation as no king ever had. He began to rule with appealing effectiveness over a modern but despotic system.

THE CONCORDAT OF 1801

Land-hungry peasants, resentful of the aristocrats with their propertied wealth and social privileges, carried out a revolution in the countryside as the old regime collapsed in 1789. They took the farms and nullified special noble rights, then became a conservative force. When the revolutionaries launched their attack on the Roman Catholic Church, much of the peasantry turned counterrevolutionary. Personally, Napoleon shared the *philosophes'* disdain for religion, but he won the hearts of the rural masses by concluding a concordat with French Catholic leaders on July 16, 1801.

The Concordat of 1801 allowed the church to resume the practice of public processions and the operation of its seminaries. It also proclaimed that Roman Catholicism was the faith of most citizens and accepted the right of the pope to dismiss bishops. The battle between the church and the revolutionary state had ended with the Napoleonic state victorious. The compromise did not accept Catholicism as the official French religion, as it had been before the revolution. Furthermore, the government kept the power to appoint bishops, left the clergy on state payrolls, and extracted an agreement that the church would accept the loss of its lands. With these few concessions, Napoleon converted the church and devotees of the faith into his allies.

HONORS AND JOBS

Although the peasants and other ardent supporters of the church required special attention, Napoleon did not forget other social groups. He established the Legion of Honor in 1802 to provide a system for rewarding exceptional accomplishments in public or military affairs. People who longed for a new aristocracy thereafter could anticipate satisfaction of their desires. For workers with the less grandiose dream of employment so that they could meet their personal or family needs, the First Consul had a reward as well. Napoleon launched a program of government-funded projects that multiplied the number of available jobs. The Consulate's military needs also guaranteed that certain industries would thrive and create still more jobs.

THE CODE NAPOLÉON

French kings in the Middle Ages and Early Modern period had gradually brought territories with varied legal systems under their control. By the 1600s, the monarchs wielded great power over the entire nation, but the diverse and contradictory judicial codes ensured unequal treatment for royal subjects. This condition heightened the anger of the populace toward the *Ancien Régime* during the Enlightenment. In a single decade, the French Revolution added an avalanche of laws and several constitutions to the accumulation of codes from previous centuries. Thus the revolution did not provide the integrated national code that France needed. It did prepare the way for this reform, however.

The revolutionaries made legal revision possible by removing the structure of the old regime. Then efforts to develop a coherent system of laws began in the mid-1790s. The work was incomplete when Napoleon seized power. By 1804, he had guided the reorganization process through a successful first stage with the production of the Civil Code. Four additional sections emerged during the next six years to produce a unified body of national law.

This five-part "Code Napoléon" reflected the authoritarian and regressive spirit of the French dictator. It legalized the supremacy of bosses over workers, men over women, and fathers over families. Male family heads could even send their teenaged offspring to jail. This provision agreed with the general spirit of the codes on crime and punishment—they called for more severe treatment of offenders than had laws in the 1790s.

Even though no hint of the Left's faith in popular sovereignty crept into Napoleon's Code, the new legal system embodied many other revolutionary principles—equal treatment under the law, personal career choice, religious toleration, private property rights, and minimal restrictions on business. Overall, Napoleon had encoded into a well-structured body of law many of the changes most desired by bourgeois liberals. It met the needs of modern France and pleased its citizenry. The Code also appealed to enlightened segments of the population in the European nations that Napoleon controlled.

PEACE IN NAPOLEON'S EUROPEAN REALM

In December 1798, a new alliance of antirevolutionary powers emerged and reinvigorated the attack on France. This "Second Coalition" included Russia, Austria, Great Britain, and several smaller states. The ability of France to survive and sometimes win remarkable victories against European alliances in the 1790s could not forever justify the costs of the war. The nation wanted peace. Napoleon delivered that and an impressive collection of subordinate territories as well.

Soon after the First Consul took power, he directed an overwhelming campaign against Austrian forces in Italy. The struggle there climaxed in victory at Marengo in June 1800. General Jean Moreau led a punishing French attack into Austria's German territories. He struck a shattering blow at Hohenlinden and then approached Vienna, the Austrian capital. Moreau had taken this enemy out of the war. In February 1801, the Austro-French Treaty of Lunéville left Italy and extensive German territory under Napoleon's sway.

Since policy differences with Britain already had caused Russia to quit the Second Coalition, after Lunéville Napoleon faced only the British. The war continued. Neither power, however, could win decisively, and they resorted to peace. The agreement arranged at Amiens in March 1802 required France to abandon none of its conquests in Europe. Napoleon thus kept Belgium, the Netherlands, Italy, and parts of Germany. The treaty also provided for the return of French colonies that Britain had taken. The Peace of Amiens ended a decade of struggle and made France supreme in Europe.

The Empire

The Consulate had taken self-government away from the French, but it provided very satisfying compensation—domestic and international peace, economic recovery, effective administration, and a European empire. In

1804, Napoleon offered the nation another prize—himself as Emperor and the founder of a new dynasty.

POPULAR MONARCHY

The revolution had removed a widely despised king and ended his dynastic line. It also brought a new but immensely popular despot to power. The First Consul arranged his transition to greater majesty by writing still another constitution that made him Napoleon I, Emperor of the French. It also specified that a Bonaparte male heir would inherit his throne. In a plebiscite, his loyal subjects enthusiastically approved the change. More than 3,500,000 voted for the new constitution; only 2,569 opposed it. A lavish ceremony in the cathedral of Notre-Dame on December 2, 1804, formally established the new order.

THE CONQUEST OF EUROPE

As First Consul, Napoleon established peace, but he longed for conquests and a European empire. The Peace of Amiens had stopped the war with Britain but not Napoleon's struggle for supremacy. He tightened his grip on Switzerland and Italy and attempted to end British commercial activity within his vast continental holdings. Great Britain responded with a declaration of war on France, May 16, 1803. By 1805, the British had drawn Austria, Russia, and Sweden into the Third Coalition against France and Napoleon's ally, Spain.

Napoleon moved swiftly against his enemies with an attack at Ulm in Bavarian Austria. In this battle on October 17, 1805, the Emperor's armies won decisively and accepted the surrender of 30,000 troops. A simultaneous attempt to overwhelm Britain failed miserably. Napoleon positioned his forces for a cross-Channel invasion, then sent his fleet toward the Caribbean. He expected the British admiral, Lord Horatio Nelson, to pursue the French navy westward while Napoleon's fleet secretly doubled back to join the attack on Britain.

Trafalgar. Lord Nelson followed his adversaries, caught them off the southwest coast of Spain at Trafalgar, and defeated the combined French and Spanish navies (October 21, 1805). Admiral Nelson died of injuries sustained in the Battle of Trafalgar, but his fleet triumphed so completely that France could no longer challenge Britain at sea. His victory left Napoleon with no way to reach Great Britain except in fantasy. The Emperor envisioned digging under the English Channel to unleash his mighty armies against his most stubborn enemy.

The Battle of Austerlitz. The Austrians continued to fight after their defeat at Ulm. The French marched to engage the armies of both Russia and Austria in the latter's territory in late 1805. On December 2, Napoleon led his forces to their most stunning victory as the French army devastated the

Russians at Austerlitz before they joined ranks with the Austrians. The French suffered about 9,000 killed or wounded, but Russian casualties numbered 30,000. The outcome convinced Austria to quit the war, a decision formally arranged on December 26, 1805, in the Treaty of Pressburg. Despite the heavy losses, Russia refused to sign the peace agreement.

The Battles of Jena and Auerstadt. Before Austerlitz, Prussia contemplated joining the Third Coalition. Instead, the battle dissolved the Coalition, and within two weeks Prussia signed a treaty, in preliminary form, with Napoleon. Months of diplomatic maneuvering followed as Napoleon tried to arrange treaties with Prussia and Russia that would give France a still stronger hold on Central Europe. The Emperor's tactics inspired Prussia to declare war on France on October 1, 1806. Since Russia and France remained adversaries, the Prussian action marked the formation of a Fourth Coalition. It posed no serious threat to Napoleon. On October 14, he turned his 200,000 battle-hardened warriors against the ill-prepared Prussians at Jena and Auerstadt. The combat at these two sites on a single day crushed the Prussians. Twenty-six days after the declaration of war, Napoleon held Berlin, the Prussian capital. King Frederick William III of Prussia (r. 1797–1840) took flight to Memel, 700 miles to the east on the edge of his realm.

The Treaty of Tilsit. Prussia had not surrendered to Napoleon, but only Russia remained actively in the war on the continent. Another deadly clash between French and Russian forces took place in Prussia at Eylau. Still the war continued. Napoleon's armies marched northeast from Eylau and subdued the Russians at Friedland on June 14, 1807. Tsar-Emperor Alexander I (r. 1801–1825) formally accepted defeat on June 21. He and Napoleon met, June 25, on a raft in the Nieman River to sign the Treaty of Tilsit. As the defeated and victorious emperors agreed to peace terms, King Frederick William waited apprehensively on the bank for Napoleon's decision about the fate of Prussia.

THE GRAND EMPIRE OF FRANCE

The peace treaties arranged and pronouncements made by Napoleon as he conquered Europe gave him control over most of the continent. At Pressburg (December 1805), Emperor Francis II of Austria surrendered his Italian province, Venetia, and his possessions on the east coast of the Adriatic. Other rulers in this region suffered more complete losses. Joseph Bonaparte took the throne of Naples in 1806, when his brother, Napoleon, decreed an end to the Bourbon dynasty's reign in that south Italian state.

Napoleon expanded his imperial authority northward also. He presented his brother Louis as ruler in the newly created Kingdom of Holland in June 1806. On July 12, Napoleon established the Confederation of the Rhine, an action by which he consolidated and subordinated most of the states of Germany. This extension of French power into Germanic territories brought

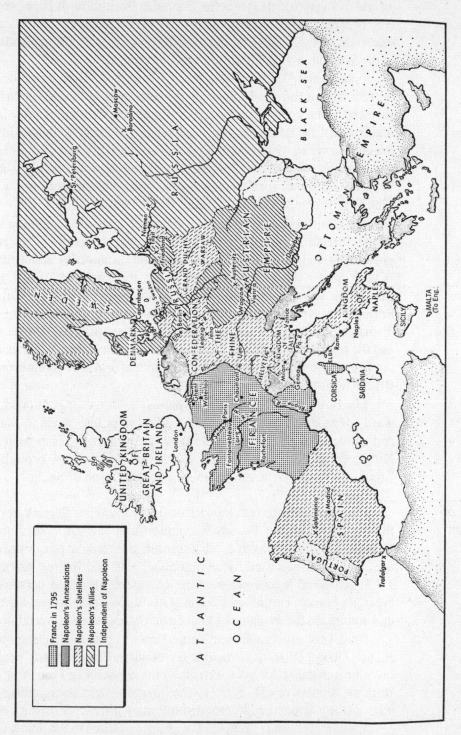

Fig. 6.1 Europe Under Napoleon, 1810

an end to a very old, if symbolic, European institution. It prompted Francis II to become simply the Emperor of Austria on August 6, as he dropped his title to the Holy Roman Empire, a formal union of the German lands founded in the 900s but a virtual fiction in modern times.

In the treaty Alexander I signed at Tilsit, the Russian Emperor accepted the new map of Europe established by Napoleonic conquests up to that time, July 1807. The agreement dictated to Frederick William of Prussia at Tilsit required that he also recognize these territorial arrangements and limit the Prussian army to 42,000 men. Prussia subsequently lost still more. Before the summer ended, the Prussians received notice that they must pay 120,000,000 francs for French war costs and surrender territory west of the Elbe River to Napoleon's Rhineland Confederation.

The Continental System. Napoleon then turned his attention westward to the Iberian Peninsula. His Berlin Decree, November 21, 1806, had ordered an end to trade between continental countries and Britain. This "Continental System" could not prevent the entry of British goods, as Europeans wanted and needed the products of British industry. When Portugal openly refused to comply with this policy, Napoleon responded by dispatching an army of occupation in November 1807. The Berlin statement and the troops in Portugal made Napoleon's policy clear. Even so, he issued the Milan Decree, December 17, 1807, to reaffirm that commerce between Britain and the continent was forbidden.

The Bonaparte Kingdom of Spain. The Emperor continued his westward advance. A French army of 100,000 swept into Spain in March 1808 and drove Charles IV from his realm. Subsequently, Napoleon gave the Kingdom of Naples to General Joachim Murat and brought Joseph Bonaparte from that south Italian state to the throne of Spain.

The Fall of Napoleon

Most of the European monarchical governments fiercely opposed the threats posed by the French Revolution and the imperial ambitions of Napoleon. Their efforts to combat this menace to their power proved futile against a nation aroused by revolutionary zeal and intense patriotism. By 1808, Napoleon held sway over the continent. He ruled personally in an enlarged France, controlled several states through enthroned subordinates, and dominated the monarchs whom he had defeated and forced into alliance.

Until 1808, the passionate dedication to country that empowered the French did not exist in the nations surrounding France. Many people in the old monarchical states even welcomed the conquering French as liberators from the repressive old regimes. The bourgeoisie in surrounding countries showed the warmest support for revolutionary principles. In the 1790s, these revolutionaries abroad accepted the French as allies in the attack on monarchy and aristocracy.

When Napoleon extended his system into Central Europe, his new subjects enjoyed the benefits of efficient administration, the Code Napoléon, the abolition of aristocratic privilege, the reduction of church influence in civic life, and the removal of traditional restraints on trade. The monarchies had no popular foundation for opposition to France. Napoleon expected the same circumstances to prevail in Spain. He was wrong.

NAPOLEON'S METHODS OF WARFARE

Napoleon repeatedly proved his military genius in the wars against monarchical armies. As a general and then as Emperor, he masterfully combined and applied the best current theories of warfare. Napoleon sometimes approached battle with widely dispersed troops to induce enemy forces to spread out. Then he suddenly merged infantry columns that could crash through thin opposing lines. The cavalry thereafter charged through the breach and wheeled to encircle the enemy. Napoleon also typically massed his cannon for concentrated, deadly fire.

The consistent use of surprise, speed, and concentration of forces did not make it easy to anticipate and counter Napoleon in battle. His meticulous plans always included many alternatives so that he could better ensure the unexpected. Napoleon increased the difficulty of successful resistance by inspiring exceptional loyalty among his troops. He went to battle and faced danger with them. A further guarantee of victory was his unconventional policy of fighting to destroy the enemy rather than taking prisoners. Napoleon's methods inspired his men and demoralized the opposition. None of this worked in the long war on the Iberian Peninsula.

THE PENINSULAR WAR, 1808–1813

The mostly peasant population of Spain supported their monarchy and despised the alien Bonaparte regime. Nobles similarly hated the elements of bourgeois liberal doctrine that Napoleon maintained in France and extended throughout his Grand Empire. Spain had no significant middle class to which French ideals might appeal. Finally, the Continental System, which Napoleon's armies had invaded the peninsula to enforce, worsened economic conditions for the Spanish. They rebelled.

Guerrilla War Against the French. Napoleon now faced a new kind of enemy that fought differently than any he had previously encountered. Guerrilla forces struck without warning against contingents of French troops as they moved about the country, attacked them in their camps, killed the wounded in their beds, and then returned to their hideouts. Poisoned water sometimes added to the toll taken by resistance fighters. Vicious suppression tactics failed against the patriotic Spanish warriors, and Napoleon could not use so effectively here the methods that gave him victory over the massed armies of a state.

Spanish Victory. Still, in the opening years of Iberian combat, Napoleon continued to dominate the continent as completely as Britain did the European seas. The Peninsular War, however, provided an opportunity for the British to alter this division of power. Sir Arthur Wellesley brought an army from Britain into Spain, and by August 21, 1808, won a battle over the French at Vimeiro. Thereafter, Napoleon engaged in a long and costly struggle against both Spanish guerrillas and the British military. It ended with Joseph Bonaparte's loss of the Spanish throne in 1813. Until that time, the war kept 400,000 French warriors south of the Pyrenees. They were needed elsewhere.

PATRIOTIC REBELLION AND WAR IN GERMANY

The lessons of the Peninsular War led the Archduke Charles, commander of the Austrian army, to call for Germans to unite in a war of national liberation. He invaded French-held Bavaria with an army of nearly 200,000 in April 1809. A few Germans responded to the Archduke's patriotic plea, but not enough. Napoleon left Spain and took Vienna, Austria, by mid-May. Seven weeks later, he dashed the Archduke's hopes with a victory at Wagram that ended the war. The Treaty of Schönbrunn on October 14, 1809, took 32,000 square miles and 3,500,000 people away from the Austrian Empire.

Patriotism in Prussia inspired a much more serious threat. The fondness for French liberalism had waned in Central Europe as Napoleon exploited his imperial territories to strengthen his state. Enforcement of the Continental System did not stop British goods from entering the region, but, as in Spain, it worked well enough to harm the economy and arouse resentment.

The presence of foreign invaders also encouraged the growth of Prussian patriotism and, among a few intellectuals, fostered a commitment to nationalism in a broader sense—they wanted to expel the French and unify Germany. In combination these influences created a potential for popular revolt, although on a smaller scale than in Spain.

Prussian leaders took advantage of the new climate of opinion in their land. They freed the serfs, ended the practice of allowing only nobles to serve as military officers, established a national draft to raise a citizen army, improved the treatment of recruits, and carried out other reforms that advanced Prussia toward the Enlightenment's modern vision of the state. When the Prussian government completed its program of change in 1813, this state stood as a more formidable enemy for Napoleon. It could fight with popular support.

THE DEADLY INVASION OF RUSSIA

The Treaty of Tilsit (1807) established peace between Russia and France but not harmony. Tsar Alexander I longed for control of Constantinople and, thereby, easier access to the Mediterranean Sea. Napoleon opposed this ambition. The French Emperor also provoked Tsar Alexander by actions that indicated the possible absorption of Poland into the Grand Empire. Other differences troubled Franco-Russian relationships but none so much as conflicts over the Continental System. This policy struck Russia with special severity since its highly agricultural economy required active trade with industrial Britain.

Alexander increasingly ignored the Continental System and finally rejected it outright. Napoleon decided to smash Russia. He marched 400,000 men to the Russian border at the Nieman River during the last weeks of spring in 1812. Behind France's Grand Army came another 200,000 reserves. In late June, Napoleon took the first of his men across the river. The Grand Army poured over the border for the next three days.

About half the men who trekked toward Moscow were French; the rest came unwillingly from client states such as Sweden, the Netherlands, Prussia, Poland, Switzerland, Austria, and Italy. The Russians retreated before them, destroying almost everything in the areas they evacuated. Napoleon had planned to live off the land.

The Battle of Borodino. Seventy miles west of Moscow the Russian general Mikhail Kutusov commanded the tsar's forces in their stand against Napoleon at Borodino, September 7, 1812. The Russians lost but took a very heavy toll among the French. Napoleon entered the Kremlin one week later. No leaders met him to surrender, and the city surrounding the Kremlin's walls lay virtually empty. Fires erupted in Moscow the next day and burned for nearly a week, taking still more of the supplies that Napoleon needed.

Russian Victory. No word of submission came from Tsar Alexander during the next five weeks. The occupying troops could not live in Moscow through the winter without provisions. French forces began their withdrawal on October 19. The position of the Russian armies compelled a retreat by the same route as the invasion. Now this land offered even less on which to live. Early snows and an unusually harsh winter compounded the misery of Napoleon's men. They fell from hunger, exhaustion, and cold, dying in the snow as their comrades trudged on. Guerrilla bands and the tsar's Cossack cavalry inflicted still more casualties. Fewer than 100,000 survived to recross the Nieman in mid-December 1812. By then Napoleon was in Paris raising an army to replace the one he had lost. He filled its ranks with many who were adolescents.

THE CONQUEST OF NAPOLEONIC FRANCE

A new and ominous coalition confronted Napoleon in 1813. Austria, Prussia, Russia, and Sweden converged on the unseasoned French warriors in Prussia at Leipzig. The battle raged for three days in mid-October and ended in devastating defeat for Napoleon. British and Spanish invaders struck France from the south during the next month. The Coalition's armies seized Paris at the end of March 1814, and the Emperor abdicated. The victors permitted Napoleon to retain his imperial title but placed him on Elba, an Italian coastal island. In France they also enthroned Louis XVIII, a Bourbon and the brother of Louis XVI.

The Hundred Days. Exile and the restoration of the Bourbon dynasty failed to remove the threat of Napoleon to monarchical Europe. On March 1, 1815, ten months after his arrival on Elba, the Emperor invaded southern France with fewer than 2,000 men. King Louis sent an army to defeat Napoleon. It met him and swore allegiance to the Emperor. Napoleon took Paris on May 20 and began a second reign of about 100 days.

Waterloo. In charge of France once more, the Emperor formed still another army and invaded Belgium. He made progress at first against the ranks of the Coalition, which now included most of the leading European states. Napoleon's assault against the British at Waterloo, June 18, 1815, brought him close to another victory. But the army under the Duke of Wellington (formerly Sir Arthur Wellesley) held firm throughout the day, and the Prussians then arrived to ensure Napoleon's defeat. He would fight no more battles. Napoleon surrendered to the British, who spurned his suggestion of retirement to Britain. They took him instead to the island of St. Helena more than 1,000 miles from the southwest coast of Africa. Napoleon died there in 1821.

French revolutionaries before 1795 destroyed the old sociopolitical order in their own country, an act of modernization that immediately threatened aristocratic and monarchical institutions all over Europe. The inherent conflict between France and the royalist states led to the bitter war that persisted throughout the years of the conservative republic, the Directory (1795–1799). The inability of this government to win either the war or wide support at home led the French to turn to Napoleon, a military hero who might give them victory abroad and an end to the domestic chaos.

The new leader turned away from both Jacobin democracy and the early liberal idea of self-government for the upper bourgeoisie. He fashioned a new system, the Consulate, with the trappings of a republic to decorate a truly dictatorial system. The ruler quickly dropped the guise of representation. In 1804 Napoleon proclaimed himself Emperor for life, the founder of a new hereditary dynasty.

In his first years, Napoleon gave his people a measure of peace that they much desired. Harmony reigned among many of the French, and malcontents were suppressed. The war ended also, for a brief time. But Napoleon would not allow this quiet on the battlefronts of Europe to endure for long, for he meant to be emperor of more than the French.

Napoleon launched a campaign of war and empire building such as the Europeans had never witnessed. French armies rolled across the continent and won control of most of the land from the Atlantic Ocean to the western borders of Russia by 1808. Subjects of the surrounding monarchs who favored the bourgeois liberal values of the French preferred their new ruler at first and so weakened the royalist potential for resistance.

When Napoleon extended control into the Iberian Peninsula in 1808, popular resistance erupted, especially among the Spanish. They preferred their king and traditional ways. Central European people turned more hostile too as French liberalism seemed increasingly alien and exploitative. Napoleon's attempts to hurt the British by cutting off the flow of their goods into the continent only angered his European subjects more because of the shortages they suffered.

Because the Russian ruler refused to support the blockade of British imports, Napoleon invaded the tsar's vast realm in 1812. The French Emperor lost most of his Grand Army to cold, hunger, and Russian guerrilla tactics. A grand coalition of European monarchical states then pursued Napoleon to his final defeat at Waterloo in 1815.

Napoleon disappeared from Europe after Waterloo, exiled to the distant South Atlantic never to return. But his blows against the Ancien Régime *continued to reverberate long after the revolutionary dictator left. The monarchies could stop Napoleon but not the forces of political modernization that he unleashed in Europe.*

Selected Readings

Bergeron, Louis. *France Under Napoleon*. Princeton, NJ: Princeton University Press, 1981.

De Caulaincourt, Armand Augustin Louis. *With Napoleon in Russia: The Memoirs of General de Caulaincourt, Duke of Vincenza*. New York: W. Morrow and Company, 1935.

Holtman, Robert B. *The Napoleonic Revolution*. Philadelphia: Lippincott, 1967.

Lyons, Martyn. *France Under the Directory*. New York: Cambridge University Press, 1975.

Markham, Felix. *The Bonapartes*. New York: Taplinger Publishing Company, 1975.

Rothenberg, Gunther E. *The Art of Warfare in the Age of Napoleon*. Bloomington: Indiana University Press, 1978.

7

The Attempt to Restore the Ancien Régime, 1814–1829

1744	Johann von Herder (1744–1803), a German cultural nationalist, is born
1774	Johann von Goethe publishes *Sorrows of the Young Werther*
1776	Jeremy Bentham (1748–1832), a liberal economist who advanced the idea of "utilitarianism," begins to influence European thought
1789	Talleyrand (1754–1838) enters diplomatic service for France; represents his country at the Congress of Vienna in 1814–1815
1790	Edmund Burke's *Reflections on the Revolution in France* is published
1798	Thomas Malthus presents his *Essay on the Principle of Population*
	Eugène Delacroix (1798–1863), a French Romantic painter, is born
1809	Metternich (1773–1859) becomes Foreign Minister of Austria
1810	Robert Schumann (1810–1856), a German Romantic composer, is born
1812	Viscount Castlereagh (1769–1822) begins service as British Foreign Minister; represents his nation at the Vienna Congress
May 1814	The Treaty of Paris is completed after the first defeat of Napoleon
September 1814	The Congress of Vienna begins
June 9, 1815	The Final Acts of the Vienna Congress are adopted
September 1815	The Holy Alliance is formed
November 1815	The Second Treaty of Paris is arranged after Napoleon's return and defeat at Waterloo

1817	David Ricardo publishes *On the Principle of Political Economy and Taxation*
October 1818	The Congress of Aix-la-Chapelle meets
1820	A liberal revolt begins in Spain
October 1820	The Congress of Troppau convenes, continues to final adjournment at Laibach in 1821
1821	The Greek independence rebellion breaks out
October 1822	The Congress of Verona meets
Mid-1823	The Continental monarchies suppress the Spanish revolt
September 1829	The Treaty of Adrianople gives Greece independence from the Turkish Empire

*D*uring *the Enlightenment, opponents and defenders of the* Ancien Régime *had fought mostly intellectual battles. The conflict became also brutally political after 1789, and it continued as a war of both ideas and politics throughout much of the 1800s. At the intellectual level, many foes of tradition after the 1790s attacked the old order with somewhat new forms of liberalism and nationalism. Others turned to an even more radical modern doctrine—socialism.*

The theories used to condemn the Ancien Régime *usually rested on Enlightenment approaches and principles such as reason and Natural Law. From the 1790s to the 1850s, most intellectuals and artists, even if they did not support traditional social institutions, rejected the Enlightenment as inhumanly mechanistic. They became romantics, theorists who believed that emotion could reveal more truth than could reason.*

As an attack on the Enlightenment, romanticism somewhat countered the intellectual assault on the Ancien Régime. *A direct and conscious effort to restore and sustain traditional ways came, however, in the form of conservatism, a new body of ideas that emerged in the 1790s.*

The post-Napoleonic political struggle to restore the Ancien Régime *began in Vienna in 1814. Representatives from every European country went to the Austrian capital that year to participate in a congress convened to restore as much of the old sociopolitical system as possible after twenty-five years of revolution and war. Many of the documents they produced, decisions they made, and events they influenced at Vienna indicated that the European leaders rejected certain modern ideas and accepted others. In most cases, they proclaimed by their words and actions a determination to fight against the ideologies of change—liberalism, nationalism, and socialism—and for conservatism.*

MODERN EUROPEAN IDEAS

The clash among Europeans in the realm of ideas during the late 1700s and early 1800s sometimes occurred within the ranks of identifiable intellectual groups such as liberals or conservatives. An important conflict emerged among liberals, for example, over the question of whether government should aid people suffering from the effects of industrialization. Usually, however, the conflicting theorists belonged to clearly separable intellectual factions.

Adherents of liberalism, socialism, and nationalism held beliefs that pitted them against defenders of the old order. Romantics scorned Enlightenment principles and advocated a very different outlook on life. Conservatives devised a modern theoretical justification for the traditional social system and thus forcefully confronted liberalism. By the 1820s, the most important intellectual conflicts were between competing modern ideas rather than between old and new views, as had been the case in the Enlightenment.

Liberalism in the Early 1800s

The liberal creed generated by the Enlightenment and applied during the moderate stages of the French Revolution (see chapter 5) suited the bourgeoisie especially well. The advocates of liberalism favored opening the way for the most dynamic and talented individuals to rise to the top of society and run the government or operate freely in business without the interference of traditional or legal restraints.

During the early 1800s, liberals in France and elsewhere typically began to concentrate on the establishment of parliaments to implement self-government and constitutions to guarantee the individual rights in which they so strongly believed—personal liberty, freedom of opinion and expression, and the profitable use of property.

THOMAS MALTHUS (1766–1834)

Confronted with the hard realities of the industrial revolution, British intellectuals in the late 1700s and early 1800s revised and sometimes gave a very new direction to liberalism. Early in his career Thomas Malthus presented a liberal vision of industrial-age economics that strongly influenced economic thought for generations thereafter. His *Essay on the Principle of Population* (1798) argued that the food supply and other life necessities increase arithmetically, adding a little at a time, while humans reproduce geometrically—they *multiply*. As a result, according to this founder of "the dismal science" (liberal economics), the laboring masses must always live in poverty. At best, they could hope for a slight improvement of their lot by controlling their sexual urges. Bourgeois liberal industrialists welcomed this argument against government aid for the poor and justification for the misery of workers. Malthus thus provided an important addition to liberal *laissez-faire* theory. At the same time, however, he turned sharply away from the traditional liberal idea of endless progress.

DAVID RICARDO (1772–1823)

David Ricardo, another liberal economist, spelled out the hard fate of industrial workers even more dramatically in his 1817 publication *On the Principle of Political Economy and Taxation.* He expanded on the views of Malthus with the assertion that whenever wages improved, laborers responded sexually, producing more children who then flooded the labor market and forced wages down. This "Iron Law of Wages" indicated the virtue of paying workers as little as possible.

THE UTILITARIANISM OF JEREMY BENTHAM (1748–1832)

Malthus and Ricardo subtracted the optimism from liberal thought. In works he produced beginning in 1776, Jeremy Bentham also responded to new intellectual trends and industrial realities but in a different way than Malthus and Ricardo. Bentham continued in a direction set by Rousseau and devised a form of liberalism that omitted Natural Law theory. He denied the existence of such natural codes but asserted that humans were controlled by an inherent tendency to seek pleasure and avoid pain.

This universal human desire for pleasure, Bentham concluded, indicated a principle that should govern the operation of society. Leaders should direct their actions so as to provide "the greatest good to the greatest number of people." According to Bentham, legislators could apply this principle of "utility" by the use of precise statistical data to determine what would give the most pleasure to the most people.

Bentham began with a rejection of the Natural Law theory held dear by Enlightenment liberals. The doctrine of utilitarianism that he presented varied from earlier liberal ideas also in its emphasis on actions to benefit "the greatest number." In this shift toward concern for the group, Bentham modified but did not reject liberal individualism. His ultimate objective still coincided with the fundamental goal of liberalism—individual freedom. Bentham also kept the faith in self-government, urging that parliamentary representatives should be the ones to decide the most beneficial social policies. Finally, despite all his significant modifications of liberalism, Bentham remained committed to one of its oldest premises, laissez-faire economics.

Socialism

A few social critics in the early 1800s rejected both the old regime and liberalism. Instead of supporting either traditional aristocratic society or a modern bourgeois alternative, they spoke for the laboring masses who seemed destined to suffer whether nobles or business leaders wielded power. These self-described "socialists" blamed the suffering of the masses on contemporaries who wrongly emphasized production rather than the fair distribution of goods, competition rather than cooperation, and individualism rather than a sense of community. The founders of modern socialism proposed a variety of solutions to this problem.

HENRI DE SAINT-SIMON (1760–1825)

The works of the French theorist Saint-Simon reflected the typical socialist faith that people are naturally inclined to humane service and that such inherent behavior could transform society. Specifically, he contended that by a scientific study of conditions, the social classes that already enjoyed the benefits of economic modernization could learn how to help the still suffering industrial laborers. Saint-Simon further asserted that once so informed, the prosperous members of society would help those in need to advance both materially and spiritually. In this way, everyone could enjoy a modern industrial paradise.

CHARLES FOURIER (1772–1837)

Fourier, another French socialist, exhibited the same confidence in the human potential for serving others, but his view of the ideal society differed considerably from Saint-Simon's. Small independent communities rather than industrial cities, according to Fourier, offered the environment that would naturally foster the kind of sharing of responsibilities and goods that would bring the ultimate happiness. The model society that Fourier recommended for the attainment of the blissful life would comprise many small communities or *"phalanges,"* each with about 400 families who jointly owned essential institutions such as schools and health facilities. *Phalange* citizens would regularly shift from pleasant work to unpleasant but necessary jobs in order to remain happy and avoid boredom. Fortunately for the adults, their occasional distasteful tasks would not have to include trash disposal. Fourier assumed that children so enjoyed plunging into filth that they would be the *phalange*'s sanitarians.

ROBERT OWEN (1771–1858)

Robert Owen prospered as a textile mill owner in Scotland, but the misery of the working class distressed him as much as it did Saint-Simon and Fourier. This manufacturer proposed small cooperative industrial communities as a model, and so somewhat combined the visions of the two French socialists. Owen applied his ideas quite successfully in New Lanark, Scotland, in the early 1800s, but his experimental industrial socialist community in New Harmony, Indiana, lasted only a few years in the 1820s before conflicts ended the effort.

Although socialism in a variety of forms won many followers by the latter 1800s, relatively few people adopted the beliefs of these first socialists. Most enemies of the *Ancien Régime* before the 1850s found liberalism, nationalism, or a combination of these ideologies more appealing.

Nationalism

Before the French Revolution, a widely shared language and a unifying culture born of a long common history had laid the foundations for nationalist ideology in that country. Once these conditions existed, nationalism emerged as the French began to think of themselves as a nation with a unique heritage.

French nationalism evolved in association with the belief that the nation and its government were the rightful possessions of all citizens. This nationalist spirit strengthened dramatically during the radical phase of the revolution as royalist foes fought to destroy the new French system. The masses and their leaders had a common and distinctly French cause for which they struggled to the utmost.

This belief in a special historic mission, often found in nationalist thinking, inspired France as this revolutionary nation conquered Europe. Then French imperialism triggered nationalist reactions throughout the continent. Thereafter, nationalism matured in other countries in somewhat the same way that it had earlier in France. Nationalists everywhere in Europe had learned much from the French about the nature and power of modern nationalism.

CULTURAL NATIONALISM IN GERMANY

Johann von Herder (1744–1803) urged Germans of all states to recognize, absorb, and develop their mutual culture. The individual, he proclaimed, could truly exist only by immersion in language, folk beliefs, and literature that she or he held in common with others.

Herder did not advocate that this cultural nation unify politically to form a state. His ideas, however, encouraged a national spirit among German intellectuals that prepared them to react to French imperialism with a call for the rise of a nation-state. Herder also had helped to plant an idea that found very fertile ground beyond Germany in the 1800s, especially in ethnically Slavic regions. This burgeoning nationalism in Central and Southeast Europe incited people to frequent revolts after 1815. The old states of the region, especially the multinational Austrian Empire, were under siege. Eventually they would fall victim to this most powerful of modern ideologies.

LIBERAL NATIONALISM

Liberal and national sentiments blended compatibly during the French Revolution in the thinking of the Girondins and others. They wanted a united nation governed by all French citizens. Liberal nationalists called for a constitution that ensured universal individual rights. They also expected the entire citizenry to mobilize for national defense or the spread of the country's way of life. The nationalists of East and Central Europe from 1815 to 1848 had a very similar outlook. They had no nation-state; therefore, they fought for its formation and for the establishment of a liberal system of government within the new nation. Throughout the first half of the 1800s, liberalism was a powerful force for change in France, while in Central and East Europe this ideology and nationalism formed an explosive revolutionary blend.

Romanticism

Liberal ideas grew out of the Enlightenment with its emphasis on reason as the preeminent human trait. Although liberalism continued to appeal to many theorists between the late 1700s and mid-1800s, the rationalism of the Enlightenment lost its supremacy among European intellectual and cultural leaders in these years. The Enlightenment gave way to the Age of Romanticism, an era when most artists, writers, and theorists denied that humanity could discover truth by reason.

Enlightenment rationalists had despised the Middle Ages for its mystical, superstitious character. Romantics considered the Middle Ages a wonderful era and disparaged the Enlightenment's overly intellectual and mechanistic view of humanity and nature.

The fondness of Romantics for that earlier age is even indicated in the origin of the word used to describe their outlook. It is derived from the label for a form of medieval literature, the narrative romance poetry of the 1100s.

Romance literature in the Middle Ages displayed a writer's emotions, all of them. Frivolity, sadness, hate, love, whatever the poet felt, deserved expression. Modern Romantics identified closely with this emphasis on emotions. The reasoning mind, they believed, served humanity in the quest for knowledge and insight, but feelings revealed far more. From the romantic point of view, therefore, the *philosophes* had both ignored the most important human quality and missed the best route to truth.

THE ROMANTIC VIEW OF THE INDIVIDUAL, NATURE, AND SOCIETY

Romantics disagreed with the Enlightenment view of humanity in other respects too. In the Age of Romanticism, the individual remained a vital concern. The newer perception of individualism differed sharply, however, from the Enlightenment idea. Romantics saw everyone as unique. People did not have universally similar endowments. Variations among humans were inevitable, for they were not intellectual machines but beings with emotions and souls. These infinitely diverse and spiritual individuals required liberty, not as an inherent right under Natural Law, but in order to explore their inner world and experience nature. In this way, the truly creative human could emerge.

Nature, from which the individual could learn so much, also appeared vastly different to Romantics than to the *philosophes*. An organic natural world—one with emerging life, growth, and mystery—appeared in the ideas of this new cultural generation. Gone were the clockwork images of the Enlightenment. God, an involved and spiritual being, made and moved this universe. The Creator was not a supreme mechanic who built the universe and left it to impersonal forces.

Romantics found as much error in the *philosophes'* idea of society as in their notion of God. In the world as conceived by these Romantics, human societies as well as nature had an organic character. They grew over time, each different from all others. Intellectuals, therefore, could not categorize them scientifically, analyze their flaws, and formulate plans for a more perfect new society. An understanding of the social order required the study of particular peoples and the examination of their outward and inner traits through folklore and history.

THE ARTS IN THE AGE OF ROMANTICISM

A reformist impulse followed naturally from the Enlightenment outlook. Eventually, even a revolutionary mood became somewhat typical. Romanticism lacked such a clear-cut inclination on social issues. Several leading Romantics rejected Enlightenment premises but adopted liberalism and even supported revolution to achieve its goals. Others ardently opposed liberalism, reform, and revolution.

A more consistent contrast existed between the *philosophes* and Romantics, in the works through which they expressed themselves. Enlightenment intellectuals usually offered dispassionate treatises on politics, society, and human nature. Romantics more often turned to the arts, especially poetry, to pour out their feelings and ideas.

Literature. When romance dominates ideas and the arts, the works that appear will emphasize emotion but not necessarily love. Romance literature, however, frequently does focus on love, as in the poetry of the Russian writer Alexander Pushkin and Johann von Goethe's German novel *Sorrows of the Young Werther* (1774). For many Romantics, a love affair with the opposite sex evoked less passionate expressions in their writing than love for nature. They wrote with intense emotion about their devotion to the natural world. The poetry of the British writers George Gordon, Lord Byron and Percy Bysshe Shelley vividly illustrate this love for the beauties and forces of nature.

Romantics perhaps did not love the unnatural quite so well, but they found it deeply interesting, an attitude reflected in Goethe's *Faust* (1808), Mary Shelley's *Frankenstein* (1818), and Michael Lermontov's *The Demon* (1841). Whatever they wrote about, Romantics consciously violated the rigid standards of composition adhered to in previous generations. Artistic revolt had a universal appeal to them that social reformism did not.

Music. The consistent tendency toward cultural rebellion affected Romantic music as well as literature. Tradition dictated that musical expression had to take certain precise forms governed by intellect rather than emotion.

Franz Schubert (1797–1828), Robert Schumann (1810–1856), Frédéric Chopin (1810–1849), and other Romantic musicians shattered this tradition. They wrote in the highly individualistic style that has come to be expected of all true artists in modern times. Above all, in contrast to the works of their predecessors, Romantic compositions conveyed feelings in reaction to exotic places, moving experiences, or whatever generated emotions worthy of expression.

Art. The same culturally rebellious and emotional spirit prevailed in the art of this era. Artists ignored the standards of the past and portrayed their diverse visions of what they saw or imagined. In response to the real sights of his times, Théodore Géricault depicted his feelings about the Napoleonic wars in paintings such as *Wounded Soldiers in a Cart*. Eugène Delacroix (1798–1863) imagined the Middle Ages in his *Entrance of the Crusaders into Constantinople*. The works of these and other Romantic painters indicate the emergence of a much more modern idea of artistic expression.

Conservatism

Despite its culturally rebellious character, Romanticism emerged as a reaction against intellectual trends that contributed to the highly revolutionary social conditions of the late 1700s and early 1800s. The trauma of social upheaval and war that strengthened the tendency of cultural leaders to question Enlightenment principles encouraged a more general reaction against the French and Napoleonic revolutions. The ideology of conservatism arose as the strongest condemnation of revolution and the most complete depiction of an alternative social vision.

EDMUND BURKE (1729–1797)

French royalists had scarcely had time to realize the horrible times that awaited them when Edmund Burke published his damnation of the rebel cause and predicted the terror to come. In *Reflections on the Revolution in France* (1790), this English theorist and political leader urged the British to recognize the madness of the notion that the old social order should be destroyed and replaced by a contemporary invention. Burke asserted that an attempt to follow the dictates of human reason rather than tradition would lead toward massive bloodshed and military despotism.

Burke demanded reverence for tradition. Whatever had evolved from the distant past became part of a living society. The removal of anything from such an organic structure, even an obviously defective institution or practice, threatened disaster. Improvement could come only by a cautiously slow process, as in the cultivation of a plant. Burke's ideas became the foundation for a widely influential ideology that flowered more fully in the 1800s.

THE PRINCIPLES OF CONSERVATISM

Conservatives diametrically opposed every central tenet of liberalism and, as in the writings of Edmund Burke, demanded worship of the traditional order. In keeping with long-standing custom, they therefore insisted that everyone accept his or her inherited position in the social hierarchy. The principle of hierarchy as well as historic precedent indicated that people must revere authority. From the masses at the bottom to the aristocrats at the top, all people had to obey their superiors, especially God's anointed supreme ruler, the king. The rejection of this tradition would lead to chaos, according to the conservatives.

The arguments for the general principles of hierarchy and authority indicated the primary concerns of conservatives in this era—the maintenance of aristocracy and monarchy. In keeping with both the abstract doctrines and their specific social values, conservatives also vehemently insisted that the historic Christian church must resume and retain its spiritual supremacy. God willed that humans live in a system of moral as well as social and political authority and hierarchy. Following the dictates of the clergy would prevent the destructive behavior of inherently evil humanity.

Most conservative ideas blended into a coherent antiliberal doctrine, a justification for thwarting the liberals who wanted to usher in a new society consistent with their own doctrines. Until after the mid-1800s, conservatives also fought tenaciously against another force for change in the traditional European order—nationalism. The rising sentiment among East and Central Europeans for the formation of states on the basis of nationality evoked an intensely hostile reaction from the defenders of the *ancien* tradition because the establishment of a nation-state system would obliterate the political structure on which they thought their way of life depended. To make matters even worse, nationalists in these decades wanted their new regimes to be liberal.

THE CONCERT OF EUROPE

Royal and aristocratic devotees of conservatism from every state that had been at war in Europe in 1814 converged on Austria's capital in September of that year. With Napoleon on Elba and Louis XVIII enthroned, the coalition that overthrew the revolutionary Emperor had invited all countries involved in the recent war, even France, to send representatives to Vienna.

Those who responded to this invitation understood that they would assemble as a "congress" to decide about the structure of post-Napoleonic Europe. Before this Congress of Vienna adjourned in June 1815, delegates agreed on state borders as expected. After the formal Vienna Congress ended, the leaders of the "Concert of Europe," as the Quadruple Alliance was also known, agreed to a more permanent system of relationships among themselves. This plan indicated that the Concert of Europe intended to change from an alliance to defeat France into an institution to preserve peace. The work of the Congress and the Concert brought forty years without a war between European states.

The Congress of Vienna

The members of the Quadruple Alliance that led the battle against France—Britain, Russia, Austria, and Prussia—dominated the proceedings at Vienna. These nations intended to balance power in Europe as a way to maintain peace. In keeping with this principle, they began their work by concluding a very lenient treaty with France so that the restored kingdom would have the strength necessary to ensure an equilibrium.

The Treaty of Paris (May 1814) that ended the war between France and the Coalition redrew French borders as they had existed on November 1, 1792. This provision gave France newly acquired areas such as the Austrian Netherlands, and returned most of the colonies lost to Britain during the wars. France also paid no damages for the destructive conflict. These peace terms indicate that conservative leaders in this era intended to restore the old order but not precisely as it had been. They would accept very significant changes and adopt new policies in order to preserve the *kind* of society they preferred. These conservatives did not resist innovation absolutely.

THE GREAT-POWER LEADERS

The representatives of Austria, Britain, Russia, and Prussia conducted their long and arduous deliberations in secret. The Austrian Emperor, Francis, provided lavish entertainment for delegates to the Congress who were excluded from the talks, but this failed to placate them. Their protests accomplished little. They went on with their dinners and dances while a handful of men decided the fate of Europe.

Prince Klemens von Metternich (1773–1859), Foreign Minister of Austria. The carefully groomed and self-assured aristocrat Metternich took charge of Austrian foreign relations in 1809. When the Congress convened in Vienna, he brought it under his command too. Metternich dominated relations among European states from then until the mid-1800s. In his conduct of affairs in Vienna, the Austrian leader followed a policy of "legitimacy" to a certain extent—he tended to support the enthronement and preservation of traditional dynasties. This principle coincided with his deep commitment to the perpetuation of the Austrian Hapsburg Empire. Yet he ignored legitimacy at times as he adhered to policies more critical to Austria's survival. In defense of the imperial realm, Prince Metternich intended above all to contain France, balance power among states so that none could conquer others, and suppress liberalism and nationalism.

Viscount Castlereagh (1769–1822), Foreign Minister of Great Britain. In 1812, as the final drive against Napoleon began, Viscount Castlereagh became foreign minister of Britain. The British spent more than the other states in this military campaign, and Castlereagh led this phase of the war. As a result of these circumstances, Castlereagh wielded great influence at the Congress of Vienna. He used his authority for the most part to support the same goals as Metternich, except that Castlereagh opposed intervention to repress liberal and nationalist movements. (This policy was influenced by the realization that the collapse of old regimes sometimes opened the door to British trade.) The British differed most noticeably from the other members of the Quadruple Alliance in Britain's lack of interest in territorial acquisitions. Russia and Prussia came hungry for land, but Britain and Austria resisted their ambitions, even to the point of threatening war.

The Russian Tsar and the Quest for Poland. Tsar Alexander I of Russia, rather than one of his officials, served as his country's negotiator at Vienna. The partitions of Poland (see chapter 4) had divided that country's land among Austria, Prussia, and Russia. Now Alexander wanted all of Poland. The tsar indicated that his control over that state would benefit its people. Although he ruled as an absolute autocrat in Russia, Alexander proclaimed his commitment to Enlightenment ideals and even to aspects of liberalism. He pledged to give independence and liberal government to Poland. Suspicions that madness gripped Alexander circulated in Vienna. Doubts also persisted that he intended anything more noble than grabbing Poland.

Prince Karl von Hardenberg of Prussia. The Prussian king, Frederick William III, left diplomatic discussions at Vienna to his representative, Prince Karl von Hardenberg. Frederick William's ardent support for Alexander's ambitions, however, governed Hardenberg's actions. Prussian leaders anticipated a considerable reward for their commitment to Russia. They would surrender the Polish territory taken during the partitions but acquire Saxony. Austria and Britain raised vehement objections to both plans for expansion. The representative of the restored French monarchy entered the diplomatic fray against Russia and Prussia.

Prince Charles de Talleyrand (1754–1838) of France. Prince Talleyrand, who represented the new French king Louis XVIII, worked as adroitly at Vienna as he had for the highly varied governments of France between 1789 and 1814. He had served as a diplomat for nearly all of them. The great powers planned no role for him in their negotiations, but that did not prevent his influence on events. Talleyrand became the unofficial spokesman for the delegations left out of the discussions. The French prince influenced certain agreements in this way but had a more dramatic effect when he sided with Britain and Austria on the Polish-Saxon issue.

THE CONFLICT OVER POLAND AND SAXONY

Congress leaders could have completed a settlement quickly on all points except the fate of Poland and Saxony. By late 1814, that conflict led to the brink of a new war. Talleyrand drew Castlereagh and Metternich into a secret agreement to ally against Russia or Prussia if either state attacked one of the three partners. Russian and Prussian leaders soon had general knowledge of the understanding among their opponents and assumed they faced a risk of war. They compromised.

THE FINAL ACTS OF THE CONGRESS OF VIENNA, JUNE 9, 1815

Before diplomats arranged the formal settlement, Napoleon began his one-hundred-day resurgence (March 1815). Negotiations stopped for a time as the Alliance resumed the war with France. The four great-power leaders still completed their diplomatic tasks in time to present the Final Acts of the Congress to all the delegations for formal signing nine days before Napoleon's defeat at Waterloo.

Russia and Scandinavia. The Acts allowed Russia to take charge of somewhat less of Poland than Alexander wanted, leaving smaller parts under Austria and Prussia. Russia also acquired Finland from Sweden. In return for the concession to Russia, Sweden annexed Norway, a Scandinavian country that had backed Napoleon.

Germany. The Congress decided to enlarge Prussia as a safeguard against French expansion. Therefore, the Vienna settlement consigned land on the Rhine River and about one-third of the German state of Saxony to Prussia. The rest of Saxony remained an independent kingdom under its former ruler. The settlement also arranged Prussia and thirty-seven other German states into a loose-knit Confederation under the presidency of Austria. Members of the German Confederation remained as independent countries joined mostly for defense. In effect, the Vienna Congress had accepted Napoleon's consolidation of scores of German principalities into fewer than forty states. They largely nullified, however, the overall unity that he had brought to the German principalities since the Confederation lacked real political cohesion.

The Netherlands, Austria, and Italy. The negotiators joined the Kingdom of Holland and the Austrian Netherlands to form an enlarged Kingdom of the Netherlands. (By this action also they intended to balance against the possible aggression of France.) For the loss of territory in the Netherlands, Austria gained Venetia and Lombardy in Italy as well as an area on the Adriatic Sea. The Final Acts also expanded Piedmont-Sardinia, a northwestern Italian kingdom that included an adjacent island. Finally, the agreement organized an enlarged south Italian state by merging Naples and the island of Sicily to form the Kingdom of the Two Sicilies.

Royal Restorations. The Congress showed little concern for the principle of legitimacy in Germany, but it did restore several ruling families that Napoleon had overthrown. During the Peninsular War, the British took the crown of Spain from Napoleon's brother and returned it to the Bourbon king, Ferdinand VII. The Congress confirmed this restoration. It also sanctioned the return of displaced ruling dynasties in Portugal, the Netherlands, Piedmont-Sardinia, and the Sicilies.

THE HOLY ALLIANCE

After the acceptance of the Final Acts, Alexander I of Russia pursued one of his mystical schemes to a conclusion at Vienna. The tsar wooed his fellow rulers with a vision of European monarchs allied in a commitment to reign in a spirit of Christian love, peace, and justice. Pope Pius VII considered such an alliance a useless attempt of secular leaders to provide religious guidance. Castlereagh dismissed it as "sublime mysticism and nonsense," and the British avoided signing. The Muslim ruler of Ottoman Turkey spurned membership in a Christian alliance. The other heads of state, however, agreed in September 1815 to join Russia, Prussia, and Austria in their Holy Alliance. This agreement had no practical effect on European diplomacy and only Alexander made any attempt to apply this mystical idea in his state.

THE SECOND TREATY OF PARIS

The Quadruple Alliance powers drew up a new peace agreement with France after Waterloo. It somewhat revised the borders they had previously arranged at Paris and Vienna in 1814 and 1815. This second treaty (November 20, 1815) included more punitive provisions than had the one in 1814. It required boundaries approximately as they had been in 1790 rather than 1792. France lost territory in the Netherlands and elsewhere. The allies also stationed troops in French territory and arranged for them to stay five years. France had to pay the cost of this occupation force and an additional penalty of 700,000,000 francs.

The Congress System, 1815–1829

On the day the four great powers concluded the Second Treaty of Paris with France, they also agreed to continue the Quadruple Alliance as further insurance against French aggression. The allies promised joint military action again if necessary to prevent French conquests. As a complementary step in pursuit of European tranquility, the Alliance decided to convene regularly as a congress to discuss mutual concerns. This unprecedented plan for a congress system converted the Concert of Europe into a more formal organization.

The British fully supported the congress system as a way to maintain a peaceful balance in Europe but refused to assist the other three powers in their efforts to suppress liberals and nationalists. On this latter issue, Britain moved further and further from Austria, Russia, and Prussia as these

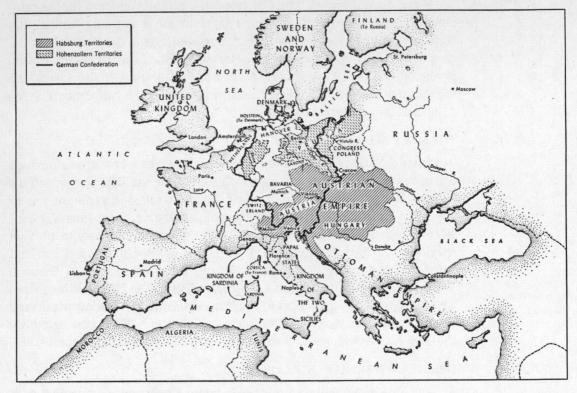

Fig. 7.1   Europe in 1815

conservative partners conducted their campaign against change after the Vienna Congress adjourned.

THE CONGRESS OF AIX-LA-CHAPELLE, OCTOBER 1818

The Concert of Europe recognized within a very short time that the behavior of France under the restored Bourbon monarchy differed greatly from the actions of its Napoleonic predecessor. Alliance members decided to gather for their first regular congress to respond to the new conditions. They met at Aix-la-Chapelle near the western border of Prussia and nullified the punishments arranged in the Second Treaty of Paris. Bourbon France then became a member of the Concert of Europe as the group expanded into the Quintuple Alliance.

THE CONGRESSES OF TROPPAU AND LAIBACH, 1820–1821

Ferdinand VII of Spain took his restoration to heart. When the Congress of Vienna gave him his throne, he canceled a liberal constitution that the Bonapartes had devised for the kingdom. The king then prepared to reconquer the Spanish American colonies, which were in the last stages of a successful revolt for independence. His order for the army to go to the

Americas provoked a rebellion among his own miserably treated troops. Riots soon erupted in cities across the kingdom. Ferdinand attempted to placate the rebels by a readoption of the liberal constitution.

The Russian tsar urged suppressive action by the Concert in Spain. Britain opposed him. When revolt exploded also in the Kingdom of the Two Sicilies in Italy and led its ruler, Ferdinand I, to grant a constitution, Metternich joined the chorus for repression. The Alliance members went to Troppau in central Prussia for another Congress (October 1820). There, over Britain's objection, they adopted Metternich's proposition that the Concert should intervene to stop revolutions anywhere in Europe. After an adjournment, the Congress reconvened farther south at Laibach. The Alliance dispatched Austria to save Ferdinand I of Sicily from liberalism. Metternich's forces rushed to the rescue, empowered Ferdinand to rescind the constitution, and on the way back through north Italy struck down rebels in Piedmont-Sardinia.

THE CONGRESS OF VERONA, OCTOBER 1822

Rebellion in Spain continued. Another Congress opened, this time at Verona in northeastern Italy, to consider further repressive moves. Castlereagh committed suicide shortly before this Congress and was replaced by George Canning when the assembly began. Canning vehemently expressed British opposition to intervention in Spain. The other Congress powers commissioned France to crush the rebellion. One hundred thousand French troops invaded Spain and accomplished this task by mid-1823. The Spanish king, Ferdinand VII, again nullified the liberal constitution. After Verona, Britain ended its participation in the Concert.

REBEL VICTORY IN THE SPANISH AMERICAN COLONIES

The conservative continental powers succeeded in Spain despite Britain's strenuous objections. They could not stop the revolt in Spain's American colonies against the will of the nation that ruled the seas. Britain asked the United States to express a common policy of opposition to European intervention in the Americas. Instead, U.S. President James Monroe announced his own policy separately (December 1823), declaring that European states must not become involved in affairs in the American hemisphere. Since Britain wanted this "Monroe Doctrine" to take effect, it did. With no chance of European intervention, the rebels in the Spanish colonies triumphed.

THE GREEK LIBERAL NATIONALIST REVOLT

The Greeks struck their first blows for national independence and a more liberal government in 1821. Even though the Ottoman Turkish Sultan was the legitimate ruler of Greece, the conservative European monarchies responded quite differently than they did to the Spanish revolt. The Russian tsar, Alexander I, advocated aid to the Greek rebels, who were led by Alexander Ypsilanti. These were Christian revolutionaries battling a Muslim Sultan. The Russian Emperor stood ready to support people of his Christian faith, and perhaps extend the influence of Russia southward at the same time. Metternich refused intervention on the side of revolution, but he also favored no assistance to the established government.

The European Attack on Turkey. When the Ottoman Empire neared victory over the rebels in 1825, Russia had a new tsar-emperor, Nicholas I (r. 1825–1855). He committed Russian forces to the rebel cause. In order to control the involvement of Russia and protect their own interests in the region, Britain and France entered the conflict too. Austria objected but to no effect. A combined allied fleet won decisively over the navy of the Sultan's ally, Egypt, at Navarino on October 20, 1827. Then the French defeated Turkish forces in Greece as the Russians advanced into the Ottoman Empire itself. Turkey submitted.

The Treaty of Adrianople, September 14, 1829. The peace settlement arranged for Russia to give up most of the territory it had conquered. But the Russians annexed some land along the Danube River and also occupied additional Danubian areas pending Turkey's payment of war damages. The treaty ended Turkish control over Greece. Members of a disunited conservative coalition had helped a liberal nationalist rebellion succeed.

*B*y *the time of the Greek rebels' triumph, Europe's modern ideologies had multiplied considerably compared to the 1790s. Theorists expanded and adjusted liberalism or turned to socialism. Intellectuals and activists transformed patriotic sentiment into an ideology of nationalism. Writers and artists established Romanticism, a new cultural movement emphasizing emotion. Romanticism dominated the arts during the first half of the 1800s. Enthusiasts for the* Ancien Régime *devised conservatism as a new complex of theories for the justification of the old social order. Thus enlarged and diversified, Modern European thought now included virtually all its main currents.*

The struggle to defend or destroy traditional systems involved much more than intellectual conflict. The European leaders of the Quadruple Alliance who triumphed over Napoleon intended thereafter to defend the Ancien Régime *politically and militarily. At the end of their arduous fight against revolutionary France, they convened a congress of all European states in Vienna, Austria (1814–1815), and took steps to restore and preserve as much of the old order as possible.*

In its Final Acts (June 1815), the Congress of Vienna organized larger and stronger states east of France and reestablished a portion of the traditional systems of government around the borders of that nation as guarantees of future peace. The great powers also pledged to take joint military action again if necessary to suppress an aggressor such as Napoleonic France. As a further guarantee of security for the established states, the Quadruple Alliance agreed to meet in regular congresses and consider problems of mutual concern.

After the great powers reached agreement at Vienna, they entered an era of unusually peaceful relationships. Even France, under a restored Bourbon monarchy, soon enjoyed completely normal diplomatic associations with its former enemies. Four of these allies—Austria, Russia, Prussia, and France—not only maintained peace but also cooperated closely in the suppression of revolts against the Ancien Régime. *The British, however, refused to support counterrevolutionary intervention since successful rebellions sometimes opened markets for industrial products.*

The four repressive monarchies succeeded in crushing rebellions in Spain, the Kingdom of the Two Sicilies, and Piedmont-Sardinia in the 1820s. They failed, however, to prevent the Spanish American colonies from winning independence because they could not act without the help of Britain, the all-powerful nation at sea.

The Greek revolt for independence from Turkey (1821–1829) came as an even more shattering blow to the defenders of the ancien *system. Unusual circumstances and conflicting great-power interests in the region where the rebellion occurred not only prevented repressive intervention but led Russia, Britain, and France to support the Greek war of national liberation. Austria opposed aid to the rebels but could not control its allies. The liberal nationalist movement in Greece triumphed.*

Spaniards, Italians, and Greeks had challenged the European status quo between 1820 and 1829. During the next two decades, liberal and nationalist rebels would repeatedly confront their conservative governments across the entire breadth of the continent. Revolutionaries choked the streets of Europe's leading cities with their barricades. Sometimes they toppled governments. Despite its diligent efforts between 1815 and 1829, the Ancien Régime *had not ensured its survival in Modern Europe.*

Selected Readings

Artz, Frederick B. *Reaction and Revolution, 1814–1832.* New York: Harper and Brothers, 1934.

Fasel, George W. *Edmund Burke.* Boston: Twayne Publishers, 1983.

Hayes, Carlton J.H. *The Historical Evolution of Modern Nationalism.* New York: R. R. Smith, 1931.

Honour, Hugh. *Romanticism.* New York: Harper & Row, 1979.

Kissinger, Henry. *A World Restored: Metternich, Castlereagh, and the Problems of Peace, 1812–1822.* Boston: Houghton Mifflin, 1957.

Kohn, Hans. *Nationalism, Its Meaning and History.* Rev. ed. Princeton, NJ: Van Nostrand, 1965.

Nicolson, Harold G. *The Congress of Vienna: A Study in Allied Unity, 1812–1822.* New York: Viking Press, 1961.

Seidman, Steven. *Liberalism and the Origins of European Social Theory.* Berkeley: University of California Press, 1983.

Smith, Anthony D. *Theories of Nationalism.* London: Duckworth, 1971.

Viereck, Peter R. E. *Conservatism Revisited.* Rev. ed. New York: The Free Press, 1966.

8

The Age of European Revolution, 1815–1848

1796	The reign of Paul I begins in Russia (1796–1801)
1797	King Frederick William III takes the throne in Prussia (1797–1840)
1801	Alexander I becomes Russian tsar (1801–1825)
1806	Francis II begins his monarchy in Austria (1806–1835)
1814	Louis XVIII is given the throne of France (1814–1824). The French king provides the Charter of 1814 as the nation's new constitution
1815	The English Parliament enacts the Corn Laws
1819	The "Peterloo Massacre" occurs in England
	The Carlsbad decrees repress reform in the German Confederation
1824	Charles X succeeds Louis XVIII in France (1824–1830)
1825	Nicholas I begins his reign in Russia (1825–1855)
	The Russian Decembrist revolt occurs
1830	Revolutions erupt in France, Italy, Belgium, and Poland
	Louis Philippe begins reign as the French "bourgeois monarch" (1830–1848)
1832	The English Reform Bill of 1832 extends voting rights
1833	The Factory Act limits hours of labor for English children in textile plants
1835	Ferdinand I starts his reign in Austria (1835–1848)
1838	The British Chartists draw up their first petition

1840 Frederick William IV succeeds to the throne of Prussia (1840–1861)

1845 The potato famine occurs in Ireland

1846 Parliament nullifies the English Corn Laws

1847 The Ten-Hours Act limits work hours for children and women in all industries in Britain

1848 Revolutions break out in France, Italy, Austria, and Germany

Francis Joseph becomes Austrian Emperor (1848–1916)

The Chartists in England present their last petition

1849 Rebels establish a republic in Rome, but France restores the pope

Austria defeats Italian liberation forces at Novara

The Frankfort Assembly ends an attempt to unify Germany

1851 Napoleon III establishes the Second French Empire

The revolution of 1789–1815 had so thoroughly demolished the Ancien Régime *in France that conservatives there could not restore the old sociopolitical system. The installment of a Bourbon monarchy at the end of the revolution, however, provided a semblance of traditional government for fifteen years. Circumstances for French aristocrats also were better from 1815 to 1848 than during the revolution, but the property and most of the privileges they had lost were gone forever.*

Elsewhere in Europe, the old regime returned to or lingered uninterruptedly in power after the defeat of Napoleon. The economic, social, and cultural conditions on which the traditional elite depended, however, continued to change in ways that undercut more of the foundations of the old order. The selected liberal reforms established during Napoleon's reign over much of the continent hastened this destruction of the Ancien Régime's *footing outside of France. Even in the regions that Napoleon never controlled, the French Revolution weakened the standing of the traditional leadership. Nearby states, such as Austria and Prussia, felt these effects the most. The stimulus France gave to change reached Britain and Russia but with lessened strength.*

As a result of long-term underlying trends and the influence of recent events in France on them, the end of the French *revolutionary era marked the beginning of the age of* European *revolution. Violent protests in Britain and revolts in Spain, Italy, Russia, and Greece between 1815 and 1830 suggested that the area susceptible to revolution had widened beyond France. Then liberal and nationalist revolutionaries struck with great force at multiple centers in the heartland of Europe during the crisis years of 1830 and 1848. In this age of European revolution, the second phase of sociopolitical modernization, the struggle between the old and new regimes climaxed but did not end.*

DEEPENING REPRESSION IN RUSSIA, 1796–1855

Even though Peter the Great (r. 1682–1725) had forcibly accelerated the transition to new ways in Russia, the country had made little progress toward economic or sociopolitical modernization by the late 1700s. A mood somewhat more conducive to progressive reform developed, however, before the turn of the century and for about twenty years affected both government programs and the behavior of small but significant social groups. Then a reactionary campaign began that virtually stopped the modernizing process until after the mid-1800s.

The Autocracy at the Accession of Paul I, 1796

The nature of Russia's government gave its monarchs the power to determine whether reform or reaction prevailed. Paul I (r. 1796–1801) had inherited the ultimate form of absolute monarchy from his mother, Catherine the Great, a system called an "autocracy" since one of the ruler's titles was autocrat. The gargantuan size of his state and the relatively low level of technology placed practical limits on Paul's authority, but he still exercised extreme power over his realm. An elaborate bureaucracy, the Russian Orthodox Christian Church, and a massive army stood ready to communicate and enforce the tsar's will.

RUSSIAN SOCIETY IN THE 1790s

During the 1700s Russian rulers greatly increased the gentry's social benefits and removed virtually all obligations of service to the state. Tsars also vastly expanded the nobility's already extreme authority over peasants. Specific gains for the gentry in the latter 1700s included greater power to exile peasants in Siberia, exemption of nobles from court-ordered physical punishment, and freedom from all taxes. The government also ended the right of peasants to bring official complaints against nobles.

PAUL I AS REFORMER AND COUNTER-REVOLUTIONARY

Paul took charge when his mother died in November 1796, and soon set about the correction of the flaws that he thought she had left in the system—Catherine had not improved the cumbersome machinery of government, and she had markedly increased noble power and privileges. Paul tried to establish a more coherent and highly centralized bureaucracy and to reduce aristocratic authority over the peasantry. He accomplished little in these attempts to reform the government and the aristocratic social structure.

Despite his interest in reform, Paul passionately opposed the spread of revolutionary influences in Russia. As his defense against contagion from the West that might induce rebellion, the tsar tried to prevent contact between Russia and the world beyond its lengthy borders. He failed. A few nobles with liberal inclinations killed Paul in 1801. They expected Alexander, Paul's son and lawful successor, to bring about the changes they desired.

Alexander I— Liberal Autocrat

Circumstances well-justified the conspirators' anticipation of liberal reform under Emperor Alexander I. The twenty-three-year-old heir to the throne belonged to the group of plotters. Alexander probably did not agree to his father's murder, but his involvement in the revolt suggested a strong commitment to change. Soon the new tsar's actions seemed to confirm the hopes of the conspirators.

ALEXANDER AGAINST AUTOCRACY AND SERFDOM

Alexander's plan for political and social reform was astounding. He began his reign as an absolute ruler over a mostly enserfed society with the declared intention of ending absolute monarchy and serfdom. But the young Emperor's reforms during his first four years of power had no clear relationship to the goal of doing away with autocracy and the serf system. He continued the effort of recent tsars to convert old monarchical institutions into a more modern professional bureaucratic structure and proclaimed his willingness to assist any nobles who volunteered to free their serfs. Government and society changed very little.

MICHAEL SPERANSKY'S DRAFT CONSTITUTION

A relatively peaceful relationship with France after 1807 enabled Alexander to devote more attention to the issue of autocracy. He commissioned his top governmental official, Michael Speransky (1772–1839), to compose a draft constitution for Russia. Speransky recommended a gradual evolution to a very limited parliamentary system of government which left the power to present legislation in the hands of an executive group (the State Council) and the tsar. Implementation of the plan got no further than the establishment of the State Council.

THE REVERSION TO ABSOLUTISM AND REPRESSION

The Final Acts of the Congress of Vienna in 1815 (see chapter 7) converted Napoleon's Duchy of Warsaw into the Kingdom of Poland, but provided for the Russian tsar to serve as the Polish monarch. Alexander gave Poland what he refused to allow in Russia, a liberal constitutional system designed according to Speransky's plan. Unfortunately for the Poles,

Alexander tended to act as though the constitutional law did not apply to him, an attitude typical of absolute monarchs.

After 1815 the tsar governed Russia in an increasingly repressive way. Religious fanatics began to act as monitors of the universities and could arrange the dismissal of professors deemed too radical or otherwise unfit. The government restricted expression for a much larger part of the educated public by tightening controls on the press.

*The
Decembrist
Revolt, 1825*

Russia had a long history of peasant revolts and palace coups. The rebels in these historic forms of attack never attempted to overthrow the *system* of government. In December 1825, when Alexander I died, revolutionaries struck with the intention of destroying the autocracy.

THE DECEMBRISTS

Education, from minimal literacy to the most advanced level, was a privilege limited almost exclusively to the nobility in Russia. This intellectual elite in the 1700s came under the influence of French thought, and many adopted Enlightenment attitudes. When the Napoleonic wars erupted, educated aristocrats comprised the officer corps in charge of campaigns in the French Empire. Thus members of the best educated and most liberal groups in Russia came into contact with life in the West, an experience that intensified their desire for sociopolitical modernization. After the officers returned home, a portion of them organized secret societies committed to such a change. These conspirators became the Decembrists of 1825.

THE REBELLION

Upon the death of Alexander I in December 1825, his younger brother, Nicholas, claimed the throne. Uncertainty about the legality of Nicholas's accession gave the rebels their opportunity. When government leaders in St. Petersburg called 3,000 troops to the Winter Palace plaza to take their public oath to Nicholas, army officers involved in the conspiracy convinced the soldiers to refuse to state the pledge. The rebels expected the stalemate to enable them to extort an agreement to constitutional monarchy.

After several hours of inaction, loyal troops opened fire with cannon, killing sixty to eighty people. The rebellion at the capital ended at once. Soon the conspiracy was suppressed everywhere. The government executed four Decembrist leaders and sent hundreds to prison or exile. The Decembrists became heroes to many Russians in subsequent decades. In 1825, few people cared about their cause.

*Nicholas I,
Guardian of
the Ancien
Régime*

Even though the repression during Alexander I's last years helped cause the Decembrist revolt, Nicholas I (r. 1825–1855) responded to it by increasing the repression in Russia. He also became a leader in the effort to defend *ancien* institutions all over the continent. European opponents of the old regime described him as "the Gendarme of Europe," the guardian against change everywhere.

HIS MAJESTY'S OWN CHANCERY AND "THE THIRD SECTION"

Nicholas reorganized the government executive council, His Majesty's Own Chancery, into "Sections" with specified responsibilities. The Third Section's duties included the creation and direction of a new security force, sometimes called the "secret police" even though they wore sky-blue uniforms. Nicholas commissioned the Third Section to watch and investigate *everything* so that it could stop any activity that might threaten the autocracy.

THE DOCTRINE OF OFFICIAL NATIONALITY

Nicholas implemented strict press censorship and presented standards for defining loyal citizens. The government's doctrine of "Official Nationality" depicted these true Russians as a people dedicated to Autocracy, Orthodoxy, and Nationality. The creed meant that loyal Russians supported the absolute power of the autocrat, accepted the exclusive spiritual leadership of the Russian Orthodox Church, and, as an inherent trait of their Russian nationality, felt an unqualified devotion to the imperial family and its government. Anyone who advocated change in these fundamental Russian ways was deemed a traitor.

THE CRITICAL INTELLIGENTSIA

The "intelligentsia" (intellectual class) of the 1800s and early 1900s produced an unusual abundance of outstanding literature and influential social thought, much of it demanding change. In their critique of Russian life, a number of these observers expressed adoration of traditional institutions but most condemned the old order. Among the critical intelligentsia, two main schools of thought emerged during the late 1700s and early 1800s.

The "Westernizers" were those who had concluded that the way of life in West Europe and the United States was vastly superior to theirs and advocated modernization along Western lines. The other group, called "Slavophiles" because they loved Slavic culture, leveled an equally sharp attack on both existing Russian institutions and Western culture. They called for a return to ancient Slavic ways. Nicholas's government worked diligently to suppress both these groups.

THE TRANSITION TO REFORM IN GREAT BRITAIN

Economic conditions after 1815 fostered a growing public demand for reform in Britain. When the need for British goods on the continent dropped sharply after the war, the economy slumped badly. Many workers lost their jobs. Plunging grain prices threatened upper-class landowners, and the government rushed to their aid with the Corn Laws of 1815. This legislation virtually prohibited grains from abroad and enabled the landlords to keep their prices high. The Corn Laws thus raised the cost of bread. Hard times for the poorer classes became harder still.

Since the few who controlled the government took care of their own needs and ignored the problems of others, postwar economic conditions provoked movements for *political* change. Discontented people wanted to share in government power so that they could help themselves as the elite did. The reformers thus set out to change parliamentary institutions.

Parliamentary Government in the Early 1800s

Parliamentary leaders (the prime minister and the other ministers of the executive Cabinet) dominated British government during the latter war years and after. Changing sociopolitical conditions and George III's intermittent insanity had stopped his attempt to reestablish monarchical control of policy. His son, George IV, who ruled from 1820 to 1830, left the monarchy still weaker. The factions that ran Parliament, therefore, again increased their power over the country.

THE POLITICAL PARTIES

The aristocracy (the titled nobles or "peers") automatically became members of the upper parliamentary chamber, the House of Lords. Property owners elected the House of Commons. Relatively wealthy country gentlemen (the gentry) and titled nobles dominated both houses and the two political parties that operated within them, the Tories and Whigs.

The Tories. Tories strongly favored religious conformity under the Church of England (Anglican Church), but their main concern after the appearance of Jacobin republicanism in France was opposition to that revolutionary view. For many years, the party was in a position to impose its creed on Britain. Lord Liverpool served as Tory prime minister from 1811 until 1828, and his party continued to control the government until 1830.

The Whigs. Very wealthy landowning aristocrats traditionally dominated the Whig Party and so held many principles in common with the Tories. But the Whigs also represented the interests of the rising industrial business class and Protestant dissenters who refused to conform to Anglican beliefs. Thus this party would defend many traditions, took a cautious approach to innovation, but inclined much more toward reform than did the Tories.

POSTWAR REPRESSION

The economic suffering that followed the Napoleonic wars inspired some political activists outside the mainstream parties to demand drastic change in Britain. The plight of the lower classes moved these Radicals, as they came to be called, to form organizations and produce publications insisting on reforms. The government had virtually no patience with such agitators.

THE PETERLOO MASSACRE, AUGUST 1819

Public protests became widespread by 1817. British leaders intensified the repression with measures such as outlawing public meetings. The dissent virtually stopped for a time. Then a worsening depression again inspired the public to act. The desperate conditions brought thousands of protesters to St. Peter's Fields in Manchester, England, in August 1819. Mounted troops arrived to seize the speaker. They rode into the crowd, killed eleven people, and injured 400 others. This "Peterloo Massacre" demonstrated the government's brutally determined commitment to preservation of the status quo. Parliament further confirmed this attitude by the passage of still more rigid laws against dissent, the Six Acts of November 1819.

Tory Reform

Both parliamentary parties included people who favored at least cautious reform. The uproar over Peterloo and fears of more serious popular action encouraged still more parliamentary support for corrective legislation. George Canning, who replaced Castlereagh as foreign minister in 1822, and other new members who soon entered the Cabinet, believed more in change than had their predecessors. Cautious reform followed.

ADJUSTMENTS IN LAW ENFORCEMENT

Sir Robert Peel, the new Tory secretary for domestic affairs in the 1820s, took charge of matters such as criminal law. Existing codes prescribed very harsh punishments. For example, they provided death penalties for over 200 crimes, even for offenses such as damaging Westminster Bridge. Peel had the laws revised so that about 100 fewer statutes called for execution. He also established a civilian police force to keep order with less chance of military violence as at Peterloo. Since Sir Robert organized the police, they became known as "bobbies."

ECONOMIC REFORM

Parliament passed a series of economic reforms in the 1820s. Until that decade, Tory leaders clung tenaciously to the import taxes and other regulations that benefited the gentry. Then the government yielded slightly to pressure from business interests and consumers for reduced tariffs on certain goods, but the Corn Laws remained untouched. In 1824, the legislators nullified the Combinations Act, a law that had prohibited the formation of labor unions. Parliament soon qualified this concession to workers by denying the right to strike. Near the end of the 1820s, the Tories even modified their stand on the Corn Laws, changing from a near prohibition of imports to a tax on such foreign products. This tariff still protected the landlords and kept bread prices high.

THE CATHOLIC EMANCIPATION BILL, APRIL 1829

English law denied Catholics the right to vote, hold public office, or serve in Parliament. A vigorous movement to end this discrimination arose in mostly Catholic Ireland in the 1820s. The more liberal Tories favored this reform but other party members staunchly resisted. The Duke of Wellington, prime minister from 1828 to 1830, and Peel secured passage of the act in 1829 after a difficult fight against stubborn Tory associates and the king. With the innovations they accepted in the 1820s, the Tories had begun the transition toward reformist politics in Britain.

Whig Reform

The Whig Party and the businesspeople who favored free trade posed the main threat to the traditions and laws that maintained the old elite of titled nobles and country gentlemen. Since the Tories who represented these traditionalist elements thoroughly dominated the British Parliament, reform of the election system became the central concern of the discontented groups.

THE ROTTEN BOROUGHS

Members of Parliament entered the legislature as the representatives of rural counties or town boroughs. Each such district sent two people to Parliament. Procedures for the selection of these representatives had remained unchanged for 150 years.

Shifts in population growth rates and settlement patterns lowered the numbers in certain districts and even emptied a few. This condition made control of elections by bribery very easy. Each of these "rotten boroughs" still had two representatives in Parliament. Rapidly growing industrial cities, in contrast, elected relatively few members to Parliament. A few cities chose none. Tradition also allowed landlords to select the representatives from certain districts, the "pocket boroughs." So long as this system remained intact, the defenders of rural aristocratic ways could keep control of Parliament and legislation.

THE REFORM BILL OF 1832

Parliamentary elections in 1830 gave fifty seats formerly held by Tories to reform-minded Whigs and others with similar attitudes. Before the end of the year, Earl Grey (1764–1845) replaced the Duke of Wellington as prime minister. A Whig now headed the government, backed by a House of Commons with a strengthened contingent of reformers.

The Subordination of the House of Lords. In 1831 the antireform Tories in the House of Lords blocked a bill that provided for a redistribution of House of Commons seats and the extension of voting rights to more people. Prime Minister Grey persuaded the king to threaten the entitlement of enough new lords to carry the vote in the upper chamber. The House of Lords surrendered on the issue rather than suffer the influx of new aristocrats.

Provisions of the New Law. The Reform Bill of 1832 took almost 150 seats from overrepresented districts, such as the rotten and pocket boroughs, and gave them to inadequately represented areas. The law also lowered the property requirements for voters sufficiently to give that right to one-fifth of the people. The body of voters thus expanded by fifty percent. These changes increased the influence of the rising urban-industrial middle-class and set a precedent for such socioeconomic electoral adjustments. The law also gave Britain the most democratic government in Europe, even though a minority still ruled.

THE ACCELERATION OF REFORM

By the early 1830s, government leaders instead of protesters took charge of the campaign to revise the parliamentary system and with the election law changes in 1832 completed the transition from repression to reform. Despite occasional lapses, Britain's government remained reformist after about 1830.

The Reform Bill of 1832 that marked the completion of this transition also provided the momentum for an accelerated pace of reform that lasted nearly twenty years. The industrial-age business interests that fought for parliamentary reform usually opposed laws designed to improve factory working conditions. Ironically, some of the Tories who ordinarily resisted political reform favored legislation to control industry. Despite their contradictory objectives, the efforts of these factions combined to launch a series of legislative innovations.

The Sadler Report. A parliamentary investigation led by Michael Sadler provided abundant evidence that large numbers of very young children worked extremely long workweeks at rigorous jobs. Sadler also discovered that cruel treatment by supervisors was all too common. Such revelations brought a growing public demand for reform, and in 1833 Parliament passed the Factory Act.

The Factory Act of 1833. The factory reform bill outlawed the employment of children under nine in the textile industry. It limited the hours of factory labor for other age groups—eight hours per day for children under thirteen and twelve hours for youths fourteen to eighteen years old. As a step toward enforcement, Parliament established a small force of inspectors to visit textile enterprises. Finally, provisions of the reform also required factory owners to provide two hours of education daily for children under thirteen.

Repeal of the Corn Laws. In 1839, the forces for free trade in grain formed the Anti–Corn Law League. John Bright and Richard Cobden added to the power of this coalition with extremely effective public speeches against the grain tariff. When the potato crop failed in Ireland in 1845 and the threat of famine haunted Britain, Prime Minister Robert Peel led a minority of his Tories to support the Whig campaign for repeal. In 1846, Parliament nullified the Corn Laws. The era of free trade had dawned in Britain.

The Ten-Hours Act of 1847. The Factory Act of 1833 had not satisfied reformers who wanted to protect women as well as children and to apply the regulations to all industries. In 1847 they induced Parliament to pass the Ten-Hours Act to set the daily maximum for women and children in factory work of all kinds. With their standard six-day week they still would carry a heavy burden of labor. But the government had drawn a line where none had existed, and in practice it quickly became the standard for men as well.

THE CHARTIST MOVEMENT

Reform in the 1820s and 1830s left many workers still deeply discontented. A labor organization in London drew up a charter in 1838 that reflected the fundamental concern of the poorer classes—a sense of political powerlessness. Designed as a petition to Parliament, this document advanced by the "Chartists" demanded voting rights for all males, equally sized voting districts, secret balloting, annual sessions of Parliament, removal of property ownership requirements for members of Parliament, and pay for legislators. The first two demands would increase worker voting power, the third would prevent powerful interests from intimidating voters, the last two would give the poor access to legislative seats, and annual sessions would increase the power of a reformed Parliament.

In June 1839, the House of Commons received the Chartists' petition with almost 1,300,000 names. The legislators expressed their contempt for the charter by voting against it 235 to 46. The petitioners took their demands to Commons again in 1842 with more than double the previous number of signers. The vote against this charter was larger than in 1839. A similar Chartist campaign in 1848 failed again, and the movement ended. Even so, the transition to reformist politics had gone far enough to ensure against revolution in Britain during a year in which rebels toppled governments all across the continent.

THE TURN TOWARD REVOLUTION IN EUROPE

The conquering troops of revolutionary and Napoleonic France transported their new ways to many parts of Europe between 1789 and 1815. During these years, Europeans other than the French showed little inclination toward revolution. Their attitudes changed quickly, however. By the 1820s, events indicated clearly that significant forces committed to a new social order had become native to virtually every society on the continent.

Metternich's Struggle for Control in Central Europe

As foreign minister and then chancellor (prime minister) for the Austrian Hapsburg Emperors Francis II (r. 1804–1835) and Ferdinand I (r. 1835–1848), Prince Klemens von Metternich's supreme concern was the perpetuation of his rulers' Central European state. The special menace that liberalism and nationalism posed for this aristocratic, monarchical, and multiethnic realm inspired Metternich's direction of domestic policies within the Hapsburg Empire. The Austrian leader also exercised a dominant influence in neighboring Italian and German states after 1815, and he stubbornly resisted liberalism and nationalism in these regions as well.

THE AUSTRIAN EMPIRE

The Hapsburg domains contained nearly a dozen ethnic groups—Germans, Hungarians, Czechs, Slovaks, Poles, Romanians, South Slavs, Italians, and others. National sentiments stirred these social elements after the intrusion and withdrawal of French revolutionary forces, and Metternich feared nationalist revolts. He scattered spies everywhere to watch potential rebels, sent soldiers to intimidate people in areas of unrest, established tight control over publications and university instruction, banned student organizations, and jailed dissidents. Metternich thus controlled his people, but anger grew among them.

ITALY

After Napoleon's conquest of a much-divided Italy, he merged principalities and left it in three larger divisions with somewhat liberalized institutions. The Congress of Vienna divided the peninsula into nine states, including the Kingdom of the Two Sicilies in the south, the Papal States in central Italy, and, in the north, Piedmont, Lombardy, Venetia, and several other small territories. Austria directly ruled Lombardy and Venetia and dominated the entire peninsula.

Although relatively few Italians cared about unity and expelling foreigners, liberalism and nationalism inspired a part of the educated minority to action against the restored system and Austrian domination. They formed secret rebel groups that sometimes met on the beaches around charcoal fires, a practice that yielded their name—the "charcoal burners" or *Carbonari*. Metternich's forces readily contained these opponents of the old regime in the 1820s, but discontented Italians increased their potential to begin a revolutionary conflagration.

THE GERMAN CONFEDERATION

When the leaders of Austria, Britain, Russia, and Prussia reorganized Central Europe at Vienna (1814–1815), they did not re-create the more than 200 separate German states that had existed before 1789. Neither did they leave Germany almost fully unified as it had been briefly under Napoleon. Instead, they established thirty-eight completely independent states and provided for their membership in a new German Confederation.

Austria and Prussia were the largest and most powerful states in the Confederation. Since the industrial revolution had made much more progress in Prussia than in Austria, the Prussians had the potential for supremacy within the Confederation. Prussia strengthened its economic advantages still more by arranging a commercial union that included eighteen German principalities but not Austria. This *Zollverein* ended all trade barriers among the member states.

Despite Prussia's apparent advantages, Austria became the dominant influence in German affairs until after the mid-1800s. The Congress of Vienna had stipulated that Austria preside over the only significant institution of the Confederation, an assembly called the Diet. The very weak structure of the Confederation left the thirty-eight states with no central government, but the feeble apparatus helped Metternich keep Austria supreme.

Conservatism among Confederation leaders and their generally submissive attitude toward the Austrian chancellor made Metternich's task easy at first. In the years just after the Congress of Vienna, he successfully pressured Frederick William III (r. 1797–1840), the Prussian king, and his fellow German rulers into refusing the liberal constitutions that many of their subjects demanded.

The *Burschenschaften*. In the universities where the ideals of liberalism and nationalism had many followers, dissidents formed *Burschenschaften* (student associations) committed to the cause of unity and liberal government. On October 31, 1817, massive demonstrations by these nationalist organizations climaxed with a ceremonial burning of conservative books. In 1819, August von Kotzebue, a well-known author of such publications, died at the hands of an assassin who belonged to a student nationalist society.

The Carlsbad Decrees. Metternich took swift and decisive countermeasures. Through the Confederation Diet he issued the Carlsbad Decrees in September 1819. This set of proclamations outlawed *Burschenschaften*, clamped stringent controls on publications, and launched an intensive campaign to drive the troublemakers from German universities. Overt liberal and nationalist activity stopped in the Confederation for several years after 1819. Despite this calm atmosphere, liberalism remained very attractive to many people within the Confederation.

The Reigns of the Last Two Bourbons in France

The coalition of European states that defeated Napoleon restored the Bourbon monarchy in France by placing Louis XVIII on the throne in 1814. The new king avoided a thoroughly reactionary policy and chose instead only a partial reconstruction of the system that had existed before the revolution.

THE CHARTER OF 1814

Louis XVIII formally established his government by presenting a new constitution for France, the Charter of 1814. This document provided for a legislature elected by a very limited body of voters, the 100,000 richest people in a nation of nearly 30,000,000. The Charter perpetuated Napoleon's Civil Code and the religious settlement he had arranged, kept education under state rather than church control, guaranteed equality before the law, and allowed those who had purchased church and noble lands to keep them.

Although Louis's constitution did not indicate that his ministers (the executives who headed the government and its various departments) would act in compliance with the will of the parliamentary majority, the prime minister eventually did govern in this way. This policy of "responsible government" became a very important political issue. Liberals favored the policy, conservatives opposed it.

THE ULTRAROYALISTS AND STRENGTHENING REACTION

Louis's acceptance of a very few liberal changes went much too far to suit the extreme traditionalists. They rejected the king's moderately reactionary policy and worked for a complete restoration of the old aristocratic and monarchical order. Louis's own brother, the count of Artois, stood at the forefront of these ultraroyalists. When the king died in 1824, Artois took the throne as Charles X. Revolutionary France had acquired a fervently reactionary master.

CHARLES X AGAINST THE TIDE

The new ruler soon attempted to turn France more directly toward the past. Within a year, his aristocratic compatriots who had lost their lands received compensation from the government. He then attempted to restore religious control over education. France erupted in protest. Opposition lessened in 1827 when Charles agreed that government executive policy should reflect the will of the parliamentary majority. Two years later, however, he reversed his stand on this issue. The Chamber of Deputies objected, and Charles responded by dismissing the legislature. If Charles expected this action to produce a more compliant Chamber, he erred.

The Revolutions of 1830

The revolution that began in 1789 had forced the modernization of the French state. Rebels struck again in France in 1830. The bourgeoisie returned to the streets to destroy a Bourbon monarchy that had begun to reverse the process of political modernization. When Louis XVI's *Ancien Regime* toppled in the early 1790s, the surrounding monarchical states took up arms and attacked to destroy the French Revolution. In 1830, the conservative monarchies of East and Central Europe had to fight at home for their own survival, for now they faced a European and not just a French revolution.

THE JULY REVOLUTION IN FRANCE

Charles X sparked revolution when he dissolved the legislature and forced the election of a new one. The enemies of royalism took more seats instead of growing weaker. Charles then issued the July Ordinances, a series of decrees that nullified the recent parliamentary elections, placed tight controls on the press, and took the vote away from 75,000 of the 100,000 eligible citizens. Most of the king's rich middle-class opponents would have no political voice if these decrees went into effect.

The bourgeoisie and their supporters among the workers of France took over the streets of Paris. The rebels ripped up paving stones, carted furniture and other objects into the narrow thoroughfares, and erected barricades. With many of their number clad in typical business attire, including top hats, the revolutionaries gathered behind their battlements and in windows along the streets to fight approaching troops. Royal forces dwindled as contingents of troops went over to the other side. The revolutionaries won Paris. As their red, white, and blue banner fluttered over the cathedral of Notre-Dame, Charles X surveyed the scene through a telescope. France's last Bourbon ruler decided to leave for Britain, and a "bourgeois monarch"—Louis Philippe—soon became "King of the French."

THE BELGIAN REVOLT

A spirit of rebellion had burned in many Belgians almost from the moment the Congress of Vienna forced the merger of Belgium and the Netherlands. The July Revolution in neighboring France intensified the Belgian desire for liberation from the dominant Dutch. Rebellion followed the next month, and Belgian nationalists won their victory by October.

Dutch opposition to Belgian independence delayed the formal recognition of the new state for almost a decade. In 1839, British and French diplomacy brought Dutch acceptance of the Treaty of London which admitted Belgium to the circle of European states. The London agreement also attempted to protect the new nation from invasion by officially recognizing it as neutral.

LIBERAL AND NATIONAL REBELLION IN GERMANY AND ITALY

By 1830, the rulers of several German states already had yielded to increasing liberal pressure and granted constitutions. The French victory over the reactionary Charles prompted German liberals to step up their demands for political liberties. Public protests quickly led rulers in four more principalities to concede constitutional rights. More than one-fourth of the Confederation states now had constitutions. Metternich's grip on the German territories had weakened but only temporarily.

In Italy, more than a decade of *Carbonari* effort had stimulated a *Risorgimento*. This "Resurgence" was a movement for political union that took its name from the view that Italians must regain the sense of common identity that held together the people of the peninsula in ancient times. Small but dedicated bands inspired by such ideas stood ready for their heroic venture.

The victory over royal absolutism in France in July 1830, provoked Italian nationalists to action. Rebels struck and took charge in the principalities of Parma and Modena in the north and in the Papal States in the peninsula's center. They anticipated victory over local rulers, freedom from Austrian dominance, and the eventual unification of Italy under a more liberal system of government.

With sentiments so similar to those of the new regime in France, the rebels expected Louis Philippe to join their battle against Metternich. They dreamed and fought in vain. France offered nothing, and Austria attacked. Hapsburg forces quickly defeated the rebels and enthroned the rulers displaced by the nationalists.

THE FAILURE OF REVOLUTION IN POLAND

The Russian tsars who ruled as kings in Poland after 1815 had always allowed significantly greater liberty for the Poles than for the people of Russia. Foreign rule bred resentment anyway, secret revolutionary organizations emerged, and Polish rebels awaited their moment. It came. Waves of revolution and protest moved out from France after July and rebellion spread into the streets of Warsaw in November. Then the forces demanding liberation began to strike elsewhere in the kingdom. The Polish legislature acted too. It declared an end to Tsar Nicholas's reign in their country.

Nicholas reacted at once. He nullified the relatively liberal Polish constitution, rushed in an army of conquest and occupation, and launched a campaign to jail or exterminate suspected rebels. It took months to subdue Poland, but the tsar won and the suppression was ruthless and complete. The uprising in Poland had ended in failure, but the European revolution would continue.

THE CLIMAX OF THE EUROPEAN REVOLUTION

Europeans committed to liberal transformation of the sociopolitical order or to national unity created turmoil on the continent in 1830 and revealed how widely revolutionary sentiment had spread since the 1790s. Yet when the conflicts subsided, little had changed.

The Reign of Metternich in Central Europe

In the Central European realms over which Metternich continued to hold sway in the 1830s, the Austrian chancellor intended to ensure that nothing about the sociopolitical system *would* change.

AUSTRIA AND GERMANY

Metternich gained the ultimate power to implement his negative policy within the Austrian Empire between 1835 and 1848 since Ferdinand I, the emperor during these years, lacked the mental capacity to exercise any authority at all. Metternich bent every effort to suppression of the discontented. These groups concerned the chancellor: the peasant masses still oppressed by obligations to the aristocracy, small contingents of miserable industrial workers, middle-class liberals, and the nationalists in every ethnic subdivision of the state.

In most respects the sources of discontent that generated opposition to Metternich's policies in Germany were the same as in Austria—an increasingly distressed peasantry, urban workers battered by the effects of first-stage industrialization, and a growing middle class committed to liberal principles and national unity. The Austrian chancellor confronted problems in Germany as he did elsewhere—with repression. He induced rulers in several states to nullify the constitutions granted in 1830 and kept potential trouble spots under watch and the threat of force. The level of public hostility continued to rise.

ITALY

The movement for Italian unity splintered after the failure of the 1830 revolts. *Risorgimento* leaders still beckoned Italians to march toward nationhood, but three factions emerged. Giuseppe Mazzini (1805–1872) challenged patriots to join his organization, Young Italy, and follow him in the formation of a fully democratic country. This kind of government, a nation-state with popular sovereignty, eventually would exist everywhere in Europe, Mazzini believed. He expected these free and self-governing nations then to recognize their common duty to serve the universal needs of humanity.

Mazzini's commitment to the Left's belief in popular sovereignty set him sharply apart from Italian nationalists attracted to liberalism but not to absolute democracy. They placed their faith in a struggle for unity led by the Kingdom of Sardinia. According to these nationalists, a Sardinian victory would give Italians a constitutional monarchy with protected liberties, especially property rights. Other nationalists rejected both democracy and liberal monarchy. Like the Guelf movement in the Middle Ages, they believed that the Roman Catholic Church offered Italy its best hope for security and progress. These "Neo-Guelfs" called for the faithful of the entire country to submit to the pope as their ruler, who then would grant their liberties. This diversity among the nationalists probably weakened the unification movement, but their common dream of liberation posed the most serious threat to Metternich south of the Alps.

The Bourgeois Monarchy in France

Charles X's abdication in July 1830 left power in the hands of the Chamber of Deputies. This legislature selected the Duke of Orleans, the former king's cousin, as the new monarch. King Louis Philippe, whose royally related family had supported the overthrow of Louis XVI (1792), ruled in the interest of the upper bourgeoisie throughout his years in power (1830–1848). The rich business and professional classes had kept their grip on the socioeconomic system after 1815. In 1830, they again supplanted the aristocrats and made the government theirs, as it had been in 1789.

REVISIONS IN THE CONSTITUTIONAL CHARTER

Louis Philippe shunned royal garb, donned the business frock of the day, and regularly joined his fellow citizens on the streets. But the king offered the French more than symbolic association. He and the bourgeois leaders of the revolt reestablished the Charter of 1814 that Charles X had nullified.

In its original form, this document guaranteed equal legal rights, permitted personal career choice, and gave the vote to the richest 100,000. In order to empower the rest of the upper bourgeoisie, the new leaders adjusted the electoral provisions of the 1814 Charter and gave the vote to about 200,000 people, less than two percent of the adult population. One of Louis Philippe's ministers said there were fewer than 200,000 who had the intelligence to vote.

THE OPPONENTS OF THE BOURGEOIS MONARCHY

Parisian workers, members of the lesser bourgeoisie, and republican idealists had joined the upper bourgeoisie on the barricades in 1830 to fight Charles X. The upper bourgeoisie then took power from Charles and gave their allies somewhat greater liberty. But when the rich elite refused to allow other social groups a part in the government, they turned against the bourgeois monarchy. The much more rapid growth of industry beginning in the 1830s expanded this hostile force by multiplying the number of workers and worsening their lives.

When citizens criticized the Charter provisions that gave the vote only to the very wealthy, Prime Minister François Guizot routinely answered, "Get rich." Political leaders watched the suffering that came with the onset of industrialization with the same cold detachment. When misery inspired rebellious behavior, the government responded with military force and strict censorship of publications. The bourgeois monarchy yielded nothing to its enemies. The rebels prepared to take everything.

1848—the Year of Revolutions

The expanded attack on the *Ancien Régime* that began in 1830 climaxed in 1848 when the most massive revolutionary wave of the period swept over Europe. Once more, the storm began in France.

THE FALL OF THE LAST FRENCH MONARCHY

As the economy worsened in the mid-1840s, suffering and discontent mounted rapidly. Restrictions on public demonstrations led rebellious citizens to the evasive expedient of holding large banquets at which they vented their rage. When Guizot decreed that such a gathering scheduled for February 21, 1848, could not be held, incensed demonstrators poured into Parisian streets.

The king removed Guizot from office, but mob action continued. Louis dispatched troops to quell the crowds on February 23. A shot of unknown origin rang out and the royal force fired at the clustered rebels. Sixteen fell dead. The suppressive violence transformed the protest into a republican revolution. Military units demonstrated increasing sympathy for the revolutionaries, and the rebels soon had the strength to take over Paris. Louis Philippe and Guizot found refuge in Britain. The nation's first bourgeois monarch thus became its last king.

The Second Republic. Revolutionaries hastily assembled to declare France a republic once more and establish a provisional government. This temporary political organization proclaimed the right of all adult males to vote in the election of a constituent assembly that would set up the permanent government—a response to the lower bourgeoisie's and labor's demand for the right to vote. As a further reward to workers, the provisional leadership also officially recognized everyone's right to a job. Many laborers insisted on more concrete benefits.

The National Workshops. Workers played a larger role in the revolution of 1848 and its aftermath than they had in 1830. Most of the 1848 revolutionaries came from other social classes, but they could not ignore the now more powerful lower classes. In the provisional government, Louis Blanc, a socialist, championed the cause of these people. He insisted on the adoption of his plan for the establishment of national workshops to provide employment for the many workers without jobs. The government complied but never put sufficient resources into the project to develop the system of thriving factories that Blanc had planned. The workshops gained reputations as centers that doled out money for needless labor. They failed.

Closure of the Workshops. The provisional government's decrees multiplied the number of voters thirty-five times. In May 1848, about eighty-five percent of the 9,000,000 eligible men voted for deputies to the constitutional convention. The assembly they elected cared deeply about bourgeois economic and professional interests but little about the plight of urban workers. The deputies voted to close the national workshops.

The "June Days." Enraged laborers answered with public protest and calls for violent action. Government forces attacked them. The street combat continued for four days in late June, killing nearly 1,500 workers and 1,000 troops. The government arrested thousands of suspects and sent many to foreign penal colonies. These actions by the Second Republic displayed the power of a united middle class and peasantry and their contempt for industrial workers.

The Constitution of 1848. When the assembly presented the Second Republic's constitution in November 1848, its provisions indicated that the entire bourgeoisie now ruled and not just the rich middle class. It guaranteed the vote to all males, established a unicameral legislature and an executive branch with extensive powers, and gave absolute protection of property rights. The constitution also protected other personal rights that liberals valued, but it rejected the idea of a right to work. As in June, a class line had been drawn.

A FLEETING REVOLUTIONARY VICTORY IN THE AUSTRIAN EMPIRE

News of the French rebels' triumph in February 1848 immediately moved liberal and nationalist subjects of the Hapsburg state to action.

Revolts in Budapest and Vienna. In a speech on March 3 in Budapest, Hungary, Louis Kossuth challenged the Magyars (Hungarians) to follow him in a battle for liberal government and reduced Austrian authority over their nation. Ten days later, demonstrators confronted the imperial parliament in Vienna, Austria, with demands for reform. An attempt by troops to suppress the protest led to chaos in the streets. Fear gripped the Austrian ruler, and Metternich lost his emperor's support. The chancellor quit his office and hastened to Britain, ending forty years of struggle against revolution. Emperor Ferdinand then proclaimed that he would submit to every demand of the Austrian populace.

An Interim of Liberation for Hungarians and Czechs. Kossuth's liberal national forces in Hungary seized their opportunity. They enacted the "March Laws" providing for an end to Austrian control over government within Hungary, although the Austrian emperor kept his title as monarch of the realm. The legislation also gave Hungarians a representative parliament, promised democratic elections, abolished serfdom and aristocratic privileges, and established freedom of the press. By early April, the Czechs who populated Hapsburg Bohemia had won concessions from Ferdinand that promised conditions much like those in Hungary.

An Austrian Constitution. The emperor's promises to his Austrian subjects in March had included allowing them to write their own constitution. Instead, on April 25, he issued his own document. It granted a representative parliament, responsible government, and voting rights for all males in Austria. Ferdinand had yielded too little to placate Austrian liberals. Rebellion simmered on and the emperor finally left Vienna in May for refuge in the calmer atmosphere of Innsbruck, Austria. The rebels took charge and by July decreed the nullification of all peasant responsibilities to their lords.

THE TRIUMPH OF AN *ANCIEN* GOVERNMENT

The revolutionaries in Hungary, Bohemia, and Austria had won their separate victories by May 1848, but since they formed no united front against the Hapsburg imperial government, the victors quickly lost political power. In June, Ferdinand's armies attacked the Bohemian capital of Prague and overwhelmed the Czech rebels.

Bourgeois liberals and peasants in Austria relished their new freedom from the social and economic restraints of the old regime, but they opposed the more democratic rebels who had helped them win control in that part of the empire. This division made the forces that wanted to continue the revolution easy prey to imperial troops as they retook Vienna in October 1848. With Austria thus subdued, Hungarian nationalists faced the imperial government alone.

Before the end of 1848, an enfeebled Emperor Ferdinand surrendered the throne to his nephew, Francis Joseph (r. 1848–1916). The young Emperor then joined Metternich's successor, Prince Felix von Schwarzenberg, in a reinvigorated reactionary campaign against the last rebel center in the empire.

Francis Joseph nullified the liberties that Ferdinand had granted to Hungary and soon invaded the region. Hungary repelled the attack and faltered only after Nicholas I dispatched a Russian force of more than 100,000 to support the Austrian Emperor. By mid-1849, Francis Joseph reigned supreme over his suppressed empire.

THE STRUGGLE FOR LIBERATION IN ITALY

In January 1848, liberals in southern Italy wrested a constitution from the ruler of the Kingdom of the Two Sicilies. The rise of the French Second Republic in the following month encouraged rebels throughout the peninsula to take action. Quickly, rulers in the Papal States and Tuscany in west central Italy and Piedmont-Sardinia to the northwest yielded to demands for liberal constitutions.

Revolution immediately followed in the Austrian-dominated states of Lombardy and Venetia in the northeast. By March 22, the rebels had expelled Austrian forces from these two principalities and Italians from many other states joined a war of national liberation against the Hapsburgs.

A bitter seventeen-month struggle ensued. The revolution at first lost momentum and Austria retook Lombardy. Then liberals won a dramatic victory in Rome in early 1849, as they expelled the pope and established a republic led by Mazzini. The war between Austria and Piedmont-Sardinia raged on in the north, until Francis Joseph's forces crushingly defeated the Italians at Novara on March 23, 1849. Republican France, after a rapid shift toward conservatism, dealt the final blow to Italian liberal nationalists with an invasion that conquered the Roman republic and restored the pope. The summer of 1849 ended with *ancien* governments reestablished in most of Italy.

THE LIBERAL NATIONALIST REVOLT IN GERMANY

The fall of the French monarchy in February 1848 intensified the revolutionary mood in Germany. In mid-March, Prussian liberals called for Frederick William IV (r. 1840–1861) to reform the state according to their principles. The king yielded nothing, however, and demonstrations immediately rocked Berlin. Frederick William then sent troops into the capital to confront the crowds. The soldiers resorted to deadly fire, and the rebels countered with barricades and violence. This chaos jolted Frederick William, and he ended it with a pledge to call a constituent assembly. During March and April the rulers of several other German principalities granted constitutionally guaranteed liberal rights.

The Frankfurt Assembly. Government liberalization pleased most German reformers, but without national unity they remained dissatisfied. The revolutionary environment of 1848 inspired nationalists to dramatic action. A group of reformers with no legal standing met in Heidelberg and devised plans for a special assembly to consider a course of action. They proclaimed that all adult males in the German Confederation could vote for representatives to this national body. The assembly of 830 mostly middle-class deputies gathered in Frankfurt on May 18, 1848.

The *Grossdeutsch-Kleindeutsch* Issue. The assembly struggled through extended debates about the best form of government for a united Germany and about the territories it should contain. The latter issue caused an especially sharp division between advocates of a Great German (*Grossdeutsch*) state that included all Hapsburg Germanic territories and a Little German (*Kleindeutsch*) state that excluded some or all of these areas. The assembly adopted a compromise that required restructuring the Hapsburg Empire. The rejection of this plan by Emperor Francis Joseph ended Austria's participation at Frankfurt and left the advocates of a Little German state in charge there.

The Triumph of Prussian Monarchy. In May 1848, Frederick William IV kept his promise to convene delegates to write a Prussian constitution. The Prussian king reverted to repressive policies in the autumn, however, and the assembly adjourned in December without producing a constitution. Frederick William then offered Prussia a narrowly liberal constitution from the throne. He also used military force to coerce the nullification of most of the liberal gains made in other German states.

Dissolution of the Frankfurt Assembly. In March 1849, the Frankfurt Assembly completed its plan for a German state that excluded Austria. The delegates agreed to form a constitutional monarchy with a parliament elected by all adult males. Then, despite the Prussian monarch's recent reactionary behavior, they invited him to become "Emperor of the Germans." Frederick William found this offer of "a crown from the gutter" easy to refuse. The assembly dissolved, its efforts to unify Germany a failure.

THE MODERN STATE AFTER THE REVOLUTIONS OF 1848

The European revolution that climaxed in 1848–1849 did not replace the *ancien* sociopolitical order with the one promised by the rebels. While they had destroyed serfdom in the Hapsburg Empire, the old government remained in power. Piedmont-Sardinia kept the liberal constitution it had won, but the middle-class revolutionaries succeeded in no other Italian state. All the German principalities acquired parliaments but not truly representative government, and the French Second Republic reflected the narrowly liberal attitudes of the middle class and peasants.

In reality, the failure of the liberal nationalist European revolution did not mean that *ancien* government and society had survived. The revolts, on the contrary, had ensured the completion of sociopolitical modernization. Since the 1400s, all European states had modernized in part, through the secularization of social institutions, the development of professional government bureaucracies, and the establishment of standing armies under the control of the central executive. By 1848, Britain and France were fully modern, which meant that each had these characteristics: consolidated territories, middle-class or joint bourgeois-aristocratic leadership, a government committed to industrialization, and an adequately large minority of the working populace mobilized in support of the state.

The revolts of 1848 at once brought the bourgeoisie of Germany and Austria into a ruling partnership with the old elites, induced governments of the region to adopt the middle-class policy of industrial development, and accelerated the movement toward German and Italian unification. Germany and Italy would complete political modernization in the early 1870s. Although several European countries at that time still did not have all the traits of a modern sociopolitical system, the transformation had proceeded far enough so as to conclude that the new form of state had become typical of the region.

*V*iolent revolts against European governments have occurred rarely in the Modern era. When such events have taken place, they usually have broken out within a single country. The history of the years from 1815 to 1848 contrasts sharply with these typical patterns and marks this as an age of European revolution. Rebellion became both frequent and widespread, especially in 1830 and 1848.

Revolutionaries in this era came from varied social backgrounds, but most were middle-class businesspeople and professionals. In keeping with bourgeois liberal ideals, they fought for self-government and personal liberty, demanding above all freedom to express their opinions and pursue business interests. In regions that lacked unity, such as Germany and Italy, revolutionaries also struggled to organize nation-states.

Liberals and nationalists won scattered victories in the 1820s and 1830s and then shocked the old regimes with smashing successes all across Europe in 1848. For the rebels, defeat followed swiftly too. Bourgeois revolutionaries in France turned against their more radical lower-class supporters once the old government fell and transformed a middle-class republic into a dictatorship that favored the bourgeoisie and peasants. Reactionary governments in Germany, Austria, and Italy struck back with a vengeance, finally unleashing their vastly superior military power. Rebels fled or were seized, and rulers nullified most of the recently granted constitutions. Soon the political and social structures of Europe showed little evidence that the revolution had taken place.

The conservative regimes standing in majestic victory after 1848 hid the true significance of the age of European revolution. New liberal or nationalist institutions had not suddenly replaced ancien *structures as the rebels had intended, but by midcentury the demise of old regimes and the triumph of modern state systems in both liberal and unexpected new forms was certain in the near future.*

Selected Readings

Briggs, Asa. *The Age of Improvement.* New York: Longmans, Green, 1965.

Brock, Michael. *The Great Reform Act.* London: Hutchinson, 1973.

Droz, Jacques. *Europe between Revolutions, 1815–1848.* New York: Harper & Row, 1967.

Hobsbawm, Eric J. *The Age of Revolution: Europe 1789–1848.* New York: Praeger Publishers, 1969.

Kraehe, Enno E. *Metternich's German Policy.* Princeton, NJ: Princeton University Press, 1963.

Langer, William L. *Political and Social Upheaval, 1832–1852.* New York: Harper & Row, 1969.

Lincoln, W. Bruce. *Nicholas I: Emperor and Autocrat of All the Russias*. Bloomington: Indiana University Press, 1978.

Robertson, Priscilla S. *Revolutions of 1848, a Social History*. Princeton, NJ: Princeton University Press, 1952.

Rudé, George F. E. *The Crowd in History: A Study of Popular Disturbances in France and England, 1730–1848*. New York: Wiley, 1964.

9

The New Nationalism,
1848–1871

*L*iberal and national idealism inspired many Europeans to struggle between 1815 and 1848 to complete the transformation of the ancien sociopolitical system. Their campaign led to revolutionary conflicts with the defenders of the old order. By the late 1840s, this era of European revolution ended with the vision of a liberal nation-state system for the continent unrealized. The revolts, however, had advanced the modernization of European institutions, even if these emerging social structures differed in important ways from the expectations of the liberal national idealists.

One important unanticipated shift toward modernity was the appearance of conservative rulers who learned from the revolts that they must court the support of the masses. In their quest for popular support after 1848, several aristocratic and monarchist leaders adopted a much more favorable view toward nationalism. These conservatives who had opposed nationalism now recognized that a people aroused in loyalty to the country could accept nobles and kings as their national leaders if not as a hereditary upper class. Members of the traditional ruling caste gained the potential to win a still broader following by their new willingness to set up institutions that would give at least the appearance of citizen influence in government.

As the old elites discovered the conservative potential of nationalism, middle-class Italians and Germans who had failed to unify their countries under liberal governments revealed their willingness to abandon liberalism for the cause of nationhood. Significant portions of the upper and middle classes of Central Europe thus grew closer together after 1850 on the common ground of conservative nationalism.

The bourgeois militants also relinquished their faith in grass-roots revolution as the means to achieve national unity and accepted state military power as the way to achieve this goal. Thus they turned to the methods the ruling elites had used in suppressing liberal rebellion during the era of European revolution. With these increasingly similar attitudes developing among bourgeois and aristocratic elements in Italy and Germany, the prospects for the emergence of new nations in these territories vastly improved.

The diminished idealism of many European liberals and nationalists after 1848 and the increasing acceptance of brute military force as the means to goals such as nationhood coincided with a striking shift in European thought and the arts in the 1850s and 1860s. A multitude of startling discoveries in the natural sciences induced leading social theorists to conclude that neither the reason of the philosophes nor the intuition of the Romantics led to truth. Science alone, in their opinion, could answer all questions about reality and thus give the only worthy guidance to human endeavors. People with this outlook frowned on idealism. Literature and art quickly began to reflect this "realist" attitude that dominated both the politics and the formal thought of Europeans after mid-century.

THE AGE OF REALISM

Throughout the 1850s and 1860s, the dominant attitude among Europeans was a commitment to whatever was practical, unemotional, and scientific. Realism in this sense thus characterized thought, the arts, and government. Remarkable progress in science during the 1800s strongly influenced this change in outlook.

Science

The scientists who jolted the minds of Europeans in this period focused attention especially on the forces and substances of the material world. Thinkers in the past had adequately explained much about the earth as a planetary body, but they provided little information about the physics, chemistry, and biology of the sphere they inhabited. Europeans in the 1800s ardently studied this neglected realm and reached conclusions about these issues. Many of their answers remain fundamental to science in the 1990s.

THE MATERIAL WORLD

European scientists in 1800 had a vast store of inherited data on the natural world. In the first half of the century, they continued to collect information in sharply focused investigations and experiments such as Michael Faraday's demonstration that magnets could produce electricity. A few scientists even began to use their findings to support broad theories. Until about 1850, however, they usually left grand generalizations about the world and life to the philosophers and political thinkers who conjured up ideologies such as liberalism, nationalism, conservatism, and socialism.

The Foundations of Evolutionary Theory. The minority of scientists who advanced broad theories in the early 1800s included two who offered important arguments about biological and geological change. Soon after 1800, Jean Baptiste de Lamarck proposed a theory of biological evolution that challenged the dominant view of changeless plant and animal forms. Similarly, Sir Charles Lyell's compilation of geological data in the early 1830s contradicted the traditional idea of an earth created suddenly in a permanent form less than 10,000 years earlier. Lyell's presentation of evidence depicted a much older planet that had changed greatly since its origins.

The Study of Matter. As geologists considered the earth's gross features and structures, other scientists contemplated the elements of which it was composed and the forces that affected them. In the late 1700s, Antoine Lavoisier presented evidence that matter was indestructible. John Dalton pursued the related problem of the structure of matter. In the early 1800s, he used modern experiments to verify the ancient theory that all matter was made up of tiny particles (atoms). The approach to the study of matter typical of this century climaxed in 1869 with Dmitri Mendeleyev's development of a table of elements based on properties such as atomic weight. A theory about the forces of nature that paralleled Lavoisier's view of matter appeared in the late 1840s. Ludwig Helmholtz concluded that the energy in nature always remained at a constant level. It could never increase or decrease.

DARWIN'S THEORY OF EVOLUTION

By 1850, science had placed Europeans on the threshold of a new form of secularism that viewed the earth and all its creatures as totally material, but made up of "immortal" substances and moved by "unalterable" forces. This intellectual climate encouraged the presentation of comprehensive theories such as Charles Darwin's conception of biological evolution.

In 1831, when the British navy dispatched the *Beagle* to South America and the adjacent Pacific waters carrying specialists to study the lands and life forms of the region, Darwin (1809–1882) was among the scientists. Information gathered on this expedition significantly influenced Darwin's thinking, but years of study followed before the publication of his conclusions.

Darwin's first comprehensive theoretical work, *On the Origin of the Species by Means of Natural Selection*, appeared in 1859. In this publication, Darwin argued that when life began on earth, there were only a few types of plants and animals. He reasoned that blind natural forces over an extremely long period of time acted on these original plants and animals to produce the great variety of species that inhabited the modern world.

According to evolutionary theory, the individual members of all species vary slightly in strength, size, health, attractiveness, and other traits. Certain individual plants or animals thus are better suited to their environments than others of the species. The less fit die younger and thus produce fewer offspring. Eventually, the less favored types cease to exist and the longer lived and more fertile organisms produce so many descendants that only their new form continues. It becomes a new species. In *The Descent of Man* (1871), Darwin applied his theories to humanity. He supported these views not only with his own research but also with recent studies by other scientists and social theorists.

DARWINISM AND THE NEW BIOLOGY

Darwinism neither accepted nor rejected the possibility of divine influence, but it directly contradicted the previously dominant conviction that God had instantly and purposely created all currently living species. Evolutionary theory also was not easily reconciled with the belief that people had been made in the image of God. Such views stirred a heated debate among supporters and foes of evolutionary ideas.

Pasteur. Darwin's provocative theory somewhat overshadowed other important achievements of the new biology after 1850. In 1861, Louis Pasteur revealed to Europeans that microorganisms caused disease, a discovery that led him thereafter to devise vaccines capable of preventing certain illnesses.

Lister and Mendel. Another revolutionary step in medical science followed in 1865 when Joseph Lister began the practice of conducting surgery in a sanitary room with sterile implements. Gregor Mendel in this same decade carried out tests with varieties of peas that enabled him to penetrate many of the mysteries of the process of heredity.

The Arts

The new scientific theories strengthened the realist mood by midcentury and helped to inspire artists and writers to reject Romantic styles. Cultural leaders began to portray the world as they actually saw it. As early as 1850, critics in France began to describe the paintings of Gustave Courbet as "realistic." Within five years it became typical for commentators to apply the word to this new form of art and literature.

REALISTIC PAINTING

Realism in art emerged and developed mostly in France. The works by Courbet that established this movement included *The Wrestlers* and *The Bathers*, both produced in 1853. In these paintings, the artist purposely violated the standards of the Romantics and their cultural predecessors by depicting grimy and tense fighters and the bodies of ordinary bathers rather than idealized men and women. Such portrayals horrified traditional observers but drew numerous young artists to him to learn.

Other important painters developed their own versions of realism. By the 1860s, the guardians of the galleries had to struggle to suppress not only Courbet's works but also those of Édouard Manet, Claude Monet, and Edgar Degas. Monet's paintings especially reflected the connection between the science and art of the day. He rendered scenes with small dots of paint and in other ways used his scientific knowledge of optics and light to depict what he saw. As a painter who captured his impression of reality, Monet in the late 1860s helped to found a new movement in art called "impressionism."

LITERARY REALISM

Realistic literature appeared in profusion all over Europe beginning in the 1850s. Leading writers in these years vividly conveyed their vision of life around them, especially the difficulties and suffering they observed. Novels served their artistic needs much better than the poetry that Romantics had favored in the previous generation.

Russian novelists in the latter 1800s lived in a very troubled society and gave the world unusual insights into human experience. Ivan Turgenev's *Sportsman's Sketches* (1852) displayed the crushing oppression of the serfs who made up half the rural population in his country. His renowned *Fathers and Sons* (1862) contained a graphic story of a rebellious younger generation's reaction to the suffering of the rural poor and other social evils.

Other Russians produced even more famous works. Leo Tolstoy used novels such as *War and Peace* (1863–1869) and *Anna Karenina* (1873–1877) to provide a very sensitive consideration of difficult questions about human traits and behaviors. In *Notes from the Underground* (1864), *Crime and Punishment* (1866), and *The Idiot* (1869), Feodor Dostoevsky depicted the emotional toll of Russia's hard reality.

The shock of social and economic revolution struck the imaginations of novelists in Western Europe after 1850. In France, Gustave Flaubert composed *Madame Bovary* (1857), the supreme example of realist fiction. This novel contained a detailed picture of a bourgeois husband's meaningless life and his wife's use of adulterous ventures to punish her boring spouse.

Several European realists wrote about the struggles and suffering of suppressed social classes. In *Les Misérables* (1862), Victor Hugo gave a moving account of the 1830 Parisian revolt. Charles Dickens in *Hard Times* (1854) and Elizabeth Gaskell in *North and South* (1855) similarly expressed their passionate reactions to the misery of the poor in Britain's industrial cities. Despite the powerful emotions that appeared to inspire realist authors, they expressed their views of society as though they were scientists obligated to report their observations exactly and in minute detail.

Social Thought

The scientific enthusiasm that encouraged the bold generalizations of the new biology and the startling realism of the arts also affected social theorists after 1850. They assumed that as thinking animals living in a fully material universe, the time for a science of society had arrived.

MATERIALIST PHILOSOPHY

European philosophers, as they considered the nature of humanity and the universe over the centuries, developed a tradition of accepting either the spiritual or material realm as ultimate reality. In any period, certain theorists incline toward idealism while others are materialists, but one of these schools of thought usually achieves dominance. The scientific environment of the mid-1800s inspired a strong movement away from the idealism of the Romantic era and toward a new form of materialist philosophy.

Leading intellectuals who considered the nature of life in this period took into account the new scientific view of matter and natural forces. By the early 1850s, one chemist had published his conclusion that matter endlessly changed from inorganic to organic and back, with life simply being the organic stage.

Materialist philosophers stated their similar conceptions of life in an especially emphatic way. Ludwig Feuerbach became a leading voice among these theorists who proclaimed that nothing except matter could possibly exist anywhere. The universe contained no God, nothing spiritual. Humans had no soul. What a person ate, in Feuerbach's view, determined what the individual became. Human nature and behavior was a matter of chemistry and nothing more.

POSITIVISM

Feuerbach thought that nutrition determined the chemical content of human minds and muscles which, in turn, decided the outcome of events such as the revolutions of 1848. In 1842 Auguste Comte, another materialist intellectual, completed a new theory of knowledge that in his view indicated how to control the course of history. Humanity in the 1800s, according to Comte, had reached the ultimate stage of development, since people in his era at last had the ability to observe society scientifically and acquire "positive" (absolutely correct) knowledge of social processes.

Comte assumed that humans had entered this positive or scientific stage of intellectual evolution after a long struggle through two previous phases of history, the theological and metaphysical stages. In the first era, observers arrived at the most backward view of events. They believed in a world controlled by supernatural forces. Life in the metaphysical (philosophical) stage seemed less mysterious than in the age of theology. With this advance in outlook, reason provided explanations of reality that at least excluded the superstitions of the past. The completion of this great intellectual journey in the 1800s brought to humanity a most wonderful prospect. Now scientific understanding in the positivist stage would lead to the perfection of the social order.

Comte's positivism influenced specialists in history and other fields in which society is studied. It encouraged them to use the methods typical of science. The "social scientists" inspired by positivism committed themselves to a quest for complete information about human issues and to an objective study of their findings. The nature of Comte's theories and the effects of his work have led scholars to consider him a principal founder of sociology.

SOCIAL DARWINISM

Whereas the disciples of Comte attempted to apply scientific methods to the study of society, other theorists simply borrowed aspects of the new science to explain social phenomena. Social theorists in the 1860s began to draw especially heavily on the works of Darwin. Walter Bagehot, for example, inserted Darwinian phrases into his commentary on international relations. He depicted nations as locked in a struggle that results in the dominance of the most powerful state. The victor thus proves its superiority, almost like a surviving species. Such misapplications of biological theory became known as "social Darwinism." Ideas of this kind were increasingly common after 1870.

REALPOLITIK

Social Darwinist notions of a brutal power struggle well suited the mood among European political leaders after 1850. They strikingly altered their principles of governance after midcentury and became devoted to the advance of their countries almost to the exclusion of all other international concerns. Highly deceitful diplomacy became typical. Officials, in fact, generally pursued the interests of their states both at home and abroad with coldly realistic considerations of power and little regard for ideals or morality.

This approach in politics meant that nothing mattered about policies except whether they worked and whether they enhanced the power of the government at home and the nation abroad. Leaders with such views took great pride that they had advanced from the idealism of the liberal nationalist era (1815 to 1850) to this new practice of "realism in politics." German officials such as Otto von Bismarck became the most dedicated followers of this policy, which they called "*Realpolitik*." The merger of the spirit of *Realpolitik* and nationalism in the latter 1800s helped to make nationalism one of the most powerful forces in modern European history.

THE TRIUMPH OF NATIONALISM

Idealistic attitudes and revolutionary methods failed the nationalists in Italy and Germany during the rebellions of 1830 and 1848. Cold political realism and state military power quickly built the modern Italian and German nations in the two decades after 1850. These victories through power politics inspired a transformation of nationalism.

The liberal nationalism of the years before 1850 included a commitment to individual rights and citizen self-government. Liberal nationalists expected to put these principles into effect by the collective action of ordinary people. After 1850, nationalists became increasingly willing to approve of expanded authority for government leaders and accept the denial of personal liberty in order to ensure national unity. Nationalists also showed much less confidence that citizen action could achieve the goals of nationhood. Instead, they placed their faith in the power of the state, and especially in its armies.

This new nationalism triumphed in Italy and Germany during the 1850s and 1860s. It became a dominant force in European affairs by the 1870s and remains a significant influence 120 years later.

The Unification of Italy

The failure of liberal nationalist rebellion (1848–1849) to end Austrian control over Italy and unite its numerous principalities discredited this idealistic campaign. Popular nationalist uprisings continued after 1850 and influenced the unification process. Now, however, these mass actions served only to support a movement for nationhood led by a single powerful state under coldly realistic leadership.

CAVOUR AND THE KINGDOM OF PIEDMONT-SARDINIA

The Kingdom of Piedmont-Sardinia, situated in northwest Italy and on a large island off its west coast, entered the national liberation struggles in 1830 and 1848. Defeat by Austria in 1849 did not prevent Piedmont's newly crowned king, Victor Emmanuel II (r. 1849–1878), from maintaining the liberal form of government his father had established. As a progressive and

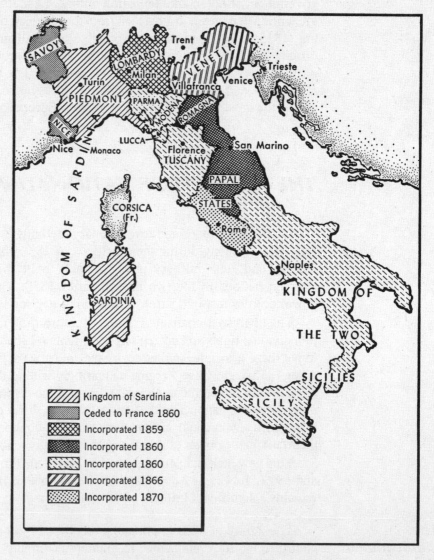

Fig. 9.1   The Unification of Italy, 1859–1870

relatively large state willing to fight for union, Piedmont had won a strong following among Italian nationalists by the early 1850s. The king appointed Count Camillo di Cavour (1810–1861), a master of *Realpolitik*, as his prime minister in 1852. Backed by the power of the Piedmont state, Cavour's methods enabled him to become the builder of the Italian nation.

Cavour typified the increasingly numerous European aristocrats who accepted moderate political liberalism and bourgeois economic values. He immediately began to govern in accordance with these modern principles as a step in his plan for Piedmont's advancement. The government actively encouraged trade and industry, expanded its railway net, and promoted agricultural production. Thus a state that already protected individual liberties, at least to a certain extent, soon had a prosperous economy and became doubly attractive to neighboring states willing to accept annexation as a step toward nationhood. Economic modernization also prepared Piedmont to produce more abundant and more lethal equipment for its expanding army. Cavour knew that power would decide the battle that had to come with Austria.

The prime minister understood as well that his state needed formidable European allies to ensure victory over the Hapsburgs. Thus in 1855 he accepted an invitation to join Britain and France against Russia in the Crimean War. (See chapter 11.) Cavour correctly assumed that even though he could send only a token force, this venture would increase the possibility of support from Britain and France when Piedmont clashed with Austria.

THE PACT OF PLOMBIÈRES

Napoleon III governed France with dictatorial authority, but he courted popularity among the masses and followed policies that in other respects were similar to those of Piedmont's rulers. He also tended to agree with the Italian nationalists who wanted to expel Austria from the peninsula.

In July 1858, Napoleon and Cavour met for several hours at Plombières and arranged a secret pact. The Emperor pledged to support a war against the Hapsburgs if the Austrians struck first. Napoleon also accepted the right of Piedmont to annex Austria's north Italian lands—Lombardy, Venetia, Parma, and Modena. The French ruler further agreed to allow the formation of an Italian confederation with the pope as president, Austria expelled from Italy, and Piedmont in control of the entire northern peninsula. Cavour, in return, offered to give Napoleon Savoy and Nice, two ethnically French sections of Piedmont. The two leaders then settled down to study a map and decide where and how Austria might be tricked into war. Thereafter, Cavour began months of effort to induce his enemy to attack. Austria obliged the following April (1859).

Battles in late May and June 1859 proved the effectiveness of Cavour's domestic and international preparations. The Austrians lost Lombardy after costly struggles. During the war, Italians began to revolt in the Papal territories and elsewhere in central Italy. They wanted to overthrow the rulers of their principalities and join the march to nationhood. Napoleon III became fearful of this rising force of popular nationalism on the southern border of France. He broke his pact with Cavour and made peace with Austria in July 1859.

Because of France's sudden departure from the war, Piedmont gained only Lombardy. Before the end of the year, however, the combined power of *Realpolitik* and mass action became evident. The Italian states of Tuscany, Modena, Parma, and Romagna overthrew their old regimes. These principalities then merged with Piedmont-Sardinia. Victor Emmanuel II and Cavour suddenly ruled a kingdom that encompassed most of northern Italy. Napoleon III accepted what Italian force had accomplished and took Savoy and Nice as his reward.

GARIBALDI AND THE CONQUEST OF SOUTH ITALY

In the age of European revolution, Garibaldi had fought to unify Italy under a more radical form of government than Cavour could tolerate. Garibaldi wanted a republic that guaranteed personal rights to everyone on a virtually equal basis. Cavour preferred a constitutional monarchy that provided for individual liberties but empowered the upper and middle classes.

The failure of Italy's liberal nationalist revolt in 1848 disheartened Garibaldi. The defeat prepared him to accept unification on Cavour's terms. When Piedmont and its methods of *Realpolitik* inspired a new and more successful struggle for nationhood, Garibaldi joined the cause.

Nationalist victories in the north in 1859 fed the flames of patriotism in the Kingdom of the Two Sicilies, a state made up of the southern peninsula and the island of Sicily. As spontaneous revolts threatened the old regime there in 1860, Garibaldi responded to directions from Cavour and led an attack on the island of Sicily. His 1,000 red-shirted volunteers ensured the rebel victory. They won the island in weeks and launched an invasion of the southern peninsula. Naples, the capital of the kingdom, fell into their hands. Garibaldi's Red Shirts marched toward Rome. He meant to wrest central Italy from the pope.

Cavour took decisive action to prevent further conquests by Garibaldi. He wanted to maintain Piedmont's control of the unification process to be sure that monarchical institutions and moderate liberalism would prevail in the new state. The prime minister also knew that Napoleon III might use his forces to stop the threat to the papacy. Cavour won Napoleon's approval for Piedmont to invade central Italy. The prime minister planned to stop Garibaldi, take part of the region, and leave the pope in charge of a state, although of diminished size. Papal forces yielded quickly to Cavour's troops. The east-central Papal States voted for annexation to Piedmont, and the pope kept the west-central region. Garibaldi and the people of the Sicilian kingdom that he had conquered accepted Victor Emmanuel as ruler.

On March 17, 1861, the new Italian parliament proclaimed the founding of the Kingdom of Italy with Victor Emmanuel as its king. Only the papal territory and Austrian Venetia remained outside the new nation-state.

THE FINAL VICTORIES FOR ITALIAN NATIONALISM

Within months after the Italian kingdom emerged, Cavour died. The leaders of the new state thereafter continued to practice *Realpolitik* quite effectively in pursuit of national unity. When war erupted between Prussia and Austria in 1866, Italy grasped the opportunity to support Prussia against the Hapsburgs. Prussia won, with Venetia falling to Italy. A military conflict followed in 1870 between Prussia and France. As a result, French forces that had remained to defend the pope left the Italian peninsula. The Kingdom of Italy then seized the last of the Papal States and established Rome as the capital of a fully unified nation.

The Unification of Germany

Prussian and Austrian monarchist forces defeated the liberal nationalist movement for German unity in 1848. In 1850, the king of Prussia, Frederick William IV, attempted to form a loosely joined reactionary Germany that excluded Austria. The Hapsburgs blocked even this conservative move toward nationhood. Liberal nationalism had suffered complete defeat in 1848, but a new conservative nationalist movement under Prussian leadership almost immediately began a march to victory.

PRUSSIA ON THE EVE OF NATIONAL TRIUMPH

A monarchy and rural aristocracy (the Junkers) with strictly *ancien* values reigned almost unchallenged in Prussia in 1850. Liberals in the age of European revolution had won a constitution that established a parliament for Prussia, which they dominated. Yet there was little of the popular involvement in political affairs that characterizes modern government. Parliament had few powers beyond approval of the budget. Furthermore, the Prussian monarchy systematically denied its citizens freedom of expression and other personal liberties.

Although Prussia was politically similar to the thirty-eight other German principalities, its *ancien régime* had built a modern economy. No other German state had. In Prussia, industry and commerce thrived, factories and banks were multiplying, and a still growing modern road system and rail net laced the prosperous state together. The Prussian economy benefited also from the influence of the *Zollverein*, a commercial union organized in 1819 that included all German states except Austria.

By the 1850s, economic modernity and the *Zollverein* gave Prussia the potential to dominate Germany either as a confederation or a nation-state.

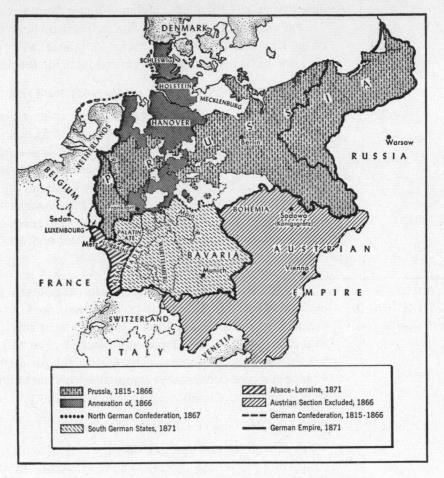

Fig. 9.2   The Political Unification of Germany

The king, however, had proved completely unwilling to challenge the
control of Austria over the German Confederation. Furthermore, Prussia's
reactionary government made many nationalists despise the idea of a German nation under Prussian rule. Prussia could not lead the way to nationhood
until a German Cavour emerged.

THE RISE OF BISMARCK

The accession of William I (r. 1861–1888) to the Prussian throne upon
the death of Frederick William, his brother, at first dimmed the prospects
that this state could lead German unification. His very conservative image
gave King William little appeal to nationalists. He added to Prussia's
political handicaps by provoking a battle with the parliament that virtually
paralyzed the machinery of government. The legislative conflict erupted

when William attempted a large-scale military modernization and enlargement program. Parliamentary liberals denied him the new taxes to pay for his venture. The conflict between the king and the liberals became a struggle for legislative supremacy in Prussia.

In 1862, William appointed Otto von Bismarck as minister-president (prime minister) to lead his counterattack on parliament. Bismarck, a relatively young (forty-seven) but experienced diplomat, had distinguished himself in 1848 by his strong opposition to German liberal rebels. The struggle of this Junker (landowning aristocrat) against the liberal nationalists indicated that he meant to maintain the social position of the aristocracy and the governing power of the monarchy. William had chosen a promising commander to fight for the interests of the king and Junkers against the parliamentarians.

Yet Bismarck differed from other Junkers in many ways. He had rejected their traditional submissiveness toward Austria and concluded that Prussia must forcibly exclude Hapsburg influence from Germany. Bismarck's belief that Prussian success required middle-class support also contrasted with the attitudes of most Junkers. He would promote continued economic modernization and accept the trappings of parliamentary government in order to win this middle-class backing. Furthermore, even though Bismarck personally cared little for nationalism, he not only joined but led the campaign for German national unity, previously a middle-class cause. In short, this supreme practitioner of *Realpolitik* accepted many aspects of modernity as a way to preserve the *ancien* institutions that he most loved.

Bismarck quickly demonstrated the effectiveness of his conservative power politics in the confrontation with the Prussian parliament. Although the assembly continued to deny royal requests for taxes to support the military program, Bismarck had the funds collected anyway. The citizens paid, and parliament yielded to this unlawful action. Thus the middle classes had their constitution and their representative body, but Bismarck had his way. This victory perpetuated monarchical supremacy and sped the Prussian climb to military leadership in Europe.

THE SCHLESWIG-HOLSTEIN QUESTION

Bismarck proceeded from his triumph over parliament to a new quest that required his political cunning and the services of Prussia's strengthened army as well. He got this first opportunity to apply *Realpolitik* in an international maneuver in 1863 when Christian IX, King of Denmark (r. 1863–1906), proclaimed his intention to annex the Duchy of Schleswig.

Schleswig, a small territory directly south of Christian's kingdom, contained a mixture of Danes and Germans. On its southern border lay Holstein, a duchy that belonged to the German Confederation even though a sizable Danish minority lived there. Holstein vigorously protested the annexation of Schleswig, and Bismarck responded by convincing Austria to join Prussia in a war with Denmark. German forces entered Schleswig in February 1864, marched into Denmark in April, and quickly subdued Christian's armies. The peace treaty permitted Austrian troops to occupy Holstein, allowed Prussian forces to hold Schleswig, and yielded the two duchies to joint Austro-Prussian control.

PRUSSIA AGAINST AUSTRIA—THE SEVEN WEEKS' WAR

The circumstances in Schleswig-Holstein at the end of the Danish war provided an ideal setting for Bismarck to provoke the battle he wanted with Austria. The prime minister's diplomatic preparations for the climactic struggle were already under way.

The Biarritz Meeting. Bismarck had courted Russian friendship in 1863 by supporting the suppression of Polish rebels who attempted to end tsarist control over their country. Then, in October 1865, Bismarck took the more important step of meeting Napoleon III at Biarritz to encourage him to remain neutral should an Austro-Prussian conflict develop. The Prussian leader most likely lured the Emperor with the prospect of territorial gains on the Rhine River. Finally, in April 1866, Bismarck secured a pledge from Piedmont to join the fight against Austria if the German war came within three months. By this arrangement, Prussia broke the German Confederation agreement that barred alliances against member states. Bismarck operated by new rules—*Realpolitik* had isolated Austria.

Bismark's Excuse for War. The Austrian Emperor, Francis Joseph, had concluded by April 1866 that Prussia left him no alternative but war. Bismarck's provocative actions in Schleswig-Holstein and in the Confederation Diet (assembly) drove the Austrian ruler to this judgment. During one dispute in the duchies in June 1866, Bismarck sent troops into Holstein. Austria got the Diet to agree to intervene militarily against Prussia, and Bismarck interpreted the assembly vote as a declaration of war.

Prussian Military Superiority. Although the Hapsburgs and other European leaders thought otherwise, Austria had almost no chance of winning. King William's military reforms had created an expanded and well-organized army. Prussia's industrial modernization had provided a rapid-fire rifle, the needle gun, and a railway system well suited to the deployment of troops. Austria had only one railway to the Prussian front and very little industry to produce its old-style muskets and other weapons. Furthermore, the Italian attack on the Hapsburgs' southern border meant that Austria had to fight on two fronts.

The Battle of Sadowa. The critical engagements occurred on the Austro-Prussian border. There the forces clashed in small battles at first. Then, in July 1866, two armies with a combined strength of nearly 500,000 fought in a brutal struggle at Sadowa. Austria suffered almost 45,000 casualties while Prussia lost fewer than one-fourth that number. This battle decided the outcome of the Seven Weeks' War, a disastrous defeat for Austria.

The Peace Settlement. Despite the smashing victory, Bismarck offered a generous peace settlement. He did not want a bitter enemy on his southern border as he pursued other Prussian triumphs. Thus he only required Austria to make a small war damages payment, yield Venetia to Italy, and accept the breakup of the German Confederation. In the afterglow of this remarkable military success, the Prussian parliament voted to legalize the unconstitutional actions Bismarck had taken in the earlier struggle with the assembly. The victories over Denmark and Austria thus increased Prussia's strength abroad and the monarchy's power over its citizenry.

THE EMERGENCE OF THE NORTH GERMAN CONFEDERATION

Austria had dominated the Diet of the old German Confederation sufficiently to have it vote for war against Prussia in June 1866. The Germans in many states of the Confederation, however, had very different attitudes toward Prussia than did their delegates to the Diet. Bismarck's acceptance of the forms of parliamentary government, Prussia's thriving economy, and, above all, the successes of the prime minister's aggressive foreign policy strongly appealed to German nationalists, especially in the north.

With Austria excluded from German affairs and Prussia's prestige among nationalists rising dramatically, Bismarck easily built a new political structure that brought most of Germany under the authority of his king. The prime minister proceeded in 1867 to organize the North German Confederation, a union of all Germanic states except the southern principalities—Hesse-Darmstadt, Bavaria, Württemberg, and Baden.

The treaties of union left the heads of the northern states in charge of domestic affairs but provided for the Prussian king to become Confederation president. In this capacity, William had full authority over the union's foreign affairs and military forces. His chief executive, Bismarck, became chancellor of the Confederation and actually governed the new organization.

THE FRANCO-PRUSSIAN WAR

The south German states had little interest in a merger with north Germany in the late 1860s. Religious differences separated the regions—the south was mostly Catholic, the north Lutheran. The Prussian tendency toward extreme monarchical power also bothered the south Germans and made them see union with the new Confederation as undesirable. Intense nationalist passions could cause the south to forget these traits of the north, but that mood did not exist at the end of the 1860s. Bismarck thought that a war with France could inspire such nationalist sentiments in the south. He began to plot a diplomatic collision course that would bring about such a conflict with France.

The Spanish Succession Crisis. The dramatic expansion of Prussian territory and military prowess alarmed Napoleon III and French nationalists. Sentiment for a war to stop the rising German threat began to grow in France. Bismarck was delighted. In June 1870, he intensified French fear and rage by convincing Leopold of Hohenzollern-Sigmaringen, a relative of the Prussian monarch, to accept the throne of Spain and persuading a reluctant King William to give the necessary approval. If this arrangement stood, it would place France between two Hohenzollern states. The French fever for war rose.

The Ems Dispatch. Since war interested William less than it did Bismarck, he tried to placate France. At the king's request, Leopold agreed not to accept the Spanish crown. William's action left Napoleon dissatisfied. In July, he sent a representative to meet William at Ems and demand a pledge that no Hohenzollern would ever take the throne of Spain. The Prussian leader would not comply and telegraphed a message about the event to Bismarck. In Berlin, the prime minister released an account of the incident to the press so worded that William and the French ambassador appeared to have had a mutually insulting encounter. They had not. The revised Ems dispatch, however, intensified the demands for war in both countries.

The Outbreak of War. On July 19, 1870, France declared the war that Bismarck wanted. The Prussian prime minister had arranged a defensive alliance with the four south German states. Now they joined the war against France. Therefore, when the "Franco-Prussian War" erupted, it involved a Prussian-led coalition of all German states, except Austria, against France. Soon after the declaration of war, Napoleon's troops marched into German territory and enjoyed success in one small-scale encounter. Then three modern armies of the German alliance responded with a stunning assault. As August ended, German forces overwhelmed the French at Sedan and seized Napoleon himself.

A New Nation, Born in War. The war continued into mid-January. By then, German control in the heart of France was so secure that the Prussian king could venture into the French royal palace at Versailles. In the Hall of Mirrors on January 18, 1871, the leaders of all the German states met to declare William the Emperor of their new nation. The war thus had enabled Bismarck to complete the process of bringing together thirty-eight German states into a unified nation dominated by Prussia. France surrendered to the new German Empire on January 28, 1871. Bismarck showed no leniency to this victim; France had to give Germany 200,000,000 francs and the important border territories of Alsace and Lorraine. The new nationalism brought great rewards and losses.

Scientific works, such as Darwin's Origin of the Species, *profoundly altered the mood of the intellectual and political elite in the 1850s and 1860s. Artists and writers expressed the new outlook in startlingly realistic paint-*

ings and novels. Courbet's artwork The Bathers *and Flaubert's story of* Madame Bovary *epitomized this effort of Europeans to bring the spirit of the new science into the arts.*

Social theorists in this era also absorbed and reacted to scientific discoveries about matter and natural forces. Feuerbach, a philosopher, declared that the universe contained only matter and not spiritual entities such as God. Comte exhibited the new enthusiasm for science in his argument that humanity had entered the "positive" stage of history, an era when scientific method could be used to perfect society. Social Darwinists offered a less thoughtful "science" of human affairs. They simply borrowed the language of evolutionary biology and applied it to social processes.

Political trends paralleled those in science, the arts, and thought. Unemotional and calculating leaders directing powerful modernizing states took control of events, especially in Central Europe, and remade the political map of the continent. Two masters of this new Realpolitik *emerged in Italy and Germany.*

As prime minister of Piedmont-Sardinia in north Italy, Camillo di Cavour followed moderately liberal government practices and accelerated economic modernization in order to win the admiration of Italians in nearby states. Then he used realistic power politics to drive Austria from Italy and achieve the success that had long eluded more idealistic Italian nationalists. By 1861, all but two small states joined the new Piedmont-dominated Kingdom of Italy. These last territories entered the union ten years later to complete Italian unification.

Otto von Bismarck, as Minister-President of Prussia, followed policies similar to Cavour's and by 1871 unified Germany under Prussian leadership. In the new German nation, however, Bismarck won mass support for his king without allowing popular influence in government even to the limited extent that Cavour had. These two leaders thus helped to create a new and much more conservative variety of nationalism that incorporated bourgeois economics, Realpolitik, *and popular authoritarianism.*

This new nationalism enabled Cavour to advance modernization in Italy without going beyond a moderate form of liberal government. Conservative nationalism provided Bismarck with a means to modernize politics and the economy in Germany with only a counterfeit version of liberal institutions. He kept the government dictatorial.

As these states achieved political modernity after 1848, economic modernization accelerated throughout Europe. The states with a head start in industry became more highly industrialized. Other states began to enter the industrial revolution. The arts of the latter 1800s reflected these changes in European government, economy, and society.

Selected Readings

Beales, Derek. *The Risorgimento and the Unification of Italy*. London: Longman, Green, 1982.

Binkley, Robert C. *Realism and Nationalism, 1852–1871*. New York: Harper & Row, 1941.

Eisely, Loren. *Darwin's Century*. New York: Doubleday, 1958.

Leymarie, Jean. *French Painting: The Nineteenth Century*. Geneva, Switzerland: Skira, 1962.

Palmer, Alan. *Bismarck*. London: Weidenfeld and Nicolson, 1976.

Pflanze, Otto. *Bismarck and the Development of Germany*. Princeton, NJ: Princeton University Press, 1963.

Simon, Walter. *European Positivism in the Nineteenth Century*. Ithaca, NY: Cornell University Press, 1963.

Steegmuller, Francis. *Flaubert and Madame Bovary*. Chicago: University of Chicago Press, 1977.

10

The Culture of Industrial Europe, 1848–1914

1848 Karl Marx and Friedrich Engels publish *The Communist Manifesto*

1856 Bessemer introduces his new method of steel processing

1859 John Stuart Mill publishes *On Liberty*

1864 The First International Workingmen's Association is organized

1865 The open-hearth steel-processing method is first used

1867 Marx publishes the first volume of *Das Kapital*

1876 Alexander Graham Bell tests the first telephone

1885 Friedrich Nietzsche begins publication of *Thus Spake Zarathustra*

1887 Gottlieb Daimler demonstrates the first successful model of a gasoline-powered automobile

1894 Sigmund Freud begins presentation of his views on the human unconscious

1895 Wilhelm Roentgen discovers X rays

1897 Joseph J. Thomson identifies electrons within atoms

1899 Gugliclmo Marconi transmits the first wireless telegraph message from France to England

1900 Max Planck advances his quantum theory

1903 The Wright brothers complete the first airplane flight

1905 Albert Einstein publishes his *Special Theory of Relativity*

1906 The British Labour Party emerges

1910   The rigid balloon airship, invented by Ferdinand von Zeppelin, carries its first commercial passengers

1913   A performance of Igor Stravinsky's ballet *Rite of Spring* inspires a riot

The triumph of the new nationalism in the latter 1800s coincided with the victory of the industrial socioeconomic order in most of Europe. Production became much more highly mechanized in countries that had industrialized first. Larger business structures emerged, new labor organizations appeared, and the economic revolution swept outward to new regions. Social theorists responded to this transformation of European life. They advanced ideologies such as welfare-state liberalism, Marxian socialism, and anarchism.

Marxism reflected the mood of scientific confidence typical of the mid-1800s. Karl Marx boldly affirmed that his "scientific socialism" perfectly revealed the past and predicted the future of humanity. This claim to certainty about society hardly agreed with the newest currents of thought in science. By the early 1900s, Max Planck and Albert Einstein, Europe's leading physicists, indicated that certainty about the substances and forces of the physical world was impossible. This change in outlook did not reduce the importance of science in European life, but a trend toward probable rather than absolute ideas had begun.

Academic social theorists, artists, and writers in the late 1800s and early 1900s were like the scientists in their increasing uncertainty about life. Psychologists and sociologists began to emphasize how little scholars knew about the mind and society. The change among intellectuals from the confidence of the mid-1800s to the uncertainty of the early 1900s troubled the educated public.

The painters, musicians, and authors who took new creative directions after 1870 probably shocked Europeans even more than did the scientists and social theorists. Leading artists produced highly abstract art. The foremost composers wrote very discordant music. Prominent writers concentrated less on what they observed in society and more on their sometimes incomprehensible impressions of the inner nature of people.

In the mid-1800s, leaders in government, business, academic life, and the arts had outlooks that differed in many ways. But they shared many attitudes too. They emphasized practical matters. They believed that they could discover the truth about the aspects of life that mattered to them. They thought that this knowledge would enable them to achieve the goals they cared about. In the early 1900s, government and business leaders remained in this practical and confident mood. Growing numbers of scientists, social theorists, and artists did not.

THE MATURATION OF THE INDUSTRIAL ECONOMY, 1850–1914

In 1850, the circle of economic modernization extended from the most developed countries, Britain and Belgium, southward through the heart of the continent to northern Italy. The industrial revolution continued to spread into new areas thereafter. By the 1890s, the economic transformation had begun in Europe's most agricultural nation, Russia. The states with the most developed economies rapidly expanded their industrial systems and advanced in technology during the latter 1800s. Before the end of the century, Germany replaced Britain as the leader in Europe's industrial race.

The Industrial Productive System

Between 1850 and 1914, industry continued its remarkable progress as the machines and processes discovered in the previous century came into much wider use. The development of new devices and methods also sped the economic revolution ahead in the latter 1800s. At the same time, the new science began to influence industry more directly and increased the effect of inventions on production. One important result of this continuing economic transformation was a 260 percent expansion of industrial output between 1870 and 1914. This great leap would have been impossible without a remarkable advance in the power that drove the machines of industry.

POWER SOURCES AND ENGINES

The number of steam engines grew rapidly after 1850. The multiplication of these machines occurred both as more factories installed them for traditional operations and as inventors discovered new applications. The innovations included a steam-driven plow, the rotary printing press, steam rollers for packing roads, and, in 1857, a steam dynamo to generate electricity.

Coal fired most of the steam engines and heated many buildings in the 1850s. By then, natural gas also had become a significant heating fuel and light source. Soon, however, industrialists began to use other forms of energy that in the next century became more important than coal and natural gas. Edwin Drake founded the new petroleum industry when he drilled a well in Titusville, Pennsylvania, in 1859. Oil use increased slowly thereafter until its boom era began in the 1920s. The electric industry advanced more swiftly. Technological improvements in the 1870s and 1880s so revolutionized this industry that by 1914 electricity provided heat and light in more urban structures than did natural gas.

TEXTILES AND INDUSTRIAL CHEMICALS

The most revolutionary changes in productive systems before 1850 took place in the British cotton textile industry. In the 1850s, Isaac Singer, an American, promoted the sewing machine. New wool processing devices became available. These technological developments encouraged a rapid modernization of the clothing and woolen industries.

Scientists gave textile manufacturing a further boost by ending the industry's dependence on natural dyes. In 1856, W. H. Perkins, a teenaged British chemist, discovered a way to produce synthetic purple from coal tar. German scientists invented a chemical form of red dye in 1869 and won a patent for it one day ahead of Perkins.

By the 1860s, chemical discoveries sped the growth of many industries. Ernest Solvay, a Belgian scientist, patented a process in 1861 that reduced the cost of producing alkali. His achievement benefited glass, soap, and textile manufacturing. Alfred Nobel's invention of dynamite in 1867 provided a low-risk way to produce an explosive of great value to the weapons industry. Dynamite also proved to be very useful in nonmilitary activities such as engineering projects.

IRON AND STEEL

Europeans produced steel before the 1850s, but this more purified form of iron cost too much to manufacture in commercially significant quantities at that time. Iron, therefore, remained the primary industrial metal until the latter 1800s even though steel was stronger and had other superior properties. The work of several technicians in the 1850s and 1860s, however, ended the supremacy of iron.

Henry Bessemer discovered in 1856 that forcing air streams through molten iron produced more and cheaper steel. This process greatly increased the metal's commercial value. An even more significant improvement came in 1865 when Pierre Martin used Wilhelm von Siemens's gas furnace design to develop the open hearth method of steel production. As a result of these discoveries, a tenfold increase in production of the metal occurred between 1865 and 1880. The era of steel had arrived.

Transportation

Only one modern form of transportation had become widely prevalent as the industrial revolution climaxed in the 1850s—the railroad. Many lines then spanned the leading industrial states; nearly all countries had begun their systems. With the introduction of the Bessemer process, Europeans began to lay steel instead of iron rails. They completed the main strands of their rail nets with a total length of more than 170,000 miles by 1900.

The railroad industry also vastly improved the safety, quality, and profitability of service during these years. Inventors and technicians introduced the Westinghouse air brake (1869), sleeping and dining cars, and refrigerated freight cars. Gradually, other modern forms of transportation began to rival trains despite these continuing improvements.

STEAMSHIPS

Steamships remained a novelty in the mid-1800s. During the latter 1800s, the development of a more efficient engine and the replacement of the paddle wheel by the screw propeller brought the new vessel into its own. It began to rise to dominance over the sailing ship on the world's seas. Steam powered more than ninety percent of the ships built in 1914. Construction materials for these vessels changed drastically too in these years. Most ships in the 1840s were wooden. Iron became the primary material in new construction by the 1860s. Shipbuilders made almost ninety-nine percent of their vessels of steel in 1898 and 1899.

URBAN TRANSIT

Steam and steel revolutionized sea travel. Somewhat more slowly, rails and electricity began to transform urban transportation as the horse-drawn cars on rails (introduced in the 1860s) gave way to electric-powered versions in the 1880s. In 1887, Gottlieb Daimler built the first successful automobile propelled by a gasoline-fueled internal combustion engine. Less than a decade later, Rudolf Diesel invented an oil-burning engine that also could be used in automobiles.

Vehicles powered by electricity, gasoline, or diesel fuel would reign supreme on city streets and country roads a few decades in the future. In the latter 1800s, however, they did not truly rival the new bicycles of the day. Inventions such as rear-wheel drive and air-filled tires greatly improved the safety and comfort of bicycles and increased their popularity. By 1900, Britain, France, and Germany each had over four million bicycles. Italians then owned two million, and other countries also had large numbers.

AIR TRAVEL

The production of marvelous new contraptions for travel on land and sea left a few inventive people still dissatisfied. Six men suspended in a container beneath a hydrogen-filled balloon used oars of silk to move their aircraft through the first human flight in history in 1784. For more than a century thereafter, the technology of air travel progressed very little.

Then science and industry quickly made flights of fancy a reality. Count Ferdinand von Zeppelin invented a balloon with an interior frame in 1898, a design so effective that such airships began passenger service in 1910. By then, a new device that showed an even greater potential to open the skies had taken flight—Wilbur and Orville Wright had completed their first successful airplane tests at Kitty Hawk, North Carolina, in 1903. The longest of the Wright brothers' first test flights lasted fifty-nine seconds and achieved a speed of thirty miles per hour. Six years later, Louis Blériot piloted his aircraft across the English Channel in thirty-seven minutes. With their incredible machines, humans had entered a new realm.

Communications Technology

Astonishing progress occurred in communications as well as transportation after 1850. The invention of the telegraph in 1844 encouraged Europeans and Americans to lay cables between countries. They completed one from England to France in 1851. Within two decades, cables also linked continents—Europe and North America in 1866, then Europe and Asia by the early 1870s.

THE TELEPHONE AND WIRELESS TELEGRAPH

Alexander Graham Bell sent the first voice message over wire with the telephone that he invented in 1876. The popularity of the new device grew rapidly. By the end of the 1800s, many government agencies and businesses regularly used telephones. In the 1890s, as the telephone became a practical tool in offices, Guglielmo Marconi invented a wireless means of sending telegraphic signals. The first coded electronic transmission flashed across the English Channel in 1899 and across the Atlantic in 1901.

BUSINESS COMMUNICATIONS AND THE MASS MEDIA

A variety of technological and organizational achievements further transformed business communication and opened the way for the development of the mass media. Typewriters and improved postal systems, for example, enhanced the operation of many enterprises by the 1870s. A series of printing press inventions that began in that decade and the cheaper paper that chemistry made possible led to the founding of the first mass-circulation newspapers in the latter 1800s. The government leaders who now typically wanted a mobilized citizenry had the means of communication they needed.

INDUSTRIAL SOCIETY

The progress of industry depended on and encouraged a wide variety of social changes. Especially dramatic alterations occurred in population trends and living conditions.

The Urban and Rural Populations

The rate of population increase that began in the Early Modern period surged higher in the latter 1800s. Between 1870 and 1914, the total number of Europeans expanded by fifty percent, from 300 to 450 million. This climb resulted in part from improved nutrition and a declining rate of death from infectious diseases. The pace of urbanization quickened even more in these years. London grew from five to seven million in the thirty-five years before 1914. Paris and Berlin experienced a similar rate of increase and in the same year had populations of three and two million, respectively.

Despite urbanization, most Europeans still lived in the country. Traditional ways changed more slowly there than in the cities, but the social influence of both peasants and landed aristocrats diminished as Europe became increasingly industrial and urban. At the same time, the urban middle classes gained in political power in several of the West European countries. In every society, the wealth of the bourgeoisie increased.

FACTORY WORK AND FAMILY INCOME

The widening gap between the wealth of the business classes and the workers increased labor discontent. Other conditions also disturbed poorer urbanites. Machines in the factories required a faster pace of work and more strength to operate than in previous decades. Work was harder. This change made it increasingly difficult for women and children to remain in industrial occupations. As a result, family incomes sometimes dropped. The more drastic swings in business cycles during the first two centuries of industrialization added to these financial woes. Inflation raised costs from the late 1840s to the early 1870s. Then, for two more decades, economic depression caused many workers to lose their jobs.

WORKING-CLASS NEIGHBORHOODS

The working classes responded to these problems in a variety of ways. Neighborhoods developed a sense of identity, sometimes provided emotional support, and offered leisure activities both constructive and detrimental. Among these diversions, socializing at the local pub became especially popular among working people. Laborers also reacted to urban-industrial conditions by establishing formal institutions such as aid societies and unions.

Labor and Business Organization

Early Modern European governments usually declared labor unions and strikes to be illegal. Britain began to ease such restraints in the 1820s by allowing workers to organize but not to strike. Parliament finally removed these restrictions on union action in 1876. France canceled the laws against strikes twelve years later. By then, Austria and the Netherlands had legalized unions, as did Germany in 1890.

THE LABOR UNION MOVEMENT

During the latter 1800s, workers did more than struggle to end laws against unions. They also found ways to form more powerful associations than in the early years of the labor movement. In the past, they had established unions limited to skilled workers in a particular craft. Laborers now began to form organizations open to all the workers of an entire industry, such as railroading.

With changes such as these, labor soon emerged as a major social force, especially in the two most industrialized countries. The German working class became especially strong and aggressive. Laborers there developed the most formidable socialist movement in Europe. British working-class power grew rapidly too. By the 1890s, laborers in Britain elected their first parliamentary representative. In 1906, they formed the Labour Party to ensure a still stronger voice in government.

CORPORATE BUSINESS ORGANIZATION

The economic and political strength of business interests spiraled upward even more swiftly than did that of labor. Governments established laws that limited the liability of company owners to the amount they had invested, thus protecting them from personal ruin if the enterprise failed. In Britain such companies were designated by adding "limited" or the abbreviation "ltd." to the corporate title. A firm with this status usually attracted greater numbers of investors.

These financial improvements gave business leaders increased power. Organizational changes during this period boosted their strength still more. Before 1850, single-owner and partnership firms were typical. Thereafter, such businesses were gradually replaced by large bureaucratic enterprises owned by numerous stockholders. Groups of trustees and a corps of managers directed these new business organizations.

The new corporate forms of business tended to expand in size and become highly centralized. They also frequently attempted to establish monopolies controlling an entire industry. The influence of these wealthy giants in government, and in society more generally, far exceeded that of the rising labor organizations.

IDEOLOGICAL RESPONSES TO INDUSTRIALIZATION

In the first decades of the 1800s, liberal and socialist theorists reacted to the rise of bourgeois power and the effects of industrialization. Ideological responses to the social effects of economic modernization sharpened even more in the 1840s and after.

The Diversification of Liberalism

Many liberals in the latter 1800s held to the traditions of Adam Smith and other founders of the ideology. They preferred to keep government involvement in the economy very limited. A leading nineteenth-century theorist, however, devised a form of liberalism with a distinctly new attitude toward the role of government in society.

JOHN STUART MILL'S TREATISE ON LIBERALISM

John Stuart Mill (1806–1873), a British scholar, argued strongly for the necessity of personal liberty, including the freedom to own and use private property. He repeated these views in several editions of his *Principles of Political Economy,* the first of which appeared in 1848. *On Liberty,* published in 1859, became an even more famous argument for these central ideas of liberalism.

THE GENERAL WELFARE STATE

Despite his commitment to fundamental liberal beliefs, Mill's ideology differed from the *laissez-faire* liberalism of his predecessors. Mill doubted that all the new machines had eased the lives of workers and urged the government to correct this injustice. His idea that the general welfare of the people sometimes required political intervention reduced the distance between liberalism and socialism. This attitude put Mill in conflict with liberals who wanted an uncontrolled business class. In ordinary usage, twentieth-century commentators have in mind John Stuart Mill's idea of the general welfare state when they refer to liberalism.

Marxist Socialism

Karl Marx (1818–1883) and Friedrich Engels (1820–1895) offered a socialist response to industrialization. They rejected, however, the theories of Proudhon, Fourier, Owen, and other founders of socialism. Marx and Engels condemned these earlier socialists' ideas as "utopian," as idealistic dreams of a society with equally shared wealth created by reform.

In place of these utopian theories, Marx and Engels offered "scientific" socialism. They called their doctrines scientific because they believed they had arrived at their conclusions through a scientific study of society. Marx and Engels also claimed that as scientists they faced the reality that justice for the working class could come about only through a violent revolutionary struggle.

THE EARLY YEARS OF MARX AND ENGELS

Marx and Engels devoted their lives to this battle against the miseries of the urban working classes. Neither of them ever experienced that life. As children, they lived in middle-class German homes—Marx's father practiced law, and Engels enjoyed the wealth from his father's textile business. Marx earned a doctorate in philosophy in Berlin. Then, under pressure from authorities who disliked his atheism, he moved to Paris in 1843. Engels eventually took charge of branches of the family business in Britain, but he too was in France in the 1840s.

THE COMMUNIST MANIFESTO

These exiles met in Paris during the troubled years before the 1848 revolt. They formed a close friendship and an intellectual association that lasted throughout their lives. Engels accepted Marx as the senior theorist and supported him financially for most of his life with funds from his family's enterprises. This dependence on capitalist profits did not lessen the rage the two socialists felt toward the bourgeois industrial system. In 1847 they began to compose a short book summarizing their theories. They published this *Communist Manifesto* in 1848.

DIALECTICAL MATERIALISM

The *Manifesto* and *A Contribution to the Critique of Political Economy* (1859) contain the fundamental Marxist ideas about society and the forces that control its development. These theories include the assertion of materialist principles similar to Feuerbach's. Beginning with such assumptions, Marx and Engels developed their doctrine of "dialectical materialism." They incorporated into this theory Hegel's idea that social change is a dialectical process: an existing condition (thesis) causes its opposite (antithesis) to emerge and the two develop in conflict until they form a new condition (synthesis).

HISTORICAL MATERIALISM

Marx and Engels used dialectical materialism as a framework for their view of history, known as "historical materialism." According to this doctrine, humanity began as primitive communists who worked together to secure the needs of life. People shared all goods equally. Life thereafter evolved through three more stages—an era of slave production, the feudal age with its farm economy and serf labor, and the capitalist industrial phase. Tools, technical procedures, and economic relationships (between worker and boss, for example) formed the "material basis" of society in each of these stages. This material foundation caused the formation of a social "superstructure" that included ideas, beliefs, art, and human institutions such as the family and social classes.

CLASS STRUGGLE

Marxist doctrine asserted that change in the substructure of tools, technology, and economic relationships caused society to proceed from one stage (thesis) to the next (synthesis). Conflict accompanied the transitions. These sometimes ruthless battles erupted because one class ruled during each stage and resisted the rise to supremacy of the next group. This inevitable "class struggle" continued, however, until the changing "means of production" (tools, work procedures, and so on) gave economic control to a new class. Revolution usually brought each new class to power.

The Bourgeoisie versus the Proletariat. Marx believed that bourgeois capitalists reigned supreme in his time because of industrialization and its resultant political upheavals such as the French Revolution. This ruling class, like all previous ones, had seized the state during its rebellion. This governing power enabled the bourgeoisie to control and profit from the labor of everyone else. The subordinate noncapitalists eventually would form a single proletariat (urban working class).

The Communist Revolution. The prophets of scientific socialism predicted that the capitalists would grow richer and fewer in number as the proletarians multiplied and sank into poverty. Ultimate victory awaited the proletariat, however, for this class truly possessed the productive means in this industrial age even if it did not own them. This economic reality guaranteed that during a subsequent revolution workers would seize the state. Then the toiling masses would take the first step toward a classless and materially equal society—the seizure of everything the bourgeoisie owned.

Disappearance of the State. After the loss of all their wealth, the business class would become proletarians or die, and only the working class would remain. Since the state, in Marx's view, was nothing but a political machine through which the ruling class controlled and used other classes, no state would exist once society became classless. Democracy in its purest form would emerge as government simply "withered away."

DAS KAPITAL

Marx moved to London in 1849 and remained in this capitalist capital until his death thirty-four years later. He relentlessly probed sources in the British Museum to discover data that supported the "scientific" revelations presented in his *Manifesto*. The first volume of his detailed analysis of the industrial economy appeared as *Das Kapital* in 1867. Engels and another Communist used Marx's notes to publish three additional volumes after his death.

Das Kapital revealed Marx's acceptance of classic liberal ideas such as Adam Smith's theory that labor alone gives value to the products of industry. Marx used these theories, however, to support his version of socialism. He claimed, for example, that while industrial workers give products their worth, capitalists sell the goods for profit (the "surplus value") and thus steal from the proletariat.

THE COMMUNIST INTERNATIONAL

Marx and Engels offered more than scholarly volumes to help the proletariat. Convinced that class loyalties rather than national feelings would seize the hearts of civilized people, Marx and Engels threw themselves into a campaign to organize a global working-class movement. They achieved a single unimpressive result before Marx died—the establishment of The First International Workingmen's Association in 1864. This loose confederation of socialist groups collapsed in 1876. Marxists thereafter organized a more successful Second International that lasted from 1889 to 1914.

Ironically, the Marxist version of socialism exhibited more strength in socialist movements at the national than at the global level. It also affected social thought and action far beyond the confines of Marxist organizations. By the end of the 1800s, Marxism had won enough followers not only to haunt capitalists but also to overshadow all other socialist ideologies on the continent.

Anarchism

Most socialists urged state intervention to force a transition to complete political and economic equality. Even though anarchists shared the socialist and communist commitment to economic and political leveling, they considered the immediate dissolution of all governments to be the only route to social justice.

MIKHAIL BAKUNIN AND TERRORISM

In the latter 1800s, increasing numbers of anarchists began to believe in terrorist violence as the best instrument to destroy the state. This ideology of violence appealed most strongly in the industrially undeveloped regions of Spain, Italy, and Russia. Mikhail Bakunin (1814–1876), a Russian theorist, bluntly expressed this anarchist commitment to violence. He defined any destructive deed as a "creative act." Such ideas helped to give anarchists the popular image as assassins and terrorists always ready to use dagger, pistol, or bomb.

SYNDICALISM

The image of anarchism as a terrorist movement blurs a much more complex reality. There were, for example, anarchists who believed in nonviolence. Sometimes militants favored massive economic demonstrations rather than individual terrorism. This idea of large-scale collective action gained a significant following in France where Georges Sorel (1847–1922) led the call for the destruction of the state by means of a general strike. Specifically, he urged a nation-wide work stoppage by all labor "syndicates" (unions). Because theorists such as Sorel believed that the masses could join worker syndicates and use a general strike to crush the state, their ideology became known as "anarcho-syndicalism" or simply "syndicalism."

MODERNISM IN THE ARTS, FORMAL THOUGHT, AND SCIENCE

The most important characteristic of a modern society is an industrial economy. The supremacy of the middle classes is a closely related trait of European modernity. Paradoxically, a great deal of the most distinctly modern literature, art, music, and philosophy during the late 1800s and early 1900s indicated that artists and writers despised the consequences of industrialization and bourgeois social dominance.

The scientists of the 1880s and after who shaped a new conception of the physical world did not intentionally reject a bourgeois outlook. Yet their ideas directly contradicted the Enlightenment conceptions that had profoundly influenced the middle-class frame of mind. This sharp contrast between the mentality of the European bourgeoisie and the intellectual elite first became apparent in literature.

The Arts

During the 1850s and 1860s, writers and artists in their realist novels and impressionist paintings depicted the bourgeoisie as a worthless class and industrial society as bleak, even horrifying. By the mid-1860s, younger members of the artistic community also adopted very nontraditional lifestyles purposely intended as an attack on bourgeois values. These cultural leaders thus expressed their rejection of middle-class society by the way they lived as well as through their creative works.

Many of these youthful rebels moved to Bohemia, in the Austrian Empire. "Bohemian" writers and artists soon launched a movement to produce "art for art's sake." This new creed meant that more of the future creative works would aim to convey beauty or other sensations and nothing more.

LITERATURE: REBELLION AGAINST BOURGEOIS SOCIETY

The realist style that became dominant in literature in the 1850s continued in the latter 1800s but in an altered form. This modified version came to be called "naturalism."

Émile Zola and Naturalist Prose. The French author Émile Zola (1840–1902) claimed that his scientific or "experimental" novels contained the perfect description of humanity. Zola believed that chemists and biologists described the merely physical traits of humans. The naturalist writer, however, could use the insights of these scientists and careful observation of life to develop a complete scientific description of "natural man." Zola offered his many novels as reports of his findings. In them he considered the lives of prostitutes, drunkards, servants, and others who experienced the worst conditions in France. *Germinal* (1885), his most praised novel, describes the suffering of miners and a strike caused by their misery.

Decadence. Several authors made the message of bohemian life-styles more direct by writing novels with heroes who lived decadent lives. One of these decadence novels, *Against the Grain* by J. K. Huysmans, presents bourgeois society as so uncomfortable for the best people that it drives them to live only for pleasure.

Symbolism. Henrik Ibsen, a Norwegian dramatist, wrote works that combined the characteristics of several late nineteenth-century literary movements. In plays such as *A Doll's House* (1879) and *Ghosts* (1881), he blended decadent, naturalist, and symbolist traits. Observers describe these works as partly symbolist because Ibsen included symbols (brief vivid descriptions of scenes from life) that were meant to reveal truths about inner human nature. The emergence of symbolism indicated that the spirit of Romanticism had strengthened again.

The combined effect of all these modern trends in literature was to widen the gulf between the creative elite and the elites of government and business. By the late 1800s, the interests and attitudes of people in the arts differed much more from the outlook of political and economic leaders than had been the case in the 1850s, in the age of realism.

ART: A CULTURAL REVOLUTION

Leading composers and painters in the half century before 1914 also confronted the conventional bourgeois world with stunning violations of cultural tradition. In contrast to Richard Wagner and other prominent composers of the period who did not seriously violate established standards, several composers produced radically discordant creations. Claude Debussy, Igor Stravinsky, Sergei Prokofiev, and Arnold Schoenberg sounded the first notes of this musical revolution. By 1913, Stravinsky measured the limits of contemporary tolerance with a ballet, *The Rite of Spring*, that provoked an audience to violent protest. Even these extremes in music did not compare to the trend in modern art. Painters made the most radical cultural turn as they abandoned standards that had held sway in Europe since the Renaissance (1400s–1500s).

The Emergence of Abstract Art. Recent findings in the physical sciences influenced the works of Manet, Monet, and other impressionist artists in the mid-1800s, but they painted to reveal thoughts or feelings about what they saw rather than to show reality precisely. This tendency toward a varied or abstract depiction of the actual world increased in the following decades. By the 1890s, an advanced guard of cultural rebels offered even less reality in their presentations and intensified the concentration on ideas or moods. These "post-impressionists" accelerated the movement of European art toward pure abstraction.

Post-Impressionism. Paul Cézanne (1839–1906), Paul Gauguin (1848–1903), Vincent van Gogh (1853–1890), and other post-impressionists blatantly violated the rules of perspective and color. For them, the realistic pictures that pleased the bourgeoisie had little to do with true art. Post-impressionists believed that their works had to be a creation of the soul unaffected by the inhibitions of industrial society. Tribal people, especially South Pacific islanders, fascinated Gauguin and van Gogh. These artists thought that such "primitive" societies allowed the free expression of creative urges and that the art of these simple societies could inspire painters of the urban industrial world. Van Gogh's self-portrait and his work *Sunflowers* illustrate the emotional and colorful results of this approach to art.

Cubism. Post-impressionist paintings contain recognizable people, scenes, and objects, but the pictures have a distinctly abstract quality. In 1905, Pablo Picasso (1881–1973) began to develop cubism, a still more abstract style that emphasized the geometric surfaces of people or objects. In his cubist works, Picasso presented whatever he painted as though it could be seen from many sides at once. The viewer of his *Damsels of Avignon*, for example, sees one figure that simultaneously displays both a full face and a profile. Many traditionalists despised this radically different art. Its appeal and influence, however, deeply affected painting both at once and throughout the century.

Pure Abstraction. A few artists rendered the final revolutionary strokes against artistic tradition with paintings that contained virtually no recognizable hint of the real world. Wassily Kandinsky (1866–1944), a Russian painter, wielded the brush at the beginning of this most extreme attack on the cultural old regime, but a fellow countryman, Marc Chagall (1887–1985), soon joined the movement to pure abstraction. The ranks of European artists committed to visual representations of mysteries from their souls swelled endlessly thereafter. By 1914, modern art indicated in an especially vivid way the extreme contrast between attitudes of the cultural and bourgeois elites.

Formal Thought

In the 1870s and after, a few influential scholars began an attack on dominant intellectual traditions that equaled the strength of the artists' assault on established values. Friedrich Nietzsche (1844–1900), a German philosopher, showed the most complete contempt for the ideas of the European bourgeoisie.

NIETZSCHE'S PHILOSOPHY OF THE IRRATIONAL

Most European intellectuals throughout the Modern period assumed the superiority of logic and reason in the search for truth and worthwhile principles. They expressed a much more limited appreciation for irrational approaches that depended on intuition, emotion, or instinct. For brief periods, as during the Age of Romanticism (1790s to 1840s), cultural leaders doubted the supremacy of reason but even then regarded it highly.

When Nietzsche published *The Birth of Tragedy* (1871), *Thus Spake Zarathustra* (1885–1891), and *Beyond Good and Evil* (1886), he started a new wave of attacks on reason that became the strongest and most lasting in European history. The confidence in reason has not returned to its former levels since the late 1800s.

Condemnation of Reason and Christian Morality. Nietzsche damned the greed of the industrial bourgeoisie and warned that European civilization was in a sharp decline. He charged that this cultural plunge was caused by a spiritual sickness that began with the ancient Greek worship of reason. These philosophers had led Europeans to reject what was most essential for the health of their souls—following primitive human instinct. Nietzsche identified a second source of the infection that threatened to kill the European soul: Christianity. Christianity's moral principles encouraged humility and meekness in a creature that naturally and instinctively was proud and power-hungry. Nietzsche concluded that Europe's salvation required the nullification of Greek rationality and Christian morality.

Affirmation of Elitism. Parliamentary government and democracy enraged Nietzsche also. These devices of popular government perpetuated mediocrity. They discouraged people of superior talents and power from gaining their rightful place at the top. The superior minority who should govern were the people capable of allowing their "will to power" to direct their lives. These instinct-driven "supermen" could lead Europeans in the creation of a superior civilization. This philosophy of primitive spiritual elitism lent itself to use by racists and aggressive nationalists, including Adolf Hitler, although Nietzsche despised racism and nationalism.

PSYCHOLOGY—THE REASONED STUDY OF THE IRRATIONAL

As Nietzsche preached the virtues of irrationality, others of his era plunged into the first scientific studies of the emotional and mental traits of humanity. The efforts of Wilhelm Wundt (1832–1920) in Germany, Sigmund Freud (1856–1939) in Austria, and Ivan Pavlov (1849–1936) in Russia to study the mind scientifically led to the establishment of psychology. During its first decades, Freud's theories and methods dominated this new field of study.

The Supremacy of the Unconscious. Freud, a Viennese physician, specialized in the treatment of nervous disorders. At first, he attempted traditional biological and chemical cures. He abandoned these approaches, however, when he became convinced that neurological maladies resulted from nonphysical causes. Freud's work with his patients indicated to him that unconscious forces within people exercise supreme control over their mental states and behavior; the reasoning mind does not. After 1894, Freud developed his theories in more detail.

Id and Superego. Freud conjectured that as a species with a long evolutionary history, humans inherited a powerful instinctive nature ("id") that compels a person to want instant satisfaction of appetites for sex, food, or whatever provides comfort and pleasure. This irrational unconscious, however, yields somewhat to "superego," a critical and punishing personality structure instilled early in life by society mainly through parental action. Superego struggles against the urges of id, an action required if civilization is to exist. Unfortunately, this suppression of natural impulses also produces emotional disorders ("neuroses") that can wreck lives and society.

Ego. The personality is completed by "ego," the conscious controlling mind. Ego must serve the difficult function of containing the inevitable war between id and superego so that the needs of both the irrational self and civilization can be adequately met. Freud devoted his life to a reasoned study of the irrational because he believed that without scientific knowledge of the unconscious, humanity certainly would fail in its ego task. Despite his confidence in the value of these insights, Freud remained doubtful that irrational creatures could maintain civilization.

Psychoanalysis. Freud had greater faith in the possibility of restoring the emotional health of troubled individuals. In psychoanalysis, the corrective method he conceived, a therapist guides patients to an understanding of the disorders that lie hidden in the unconscious. In this procedure, the psychoanalyst elicits free-flowing conversations and dream descriptions, then interprets them to provide self-knowledge and, thus, a sound personality.

Science

Despite Freud's qualified affirmation of the value and power of reason, he contributed to a growing sense of uncertainty among Europeans about their ability to understand human nature and the social order. Physicists in the late 1800s and early 1900s did even more to undermine long-established convictions about an orderly and knowable universe.

REDEFINING MATTER

The frontiers of knowledge in geology, biology, and chemistry expanded with unprecedented speed throughout much of the 1800s. A similarly explosive rate of discovery began in physics in the 1890s and almost immediately changed the scientific view of matter that had prevailed throughout the century. The transformation in this aspect of science resulted from these developments: Wilhelm Roentgen's discovery of X rays in 1895; subsequent investigations by Henri Becquerel and Marie and Pierre Curie into the nature of radioactive emissions; and, in 1897, Joseph J. Thomson's proof of electrical particles (electrons) within atoms.

In combination, the work of these physicists confirmed that electricity is a component of all matter. This conclusion led scientists to view atoms as tiny solar systems rather than impenetrable solids. This revised notion of the structure of matter at the end of the 1800s left scientists still highly confident that atoms are indestructible and, with further study, fully understandable.

Ernest Rutherford's discovery in 1911 that atoms contained a center or nucleus composed of positive electrical particles (protons) around which electrons revolved seemed to justify the belief that science might soon yield complete knowledge of matter. The mood of high confidence, however, would not last much longer.

QUANTUM THEORY—A SCIENCE OF PROBABLE TRUTH

Max Planck (1858–1947) ushered in the twentieth century with a refutation of a fundamental natural law—the conviction that energy release, as in heat from matter, always occurs in an even flow. The quantum theory that he presented in 1900 held that energy bursts from its source not as an unbroken line but like a series of dashes or packets (quanta) of power.

Thirteen years later, Niels Bohr used quantum theory to support his conclusion that Newtonian physics, established in the latter 1600s, explained the movement of planets but not of electrons. Bohr affirmed that the motion of particles inside the atom cannot be predicted. Physicists can do no more than estimate the action of subatomic particles within certain limits of probability. Further consideration of the implications of quantum physics during the next fifteen years indicated that science yields only probable truth, not absolutely correct answers.

RELATIVITY THEORY—A SCIENCE OF TEMPORARY TRUTH

Planck's revelations dissolved scientific certainty about the smallest particles in nature. Other scientists demonstrated that an honest science requires an equally imprecise idea of the larger universe.

The Michelson-Morley Experiment. For over 200 years, experts had assumed that the movement of structures such as planets could be measured with perfect accuracy because they traveled through ether, a motionless space substance. A single test, the Michelson-Morley experiment in the United States in 1887, simultaneously proved that the earth's rotation does not influence the speed of light and that ether does not exist.

Einstein's Theory of Relativity. In his *Special Theory of Relativity* (1905), Albert Einstein (1879–1955) contended that no object or force in the universe affects the speed of light, that light's rate of motion is the single absolute in nature, and that all scientific laws are valid for objects traveling at the same speed. This comprehensive proposition confirmed and expanded on the Michelson-Morley discovery and required a radically new view of reality.

The Implications of Relativity Theory. Einstein's calculations indicated that as speeds increase, objects shorten and time slows. For example, a person moving at nine-tenths the speed of light ages half as fast and is half as tall as at ordinary speeds. Relativity theory, furthermore, revealed that space and time do not exist apart from objects. If matter disappears from the universe, so do space and time. Every fact and law in the natural world, therefore, has validity only under specific conditions of space, time, and speed. All truth is temporary. With the new physics of Planck and Einstein, the modern scientific view of reality had become as divorced from the commonsense world of bourgeois industrial Europe as abstract art.

*M*ost *of Europe's industry remained concentrated in Britain, the Netherlands, Belgium, Prussia, and France in 1850. During the next sixty-five years, this region became more highly industrialized. Meanwhile, the new productive system began to emerge in the rest of the continent. Technology advanced rapidly as industry intensified and expanded across Europe. Builders and manufacturers increasingly made structures and devices of steel instead of wood or iron. The growing chemical industry yielded synthetic dyes, dynamite, better soap, and cheaper paper. Inventors enhanced the comfort, safety, and speed of rail transportation and produced the first automobiles and airplanes. They also made electricity a commercially useful source of power for the first time.*

A social transformation accompanied the maturation of the industrial economy. Urbanization proceeded at a rapid pace. In the growing cities, the middle classes continued to gain social and political influence, and their power, or at least their values, became dominant in most of Europe. Financiers and industrialists also strengthened their grip on the economy by the organization of large corporate structures. A rapidly expanding industrial labor force could not seriously challenge the authority of the business classes, but workers built stronger unions and won the right to strike in most of the industrial states.

In the fifty years before 1914, even more drastic change occurred in the realms of art and science than in the socioeconomic order. Leading writers and painters turned away from realistic works to such extremely personal and abstract expressions that they alienated the middle and upper classes who usually patronized the arts. This consequence suited many in the cultural elite since they had come to despise the bourgeoisie and the effects of industrialization.

Scientists and industrialists formed a lasting partnership in these years, much to the benefit of modern business. At the same time, however, new developments in physics created an abstract perception of the material world that was as incomprehensible to the bourgeois mind as the revolutionary new art. The outlook of the scientific and cultural elite thus contrasted sharply with the attitudes of Europe's socioeconomic leaders by 1914.

Several leading intellectuals also produced social theories alien to the contemporary middle-class way of life. In his philosophical treatises, Nietzsche described a bourgeois-dominated civilization made sick by a rational and Christian approach to life. He pled for a willful, instinct-driven elite to rise and restore humanity's natural, primitive condition. Marxists also attacked the bourgeois system, but they wanted a revolution that would complete the modernization of the human order through the establishment of a classless society of workers who shared authority and wealth equally.

The artistic elite's rejection of the middle class and the brilliant anti-bourgeois attacks of Nietzsche and the Marxists hinted at the very troubled times that would come in a more distant future, after 1914. More immediately, the socioeconomic trends between 1850 and 1914 revealed the nearly complete triumph of the modernizing bourgeoisie. These were, on the whole, glorious times for the European middle classes. The history of government affairs in Europe, 1850 to 1914, will further confirm this pattern of bourgeois triumph.

Selected Readings

Berlin, Isaiah. *Karl Marx: His Life and Environment.* 4th ed. Oxford, England: Oxford University Press, 1978.

Bradbury, Malcolm, and James McFarlane, eds. *Modernism, 1890–1930.* Atlantic Highlands, NJ: Humanities Press, 1978.

Freud, Sigmund. *On Dreams.* New York: Norton, 1952.

Gay, Peter. *Freud: A Life for Our Times.* New York: Norton, 1988.

Hamilton, George H. *Painting and Sculpture in Europe, 1880–1940.* Baltimore: Penguin Books, 1972.

Hayes, Carlton J. H. *A Generation of Materialism, 1871–1900.* New York: Harper and Brothers, 1941.

Henderson, W. O. *The Industrialization of Europe, 1780–1914.* London: Thames and Hudson, 1969.

Howe, Irving, ed. *The Idea of the Modern in Literature and the Arts.* New York: Horizon Press, 1967.

Hughes, H. Stuart. *Consciousness and Society: The Reorientation of European Social Thought, 1890–1930.* New York: Vintage, 1961.

Joll, James. *The Anarchists.* Cambridge, MA: Harvard University Press, 1980.

Kaufmann, Walter. *Nietzsche: Philosopher, Psychologist, Antichrist.* 3rd ed. Princeton, NJ: Princeton University Press, 1968.

Marx, Karl, and Friedrich Engels. *Basic Writings on Politics and Philosophy.* Ed. L. S. Feuer. Boston: Peter Smith, 1975.

Mill, John Stuart. *On Liberty.* New York: Norton, 1975.

Millward, Alan S., and S. B. Saul. *The Development of the Economies of Continental Europe, 1850–1914.* Cambridge, MA: Harvard University Press, 1977.

11

The Era of the Nation-State, 1850–1914

1852 Napoleon III establishes the Second French Empire

1854 Beginning of the Crimean War, fought by Russia against Turkey, Britain, and France until 1855

1861 Emancipation of Russia's serfs by Alexander II

1867 All urban and some rural males received the right to vote

The Hapsburgs reorganize their empire into the Dual Monarchy

1870 The Second Empire collapses in France, and the Third Republic is established

1871 Formation of the German Empire with Bismark as chancellor until 1890

Revolt of the Paris Commune

1872 The German anti-Catholic *Kulturkampf* begins

1884 Parliament establishes male suffrage in Britain

1894 Nicholas II, the last Russian tsar takes the throne

1903 Russian Communists divide into Lenin's Bolsheviks and the Mensheviks

1906 The British Labour Party emerges

1911 The Parliament Bill of 1911 elevates Commons to more complete supremacy over Lords

1928 British women twenty-one and over gain the vote

The rebels of Central Europe who struck their blows for liberal government and national unity in 1848 lost decisively. The middle-class forces who made this revolutionary attempt in Italy and Germany realized their dream of nationhood within the next two decades, however, by compromising or abandoning liberal political principles to make common cause with upper-class traditionalists. For their part, the old elite accepted nationalism, a change that enabled them to keep a share of power.

This joining of middle- and upper-class leadership in Central Europe under the banner of conservative nationalism encouraged the spread of bourgeois values and the industrial economic system across the entire continent. As the European states became more economically alike, however, the region fragmented politically more than ever in modern history. Previously, monarchical and aristocratic family ties, common upper-class values, and nearly universal religious institutions had fostered a unitary spirit that somewhat qualified the sovereignty of individual countries.

The Concert of Europe (see chapter 7) reflected the persistence of this internationalist outlook in the first half of the 1800s. This system collapsed, however, in the 1850s, and most Europeans developed a new political attitude. They came to believe that the national group should form the basis of the state and that citizens owed absolute loyalty to the country.

As a result of this trend, by the 1870s the entire industrial heartland of Europe was organized politically as nation-states. The Austrian and Russian empires had not yet taken this national form, but they at least had to adjust their policies and institutions to draw on or counter the power of nationalism in the interest of the state. This transition to an industrialized nation-state system left little of the *ancien* political order intact.

Contrary to the traditions of the old regime, these late nineteenth-century states usually involved citizens in public affairs by extending voting rights to more of the population and by establishing representative assemblies. In Germany, Austria, and Russia, these new popular institutions allowed citizens to exercise very little real power, and even in the more democratic states, large segments of the populace usually lacked political rights. Still, these institutional changes and the spirit of the new nationalism encouraged a much wider circle of devotion to the country. This political mobilization of the masses within a nationalist state structure is the hallmark of modern government, a development that is the central feature of European public affairs between 1850 and 1914.

THE COLLAPSE OF ANCIEN INTERNATIONALISM

The Concert System arranged by Europe's *Ancien Régimes* at Vienna in 1815 kept the continent somewhat unified and helped to maintain international peace until the 1850s. This traditional form of European internationalism then collapsed.

The European States at Odds in the Near East

In the decades after Napoleon's defeat in 1815, there was a high potential for a clash among European states over policies and actions related to the Near East, the region between the Caspian and Mediterranean seas.

EUROPEAN NEAR EASTERN INTERESTS

France and Britain saw the area as a vital link to parts of the world where they had imperial or trading interests. The tsars had expanded in that direction for years and longed eventually for a standing there that would give Russia secure water routes from the Black Sea into the Mediterranean.

THE INFLUENCE OF RELIGION ON NEAR EASTERN RIVALRIES

The Ottoman Turkish Empire stretched across this region on the southeastern borders of Europe. This Muslim state contained large groups of Orthodox Christians and Catholics. Russia claimed protective rights over the Orthodox populations there as the French did for Catholics. Since Turkey was in decline and thus vulnerable to encroachment from the outside, the chance that the competing interests of the Europeans might lead to conflict gradually increased.

The Crimean War, 1854–1855

The incidents that led directly to the first European war in nearly forty years began in the Turkish Empire in 1850. A conflict erupted between Orthodox and Catholic Christians over access to sacred sites in the Holy Lands. France proclaimed its intention to support the Catholics there, and Russia responded in kind for the Orthodox Christians. Turkey and Russia began a lengthy struggle over this issue that finally led to war between them in October 1853. The following March, France and Britain entered the war against Russia.

THE MILITARY CAMPAIGNS

Once the British and French entered the war, a few small-scale naval actions occurred as they made coastal attacks on Russia. Heavy and protracted battle then followed on the Crimean Peninsula in the Black Sea. Russian defensive preparations and strategies at the Crimean port of Sevastopol held against the combined assault forces for nearly a year.

By the time the Russians abandoned the city in September 1855, their cause was lost. All the combatants suffered heavy casualties, but the course of the war and its outcome demonstrated the marked technical and organizational superiority of the more industrialized states, Britain and France. Despite Russia's fierce resistance at Sevastopol, the Crimean War exposed the serious backwardness of that nation's economic, political, and military institutions.

THE TREATY OF PARIS

Tsar Nicholas I of Russia had died in March 1855, as the battles raged on at Sevastopol. To his successor, Alexander II, the condition of his country was obvious. The new tsar wanted peace at once. The treaty negotiated at Paris during February and March 1856 ended Russian control of important territories on the Danube River and denied Russia the right to have Black Sea naval forces or fortifications. The defeat was complete, and the Concert of Europe was dead. For many European leaders, the interests of their nation-state were beginning to override all other concerns and loyalties.

THE NATION-STATE UNDER POPULAR DICTATORSHIP

Nationalist sentiments and state power rose to new heights between 1850 and 1914. Soon after the revolution of 1848 in France, a new government emerged that provided a model for one very effective form of nation-state—popular dictatorship.

The Second Empire in France, 1848–1870

The revolutionaries who toppled the upper-bourgeois monarchy of Louis Philippe in 1848 produced a plan for a second French republic. They arranged for a parliamentary government led by a president who could serve only one four-year term. The revolutionary assembly also gave the vote to all adults and arranged for a presidential election in December 1848. All the candidates except one had unfamiliar names. Louis Napoleon Bonaparte, Emperor Napoleon's nephew, did not suffer that handicap. He won decisively.

The next spring, voters elected a legislature dominated by monarchists. A democratic vote produced this result because most citizens were peasants who revered tradition and still more of the electorate feared further rebellion by urban lower classes. Although President Bonaparte's family heritage suggested that he might be an authoritarian willing to suppress rebels, monarchist legislators wanted a genuine king, not a Napoleonic emperor.

Thus when the president asked for a constitutional change so that he could stand for reelection, the assembly refused.

Louis Napoleon struck back. His troops marched into the capital on December 1, 1851, and the next day the president dissolved the legislature. Then he turned to the French people for approval of his unconstitutional acts. The new Napoleon had established a dictatorship, but he intended to have the support of the masses.

THE CREATION OF THE SECOND EMPIRE

Before its dissolution, the legislature had decreed an end to universal voting rights by stipulating that if citizens changed residences within three years before an election they could not vote. Louis Napoleon presented himself in the struggle against parliament as the champion of democratic elections and also advocated industrial development, farm subsidies, and assertiveness in international relations. Liberal intellectuals and republicans still opposed him because of his authoritarianism. Within days after Louis Napoleon's seizure of power, a few members of the republican opposition organized disruptive public protests.

Swift and brutal military suppression killed 200 of the ruler's foes. This slaughter alienated and embittered some citizens, but rural France liked the president's tough law-and-order measures. The economic policies that he promised to carry out also appealed to many businesspeople and peasants. Bonaparte had won over most of the nation.

The president reigned supreme after the first days of December 1851. No legislature existed to challenge him. Furthermore, the specter of 200 dead intimidated other potential opponents. This makeshift dictatorship, however, left the leader dissatisfied. He wanted a formally structured popular authoritarian system. Louis Napoleon turned to the people and asked for a vote of approval that would empower him to write their new constitution. The plebiscite on December 21, 1851, granted this authority to the president with the support of more than ninety percent of the 8,000,000 voters.

A New Constitution. The new system of government changed the presidential term from four to ten years and gave the executive full control over legislative proposals, diplomatic relations, and the military. The constitution also established a bicameral legislature with a Senate appointed by the president and a popularly elected Legislative Body. All males had the right to vote. Lawmaking procedures ensured that the president's legislation always would pass and with no changes other than those he approved. Constitutional provisions indicated that this all-powerful executive had to answer to the people, a duty that he would meet in part by seeking approval of his actions through plebiscites—a yes-no vote on issues.

A New Emperor. Louis Napoleon's willingness to appeal to the masses indicated his desire both to rule in the public interest and to involve the people in political life. The French responded warmly to their leader and supported his moves to expand presidential authority. On November 21, 1852, in a plebiscite on whether France should become an empire, more than ninety-nine percent of 8,000,000 voters favored the change. The French who longed for an emperor considered Napoleon I's son, who never reigned, to have been the second Bonaparte dictator; thus the president became Napoleon III by decree on December 2, 1852.

DICTATORSHIP AND MODERNIZATION, 1852–1860

Although the new dictator allowed practices that suggested democracy, he kept power fully in his hands. The constitution made the executive supreme within the government; the Emperor had the army and a controlled press to ensure that popular opposition had little chance to develop. The new dictator sincerely intended, however, to have government for the people if not by them, an attitude demonstrated by a very effective program of economic modernization.

The *Crédit Foncier* and the *Crédit Mobilier*. The imperial government accelerated the growth of a modern industrial economy by actions that made huge sums of money available for business investment. In 1852, public funds flowed into two private financial institutions and made the government a virtual partner in their operations. The empire pumped money into the *Crédit foncier,* for use in lowering the interest on loans to commercial enterprises and farmers. *Crédit mobilier,* a firm that managed business stocks, received government aid to facilitate the expansion of existing enterprises and to encourage new businesses. This banking institution collapsed in 1867, but *Crédit foncier* continues to operate today; both these organizations stimulated French economic development. Utilities, railroads, and other transportation facilities especially benefited from their support.

Public Works. Napoleon III launched government programs to improve both rural and urban life. In the countryside, he took action to reclaim abused land, drain swamps, protect forests, and promote farm modernization. The Emperor demonstrated his special concern for progress in the cities by even more massive projects to rebuild and beautify urban France.

Baron Haussmann and the Reconstruction of Paris. Napoleon III and Baron Georges Haussmann, his chief administrator for the district surrounding Paris, carried out a bold renewal plan for their capital. They cleared away vast sections of old buildings and restructured the city along widened streets and attractive new boulevards. The Emperor probably took this action in part to make street barricades extremely difficult for rebels to build. More noble motives appeared to inspire his efforts too, however, since he provided beautiful new public buildings and modernized the water and sewage systems, improvements that had little to do with the suppression of opposition. The reconstruction created a healthier environment and made the capital a showplace of Europe by the end of Napoleon III's reign.

THE LIBERAL EMPIRE, 1860–1870

In the 1850s, the French economy advanced and life generally improved. Even the setbacks from a surge of floodwaters and a few poor harvest years did not seriously undermine the popular authority of the Emperor. Yet citizen support for Bonaparte weakened sufficiently by 1860 to concern him. He immediately began to adjust imperial practices in keeping with certain principles of European liberalism and continued on this new course throughout the decade.

Napoleon III began by expanding the rights of legislators and citizens to discuss public affairs and by allowing greater freedom of the press. In 1862, he surrendered part of his authority over the budget to the Legislative Body, and thereafter in other ways shared power with appointed and elected officials. French workers also gained new avenues through which to pursue their interests as the Emperor legalized unions and strikes in 1864.

GLOBAL IMPERIAL ADVENTURES

True to the traditional spirit of empire, Napoleon III dreamed of pursuing power and glory beyond the borders of his state. This vision of global greatness probably significantly increased his appeal to the citizens. An early attempt to make these hopes become a reality involved France in the brutal Crimean War, a conflict with no real victors that yielded no grand imperial image.

A more successful adventure for France began in the same year as the Crimean War when Napoleon III supported Ferdinand de Lesseps's plans for a canal to connect the Mediterranean to the Red Sea. This project, completed in 1869, helped to make France a leading influence in eastern Mediterranean affairs until the 1950s. French imperial forces also moved into Asia and took Indochina during the decade after 1859. (This peninsula encompasses Laos, Cambodia, Thailand, and Vietnam.) In these same years, France developed small settlements and spheres of influence in East and West Africa that became the foundations for a vast empire on that continent in later years.

Napoleon III's attempt to extend his realm into the Americas led to a fiasco. France, as well as Britain and Spain, sent forces into Mexico in 1861 because of that country's unpaid debts to the European states. The French ruler, however, planned to take more than money. His forces overthrew the Mexican government and enthroned the Austrian archduke Maximilian in an effort to establish a French-influenced empire in Central America. When the United States ended the Civil War in 1865, its federal government could resume enforcement of the Monroe Doctrine. France responded to threats from the United States by withdrawing imperial troops in 1866. The Mexicans then executed Maximilian. This outcome damaged Napoleon III's image in France.

Despite the mixed success of Napoleon's imperial adventures and the increasing opposition to authoritarian government, the dictator remained quite popular in 1870, after two decades in power. Bonaparte had succeeded quite well in further modernizing the French political system by tying the national masses more tightly than ever to the state.

The New German Empire, 1871–1914

Napoleon III's approach to political modernization, blending authoritarian and somewhat democratic institutions, illustrates the approach used quite effectively beginning in 1871 in the newly united German Empire. Otto von Bismarck, as chancellor of Germany, developed a popular authoritarian system and ran it for Emperor William I from 1871 to 1890.

The German constitution, adopted in April 1871, established a parliamentary structure that gave the appearance of truly representative government. The constitution also provided the legislators a significant if very limited degree of influence over public affairs. An upper house, the *Bundesrat,* was made up of representatives of the separate German states, such as Prussia and Saxony, that had united in 1871. Prussia, with its conservative and authoritarian traditions, dominated this body. Representatives in the lower chamber (*Reichstag*), elected by universal male suffrage, had the power to approve or reject the national budget and could amend or stop legislation. This system left the chancellor and Emperor with a limited dictatorship, but a dictatorship nevertheless.

BISMARCK'S POLICY ORIENTATION

Bismarck had used diplomacy and warfare with little regard for ethics in order to form a unified Germany dominated by Prussia and its somewhat modernized Junker (landowning aristocratic class) traditions. As chancellor, he intended to preserve the new empire without further expansion of its borders. War no longer suited his purposes, so he maneuvered to keep a peaceful international structure in Europe. Bismarck also expanded the German army to almost 500,000, an implied threat intended to further guarantee the empire's security.

Within the new Germany as within Prussia before, Bismarck accepted the need for certain adjustments in *ancien* tradition, such as allowing a more active political role for social elements previously ignored by the aristocracy. The chancellor meant to ensure, however, that the Prussian Junkers and monarchical dynasty reigned supreme within Germany. He stood ready to fight diligently against any threat he perceived to these interests.

Fig. 11.1   Europe, 1871–1914

THE *KULTURKAMPF*—A STRUGGLE AGAINST CATHOLICISM

Bismarck considered Lutheran Christians, the religious majority in Germany, to be loyal citizens, but he viewed the almost equally numerous Catholics as a treasonous menace. This international Catholic Church led by a pope who claimed infallibility appeared to require the total devotion of members everywhere. Would the Catholic Center Party in Germany or other papal loyalists obey the Emperor if the head of the Catholic church decreed otherwise? Bismarck launched a "struggle for civilization" (*"Kulturkampf"*) to ensure that Catholics would submit to the German ruler.

The chancellor's anti-Catholic campaign began in 1872. His steps to nullify the influence of church leaders included denial of the right of the clergy to criticize the government and the expulsion of the Jesuit teaching and missionary order from the country. The government also closed schools established for the clergy and forced these churchmen into secular educational institutions. Other measures against Catholic influence, such as requiring marriages to be legalized by the state, continued throughout the 1870s.

THE CAMPAIGN AGAINST SOCIALISM

Despite the moderate behavior of German socialists, their revolutionary ideology and image made them an easy target for Bismarck when he wanted to encourage citizen loyalty by attacking a "public enemy." The chancellor charged the socialists with plotting to assassinate the Emperor and demanded the dissolution of the Social Democratic Party.

With some difficulty, Bismarck finally convinced the bourgeois Liberal Party to support legislation to outlaw the Social Democratic Party. The Anti-Socialist Law passed in 1878 and remained in effect until Bismarck's resignation from office in 1890. These crusades against Catholics and socialists might have encouraged stronger loyalty to the state, but they did not weaken the movements that Bismarck attacked.

BISMARCK'S WELFARE-STATE PROGRAM

Bismarck not only fought relentlessly against potential competing loyalties that might weaken the state but also offered the most generous welfare program in Europe as an enticement to the citizenry. An 1882 law required a sickness insurance program for all workers to be paid for jointly by employees and employers. Seven years later, an old-age pension program funded in the same way went into effect. The government also established accident insurance for laborers in 1884 with all costs to be covered by employers. While Bismarck courted workers with this welfare program, he successfully promoted trade and industrial development, to the benefit of the business community.

THE GERMAN NATION-STATE WITHOUT ITS FOUNDER

In 1890, a brash young ruler took the imperial throne as William II (1859–1941). This grandson of William I pressured Bismarck into retirement before the end of the year. The Emperor's chancellors thereafter took instructions from the throne. Certain Bismarckian policies continued in effect after the founder of the nation-state left office. Workers still enjoyed the welfare program begun in the 1880s and witnessed the passage of more laws to protect laborers and advance their influence in the workplace.

William II also took up Bismarck's campaign to strengthen the military. In this case, however, the Emperor's expansion of the army and drive to build a navy superior even to Britain's made Germany seem aggressive and militaristic, images that Bismarck had carefully avoided. The Emperor heightened the troublesome diplomatic effect of his military policies with belligerent public statements. Britain responded by turning from its traditionally close association with Prussia and Germany and cultivating better relations with France.

Despite the decline in the quality of German leadership after 1890, the popular authoritarianism of Bismarck and his successors had quickly built a remarkably prosperous and strong modern state. The British, and eventually other West Central European states, followed a different course to political modernization and power.

THE DEMOCRATIC NATION-STATES

Before 1851, France sporadically used democratic institutions to achieve the modern political goal of citizen involvement in public affairs. Britain became the first European state, however, regularly to maintain a system with a significant degree of democracy. Parliament built an important part of the British structure of popular sovereignty as early as the 1830s, and then continued this work of democratization into the next century.

Parliamentary Democracy in Britain, 1848–1914

Whig and Tory Party leaders both contributed to the carefully limited expansion of popular authority in 1832. (See chapter 8.) Both parliamentary parties went through a period of reorganization in the 1850s, and the cause of democratization languished.

EMERGENCE OF THE LIBERAL AND CONSERVATIVE PARTIES

Restructured and reinvigorated political organizations emerged under effective new leaders in the 1860s. John Bright and William Gladstone (1809–1898) reshaped the Whigs into the Liberal Party as Benjamin Disraeli (1804–1881) molded his Tories into the Conservative Party. Liberals and Conservatives alike then promptly entered a campaign to extend voting rights with the expectation that new citizens would support their party.

THE REFORM BILLS OF 1867 AND 1884

Once the parties had emerged in their new form, Liberals under Gladstone's influence and inspiration entered the battle for democratization. A Conservative-dominated Parliament at first blocked this Liberal program of electoral reform. Prime Minister Edward Derby, however, eventually yielded to Disraeli's call for their party to support a broadened franchise rather than allow the Liberals to win the masses with this issue.

The Reform Bill of 1867 that emerged from this partisan struggle approximately doubled the size of the electorate. It allowed all males who owned a house to vote. Men in the cities who rented homes also gained the franchise. The act was thus more restrictive for rural than urban males, it discriminated against the poor of country and city, and it excluded women completely.

During the next seventeen years, both the Gladstone and Disraeli administrations failed to extend voting rights any further. Then Gladstone's Liberals secured passage of the Reform Bill of 1884, an act that applied the same standards to rural males that were established for urban ones in 1867. This new law enfranchised all men except migrant workers, servants, and single males living with their parents. For another thirty-four years, all women continued to be barred from participation in national elections. Nevertheless, these two voter reform bills made Britain more democratic, but without creating a democracy.

A NEW TIDE OF REFORM

Periodic surges of reform became characteristic of the British system during the early 1800s. The first such wave of change began in the 1820s and subsided in the 1840s. When a second phase began in the 1860s, political leaders concentrated on electoral issues, as they had before 1850. The passage of the Reform Bills of 1867 and 1884 indicated this persistent special interest in the franchise question, but other matters did capture the attention of the parties.

In 1870, with Gladstone and the Liberals in power, an executive decree made government jobs open to all citizens, with selection to be determined by examinations. This reform reduced the tendency to hire people because of their "connections" rather than their ability. The government similarly loosened the control of traditional social forces over access to higher education and the military officer corps.

Laborers also benefited from the Liberals' interest in disadvantaged groups. A secret ballot law passed in 1872 freed workers from the risk of economic reprisals when they voted contrary to the interests of employers. After the Conservatives won control of Parliament in 1874, Prime Minister Disraeli and his party continued this trend of reform in the interest of the masses. Two laws passed in 1875 established programs to improve public sanitation and the housing of the poor.

EMERGENCE OF THE BRITISH WELFARE STATE

The pace of reform slowed drastically by the 1880s and did not quicken again until the early 1900s. Conservatives lost much of their drive for innovation when Disraeli's leadership ended in 1880. Gladstone dominated his party until 1894, but he guided the Liberals toward causes that produced little reform legislation.

A new generation of Liberal Party leaders resumed the campaign to transform Britain when they took control of Parliament in 1905. These Liberals turned away from the party's laissez-faire traditions and advanced a program of welfare legislation similar to Germany's. Between 1906 and 1912, they established worker accident insurance, an old-age pension plan, health insurance for all citizens, unemployment insurance, and a minimum wage law.

THE SUPREMACY OF THE HOUSE OF COMMONS

The expense of this welfare-state program helped to provoke a budget crisis, the resolution of which elevated the House of Commons to full supremacy over the House of Lords.

The People's Budget of 1909. This struggle erupted when Chancellor of the Exchequer (treasury minister) David Lloyd George (1863–1945) introduced a People's Budget in 1909. His proposal included a progressive income and inheritance tax designed to take more of the cost of welfare from the richer citizens. The House of Commons passed the bill, but the House of Lords blocked it, the beginning of an eighteen-month deadlock on this issue.

The Parliament Bill of 1911. Commons resorted to a formidable weapon. In 1910, the lower house proposed to nullify the Lords' power to stop its budget laws and leave them with the authority to do no more than delay other legislation. The upper house accepted this measure as the Parliament Bill of 1911. The Lords yielded when Liberal Prime Minister Herbert Asquith (1852–1928) warned that, if necessary, the king would appoint enough new nobles to secure passage. The popularly elected house had completed its long transition to sovereignty.

EMERGENCE OF THE LABOUR PARTY

Neither the democratization of British government nor the Liberals' welfare-state plans convinced working-class leaders that they had sufficient political authority. The labor movement in the latter 1800s reflected this belief that the two leading parties did not respond adequately to its needs.

A group of intellectuals who sympathized with laborers formed the Fabian Society in 1883. This organization advocated complete democracy and a socialist economy. Fabians soon began to insist that workers should establish their own party and support this quest for social equity.

In 1893, Keir Hardie (1856–1915), a Scottish miner, reached the same conclusion as the Fabians and organized a fledgling political group. The rapid growth of unions made up of unskilled workers indicated that the masses in the factories as well as labor leadership elements wanted increased power in Britain. These forces merged to form the Labour Party in 1906. Liberals and Conservatives now faced an organization devoted to the cause of the working class. Within two decades, this socialist party and the Conservatives dominated Parliament.

THE MOVEMENT FOR WOMEN'S RIGHTS

When the Labour Party emerged to support the interests of workers, women still could not vote in national elections. Advocates of women's rights hardly accepted their disenfranchisement quietly. The men and women who took up the feminist banner met stubborn, even brutal resistance, and resorted to militant tactics.

The Pankhursts and the Feminist Protest. Emmeline Pankhurst and numerous determined women, including her two daughters, guided and inspired the attack on British male supremacy. They voiced their demand for the right to vote by such actions as storming Parliament, chaining themselves to government buildings, and burning mailboxes. Opponents answered their protests by jailing and beating the feminists. When imprisoned women used hunger strikes to protest this treatment, authorities sometimes force-fed them.

The Climax of Democratization. Victory still eluded feminists when Europe entered the World War in 1914. The remarkable contribution of women to the four-year campaign against Britain's enemies convinced the men in Parliament that voting rights should be extended to the females now deemed worthy. In 1918, they granted the franchise to women thirty and over. The same law allowed all men twenty-one and over to vote, thus extending the right to previously excluded male groups, such as migrant workers. Legislation in 1928 lowered the voting age for women to twenty-one. British political democracy was complete.

THE IRISH QUESTION

A century before Britain ended the exclusion of women from national politics, the government abolished the laws denying all political rights to Catholics. The 1828 act that ended political discrimination against Catholics especially affected Ireland, since most people there were of that faith. This change meant that for the first time Irish citizens could vote on members of the House of Commons. The newly enfranchised region exhibited little appreciation, since the opportunity to send a few representatives to Parliament meant little to a people who considered themselves victims of centuries of English exploitation.

The sense of economic misuse at the hands of the English resulted especially from extremely high rents and other absentee-landlord practices that for many generations had kept Irish tenants impoverished. These feelings of abuse deepened in the 1800s when famines struck and caused thousands to starve while English leaders refused to change trade policies so that food prices would drop.

Gladstone opened his first administration in 1868 with an energetic effort to overcome Ireland's economic problems. Life improved somewhat, but discontent persisted. Irish immigrants to the United States supported a movement for "home rule" in Ireland. They wanted their native country to have its own separate institutions of government. The Finian movement in Ireland took up this cause too. Soon Charles Stewart Parnell joined the home-rule struggle as leader of the small Irish contingent in Commons. Even though these independence advocates gained a formidable ally when Gladstone sided with them in 1886, success still eluded them when his career ended a decade later. Other Liberals, however, resumed the campaign for home rule after the turn of the century.

The Conservative Party opposed this reform. The predominantly English and Protestant region of Ulster in Northern Ireland also staunchly resisted allowing Irish Catholics to govern the island. These forces stalled successive home-rule bills in Parliament until the outbreak of war in 1914 overwhelmed the legislature with other concerns.

Democracy in the European Heartland, 1870–1914

France restored republican government for a third time in 1870 and, thereafter, gradually empowered its citizenry through legislative institutions as had Britain. Italian unification efforts finally succeeded in the same year that the Third Republic emerged in France. Italy also inclined toward a parliamentary government that responded to popular forces. Democracy in these two West Central European states evolved somewhat differently than in Britain, but the tendency in Italy and France was toward self-government.

THE COLLAPSE OF THE SECOND FRENCH EMPIRE

Napoleon III instituted a largely successful program to improve life within France. His foreign adventures more often failed and eventually brought disaster. The Emperor expected a glorious military triumph when a diplomatic conflict brought about the Franco-Prussian War in 1870. Instead of emerging a hero, however, he quickly became a captive of the Prussians. Upon release, Napoleon fled into exile in Britain. A provisional government immediately took charge in France and resumed the war against Prussia. France still failed miserably in battle. A humiliating treaty required the surrender of important French territory (Alsace and part of Lorraine) to the new German Empire and the payment of a large indemnity as well.

THE REVOLT OF THE PARIS COMMUNE, 1871

When the French provisional government began to plead for peace, militant patriots in the capital attempted to continue the war with Germany. The French rebels also wanted a republic and considered provisional leaders to be against popular government. Like the zealots of 1792, these determined French republicans organized as the "Paris Commune" and prepared to fight against Germany and for representative government. The provisional administration further enraged the Commune by ordering citizens to accept a heavy financial burden, the payment of taxes and rents ignored during the war.

By February 1871, the provisional leaders had arranged the treaty with Germany and, in March, they sent troops to disarm the Paris Commune. Parisians resisted these forces and killed the commander of the military group. Adolphe Thiers, the head of the temporary national government, responded with a military assault on the city in May. More than a week of ferocious combat left thousands dead and the Commune smashed. Provisional forces then executed thousands without trial, took others to court and sentenced them to death, and imprisoned still more. In the turmoil of a losing war and brutal civil strife, a new French government had begun to emerge. The builders of this new political structure now faced a long if less bloody struggle.

EMERGENCE OF THE THIRD REPUBLIC IN FRANCE

The Germans had allowed the French to elect a representative assembly before the end of the Franco-Prussian War so that this provisional government could negotiate for peace. A minority of citizens, ardent republicans and a few socialists, shared the feelings of the Paris Commune. Most, however, desperately wanted to quit the war and restore a conservative and orderly system. As a result monarchists won a majority of the seats in the assembly.

When the representatives met to organize a new government, they established the Third Republic. This somewhat surprising development resulted from a royalist split. One faction demanded a king in the tradition of the *Ancien Régime*. The other longed for a monarch who would govern in the interest of the wealthy business class as Louis Philippe had (1830–1848).

The royalist stalemate enabled a republican minority to dominate the assembly and arrange a government similar to Britain's. In the structure established in 1875, a president formally ranked as head of state but had no more power than a British monarch. Legislation also provided for a powerful parliamentary body that included an upper house (Senate) and a Chamber of Deputies. All males had the right to vote for Chamber members, a degree of democracy not achieved in Britain until a decade later.

Once the system was in operation, the party, or more typically the coalition of parties that held a majority in the legislature, selected an executive body. This cabinet of ministers included a chief executive, the prime minister. These executives held positions of great authority, but the Chamber remained supreme.

With a multitude of parties rather than two clearly dominant ones as in Britain, French prime ministers often could not maintain a coalition and win majority votes for legislation. Third Republic ministries thus frequently collapsed to be replaced by a cabinet supported by a new combination of deputies. In this respect, French government differed markedly from Britain's in this era.

THE FRENCH REPUBLIC AT RISK

Executive instability troubled the new republic in France, with many other problems compounding the threat to popular government. Discoveries of corrupt financial practices involving Chamber members weakened public support for the system. This discontent with republican leadership strengthened the tendency of French citizens to long for popular authoritarianism. In the latter 1880s, a wide following developed for a famous military leader, General Georges Boulanger. The expectation grew that he would seize power. Instead, he left the country in 1889 and killed himself on his mistress's grave in Brussels in 1891.

THE DREYFUS AFFAIR—A TRIAL FOR THE THIRD REPUBLIC

Captain Alfred Dreyfus faced charges in 1894 that he had spied for Germany. The actual traitors in the officer corps needed a scapegoat. They selected Dreyfus as the victim, in part, because he was a Jew among peers who tended toward anti-Semitism. The conviction of this innocent officer and his imprisonment on Devil's Island provoked a crisis that threatened the existence of the republic more seriously than any of the previous problems.

Defenders of the captain fought for his release but also for the survival of the government because Dreyfus's opponents used his case in an anti-republican smear campaign. These anti-Dreyfusards—monarchists, anti-Semites, Catholic leaders, and conservative members of the armed forces—kept Dreyfus imprisoned and the Third Republic on trial for years. Dreyfusards could not win his pardon until 1899, and it required another seven years to have the conviction nullified. The Third Republic had suffered but triumphed.

LAWS OF THE NEW ORDER IN FRANCE

Victory for the Dreyfusards encouraged the republic's supporters to strengthen laws against one opposition faction, the Catholic clergy. Legislation passed in the 1880s had weakened church influence by restricting its organizations and establishing a system of free public education in which religious teaching was banned. New measures in the early 1900s further limited Catholic secular activities and decreed the full separation of church and state.

The government exhibited a more benign attitude toward the working class and legalized unions in 1884. The labor movement then regained momentum after years of weakened influence. Socialism also made progress in the Third Republic and increased the pressure on the republic for welfare-state programs. The forces of labor failed, however, to win the kind of public aid provided in Germany and Britain, thus continuing a government tradition of ignoring working class demands.

Labor adhered to its traditions too, as workers turned to direct-action tactics, especially after 1906. Strikes multiplied and syndicalism emerged with its demand for a general strike as an instrument of revolution. Obviously, the democratic nation-state, as it evolved in the Third Republic, had politically mobilized the masses, but not always in support of its government. The commitment of the masses to France had strengthened dramatically, however, as they would demonstrate in a great war that loomed before them.

DIVISIONS IN A UNITED ITALY, 1870–1914

Revolutionary France had given German and Italian nationalists lessons in the power and glory that a united and politically aroused people could achieve. In 1870, therefore, a new Kingdom of Italy anticipated such rewards for its generations of sacrifice. A multitude of social divisions prevented the realization of these dreams during the next forty-five years and raised questions about the reality of Italian nationhood.

Many leaders in the drive for unity had intended to establish a secular state true to the principles of liberalism. Catholic clerics firmly resisted; after unification, they continued to oppose the nation-state. Church opposition made real unity difficult to achieve, especially since peasants, the majority of the population, remained very loyal to the faith. The disaffection of peasants had further significance since they were concentrated regionally, in the south. Italy's religious, social, economic, and regional divisions remained a serious problem in 1914.

ITALY'S INFANT DEMOCRACY

Whatever the social divisions, Italian government embarked on an experiment in democracy that affected people all over the peninsula. Many of them remained more loyal to their separate states than to "Italy," but the nation had a common system of government with a structure much like that of the French Third Republic.

The king, Victor Emmanuel II, held a position equivalent to the French president. The Senate had a unique composition in that its members were either relatives of the king or his appointees. The Chamber of Deputies, however, was elected, as in France, although the electorate remained very small until 1912. In that year, Italy instituted universal male suffrage, a right established in France in 1848 and in Britain in 1884.

Since Italy's limited democracy gave little power to the lower classes before 1914, social legislation received even less attention than in France. Instead, leaders devoted their efforts to controlling militant labor and attracting a devoted following to the glorious cause of empire building, mostly in North Africa. The young Italian nation-state and even younger democracy did not succeed as well as Germany, Britain, and France in activating its citizenry, even when imperial adventures brought a measure of success. Despite their problems, by 1914 Italians had laid the foundations of a more fully modern nation-state.

MULTINATIONAL AND DYNASTIC NATIONAL STATES

The countries on Europe's eastern and western borders responded to the social forces that reshaped governments in Britain and the continental heartland after 1848. Leaders in these regions, for example, recognized the need to elicit mass political support. In various ways they utilized nationalism in their efforts to engage the citizenry. Yet these countries—Portugal, Spain, Austria, and Russia—did not become modern nation-states. Spain and Portugal had made only the first faltering steps toward sociopolitical modernity by the second decade of the twentieth century. Older political institutions remained even more firmly entrenched in the Austrian Hapsburg and Russian Romanov multinational empires.

The Iberian Kingdoms

Social divisions similar to Italy's hindered the progress of sociopolitical modernization in Portugal and Spain between the 1850s and 1914. These Iberian states differed from Italy, however, in that their advance toward modernity occurred at an even slower pace, leaving their kings or other authoritarian leaders with considerable power through most of this period. Still, both nations established self-governing institutions that had begun to have significance before 1914.

PORTUGAL—FROM AUTHORITARIAN MONARCHY TO REPUBLIC

Years of social strife ended in the early 1850s in Portugal, but rigidly authoritarian rulers established and maintained this civil peace. Governmental institutions structured much like Britain's constitutional monarchy gave the appearance if not the reality of modern self-government. Either the kings themselves or their appointed prime ministers reigned as dictators over the nation until 1908.

From 1908 to 1910, a new ruler, Manuel II, provided genuine constitutional monarchy. Then a revolt drove him from power and established a republic. The new government ended the civic power of the Catholic Church and enacted a truly liberal constitution. After the founding of this modern national structure, attacks from royalists and a still dissatisfied working class hindered its further development.

CONSTITUTIONAL MONARCHY IN SPAIN

Spain suffered the strain of civil conflicts almost continually from the 1830s to 1870s. The reign of the Bourbon king Alfonso XII (1874–1885) finally brought a period of political stability and a return to constitutional monarchy, a system tried intermittently earlier in the century.

The government issued a new constitution in 1876 that specified restrictions on royal authority, provided for an executive cabinet, and established a legislature consisting of a Senate and House of Representatives. Property limitations on the right to vote, however, excluded all but a tiny minority from participation in House elections.

This essentially royalist and aristocratic system remained intact under the king's son, Alphonso XIII, who held the throne until the monarchy fell in 1931. Leftist opposition to this government grew increasingly vicious from the 1890s onward, with assassination attempts, especially by anarchists, becoming almost commonplace. Alphonso XIII survived at least ten such attacks by these violent foes of authoritarian government, but he did not yield additional power to the citizens. Spain had moved toward modern self-government since 1874, but not very far.

The Establishment of Dual Monarchy in Austria

When the new German nation emerged in 1871, the Austrian Hapsburg Emperor was left in charge of an empire with a large German population in the north, but with many other national groups in his realm. The most powerful non-German nationality, the Magyars, gained a special position in 1867 and thereafter had control over internal affairs within their section of the empire. This Magyar region, known as Hungary, accepted the Hapsburg ruler as king. In Austria, the same person ruled as Emperor. The Hapsburg realm had evolved into a Dual Monarchy—Austria-Hungary.

MAGYARIZATION IN HUNGARY

Once the Magyars won rights for their nationality, they forcefully denied the same privileges to all other ethnic minorities (Croats, Romanians, Serbians, Slovaks) within the Hungarian kingdom. In fact, they vigorously pursued efforts to impose the Magyar language and culture on these groups, a policy of "Magyarization."

NATIONAL MINORITY DISCONTENT IN THE AUSTRIAN REGION

The German majority in the Austrian part of the empire followed a more tolerant minorities policy. Hapsburg leaders adamantly refused, however, to grant other groups the special status enjoyed by Magyars. The Czechs (a Slavic people) struggled valiantly but in vain for such a privileged position. Various South Slavic nationalities in Austria reacted in similar ways to life within a German-dominated state.

These South Slavs posed a special problem for Austria because people of their ethnic group had formed the nation-state of Serbia on the southern border of the Hapsburg realm. Many Austrian Slavs thus longed to separate from the empire and merge with Serbia. Imperial leaders would go no further than they had in 1867 to placate the political aspirations inspired by the age of the nation-state. The lack of a solution to this problem doomed the 700-year-old empire.

Romanov Russia—an Empire of 200 Nations

When Alexander II (r. 1855–1881) became tsar of Russia, he ruled the largest state in the world and governed an estimated population of 75,000,000. Unfortunately, his realm was less socially cohesive than any other country on the European continent.

This disunity resulted in part from the great cultural diversity of the tsar's subjects. The nationalities within imperial borders numbered from 120 to 200, depending on the defining criteria. The majority nationality, the Great Russians, had forged the empire over many centuries, and its ruling class was largely Russian. By the 1700s, the Great Russian tsars adopted a policy of sociocultural conversion or "Russification" of the minorities to better ensure the unity of the empire. No other European national minorities in the Modern era felt more pressure to surrender their culture to the majority.

Social fragmentation of another kind concerned Alexander II even more than did the national divisions. The new ruler believed, in fact, that the split between the masses of impoverished peasants and the small, highly privileged aristocracy might doom the empire if he did not effect sweeping social reforms.

THE PEASANT PROBLEM

The Emperor, the intelligentsia, and many aristocrats knew that the increasingly rapid industrialization of most European states had greatly increased their power and reduced the influence of Russia in international affairs. Concerned leaders also recognized the much greater prosperity of other European states. These Russians believed that the peasant problem prevented the technical and economic modernization so desperately needed by their nation.

Reform advocates saw conditions in rural Russia as a "problem" in part because the farmers (over eighty percent of the population) produced far too little to feed an urbanizing society. With their old-fashioned ways, peasants also could never grow a surplus to sell for industrial investment funds. Half these peasants, moreover, lived in the virtual slavery of serfdom and worked even less effectively than free farmers. Worst of all, without an end to serfdom and other steps to modernize agriculture, the empire could not find enough workers for a factory system.

By the mid-1800s, many Russians asserted that the horrible immorality of possessing serfs demanded action, regardless of economic considerations. This argument certainly intensified the demand for emancipation. So too did fears of massive serf revolt, although this belief influenced attitudes less than the economic and moral aspects of the peasant problem. The tsar himself warned aristocrats that the liberation of the serfs would come "from below," if others did not liberate them "from above."

EMANCIPATION OF THE SERFS, 1861

Alexander moved as swiftly as he could against the resistance of gentry elements who feared the economic loss and social disorder that emancipation of their serfs might bring. A decree of emancipation in 1861 freed all serfs, but responded to the economic concerns of their former masters by paying the aristocracy for the land and workers they surrendered.

This money for the nobles came from the government, but freed serfs had to repay the state in annual fees for forty-nine years. The heavy debt and the allotment of about twenty percent less land to the peasants than they had farmed as serfs greatly diminished the beneficial effects of freedom. Many reformers denounced emancipation and raised the cry for revolution. This opposition persisted even though Alexander II went on to complete a series of reforms that increased popular influence at the local level, modernized the military, and expanded educational opportunities.

The Burgeoning of Russia's Revolutionary Movements

Conditions during the reigns of Alexander II and his son, Alexander III (1881–1894), encouraged numerous movements committed to drastic reform or revolution. An unusually large force of political activists who were determined to destroy the old regime emerged.

THE POPULIST MOVEMENT

Revolutionary movements committed to the overthrow of the *ancien* social and political order began in Russia under the influence of alienated intellectuals (the intelligentsia) in the early 1800s. Until after the mid-1800s, these rebellious leaders had no popular following.

In the 1860s, such movements broadened somewhat as idealistic university students and others became committed to the theory that Russian peasants had a natural ability to create and live in a rural socialist society. The intellectuals who held this belief became known as "populists." In the 1870s, some of them attempted to go to the countryside and inspire revolution. The peasantry did not respond as the rebels anticipated. Rural Russians did not understand the intentions of these strange newcomers. In some cases, the peasants turned the populists over to the police.

TERROR AND REPRESSION

The populist movement fragmented after the failure of these early idealistic actions. Many populists remained convinced that the rural masses could be enlightened and peacefully transform Russia. Others insisted that, on the contrary, only violence could destroy the oppressive system. In 1881, members of a militant faction, the People's Will, succeeded in assassinating Tsar Alexander II. Brutal repression followed under the new Emperor, Alexander III, but during his reign the movements for reform or revolution continued to develop, usually working in secret or in exile.

RUSSIAN MARXISM

Georgi Plekhanov established the first Russian Marxist organization in 1883, the year Marx died. By the 1890s, Marxists had become a significant element among Russian revolutionaries. They met at Minsk in 1898 and established a communist party, the Social Democrats (SDs). They promoted their ideas through underground publications such as their journal *Iskra* (*The Spark*).

VLADIMIR LENIN—FOUNDER OF RADICAL RUSSIAN MARXISM

Vladimir Ilyich Ulyanov (1870–1924) took the pseudonym "Lenin" during his early years of revolutionary activity. Although he came from an economically comfortable family (his father was a school administrator), Lenin's older brother identified with the suffering masses. The government executed him in 1887 for involvement in a conspiracy to kill the tsar. This event perhaps contributed to Lenin's lifelong dedication to revolution, a commitment that led him to form a distinctly Russian and radical variety of Marxist communism.

Lenin plunged into antigovernment activities as a young law student. Despite expulsion and government restrictions on his admission when he tried to change schools, he finished his degree. He also continued in his radical ways. After several arrests and imprisonments, Lenin fled abroad. At various sites in Europe, Lenin worked with the Russian SDs to advance the cause of communism in his homeland.

Lenin devoted much of his energy to organizational work, political journalism, and writing. In 1902, he wrote one of his most famous works, *What Is to Be Done?* This booklet enthralled the radicals in his country. In its pages, Lenin poured out his hatred for "the shame and curse of Russia" and demanded destruction of the contemptible system. Lenin contended that this revolution required a small, secret group of dedicated rebels rather than a huge party operating in public. In his view, a highly professional band of revolutionaries could lead the small urban proletariat and the masses of poorest peasants to a sweeping communist victory over the old regime. The oppressed, he proclaimed, must not wait for the bourgeoisie to take over and have their day. No other leading Russian dissident offered such a radical revolutionary vision.

THE COMMUNIST SPLIT—BOLSHEVIKS AND MENSHEVIKS

Russian Marxists held their first international conference in 1903 in Brussels, Belgium. By this time, Lenin stood as the leading figure in the Social Democratic Party.

SDs often engaged in heated ideological battles when they convened. At Brussels, Lenin led a faction that demanded adoption of a radical approach to party operation—dictatorship of the leaders over the rank and file. He won the vote and subsequently called his group "Bolsheviks," Russian for "people of the majority." The opposing group that favored more democratic party procedures became known as "Mensheviks," or "people of the minority."

These two factions evolved into separate parties, with the Bolsheviks fighting for an elite-led armed workers' revolution with no intervening era of capitalism. Mensheviks held to a more moderate and traditional Marxist doctrine. From 1903 on, Lenin overshadowed other Russian Marxists as he built the more radical communist force that would achieve power in 1917.

THE SOCIALIST REVOLUTIONARIES

Although the Bolsheviks won a strong following among workers in cities (where the outcome of revolutionary struggles are usually determined), another group had the strongest following among the peasants. In 1902, populist elements organized the Socialist Revolutionary (SR) Party and became a frontline force in the battle to destroy autocracy.

The new party showed its populist spirit in its commitment to the creation of a peasant socialist society, rather than the urban industrial socialist society favored by Marxists. SRs varied in their preference for methods, but the party generally inclined toward terrorist tactics. They especially favored the assassination of government officials as a way to destroy the Russian system.

RUSSIAN LIBERALISM

In the 1880s, Russia lacked the usual conditions necessary for the emergence of liberalism—it had little industry and only a shadow of a middle class. The local government reform during the reign of Alexander II, however, produced a core of experienced officials and staff professionals who adopted views typical of nineteenth-century liberals. In 1905, this small but growing force established a political party, the Constitutional Democrats ("Kadets" or "KDs" in Russian). Liberals were ready to support thorough reform of the old order.

The Soldiers of the Russian Revolution on the Attack

Social critics committed to reform or revolution had an increasingly responsive public in Russia in the late 1800s and early 1900s. Harsh conditions in the factories and on the farms, advances in the educational level of workers, and the increased political awareness of peasants prepared the masses to respond to revolutionary leaders. The onset of rapid industrialization in these years had strongly influenced the development of these conditions favorable to the recruitment of masses of revolutionaries.

NICHOLAS II AND THE ACCELERATION OF INDUSTRIALIZATION

Rapid industrialization did not begin in Russia until the 1890s. The acceleration of economic modernization resulted mostly from government programs instituted in the reign of Nicholas II (1894–1917). This last tsar, a devoted father and well-intentioned ruler, lacked the talent to govern, especially in an autocracy. At first, however, he appointed and supported a few capable administrators. One of these officials, Sergei Witte, laid the foundations of modern industry during the tsar's first decade in power.

Although industry grew much more quickly under Witte's influence, the factory work force remained small (only about two to three percent of the population even in 1917). Surprisingly, however, urban labor became a significant revolutionary force by the early 1900s. This radical potential resulted from the proletariat's close ties to the revolutionary peasantry and the Russian practice of building huge factories. Many plants employed over 1,000, and, with the horrible conditions typical of industry at that time, they offered an excellent environment for radical organization.

THE REVOLUTION OF 1905

Russia went to war with Japan, an imperial rival to the "east," in 1904, and by the next year the tsar's forces had suffered a severe and humiliating defeat. The burden of war intensified the material suffering of the Russian masses and dramatized the horrible inadequacy of the country's leadership.

Bloody Sunday. Petersburg workers responded to this increased misery in January 1905 by joining a peaceful demonstration intended to communicate to the tsar their plea for factory reforms (such as an eight-hour workday) that would ease their hardships. Under the leadership of a priest, Father Gapon, 200,000 people marched to the tsar's palace in the heart of Petersburg. Slaughter ensued. Nicholas's troops killed about 500 people and injured thousands. The day became known as "Bloody Sunday."

The Emergence of Revolutionary Soviets. Widespread rebellion followed the massacre in Petersburg. The government promised a few reforms, but in September the tempo of strikes in the capital increased, mobs took over streets, and finally a general strike of historic dimensions occurred. Rebels in Petersburg, Moscow, and other large urban centers began to organize politically to deal with the government. They formed workers' councils ("soviets") that rivaled government authority in cities such as Petersburg.

The October Manifesto. Finally, Nicholas II pledged more drastic reforms. He declared his intentions in a decree ("manifesto") in October 1905. Partly as a result of the tsar's concessions, the revolt in the cities subsided by early 1906, but the rural revolution continued during that year.

The Fundamental Laws. The October Manifesto amounted to a declaration that Russia would be a constitutional monarchy. The government presented the details of a reformed system in the Fundamental Laws (May 6, 1906). Even Nicholas's concessions left him with sweeping authority to implement all laws, control the military and direct foreign relations, lead the Russian Orthodox Church, and assemble and disband the new legislature (Duma). He even had the right to nullify any laws passed by the Duma. But there *was* a Duma. No Russian national parliament, however limited, had ever existed before. The members of the Duma, moreover, would be elected.

The Last Years of the Russian Autocracy

The First Duma seemed to promise something much more than sham reform. Nearly all males gained the right to vote for assembly members, and they elected a strongly reformist legislature instead of the conservative one expected by the government.

SUBDUING THE DUMA

Duma members proposed giving government, church, and noble lands to the peasants, and writing a new constitution. Nicholas II would have none of this, and he dismissed the assembly. The government worked diligently to control the Second Duma elections and make certain that it was "Right."

When the new Duma met on March 5, 1907, it was even more reformist than the first. The new prime minister, Peter Stolypin, disbanded it. On the day of the Second Duma's dismissal, a new electoral law made reformist control over future assemblies impossible. Thus, when the Third Duma met in 1907, over 300 of the 442 representatives were government loyalists.

The Fourth Duma (1912–1917) had the same conservative outlook. Even though the Right dominated these assemblies, moderate liberals had considerable influence. These liberals of sorts were the Octobrists, a party that accepted the constitutional monarchy promised in the October Manifesto of 1905. They spoke for moderate reformist nobles and businesspeople.

The few Kadets in the Duma became the main critics of the government in the assembly. They represented professional people in particular but also had significant support among middle-class groups. Even some nobles backed the Kadets. Despite the Kadet presence, the Duma no longer had a real potential for sharing in control of Russia.

TERROR AND REPRESSION IN THE ERA OF STOLYPIN

Revolutionaries had no place in the Duma. They continued their assault on the system, however. Their terror killed 1,400 victims in 1906 and 3,000 in 1907. The rebels went after any and all government figures, with little regard for innocents who might die in their attacks. An explosion they set off in one of the prime minister's homes in 1906 took more than thirty lives. Two of Stolypin's children died in this blast, but not the prime minister.

"Stolypin's Neckties." Stolypin answered with both repression and reform. He established virtual martial law in part of Russia and set up courts there to carry out trials. These courts showed little concern for the law. Hastily conducted trials led to the execution of more than 1,000. (Russians began to refer to executioners' nooses as "Stolypin's neckties.") The repression generally accomplished its purpose, at least in the short run. For a time, terrorist acts diminished.

Conservative Land Reform. Stolypin's reform program focused especially on his effort to redistribute a portion of Russian land. He wanted to create a conservative body of private farmers who would support the system. This land policy did not really amount to a socioeconomic transformation in the interest of peasants, however. It could not, since the prime minister refused to take any land away from the nobles without full payment for the property. His primary goal was to preserve the old order.

The Assassination of Prime Minister Stolypin. An ironic climax came to the Stolypin era of repression. A police agent working under cover in a revolutionary group shot and killed the prime minister on September 14, 1911. Thereafter, much less effective officials struggled to hold a vast, diverse, and troubled empire together. Then, in 1914, the Romanov dynasty led divided Russia into a four-year multinational European war.

*M*ost *kingdoms in North and West Europe emerged during the Middle Ages as territorial states containing one dominant sociolinguistic group (nation). The masses in these states felt mostly local instead of national pride or loyalty until the 1800s. By the latter nineteenth century, nationalism enthralled many of these Europeans and inspired them to believe in their country's superiority to all other states. This spirit inspired the politically divided Italians and Germans to engage in a struggle to unify their nations that lasted through most of the 1800s. By the early 1870s, these movements succeeded in both Italy and Germany.*

The exceptional strength of nationalism and the growing numbers of people committed to this secular faith in the latter 1800s enabled nation-state leaders to mobilize human and other resources as never before. The involvement of the masses that made this fuller utilization of state potentials possible is the most outstanding trait of modern government.

Europeans increased citizen participation still more between the years 1848 and 1914 by the development of parliamentary and democratic or seemingly democratic institutions. Nation-states with systems that had the appearance but not the reality of citizen self-government were France under

Napoleon III and Germany under Bismarck and his successors. Britain, France, and Italy had more genuine parliamentary democracies.

The aspirations for nationhood and self-government that affected the European heartland so deeply after 1848 also influenced events in the continent's western borderland states. National self-consciousness intensified in Portugal and Spain but continued to lack the strength to unify these states to the extent that it did in Britain and France. Portuguese and Spanish leaders also responded relatively late and not very adequately to the longings of those citizens who wanted representative government. Even so, both countries had begun to provide self-governing institutions before 1914.

After the mid-1800s, nationalist and democratic forces threatened to shatter the Austrian and Russian multinational dictatorships in East Europe. The Hapsburg dynasty in Austria adjusted well enough to survive by yielding control of domestic affairs to the Magyars in their region, which remained within the empire but became the Kingdom of Hungary. The dominant Magyars and Austrian Germans then refused significant concessions to the many other national minorities within their territories, but the possibility of revolt and fragmentation still haunted imperial leaders.

The Romanov dynasty in the Russian Empire controlled a vast state inhabited by over 100 nationalities. The tsars belonged to the largest of these, the Great Russians, and found it unnecessary to compromise with any of the minorities even to the extent that the Hapsburgs did. (The dangerous potential of nationalism to the realm remained largely hidden until after 1914.) But the growth of revolutionary movements and a popular revolt that almost toppled the government forced the Romanovs to take action on other social and political issues. In response to these pressures, they freed the serfs and carried out other reforms that gave at least the semblance of self-government. As a result, revolutionary forces remained under control but highly dangerous.

Developments during this era of the nation-state brought the countries of this region to the zenith of their power, despite serious problems that persisted, especially in the Russia and Austrian Empires. Most of them used this exceptional strength to conquer vast realms in Asia and Africa between 1870 and 1914. Then, in the four years that followed, they unleashed their forces within Europe to wage a war on one another that wreaked more destruction than any in previous history.

Selected Readings

Chapman, Guy. *The Dreyfus Case: A Reassessment*. Westport, CT: Greenwood, 1979.

Kann, Robert A. *The Multinational Empire*. New York: Octagon, 1964.

Mack Smith, Denis. *Italy: A Modern History*. Rev. ed. Ann Arbor: University of Michigan Press, 1969.

May, A. J. *The Hapsburg Monarchy, 1867–1914*. Cambridge, MA: Harvard University Press, 1951.

Miller, Forrestt A. *Dmitri Miliutin and the Reform Era in Russia*. Nashville, TN: Vanderbilt University Press, 1968

Mosse, Werner E. *Alexander II and the Modernization of Russia*. Rev. ed. New York: Collier Books, 1962.

Palmer, Alan. *Bismarck*. London: Weidenfeld and Nicolson, 1976.

Pushkarev, Sergei. *The Emergence of Modern Russia, 1801–1917*. New York: Holt, Rinehart, and Winston, 1966.

Robinson, Gerold T. *Rural Russia Under the Old Regime*. Berkeley: University of California Press, 1967.

Simon, Walter M. *Germany: A Brief History*. New York: Random House, 1969.

Thompson, David. *Democracy in France since 1870*. 5th ed. Oxford: Oxford University Press, 1969.

Thompson, James M. *Louis Napoleon and the Second Empire*. New York: Noonday Press, 1955.

Yarmolinsky, Avrahm. *Road to Revolution: A Century of Russian Radicalism*. New York: Collier Books, 1962.

12

The New Imperialism and the Great War, 1870–1918

1857 The Great Rebellion (Sepoy Mutiny) against the British takes place in India

1859 French conquests in Indochina begin

1865 The Russians capture Tashkent in Central Asia

1876 Leopold II of Belgium establishes a colony in the African Congo

1882 Germany, Austria, and Italy form the Triple Alliance

1884 The Berlin Conference stipulates rules for colonizing Africa

1907 France, Russia, and Britain organize the Triple Entente

1908 Austrian annexation of Bosnia provokes a Balkan crisis

1912 Balkan wars begin and continue into 1913

1914 The assassination of Franz Ferdinand, heir to the Austrian throne, on June 28 leads to the outbreak of the First World War on July 28

1916 The battles of Verdun and the Somme occur

1917 The United States enters the war on the Allied side

1918 An armistice on November 11 ends the First World War

1919 Germany signs the Treaty of Versailles, accepting peace terms prescribed by the Allied Powers (June 28)

*E*urope's lengthy process of modernization climaxed in the late 1800s and early 1900s. The countries of this region achieved peak strength with the emergence of a system of nation-states empowered by industrial economies, well-organized central governments, massive military forces, and broad citizen involvement in public affairs. Whatever great achievements other cultures of the world had realized by this time, these circumstances meant that none had the power of Modern Europe in the 1870s.

During the latter 1800s and early 1900s, Europeans used their exceptional strength to seize control of much of the rest of the world. They conquered virtually the entire African continent, large Asian territories, and islands scattered throughout the Pacific, completing most of this assault on the globe within thirty years. In addition to territories taken in these forced annexations, Europeans subordinated other areas, including vast portions of China and the Middle East, by political and economic arrangements extorted under threat. The United States joined the Europeans in this wave of imperial expansion in Asia and similarly encroached on Caribbean islands and Central America.

The imperial onslaught slowed somewhat during the early 1900s. Crises then began to erupt in southeastern Europe, in the Balkan Peninsula. Imperial rivalries, struggles to maintain or increase state power, fiery nationalist attitudes, the tensions between two competing alliances, and a raging arms race generated these conflicts and led finally to a cataclysmic war among the Europeans in 1914.

The four years of carnage that followed this outbreak drastically altered the history of Modern Europe. Even before the war ended, the German imperial government and the Austrian and Russian Empires collapsed. Then, the victorious powers gathered after the fighting stopped and attempted to arrange an enduring structure of peace. After negotiating for months, they finally completed treaties to implement the peace plans they had conceived. And they hoped. In most respects, they longed in vain for the success of their peacemaking efforts, as the aftershocks of the war continued to reshape events in ways they could neither anticipate nor control.

THE NEW IMPERIALISM

In the late 1400s and early 1500s, the Europeans' gunboat-era military technology and centralized monarchical states enabled them to conquer the Americas and parts of Africa and Asia. Europe's aristocrats and merchants expected these imperial ventures to bring highly profitable products from the colonies. Royal governments believed the wealth that poured in would make them powerful. The maturation of the industrial economy and the modern nation-state system in the latter 1800s led to a new era of imperialism with related but significantly different causes and effects.

The Rebirth of the European Imperial Spirit

European encroachments on the outside world begun in the Early Modern era never completely stopped, but aggression against other societies waned for about a century before the 1870s. A renewed, more forceful, and more successful imperial expansion began in the latter 1800s. Several trends converged to inspire this second phase of global conquest.

THE PROFIT MOTIVE FOR EMPIRE

Britain, Belgium, the Netherlands, Germany, and France had well-developed industrial systems by the 1870s, and economic modernization had begun in other European states. Many businesspeople somewhat unreasonably feared that natural resources and markets for products might soon become insufficient to sustain economic growth as Europe became mostly industrialized. The belief that their nations must acquire territories that contained both essential raw materials and captive customers for factory products led some industrialists to campaign for imperial conquests.

Large investment firms increasingly controlled European industrial enterprises and economic development during these years. As the Modern economic system began to mature, financiers and individual investors had a strengthening desire for profitable ventures that Europe seemed too small to satisfy. There was a world of financial opportunity abroad.

THE NATIONALIST PASSION FOR COLONIES

Government leaders, such as Bismarck, sometimes at first opposed this imperialist urge from business and other quarters, then yielded. The susceptibility of government officials to these demands resulted in part from the need of the now maturing nation-state system to win and sustain the support of the business community and other segments of the middle class that shared this outlook. Without the favor of these richest, most educated, and most politically active social forces, even the authoritarian nations would suffer reduced strength. The democratic states had to follow the will of such influential pressure groups even more energetically.

Nor were all governments resistant. The new nationalism of this era burned in the hearts of political leaders even as it inflamed the souls of businesspeople, intellectuals, religious leaders, and many other citizens. Convinced of the superiority of their national cultures and the states that embodied them, enthralled leaders and masses stood ready to join in a common imperial adventure and prove their greatness by conquering and colonizing foreign lands.

THE STRUGGLE FOR STRATEGIC SUPREMACY

The sociopolitical modernization of Europe entered its final stage when the French Revolution began in 1789. For the next twenty-five years, the European state structure underwent rapid change as France conquered, politically transformed, then lost most of the continent. Conservative European powers kept the region's territorial organization stable from 1815 to 1848, but liberal and nationalist forces fiercely besieged the system. Italian and German unification movements escalated this war against the old state order in the 1850s and by 1871 had resulted in a drastic revision of the political map of the continental heartland.

The eighty years of transformation that began in 1789 had yielded a much simplified system of relatively large states. The European nations could not continue traditional diplomatic relationships, since Italy and Germany had completed their unification movements and absorbed many older principalities. The quest for a new balance of power in an age of militant nationalism led to a struggle for supremacy among the states of Europe. This competition for superiority required secure supplies of the materials needed to build and maintain economic and military strength. Each European state also wanted to ensure its potential to field a larger army and conduct more successful naval operations than any rival.

For many Europeans, a global empire seemed an effective way to help meet these strategic needs. They could take lands that had manpower for their armies and vital raw materials. Their military forces also could establish the bases necessary to expand and project the nation's power.

THE DESIRE TO SUBDUE PRESUMED INFERIORS

Social Darwinism and racism exerted a powerful influence on Europeans by the latter 1800s and fed their passion for empire. Distortions of Darwin's theories encouraged the commitment to a global struggle among nations to prove their superiority—the "fittest" state would triumph over the inferior people it went out to conquer and would surpass its European rivals in imperial competition. Social Darwinism and other intellectual currents of the era also fostered racism, the belief that certain races are innately superior. Certain of the supremacy of their white race (or German or British race, as some thought), European racists proclaimed it their duty to send the best of their breed to subdue lower humans abroad.

Other Europeans who did not exhibit such overt Darwinist or racist attitudes simply became convinced that their civilization surpassed all others materially, morally, and spiritually, an achievement that obligated them to "uplift" backward people elsewhere. They supported the extension of European power, that is, in order to take to these unfortunates the comforts, humane values, and faith of a superior civilization. Imperialist impulses of this kind persisted even when the intended recipients of the new ways resisted and had to be forcefully conquered.

The Completion of Europe's Global Conquest

When the European imperial surge intensified in the 1800s, it struck with greatest force in the regions where Europeans previously had made only small incursions—Asia, the islands of the Pacific, and Africa.

THE BRITISH IN INDIA

Portugal led the Early Modern imperial attack on India, but British private-enterprise interests, organized as the East India Company, moved in and dominated the continent by the late 1700s. Company control depended on the loyalty of native troops (*sepoys*) who policed the Indian territories

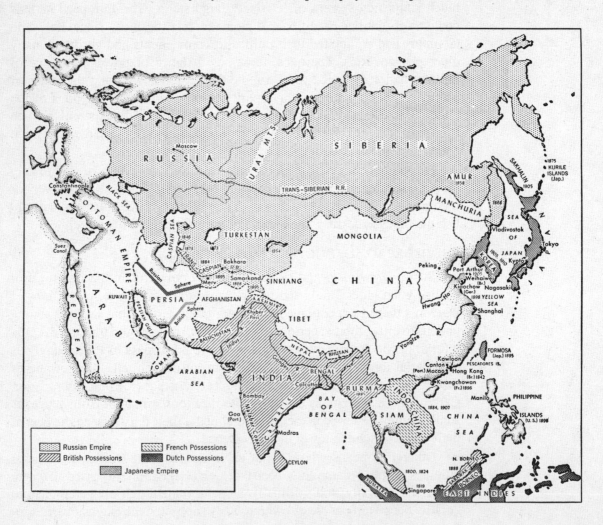

Fig. 12.1   Imperialism in Asia to 1914

exploited by the British. In the Great Rebellion of 1857–1858 (known to the British as the "Sepoy Mutiny"), these native armies joined in an attempt to overthrow the colonial company. Superior imperial forces subdued the rebels and brutally punished them. Thereafter, the British government ended the reign of the company and took direct control of the colonies in India.

During the late 1800s and early 1900s, a few thousand British administrators and about half a million native civil servants erected a colonial bureaucracy that governed about two-thirds of the huge subcontinent and indirectly influenced public affairs in the rest of India. A subjugated population of 200 to 300 million both benefited and suffered from policies over which they had no control.

British rule, for example, accelerated the development of modern government, economic, and medical practices. These changes soon improved the health and enhanced the civil security of small numbers of people. Imperial authorities also attempted to end certain traditional practices such as *suttee*, the burning of living wives along with the bodies of husbands who predeceased them. Potential victims of *suttee* might have appreciated this alteration of custom, but assaults on tradition generally provoked a negative reaction. British racism and exploitative economic practices probably incensed Indians even more. The resultant sense of oppression inspired an Indian nationalist movement by the latter 1800s, and it soon gained massive support.

RUSSIAN AND FRENCH ANNEXATIONS IN ASIA

A Russian Orthodox Christian chaplain, with cross raised high, rushed into Tashkent in the vanguard of warriors who conquered the city in June 1865. They had captured this Muslim center for Tsar Alexander II, his first city in a large Central Asian region known then as Western Turkistan. Within a decade, the Russian Empire absorbed this entire Muslim Turkic territory.

By 1875, Russia also had obtained additional holdings east of Central Asia. Under simultaneous pressure from Britain, France, and Russia, China signed treaties in 1858 and 1860 that surrendered territory to the tsar. Russia then ceded a chain of small Pacific islands to Japan in return for the southern half of Sakhalin, a large island near the southeastern Russian coast. Imperial expansion under Alexander II climaxed a long history of conflict between the Russians and the Turkic and Asian peoples of this region. The imperial invaders had loudly proclaimed their religious motives. They probably cared mostly about profits and border security. Regardless of the Russians' intentions, life in the region changed very little by 1914.

As Alexander II expanded his empire into North Asia, Napoleon III secured a new colonial realm for France in the south. A show of force by his navy at Saigon, a coastal city on the peninsula of Indochina, signaled the beginning of a French imperial campaign in that region in 1859. The

Emperor's forces ruled all of Indochina ten years later. Imperial agents of the Second Empire and the Third Republic made a more concerted effort to convert native Asians to the European way of life than did the Russians or British. The French, however, treated the Indochinese as conquered and inferior people. Anticolonial nationalist movements soon emerged there, as they had in India.

CHINA'S LOSS OF SOVEREIGNTY AND THE RISE OF JAPAN

Business activities conducted by the British East India Company in the early 1800s included taking opium into China to sell. The rulers of China tried to stop this trade, and the British countered with military force. Britain won these "Opium Wars" (1839–1842) and wrung a partial surrender of sovereignty from China. The victors extorted the right to continue their opium business, set tariffs on British goods sold in China, and apply British rather than Chinese law to British citizens in China.

Subsequently, France, Russia, and the United States further humbled China by taking the same tariff privileges and legal rights for their citizens. The Japanese probably would have suffered a similar reduction of sovereignty if they had not "westernized" their economic and military institutions sufficiently to fend off the Europeans and Americans. Japan's advance in power even enabled this Asian nation to begin its own empire building in the region and to defeat a European giant in the Russo-Japanese War (1904–1905).

The Colonization of Africa

In 1800, a little over 300 years after the Portuguese and Spanish first began taking small coastal colonies in Africa, the Europeans still held very little of the continent and knew almost nothing about its social or physical geography. They gradually increased the tempo of their learning and conquests during the next seventy years and then joined a competitive rush to take the entire continent.

ONSET OF THE NEW IMPERIALISM IN AFRICA

Dutch imperialists in the Early Modern period secured a large colony, the Cape of Good Hope, on the southern tip of Africa. In 1806, the British acquired Cape Town, a port in this region, and began to expand inland. Dutch settlers ("Boers") chafed under the control of the new imperialists, especially after the British decreed an end to slavery in 1834. Boers migrated inland to escape the British (the "Great Trek" of 1835–1837); there they organized two republics. Conflicts persisted between the old and new European intruders. Superior British force eventually settled these differences in the brutal Boer War (1899–1902).

A French invasion that began on the coast of North Africa in Algeria in 1830 brought an even more hostile reaction than Britain faced in the south

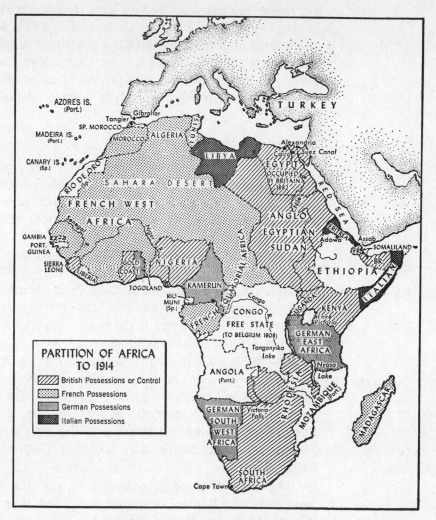

Fig. 12.2   The Partition of Africa to 1914

at this time. Thirty years of difficult struggle with the Algerian Muslims followed before France gained a sure hold on the region's coastal fringe. Napoleon III's Suez Canal project, completed in 1869, indicated the broader African imperial interests of the French. Britain, however, immediately challenged the movement of France into the northwest corner of the continent and even took control of the Canal (1872). Franco-British rivalry intensified dangerously in the area thereafter.

As British and French forces pressed into North and South Africa, Belgian King Leopold II (r. 1865–1909) plunged in to take the heart of the continent as his personal possession. Dr. David Livingstone, a medical doctor and missionary from Britain, had entered Central Africa in 1841. As a device to entice readers, the New York *Herald* sent H. M. Stanley to search for Dr. Livingstone, a task he completed in 1871. Stanley then began to promote ventures in the Congo River territories he had explored. By 1876, Stanley had enticed Leopold to take a large area south of the Congo and develop rubber plantations as a private business activity. France at once charged in to claim territory north of the river. A massive imperial assault had begun.

THE FALL OF AFRICA

Leopold's new Central African realm was a personal colony, not a Belgian possession. It contained lands also claimed by France, Britain, Portugal, and Germany. European leaders decided to hold a conference to resolve these differences and regulate the colonization of sub-Saharan Africa.

The Berlin Conference of 1884. In their discussions at Berlin, the participants agreed that Leopold's African colony belonged to him personally and would not be controlled by Belgium or any other state. The diplomats also defined mutually acceptable perimeters for Leopold's personal colony. The conferees declared that in the future, imperial states could claim only the areas that they actually occupied.

The Belgian Congo. After the Berlin Conference, Leopold continued as before to operate his rubber plantations with barbaric forced-labor methods. Reports on conditions in his "Congo Free State" filtered out over the years and led to an international investigation. The continuing critical attention of the world community to the king's project finally led his government to take charge of the colony in 1908. It became known as the Belgian Congo.

The Final Conquests in South Africa. The frantic land-grab that precipitated the Berlin Conference continued after its adjournment. The British colonized northward from the Cape until they encountered territories taken by the Germans, Portuguese, and Belgians.

The British and French Triumph over North Africa. North of the band formed by German East Africa, the Belgian Congo, and Portuguese Angola, Britain took two more colonies (Kenya and Uganda) and forced Egypt and the Sudan into subordination as "protectorates." Most of East Africa thus belonged to the British. France brought almost all of the western two-thirds of the continent into its empire and would have continued eastward to the Red Sea if not blocked by Britain.

The Lesser Powers in the North. Spain, Germany, and Italy held relatively small territories in North Africa. The Italians had possessed nothing at all until 1911 when they conquered Tripoli (which they renamed Libya). After the fall of Tripoli, only Ethiopia in East Africa and Liberia on the west coast remained independent. The Ethiopians remained free after defeating Italian invaders in 1896. The imperialists left Liberia, a state established for freed slaves from the United States, untouched. The Europeans had conquered most of the world by 1914. Then they began to conquer themselves.

THE FIRST WORLD WAR

In the late 1800s and early 1900s, Europeans glorified violent struggle and believed it to be right for "superior" nations to dominate inferior peoples. These attitudes had encouraged the new imperialism, and empire building strengthened such beliefs still more. Most of the societies in which this mood prevailed had well-developed industrial economies that greatly increased their potential for destructive combat, as their imperial assault on the world had proved. These circumstances alone made the early 1900s dangerous times.

**The Origins
of Europe's
"Great War"**

Conditions in Europe in the early 1900s raised the probability of military conflict but did not make a highly destructive four-year conflagration among the leading continental powers inevitable. Such a large-scale European struggle came about especially as a result of intense nationalism and the influence of two rival alliance systems.

NATIONALISM AND THE AUSTRO-RUSSIAN CONFLICT

Militant nationalism affected circumstances in Southeast Europe in a particularly dangerous way. Germanic Hapsburgs had created the Austro-Hungarian Dual Monarchy in 1867 to placate Magyar nationalists. Austrian leaders believed, however, that similar concessions to any of the numerous other nationalities within the empire would foment independence movements and shatter the state. South Slavs under Austrian power posed the gravest threat, since Serbia stood on the southern border of the empire as a model of the Slavic nation-state they wanted to form.

Russian support for the national ambitions of the Slav minority in Austria magnified the threat beyond calculation. The Tsarist Empire created an especially explosive problem simply by standing as a great power behind the South Slav nationalist movement. Russia further elevated the risk to Austria by the evident motive for this pro-Slav policy. Romanov officials not only expected to bring about the liberation of ethnically related South Slavs, the Russian leaders planned to dominate the Balkan Slavs and thereby gain supremacy in the region south of Austria. Such an outcome would be a doubly severe blow to the Hapsburgs.

Fervent nationalism had a critical influence on the Austro-Russian conflict in the Balkans, and this clash brought war between these powers in 1914. The extremely militant nationalist spirit that had captivated the Germans, French, British, and Italians since 1848 ensured that the war would not remain a small East European affair.

DEFENSIVE ALLIANCES AS AN INCITEMENT TO WAR

The combination of Russian might and South Slav nationalism posed a threat that the Hapsburgs alone could not counter. But Austria had a powerful ally—Germany. When the German Empire emerged in 1871 it was at once the strongest nation on the European continent. Since Imperial Chancellor Bismarck had achieved the place for Germany that he wanted, he set out to protect the nation's interests by setting up an intricate system of alliances designed to guard against France in particular.

The League of Three Emperors. While he was in power, Bismarck managed to keep both Austria and Russia tied to Germany, thus denying France a strong ally on the continent. He achieved this result through most of the 1870s by organizing the League of Three Emperors, a loose association of Germany, Austria, and Russia. Conflicts between the Romanov and Hapsburg Empires caused Russia to bolt from the League in 1878, but Bismarck found another way to prevent a Franco-Russian association.

The Dual Alliance. German interests required above all the maintenance of ties to Austria. Bismarck, therefore, arranged a secret Dual Alliance with the Hapsburg Empire in 1879. The two powers pledged to fight together against Russia if that country attacked either Germany or Austria.

The Triple Alliance. In 1882, Italy joined the Austro-German diplomatic-structure, creating the Triple Alliance. The secrecy of these agreements and skillful diplomatic maneuvers enabled Bismarck to keep Germany and Russia on very friendly terms throughout the 1880s, even though the Alliance designated the Russians as potential enemies. The security structure changed quickly and dangerously, however, after Bismarck's retirement in 1890.

A Franco-Russian Alliance. Bismarck's successor, Leo von Caprivi, had no interest in continuing friendly relations between Germany and Russia. He allowed the understandings with the Russians to lapse, and in 1894, the tsarist government formed an alliance with France. From the 1890s onward, Germany used the Dual Alliance to promote aggressive Austrian moves rather than restrain them. As a result, Austria's treatment of Russia became more reckless.

The Triple Entente. The evolving power structure on the continent posed serious problems for Britain. Imperial rivalries had kept the British in conflict with the Russians and French, but Germany's rapidly growing military power and its great advances in international trade eventually concerned Britain above all else. In 1904, therefore, the French and British arranged the "Entente Cordiale," a mutual defense understanding but not technically an alliance. These two nations formed similar ties to Russia in 1907 and, thus, created the Triple Entente. The great powers of Europe were now divided into two alliances. This diplomatic structure almost guaranteed that if any nation plunged into the abyss of war, all the rest would follow.

A SEASON OF CRISES—THE IMMEDIATE CAUSES OF WAR

A series of rapidly developing international crises encouraged the formation of alliances designed to yield greater security for the member states. As clashes continued, they affected the relationships within and interactions between the rival groups—the alliances tightened and the two sides became more belligerent.

The Moroccan Crises. France's African empire included most of Morocco on the northwest coast. Emperor William II of Germany traveled to Tangier, Morocco, in 1905 and pronounced his commitment to Moroccan independence from France. He intended to demonstrate that in such a confrontation, the French could not count on support from Britain, their partner in the new Entente. An international conference in Algeciras, Spain, in 1906 proved the contrary to be true. Britain not only fully supported France's right to control Morocco but also began to plan ways to cooperate militarily if war with Germany erupted. A similar Franco-German clash over Morocco in 1911 further strengthened the Entente's military relationship and increased its hostility toward the Triple Alliance.

The "Balkan Powder Keg." The international conflicts that precipitated the Great War in 1914 occurred on the Balkan Peninsula in Southeast Europe. The region thus earned its description as the "Balkan Powder Keg." The components in this "bomb" included: the struggle of small states (Greece, Serbia, Bulgaria, and Montenegro) to expand their power or territory at the expense of one another, Austria, or Turkey; the Ottoman Turks' fight to keep as much of the Balkans as possible; Russia's attempts to increase its influence in the region; and Austria's battle to preserve itself against the threats of Russian and nationalist forces in the Balkans.

The Bosnian Crisis. The first Balkan crisis began with Austria's abrupt annexation of Bosnia-Herzegovina in 1908, a move intended to block Turkish or Serbian ambitions in the area. Serbia could do nothing since Russia, weakened by a recent war with Japan and the Revolution of 1905, offered no assistance. German forces, however, stood ready to fight for Austria if necessary, and the Hapsburg venture succeeded. This outcome made Austria even less cautious and the empire's enemies more hostile.

The Balkan Wars. After four years of relative quiet in Southeast Europe, two Balkan wars flared up in quick succession. The first came in 1912 as Serbia, Greece, Bulgaria, and Montenegro combined forces to win lands from Turkey. Within a month after fighting stopped, strife over the division of spoils brought war between Bulgaria and its allies. Bulgaria lost. Austrian threats, however, kept the Serbs from benefiting from this victory as they wanted. Serbia viewed this outcome as another affront, and the Balkans became still more explosive.

MILITARISM AND THE ADVANCE TOWARD WAR

During the decades before the battles began in 1914, Europeans adored the idea of military power as never before in their history. This enchantment derived in part from the emotional pleasure of watching military display and knowing that massive forces supported the country's interests. Experience also suggested practical reasons for this devotion to military power. Wars since the mid-1800s usually had seemed quick and decisive affairs that brought desired results at a relatively low cost in funds and lives.

Confidence in the great value of military power led the European states to enter an arms race that produced the largest and most lethally equipped forces ever. The size and industrial-age equipment of these military forces necessitated careful planning for their mobilization; alliance commitments added other complexities to strategic designs. German leaders, for example, had to prepare for a two-front war. They assumed the necessity of defeating a fast-moving France first and then turning all their forces against Russia.

These circumstances resulted in intricate and rigid strategies and mobilization procedures that would be difficult to alter once started. Even if the purpose of this martial competition was primarily defensive, this combination of circumstances intensified national fears and hatreds and magnified every crisis.

The Conflagration, 1914–1918

The Balkan crisis that led to the First World War began on June 28, 1914. On that day, in Sarajevo, Bosnia, an assassin killed Archduke Franz Ferdinand, heir to the Austrian throne. Austria blamed Serbian-inspired Slav nationalists for this terrorist act and made demands on Serbia designed to provide an excuse for war. The Hapsburg government had decided to smash the Slav threat forever, and Germany once more promised to back its Austrian ally. Russia could not fail its South Slav associates again and assured support to Serbia. Exactly one month later, the Great War began in a chain reaction of mobilizations.

Austria's declaration of war on Serbia, July 28, 1914, prompted Russia to order the movement of its armies toward the borders of Austria and Germany on July 29. Two days later, Germany demanded that France announce its intentions and sent a sharp warning that Russia must stop mobilization. Since the tsarist government ignored this message, Germany declared war on Russia on August 1.

On the same day that Germany and Russia went to war, French forces began to mobilize. Germany launched its strike through Belgium toward France two days later. The British proclaimed that an 1829 treaty required them to defend neutral Belgium and entered the war against Germany on August 4. The war plans of all these combatants assumed swift victories and thus a short war. The projections proved tragically wrong.

THE WARTIME ALLIANCES

When the Triple Alliance and Entente powers unleashed war, Italy at first remained neutral. Germany and Austria found other allies, however. Turkey joined them in November 1914. Then Bulgaria allied with Germany and Austria the following year. These four "Central Powers," grouped together in mid-continent, had the strategic advantage of relative ease in coordinating military operations. A more significant disadvantage was the draining effect of a two-front war.

On the Western Front where the outcome of the war was decided, Germany faced three of the "Allied Powers"—France, Britain, and, after May 1915, Italy. The United States became an "Associated Power" on the Allied side in 1917. Other Allied and Associated Powers by 1917 included Romania, Greece, Portugal, and many Latin American states. On the Eastern Front, Russia bore the brunt of the fighting for the Allies against the Central Powers.

THE WESTERN FRONT

Within a few weeks after the invasion of France, the failure of the German offensive on the Western Front became apparent. The forces there then settled down to a grinding stalemate war with little movement and much slaughter. The opposing armies dug a series of trenches along lines that stretched for about 500 miles through eastern France. They faced each other across a "no-man's-land" of shell-churned soil over which lay coils of heavy barbed wire. Machine guns, the "queens of the trenches," positioned to cover the lines with cross fire made assaults extremely deadly. Heavy-artillery barrages, the weather, and rats made the ditches a virtual hell on earth. New military technology such as poison gas, tanks, and airplanes compounded the horrors of trench warfare.

The Battle of Verdun. Two of the most important battles on the Western Front illustrate the nature and consequences of combat under these conditions. After vicious and costly fighting throughout 1915 with virtually no movement of battle lines, the German command decided in 1916 on an attack at Verdun designed more to kill French troops than to break through. Almost a year of assaults "bled France" as intended, taking nearly 350,000 lives. But the Germans bled themselves too. They lost almost the same number.

The Battle of the Somme. As the battle raged at Verdun, Britain launched an offensive on the Somme River; 70,000 British soldiers died before the first one reached German lines. A Canadian battalion lost 90 percent of its 800 men on its first day in combat. The Allies never advanced more than seven miles, won nothing of importance, and lost over 600,000 lives in the six-month Somme campaign. Germany lost almost 700,000.

THE EASTERN FRONT

On the Eastern Front the forces fought a more mobile war. During the first year, however, results differed little from those in the west—heavy losses and no clear victory emerging in the struggle between Russian and Austro-German forces. By 1916, however, the tide seemed to turn in favor of the Germans (who carried the brunt of the Triple Alliance effort). As the Russian economy and then its sociopolitical order began to collapse in 1917, it appeared that Germany soon might be free to move all its troops to the Western Front.

THE SEA WAR

Britain ruled the surface of the seas almost from the beginning of the war and used this control to blockade the Central Powers. Eventually,

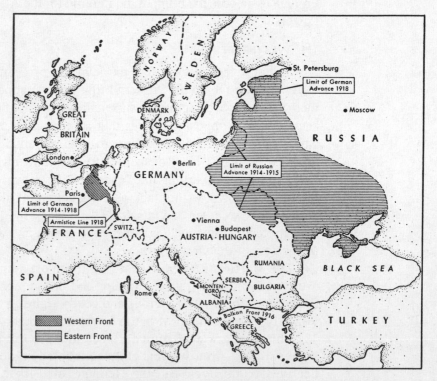

Fig. 12.3   World War I, the Western Front, 1914–1918

shortages of raw materials and food seriously hampered the war effort and caused real hunger. German submarines dominated beneath the sea's surface and had the potential to blockade Britain but only by unrestricted war on all ships, including the vessels of neutrals such as the United States. Germany had long hesitated to allow its submarines to conduct this kind of war at sea since attacks on the ships of noncombatant nations almost certainly would cause the Americans to declare war on the Central Powers. But as prospects for victory for Germany improved in 1916–1917 and the effects of war began to exhaust the German people, unrestricted submarine warfare began.

THE ENTRY OF THE UNITED STATES

The United States declared war on the Central Powers in April 1917 and the conflict became "a moral crusade," reflecting President Woodrow Wilson's attitudes toward this military campaign. Wilson depicted the conflict as a struggle for democracy, "freedom of the seas," national self-determination, and a world governed by honest and open diplomacy under the guidance of a "League of Nations." He summed up such ideals in his "Fourteen Points," and promised that this conflict would be a "war to end all wars" and "make the world safe for democracy."

RUSSIAN DEFEAT ON THE EASTERN FRONT

A revolution in Russia in March 1917 replaced the autocracy with a government that seemed headed toward parliamentary democracy. The new leaders, however, had little popular support and no other foundations for power. They erred also in staying in a war no longer tolerable to most Russians. Thus a second upheaval came in November 1917 and brought to power a government committed to withdrawal from the war. Russia surrendered in early 1918.

ALLIED VICTORY AND THE ARMISTICE

Even with no war on the Eastern Front, Germany could not win against the combined forces of the western Allied Powers. A German offensive in the spring and summer of 1918 stopped fifty miles from Paris, and then an Allied counterattack began. This offensive led to victory by autumn. On November 11, 1918, Germany signed the armistice that ended the war.

The Peace of Paris and the Aftermath of War

President Wilson went to Paris to join in the peace negotiations as head of his nation's delegation. Wilson took this unprecedented step for a president of the United States because he intended to ensure that his peace goals would be embodied in the treaties. French Premier Georges Clemenceau, however, represented a nation determined to punish the defeated Germans. Wilson's idealistic plans stood in the way of such a punitive treaty. The

Prime Minister of Britain, David Lloyd George, came to Paris with intentions more compatible with Clemenceau's than Wilson's.

THE TREATY OF VERSAILLES

The Peace of Paris that emerged resulted in five documents, beginning with the most important, the Treaty of Versailles with Germany, signed June 28, 1919. This settlement, and those with the other Central Powers, embodied many elements that Wilson believed necessary. But the attitudes of the French and British, as well as other problems, prevented the full realization of Wilson's goals. The intermingling of national groups across East Europe, for example, prevented consistent application of his idea of national self-determination.

The extent to which Wilson succeeded can be measured in part by a review of the main provisions of the Treaty of Versailles. Wilson wanted a peace with as little punishment in it as possible; that vindictive spirit was reduced by his efforts but not removed. The treaty arranged for the victors to occupy the industrially and strategically valuable German Rhineland for fifteen years. Altogether, the settlement caused Germany to lose territory containing one-tenth of its people. In addition, the German military was to operate without a general staff and no more than 100,000 troops. Germany was barred from the new League of Nations, and imperial colonies had to be surrendered to victor and League control.

Versailles Treaty Article 231 dealt the Germans an especially severe blow. They had to accept a clause declaring German responsibility for all the war destruction. Germany also had to promise to pay for this destruction ("reparations"). When the German delegation objected to these terms, the Allied Powers ordered them to accept. Embittered German nationalists soon began to attack this humiliating, "dictated" treaty. They also denounced their government for accepting it. Whatever Wilson's intentions, the Germans certainly felt punished.

THE TREATIES WITH GERMANY'S ALLIES

By the time the diplomats finished their work, nationalist forces had succeeding in shattering the Hapsburg Empire. The Allied Powers required Austria, now one-fourth its former size, to sign the Treaty of St. Germain and required the new state of Hungary to accept the Treaty of Trianon. These documents contained punishing and restrictive provisions similar to those in the Treaty of Versailles. Turkey and Bulgaria received similar treatment.

THE IMMEDIATE CONSEQUENCES OF THE GREAT WAR

When the First World War ended, it had taken about 110 million lives and cost almost $400 billion. Russian losses were especially great. In fact, the death, destruction, and expense suffered by the Romanov Empire made its survival impossible. The collapse of tsarist Russia then led to the emergence of Soviet Russia as the first Communist state, while enabling Poland, Lithuania, Latvia, Estonia, and Finland to become independent countries.

The war shattered a second large state—the Austrian Empire. South Slav minorities thus were freed to merge, forming the new state of Yugoslavia. The Czech minority also broke from Austria and established their own nation, Czechoslovakia. An old dynastic state had disappeared from Central Europe. The region had assumed the nation-state structure that would endure until the 1990s.

Modern governmental and economic systems provided late nineteenth-century Europeans extraordinary power. The mood of the times—elitist, racist, militarist, aggressively nationalist—helped to inspire the use of this strength in a new surge of imperialism, beginning in the 1870s. With exceptional swiftness, explorers, merchants, missionaries, imperial administrators, and conquering navies and armies lunged into the non-European world. By 1914, Britain held India; the British, French, Russians, and Americans controlled most of the rest of Asia; and Britain, France, Germany, Portugal, Belgium, Italy, and Spain had taken Africa.

The "new imperialism" brought limited economic, technological, and political modernization to the new colonies. The subject peoples in these conquered lands perhaps realized certain improvements in their lives. For the most part, however, European imperialism again proved to be brutal and exploitative. The inability of the Europeans to establish and maintain these empires without force and violence indicated that the colonists did not think that life improved after foreigners took their land.

The imperialist nations exhibited intensified hostility toward one another as they competed to take over the world. Yet they fought relatively little in their colonial realms; in fact, they usually succeeded in ending contention diplomatically, as in the Berlin Conference in 1884. In contrast, the resolution of their conflicts in Europe proved exceedingly difficult to achieve by negotiation. The most intractable problems developed in Southeast Europe in the Balkan Peninsula. There, Serbia struggled to take in all territory inhabited by South Slavs, an action that threatened to fragment the Austrian Empire. Austria's determined fight against Serbia and Russia's support for Slavic national independence made the Balkan "powder keg" truly explosive.

A blowup involving Austria and Serbia might have remained a local conflict. Even a war that drew in the Russians could have occurred with little effect on the rest of Europe. Instead, in 1914, a crisis in the Balkans ignited a conflagration that engulfed all the great powers. This larger war came as a result of the virulent nationalism that inflamed all Europeans, the existence of two rival alliances that connected most nations to the conflicting South-east European states, and the widespread confidence in military solutions to international differences.

In the First World War, the Central Powers (Germany, Austria, Turkey, Bulgaria) and the Allied Powers (France, Russia, Britain, Italy, and later the United States) fought tenaciously for four years. Battle lines moved little and losses in lives and resources were exceptionally high. These sacrifices broke Russia first. In the throes of a revolution, this nation surrendered to Germany in early 1918. But with enemies on two fronts for most of the war and with coasts blockaded by the British navy, the Central Powers eventually could not sustain a campaign so costly in human and material resources.

The victorious Allies convened in Paris after the armistice in November 1918 to decide treaty terms that they would force the Central Powers to accept. European Allied leaders wanted reparations and revenge included among the rewards of victory. American President Woodrow Wilson hoped that his idealistic Fourteen Points would shape the settlement and ensure against another world war.

The Peace of Paris completed in 1919 did reflect Wilson's influence, especially in the provisions for a League of Nations. Yet vindictiveness was much more evident than such idealism, especially in clauses blaming the Central Powers for the war and charging them for its costs. These treaties and the larger consequences of the war drastically affected events in Europe for the next seventy years. That the Great War was a watershed in Europe's history became most immediately evident in Russia where a new Communist state rose in the social and political rubble left by the awesomely destructive conflict.

Selected Readings

Ashworth, Tony. *Trench Warfare, 1914–1918: The Live and Let Live System*. New York: Holmes and Meier, 1980.

Fay, Sidney B. *The Origins of the First World War*. 2nd ed., rev. New York: Free Press, 1966.

Hoehling, Adolph A. *The Great War at Sea: A History of Naval Action, 1914–1918*. New York: Crowell, 1965.

Joll, James. *The Origins of the First World War*. New York: Longman, 1984.

Lafore, Lawrence D. *The Long Fuse: An Interpretation of the Origins of World War I*. 2nd ed. New York: Lippincott, 1971.

Leed, Eric J. *No Man's Land: Combat and Identity in World War I*. New York: Cambridge University Press, 1979.

Porter, Bernard. *The Lion's Share: A Short History of British Imperialism, 1850–1893*. New York: Longman, 1984.

Robinson, Ronald E., John Gallagher, and Alice Denny. *Africa and the Victorians: The Official Mind of Imperialism*. New York: St. Martin's Press, 1961.

Schmidt, Bernadotte E., and Harold C. Vedeler. *The World in the Crucible, 1914–1918*. New York: Harper & Row, 1984.

13

The Emergence of the USSR, 1914–1941

December 1916	Assassination of Rasputin
March 1917	The Romanov autocracy falls
April 1917	Lenin presents his April Theses
July 1917	An uprising against the Provisional Government takes place
August 1917	Kornilov attempts to take power
November 1917	The Bolshevik Revolution occurs
January 1918	Dissolution of the Constituent Assembly
March 1918	Russia surrenders to Germany at Brest-Litovsk
Mid-1918	The Allies intervene in Russia and civil war begins
July 1918	Execution of the tsar and his family
Late 1920	The Communists win the civil war
March 1921	The Kronstadt naval garrison revolts
1921	Lenin establishes his New Economic Policy (NEP)
January 1924	Lenin dies
1928	Stalin begins his rule
1931	A famine begins in the Ukraine
December 1934	Kirov's murder marks the onset of Stalin's purges
1936–1938	The Great Purge takes place

The Russian Ancien Régime *remained nearly intact throughout the Modern era. No other European state had such antiquated institutions. Severe stresses built up during the 1800s as this system became less and less adequate to meet the needs of Russian society. Reformers and rebels tried to change or destroy the tsarist structure, and by the latter 1800s even the imperial government took up the cause of modernization. Industry progressed rapidly as a result, but sociopolitical institutions remained too archaic. Revolutionaries and the ruling regime continued their brutal fight.*

The persistence of backward conditions in Russia in the early twentieth century and the bitter struggle of forces contending to save, reform, or destroy the old regime made the state extremely fragile. In this weakened condition, the empire marched enthusiastically into the First World War in 1914. This great conflict killed masses of Russians, depleted national resources, and wrecked the economy. Under the strain of this massive crisis, the autocratic state collapsed in early 1917.

The leaders who first took charge after the overthrow of the tsarist system favored the construction of a parliamentary and capitalist state. Within months, another revolution swept this liberal regime from power. The new rebels then began to build the world's first Communist state.

WAR AND THE RUSSIAN REVOLUTIONS OF 1917

The First World War opened in Russia, as elsewhere in Europe, to the joyous shouts of patriotic citizens of all classes. The cheering soon died.

An Old Regime in a Modern War

Attitudes changed because war's reality quickly confronted Russia. A frightening hint of future horrors came when the government sent about one-fourth of the troops to the front without weapons during the first months of combat. Officials told them to take up the guns of fallen comrades.

By 1917, the empire's industry, agriculture, and transportation facilities were in desperately bad shape. Losses mounted to staggering proportions. Over 15,000,000 men had entered service by the end of the war. Nearly 4,000,000 suffered nonlethal wounds, about 2,500,000 were captured, and over 1,500,000 died. No other state in the war had so many casualties.

AUTOCRATIC MISGOVERNMENT

The horrible spirit of the war visited civilians too, in part as a result of the inadequate leadership of the tsarist government. Within Russia, food and fuel supplies dwindled to painfully low levels and living costs skyrocketed. To make matters worse, in August 1915 Tsar Nicholas II took direct control of the Russian war effort nearer the front and left the Empress Alexandra and a peasant religious mystic, Gregory Rasputin, in charge of the bureaucracy within Russia.

Nicholas lacked the talent to rule. Not only did the tsar have still less skill as a military leader, but now he commanded a losing army at war. Simultaneously, Nicholas fully yielded government in Russia to a woman more lacking in political competence than he. The Empress, in turn, submitted completely to the authority of Rasputin, a strange spiritual leader with no competence to govern and a well-deserved reputation for corruption, promiscuity, and drunkenness. He had won his completely undeserved trust from the royal couple ten years earlier by convincing them that he could control the bleeding of their hemophiliac son.

THE ASSASSINATION OF RASPUTIN

With this trio in command, conditions became so desperate that even leading aristocrats decided to resort to terror against the government. In December 1916 a group of nobles assassinated Rasputin in an effort to bring the Romanovs to their senses and save the old regime. This act also indicated that all segments of society had abandoned the tsarist system as it was then constituted.

The Fall of the Autocracy, March 1917

With even aristocratic support waning, the end for tsardom came quickly. Ordinary people, however, brought down the old regime. Inadequate supplies of bread and fuel led segments of the hungry and cold population of Petrograd to go on strike. (Soon after the outbreak of war with the Central Powers, the government had given the capital the Russian name "Petrograd" instead of the Germanic "St. Petersburg.")

THE PETROGRAD WORKERS' STRIKE

The forces of popular revolution surged into the streets of the capital on International Women's Day, March 8, 1917 (February 23 on Russia's "Old Style" calendar, which stayed in effect until after the Communist Revolution). A contingent of women acted first. They took up protest banners and marched, even though the leftist parties, including the Bolsheviks, had advocated caution and opposed the action. Army units ordered to stop such behavior joined the strikers. Even the usually dependable Cossack horsemen, when called to suppress the rebellion, not only refused to act but sometimes attacked the members of the militia who tried to stop the protests.

Almost 90,000 demonstrated on the first day. Then, on the second day of protest, twice that number filled the streets. Soon virtually all the workers stormed through the avenues—about 250,000 laborers. Middle-class people and university students cheered them on and sometimes joined the marchers. Government officials and the police fled.

ABDICATION OF THE TSAR

The government tried and failed to suppress the revolt with force. On Alexandra's advice, Tsar Nicholas resorted to his ultimate weapon—he simply ordered the rebels to stop. They ignored him. Then leaders of the Duma (parliament), which always before had been a pliant tool of the tsar, took action against their ruler. On March 12, they organized a Provisional Government with about twenty members. Most of these men were bourgeois liberals, but the group included a prominent moderate Socialist Revolutionary (SR), Alexander Kerensky. These leaders intended to end autocracy and establish parliamentary government. Nicholas II had no choice. He abdicated on March 15.

THE PETROGRAD SOVIET

On the day of the creation of the Provisional Government, a competing power center emerged—the Petrograd Soviet of Workers' and Soldiers' Deputies. As in the 1905 rebellion, popular forces established this revolutionary city council as an agency to express their will. The Petrograd Soviet began with the backing of impressive numbers of workers and soldiers, but it did not try to seize control of Russia. Instead, the Soviet accepted the Provisional Government as the historically correct political authority. The workers' council had a moderate socialist outlook but believed that Russia had not then reached the stage where a socialist revolution could succeed.

Yet the Soviet exerted much influence over events. Its power extended especially to the military. Since the war had brought a flood of peasant and many urban workers into the army, the troops identified with the Soviet and obeyed it. They complied, for example, with the council's "Order Number One," issued on March 14, 1917. This decree called for soldiers to elect representatives to command their units, except in combat when officers could take charge. The Soviet also instructed the military rank and file to obey Provisional Government orders only when the Soviet also approved its commands.

THE FIRST CONGRESS OF SOVIETS

Soon, similar revolutionary Soviets formed across Russia. Representatives from these local councils met at Petrograd on June 16, 1917, in the first All-Russian Congress of Soviets. Those who gathered (285 SRs, 245 Mensheviks, 105 Bolsheviks, and a few other socialists) set up a Central Executive Committee to act as its continuing leadership. These Soviets had a significant popular following. The Provisional Government did not.

The Failure of the Provisional Government

The failure of the Provisional Government to win support resulted from several policies and from an inability to cope with persistent serious problems. The new leaders, for example, offered land reform in the future rather than at once as the peasant masses wanted. Everyone continued to suffer, moreover, from rampant inflation, plunging industrial production, and a wrecked transportation system. Above all, the government alienated the populace by committing itself absolutely to the war alliance, despite Russia's increasingly evident inability to win. As the Provisional Government continued policies that drove the people to oppose it, the Bolsheviks positioned themselves to take control.

THE GROWTH OF BOLSHEVIK STRENGTH

The Bolshevik victory depended a great deal on Lenin's policies and actions. When the revolution broke in March 1917, he was in Switzerland in exile, as usual, working on his theories and on Party organization. Lenin traveled to Russia in April 1917 and presented his "April Theses." This policy statement demanded peace at once, peasant possession of all the land, and complete governing power in the hands of the workers' Soviets. These views were significantly more democratic than the ideas Lenin expressed in the early 1900s.

Most Bolsheviks strongly opposed the Theses. The majority of Party leaders shared the Petrograd Soviet's view that a socialist revolution could come only after passage through a capitalist era. Lenin seemed to want to rush history, in violation of Marx's ideas. With great difficulty, Lenin finally convinced the Party to accept his principles. This Bolshevik platform had a much broader appeal than did the policies of the Provisional Government. Party membership began to grow rapidly, especially in cities such as Petrograd where workers flocked to the organization. The Bolsheviks even began to increase their popularity among peasants.

THE "JULY DAYS" REVOLT

The Provisional Government's problems reached serious proportions as early as May 1917. By then economic troubles and an impossible military situation led to a change in the composition of the leadership group. More socialists came in, and Kerensky, the SR, took over the ministries of the army and navy. He soon launched an offensive on the southwestern front. Disaster followed there. At the same time, rebellion seethed among the national minorities. In rural Russia, a socioeconomic revolution was underway as the peasants seized the land. Ethnic non-Russians and the farmers would not wait for a new government and its reform legislation.

Even more ominously, food shortages created utter turmoil in the cities, the critical centers of government control. Rebels in military units stationed in Petrograd shared the peasants' impatience. They began their assault on the Provisional Government on July 16, 1917, and the Bolsheviks reluctantly followed them in rebellion. By July 18, this venture had collapsed. A few troops loyal to the government and public disinterest in the coup sealed the fate of "July Days" rebels.

Not only did the revolt fail, as the Bolsheviks expected, but they also were charged with treason. The Provisional Government used the outbreak as an excuse to spread the false charge that the Bolsheviks had "German" support. This traitorous image made it easier for Provisional leaders to suppress these enemies on the Left.

THE KORNILOV AFFAIR

Bolshevik popularity dropped sharply for a while after July 1917. But events soon reversed the fortunes of the Party. Alexander Kerensky became Provisional prime minister in July, and the following month, he sent a military force under General Lavr Kornilov to the capital. Kerensky's aim perhaps was to suppress the Petrograd Soviet. Kornilov probably wanted personal power and the restoration of a more traditional authoritarian government.

Whatever the intentions of the general and the prime minister, by the time Kornilov reached Petrograd with his troops, Kerensky had decided the general was an enemy. Kerensky called on the people of Petrograd to stop Kornilov and prevent his destruction of the revolution. Petrograders prepared to defend their rebel stronghold as Kornilov approached. Local authorities freed Bolshevik leaders from prison, and the Party took up weapons to join the revolutionary guard. They never had to fight the general. Facing strong citizen resistance, Kornilov gave up the cause before reaching Petrograd. The affair left the Bolsheviks popular and rearmed. Provisional Government support plummeted.

The Bolshevik Victory

Within weeks after the Kornilov affair, the Bolsheviks had won a majority in the Petrograd and Moscow Soviets, though not in the Central Executive Committee of the All-Russian Congress of Soviets. Across the country as well their popularity mounted.

THE "OCTOBER" REVOLUTION

Lenin, hiding out in Finland after the failed July revolt, sent messages after the Kornilov debacle urging his Party to take over the country. On November 5, he returned in disguise to Petrograd and with difficulty got the other Bolshevik leaders to go along with the idea of an armed insurrection. Leon Trotsky, a long-time Marxist but recent convert to Bolshevism, proved to be Lenin's most enthusiastic supporter in the quest for revolution.

On the night of November 7, 1917 (October 25, on the Old Style Russian calendar), rebel troops took control of the centers of transportation and communication in the capital. In the early morning darkness of November 8, a "Red Guard" formed by city workers, a Petrograd army unit led by

Bolsheviks, and militantly proletarian sailors from the nearby Kronstadt base attacked the Winter Palace, where the Provisional Government had set up its headquarters. They encountered almost no opposition. In a virtually bloodless coup, the Provisional Government fell and working-class forces took over. Despite this gentle collapse, a brutal transition was in store for the Russians.

FORMATION OF THE COMMUNIST GOVERNMENT

Throughout the months from the March to the November revolutions, the Provisional Government had officially led Russia, but the revolutionary councils, and especially the Petrograd Soviet, had assumed partial control. The Bolshevik Party also became an increasingly important center of authority before the autumn revolution. Once the Provisional Government fell, the Bolshevik Party and the network of Soviets that it dominated completed the transition to power.

Although the new ruling system remained in flux throughout the twentieth century, the fundamental structure of the new state emerged during these early years and persisted thereafter. The Party and the Soviets evolved as dual, overlapping hierarchies, with the Party reigning supreme and authority in both pyramids concentrated at the top.

The Communist Party. In March 1918, the Bolsheviks renamed their organization and became the Communist party. Three small groups held the uppermost positions in this organization. These executive agencies were the Political Bureau (Politburo), the Secretariat, and the Organizational Bureau (Orgburo). The Politburo and Secretariat typically possessed the highest authority, even though Party rules stated that a larger Central Committee controlled them. Theoretically, the mass of Party members selected and guided these leaders. Beginning in small local Party organizations (cells) at the bottom, Communists supposedly chose delegates from their group to act for them at the next higher level through a succession of tiers to the national Party Congress and its Central Committee. In practice, the top authorities designated Party leaders above the local level and decided policies without regard to the wishes of lower-ranking people.

Soviet Government. Although the supreme power belonged to the Party after the revolution in November 1917, the structure of Soviets technically comprised the government. In July 1918, the leaders of the new state adopted a constitution that described the formal system of this "Russian Soviet Federated Socialist Republic" (RSFSR) that had replaced the autocracy and the Provisional Government. Soviet government organization and its operating principles repeated those of the Party in that lower councils, in theory, sent delegates to successively higher levels up to the national All-Russian Congress of Soviets. Once more, top officials actually controlled most elections and policy making. (As Soviet officials composed the constitution through the early months of 1918, they also moved the capital of the new RSFSR to Moscow.)

Party-State Relations. Since the Soviet Congress met only periodically, it elected a Central Executive Committee and a Council of Peoples' Commissars (Sovnarkom) to work as permanently operating governing agencies. (The Council of Peoples' Commissars roughly paralleled a cabinet of ministers in a parliamentary system.) The members of these Soviet executive agencies ranked high in the Party. (Lenin, for example, led both the Party Politburo and the government Sovnarkom.) This practice blurred distinctions between the two systems at the top, but organizationally the Party dominated the government and controlled the Soviet state.

ENACTMENT OF THE REVOLUTION

During its first months in power, the new government decreed a socioeconomic revolution. It finished the dissolution of the old regime by outlawing titles of nobility and seizing the property of aristocrats, some middle class people, and the churches. Communist leaders also began to socialize the economy by means of seizing peasant land, turning control of factories over to the workers, and converting all banks and large industries into government enterprises. These and other more revolutionary measures enacted by 1921 often were not fully implemented, but a drastic transformation had begun.

Such sweeping changes decided by a single party provoked opposition. Communists responded by suppressing all parties, other than the leftist Socialist Revolutionaries, by the beginning of 1918. Within months thereafter, the leftist SRs abandoned the Communists and all opposition parties were outlawed. As a further guarantee of power, Soviet leaders established a security force, the Cheka, in December 1917. This organization, headed by Felix Dzerzhinsky, was the parent of "secret police" agencies that operated under various titles until the demise of the KGB in 1991.

THE CONSTITUENT ASSEMBLY

Lenin's Party and government had strong support among the 500,000 Russian city workers and among rank-and-file members of the military. By late 1917, the Communists had won a significant peasant following, but most of the 120,000,000 rural people still backed the Socialist Revolutionaries. Since most voters were peasants, the elections sent over 400 SRs, 170 Bolsheviks, 34 Mensheviks, and 100 other socialists to the Constituent Assembly that met in January 1918.

From the Communists' point of view, they represented the proletariat, the class to which every citizen would belong in the future. The SRs and others had won more votes from the 1917 citizenry, but support of classes still tied to the past meant nothing. The Communists dissolved the Constiuent Assembly on the day it first met, January 18, 1918. For the next seventy-two years the Party would share power with no other political organization.

THE TREATY OF BREST-LITOVSK WITH GERMANY

The new Communist government had one overriding international concern at first—to end the war with Germany. Trotsky, as Commissar of Foreign Affairs, led a delegation to Brest-Litovsk in western Russia to hold peace talks with the Germans.

The harsh terms that Germany offered shocked the Communists. Trotsky, as well as many other Party leaders, opposed acceptance. Lenin believed, however, that the insecure position of his new government at home and the complete inadequacy of the Russian military allowed no choice but surrender. On March 3, 1918, the Treaty of Brest-Litovsk ended the devastating war but also took away 1,000,000 square kilometers of territory with over 50,000,000 inhabitants and many valuable industrial facilities.

THE ERA OF CIVIL WAR, 1918–1920

After nearly two decades of struggle, the Communists finally won power with relative ease in November 1917. The coup itself, moreover, caused few deaths and little destruction. Peace with Germany the following March required acceptance of humiliating terms but ended a costly siege. Despite these mostly promising developments, a civil war erupted in Russia in the summer of 1918. A desperate struggle ensued that caused more widespread suffering than the Great War and very nearly destroyed the new government.

The Enemies of the Russian Communists

No movement could equal the political and military strength of the Communists in Russia's great cities by late 1917. The Party gained additional power from the solid support of the working masses in these urban centers. These circumstances enabled Lenin's forces to take control, but an array of enemies fought from the outset attempting to ensure that the Communists would not continue to rule Russia. The "Whites," reactionaries who wanted to return to a more traditional sociopolitical system, rose as the greatest threat to the Communist "Reds."

THE WHITE FACTIONS

The Soviet government's reactionary enemies emerged in many different regions around the Communist stronghold in central Russia. General Anton Denikin took command of White troops in southern Russia early in the Civil War. Several reactionary factions appeared to the east of the

Russian heartland. The most important of these groups, led by Admiral Alexander Kolchak, operated in western Siberia at the beginning of the conflict. In Estonia in the northwest, General Nicholas Yudenich directed a White movement that eventually threatened Petrograd itself.

These White factions, and others that formed as the war proceeded, shared little but their opposition to the Communists and the determination to restore the power of former privileged groups. Beyond these sentiments, they had no common beliefs about a new order to establish in place of the Soviet state. Despite such handicaps, the Whites had the potential to destroy the Red state. Other opponents lacked this deadly strength but did heighten the danger to communism.

THE REBELLIOUS NATIONAL MINORITIES

Among the nearly 200 national minorities within the Romanov Empire in 1917, those on the southern, western, and northwestern borders exhibited an especially strong desire for independence. They began their drive to separate from Russia during the tumultuous transition after the Bolshevik Revolution. Nationalist rebellions broke out in Central Asia and in the southwest in a region the tsars had organized as the Transcaucasian Federation. The Soviets quelled these revolts by the mid-1920s, but they could not suppress outbreaks in Poland, Lithuania, Latvia, and Finland. These western and northern nationalities won full independence. By 1919, the new Polish state had sufficient power to invade Soviet territory and occupy parts of Byelorussia and the Ukraine during the Civil War era.

FOREIGN INVADERS

Soviet Russia's exit from the war in March 1918 gave the other Allied Powers an excuse to send troops into the Communist state. For France and Britain, the main objective of Allied intervention was the overthrow of the Communists, even though official statements claimed the goal of preventing German seizure of military goods. The declared rationale for entry somewhat more accurately reflected the motives for American intervention. Twelve other countries also sent in troops, most of them in an attempt to seize territory.

The foreign intervention that heightened the danger to the Communist government involved these forces: 60,000 from Japan, 40,000 British troops, a Czechoslovak "legion" of 30,000 or more that had fought for the tsar in the Great War, a contingent of 10,000 from the United States, several units from France and Greece, and smaller numbers from nine other countries. The Japanese and Czechs fought the Reds, but the other powers opposed the Communists mostly by providing money and supplies to the Whites.

The Reds and Whites at War

The Communists and the Whites engaged in full-scale war from mid-1918 to late 1920. Red forces had the advantage of a consolidated territory and strong commitment to a cause. Even so, the scattered and uninspired Whites almost conquered the Communist state in the first year of the struggle.

THE WHITE OFFENSIVE

Leon Trotsky demonstrated genius as the organizer and commander of the Red Army, but in the early stages of the Civil War his talents seemed to matter little. The Whites pressed in on the Reds from several directions and greatly diminished their territory. One anti-Communist operation in July 1918 brought a combined White and Czech force near the place where the Soviets held the tsar and his family. On orders from Lenin, the Romanovs' captors executed Nicholas II, Empress Alexandra, and their five children. The Whites continued their advance and by October 1918 Yudenich's army approached Petrograd as Denikin's troops neared Moscow. Soviet enemies thus stood poised to take the two major Russian cities.

THE RED VICTORY

Fortunes then changed for the Red Army. Under Trotsky's guidance, the Communist military had improved rapidly. Yudenich's attack on Petrograd failed. The Communists dealt Kolchak a smashing blow before the end of 1919. Then the reds drove Denikin back far to the south in early 1920. At that point, Poland attacked Russia, forcing the Reds to ease pressure on Denikin. Thereafter, General Peter Wrangel replaced Denikin as leader of the Whites in the southwest. Wrangel began an offensive in that region that at first made progress. By autumn 1920, however, Poland quit the war and Wrangel began to lose ground. The navy of the Allied Powers, operating in the Black Sea, subsequently evacuated Wrangel and his army. The Reds had secured their victory by the end of 1920.

WAR COMMUNISM

The new Communist state continued to develop during the Civil War. Russia's authoritarian tradition influenced this process, despite the revolutionary spirit of Communism. Party ideology and the events of the Civil War had an even more profound effect on the evolution of the Soviet system between 1918 and 1921. All these forces—Russian culture, Communist philosophy, and the demands of the civil struggle—drove the new government toward political dictatorship. These same influences, but especially the battle with the Whites, prompted the Party to devise policies that it described as "War Communism."

Before the Civil War, Soviet leaders had acted on their commitment to the formerly oppressed working classes by turning control of factories over to the laborers and allowing farmers to take the land. The workers ran plants badly, however, and the needs of the embattled Red Army made this experiment impossible to continue. In the era of War Communism, the Party decreed an end to proletarian management and declared that the government thereafter would own and control virtually all industrial and financial institutions. In order to provide the food and other farm goods needed by factory workers and the Red Army during the Civil War, Soviet leaders also commanded that peasants surrender all products that the government considered to be "surplus." Rural War Communism produced especially serious abuses as government agents seized even necessities from the farmers.

THE CRISIS OF 1920–1922

Red Army operations and the implementation of War Communism gave the Soviet government its Civil War victory but left Russia on the brink of disaster. Industrial and farm production had dropped sharply. Prices had spiraled rapidly upward. Severe dry weather produced a famine in 1921–1922 and greatly intensified the misery. The combination of Civil War, hunger, and disease killed 20,000,000 Russians between 1918 and 1922.

Finally, the suffering became unbearable, and the toiling masses revolted against the self-proclaimed workers' state. Peasants turned to armed rebellion, especially in the area south of Moscow. In the north, near Petrograd, the naval garrison at Kronstadt delivered the Soviet government an even more staggering blow. Communists had recognized the sailors at this base as some of the greatest heroes of the Bolshevik Revolution. In March 1921, the Kronstadt garrison revolted. Trotsky led the Red Army in a brutal suppression of these proletarian rebels. The conditions and events of 1920–1921 stunned Lenin. He responded with an almost revolutionary revision of Soviet policy.

THE FORMATION OF THE USSR, 1921–1928

Even though Communist leaders had to deal with the crisis of 1920–1922, they soon were able to devote much more attention to the construction of the new order. By the end of the decade, they had largely completed the formation of their new state, the Union of Soviet Socialist Republics (USSR). Communist authorities for many years thereafter had an extremely powerful government to execute whatever policies they chose.

The New Economic Policy

In 1921, Lenin proposed drastic measures to end the suffering and turmoil left by the Civil War and War Communism. He called his plan the New Economic Policy (NEP), and it horrified many Communist leaders. NEP repelled numerous Party officials because it entailed a retreat from the

extremes of War Communism to a system that combined dictatorial socialism and capitalist private enterprise. Lenin's opponents finally yielded to
his arguments that nothing but this adoption of limited bourgeois practices
would restore the economy quickly enough to save the Soviet state.

INDUSTRY AND COMMERCE UNDER NEP

The 1921 reform program permitted the resumption of private retail
sales in stores and on the streets (by "Nepmen" who bought and sold almost
everything)—practices punishable by death during the Civil War. The NEP
even restored the right to operate small private industries (no more than
twenty employees). Although Lenin refused to end government ownership
of large factories, the banking system, public transportation, and wholesale
and foreign trade, his policy did reduce the authority of state bureaucracies
over these enterprises.

AGRICULTURAL NEP

The change for peasants from the days of War Communism was even
more drastic than for urban workers and entrepreneurs. The forced requisi-
tioning of produce ended, replaced by a provision for farmers to pay taxes
(at first in produce, later in money). The NEP rules also allowed peasants to
use or sell everything they produced in excess of tax obligations. Before the
end of the 1920s, peasants gained the right to lease land and hire workers (a
practice previously condemned as "wage slavery"). Under these conditions,
the number of relatively prosperous farmers (known as "kulaks") multiplied
rapidly.

The overall effect of NEP meant that Soviet Russia's 20,000,000 family
farms operated under a private enterprise system, despite the theory that the
state owned the land. Lenin's plan succeeded remarkably well. It brought a
quick end to the famine conditions of the early 1920s, and by 1928 the
amount of land under cultivation exceeded 1914 levels for the first time
since the Great War began. Industry recovered in a similar fashion.

The New Political Union

By the end of 1922, nationalist rebels in Byelorussia, the Ukraine, and
the Transcaucasian Federation had lost their bid to follow the path to
independence opened by Poland, Lithuania, Latvia, Estonia, and Finland.
Byelorussia, the Ukraine, and Transcaucasia accepted their status as
"republics" annexed to the Russian Republic to form the Union of Soviet
Socialist Republics. Communist leaders then revised the 1918 constitution
to describe the structure and laws of this new larger union.

THE CONSTITUTION OF THE USSR

The constitution adopted in 1924 provided Soviet government structures
for the new republics patterned after Russia's, as described in the 1918
constitution. The addition of these three regions to the state necessitated

changes in the central institutions of government. The All-Russian Congress became the All-Union Congress of Soviets, and its Central Executive Committee (CEC) changed to a two-part agency consisting of the Council of Union and the Council of Nationalities. The Congress with more than 2,000 representatives met annually but had no real authority. The CEC with its hundreds of members also did not truly administer Soviet affairs. Instead, two smaller CEC committees—the Presidium and the Sovnarkom—led the government but took their orders from the top Party agencies.

DICTATORSHIP AND LIBERTY IN THE NEW SOVIET UNION

Not a word about the Communist Party appeared in the Constitution of the USSR. Despite this omission, the 472,000 Communists ruled the nation of 150,000,000 in 1924. The Party, moreover, decided who entered its ranks. These half million self-selected Communists, though supreme among the citizens, possessed very uneven powers within the Party. A national Party Congress held ultimate authority, according to stated principles, but in practice a few leaders (under 100) in four small executive agencies exercised dictatorial control over the Party and the state. The most important of these Communist chiefs were the General Secretary and the members of the Politburo (seven people in 1924).

The denial of political influence to almost all the millions of Soviet citizens meant that several impressive constitutional provisions, such as the right of free speech, had limited meaning. These articles in the 1924 document, however, suggested a very new social reality that lasted until the end of the 1920s—greater personal liberty for the masses than Russians had ever enjoyed. Literature, art, the cinema, theater, and especially music benefited from this greater freedom of the early Soviet years.

The Grasp for Ruling Power After Lenin's Death

Lenin suffered a stroke in May 1922, and thereafter only intermittently and briefly recovered enough to resume his duties. A massive brain hemorrhage killed him on January 21, 1924. Hordes of ordinary people braved severe cold weather to join in an orgy of public mourning. Party executives led the ceremonial grieving but probably cared much more about the struggle, already under way, to take Lenin's place. They faced a long and uncertain battle. With no legally established way to select the actual chief executive of the Soviet Union, Lenin's successor would be whoever could seize power.

THE CONTENDERS

In the months after his first stroke, Lenin wrote two instructional statements to the Party that included brief estimations of the leadership potential of six people. He noted the talents of all these men but implied that no single person could take his place. Although no individual met Lenin's prideful standards; he referred to Gregory Zinoviev, Lev Kamenev, Nikolai Bukharin, and Gregory Pyatakov because they were among the contenders to succeed him. His remarks accurately suggested, however, that two other people overshadowed all the competitors.

Leon Trotsky appeared to have the greatest advantages in the rivalry. His intellectual brilliance and persuasive speaking and writing ability helped catapult him to the top of the Party, even though he did not join the Bolsheviks until 1917. After Trotsky commanded the Red forces in the October Revolution and the Civil War with such mastery, only Lenin inspired more awe among Communists.

Joseph Stalin (1879–1953) lacked Trotsky's impressive public image, but by 1924 he had more influence over the rapidly swelling ranks of full-time Party workers than anyone, even Lenin. Stalin began his climb to this powerful position at age seventeen when he quit the seminary to work for revolution. He soon joined the emerging Bolshevik movement and fought daringly for it, robbing banks to provide Party funds. Such operations often landed Stalin in jail. He always escaped and returned to the struggle. His dedicated Party work placed Stalin among the leaders in the revolutionary and Civil War battles of 1917 to 1921. By 1924, Stalin held office in every top Party agency.

THE ISSUES

Policy debates gained much attention in the struggle for power. Rivals fought by claiming to know the right course for the Party to take. Trotsky and Stalin conflicted most sharply over whether Communism could succeed in Soviet Russia without also having a global Marxist revolution in the near future. The traditional Party belief that success in the USSR required a worldwide proletarian victory appealed to Trotsky. He defended the view vigorously.

Stalin countered that Communism certainly could succeed in the USSR with a triumph abroad in the distant future. An increasingly nationalistic Soviet Communist Party found Stalin's idea of "socialism in one country," as he called it, very appealing. The evident failure of Communist revolts elsewhere intensified the allure of Stalin's doctrine. Relatively few Party members wanted to believe that world circumstances doomed their cause.

Trotsky and Stalin clashed over another issue—whether to continue NEP or force a rapid change to complete socialization in the USSR. This question had the utmost significance for the future of Soviet Russia. It received less attention in the leadership fight, however, than did ideas about world revolution. Nevertheless, Stalin's support for NEP helped his cause. The stand he took placed him in the camp with Bukharin and several other Party veterans. Trotsky opposed them and called for hasty socialization, a policy favored by Zinoviev. Many Communist officials who had joined the

Party in 1917 and after agreed with Trotsky and Zinoviev, but these novice bureaucrats owed their jobs to Stalin and wanted him at the top of the structure.

THE VICTOR

Stalin held more high positions in the government and the Party than any of his rivals—Commissar of Nationalities, member of the Politburo and Orgburo, and General Secretary of the Party. The latter three offices gave him control over the development of the Party structure and the power to appoint most important Communist bureaucrats. These Party workers remained submissive to established superiors, but during the transition after Lenin's death, they largely decided who would rule. They chose Stalin.

Loyal Stalinists carried their champion to power by voting with him on critical issues in the meetings of top Party organizations. The victory came in a Party Congress in December 1927. The deputies at this session ruled that no one could vary from Party policy as defined by Stalin. His rivals adopted his positions or were expelled at least from office and sometimes from the Party. Trotsky suffered complete exclusion and fled the Soviet Union in 1929. Stalin had him assassinated in 1940.

THE STALINIST SUPERSTRUCTURE, 1928–1941

Soon after Stalin began to run the Party in early 1928, his actions indicated that he was prepared to force the rapid development of a state with a completely socialized industrial economy. Stalin's methods revealed almost as quickly that he would exercise absolute control over the government, its economy, and every other aspect of life that he could. By 1941, the new Soviet dictator had largely achieved this goal of building a "totalitarian" system. The political, economic, and social superstructure that took shape under his command during the 1930s changed considerably after Stalin died in 1953. It remained mostly intact, though, until the late 1980s.

Soviet Russia's Industrial Revolution

By the late 1920s, manufacturing had finally returned to 1914 levels of production. This "recovery" left Soviet Russia still an almost completely agricultural nation. The NEP farm system ensured a relatively slow transition to an industrial economy.

The NEP allowed rural families to tend their lands and, for the most part, dispose of their crops as they wished. Poorer peasants produced enough to take care of themselves. The more prosperous kulaks' larger yields fed the relatively small population of urban workers. But the farm system in the late 1920s would neither take care of a mostly urban society nor supply products to sell abroad and pay for an industrial buildup. Peasants might eventually change on their own and fulfill the needs of a modern economy, or in time Soviet leaders might teach them these new ways. Stalin decided he would not wait for such an evolutionary process to occur.

THE FIVE-YEAR PLANS

In the struggle with Trotsky, Stalin had demanded the perpetuation of NEP. He reversed his position in 1929 and ordered a swift expansion of industry, a change that would require complete socialization. Stalin at the same time decreed farm collectivization. This policy meant that the more than 20,000,000 private family farms would cease to exist as soon as possible. Most peasants would remain in their present villages and homes, but rural workers would merge family plots into collective fields.

Stalin and his supporters claimed that new economic difficulties and foreign threats required this nullification of NEP's urban private-enterprise and small family farm system. Above all, they wanted agricultural collectivization so that the government could forcibly take the goods it needed to carry out an industrial revolution. Lenin had used similar methods during the Civil War, but then restored private farming in the NEP era and eventually decided that a gradual shift to rural socialism would be best for Soviet Russia. Bukharin and other Party veterans also wanted NEP and a slow change to collective farms. Neither Lenin's conversion to NEP nor the views of revered leaders such as Bukharin mattered anymore. Stalin and his new bureaucrats ruled the Party.

Elaborate statements of goals and timetables confronted everyone involved in Stalin's projected industrial revolution. Soviet leaders presented these economic schedules regularly for the next six decades, almost always as "Five-Year Plans." They served mainly to increase government control over the economy and the citizenry rather than to provide general material prosperity.

Stalin advanced his first Five-Year Plan in 1929. It contained these projections for 1933: collectivization of twenty percent of peasant farms, an increase of about 250 percent in steel production, and an advance from 1,300 new tractors per year to 170,000. The Plan called for equally incredible increases in the output of iron, cement, cloth, electricity, and other goods.

The 1929 economic schedule and all subsequent ones until the late 1980s strongly emphasized the development of heavy industry. This policy meant a concentration on the production of electricity, oil, industrial and construction machinery, modern hauling systems, military hardware, and large mechanized farm implements.

AGRICULTURAL COLLECTIVIZATION

Most Soviet farmers hated collectivization. Ukrainian peasants who tilled the richest agricultural land especially despised the new policy. Farmers across the country stubbornly resisted; they ate and otherwise consumed everything they could to prevent requisitions. They destroyed farm animals, equipment, and other property in an effort to wreck the collectivization drive. Farmers even attacked and sometimes killed local officials who directed the change.

Red Army contingents ordered out to suppress resistance and force submission would not always fire on the peasants. They had good reason not to shoot. Many soldiers came from the farms and sympathized with the protesters. When other means failed, Soviet officials sent in OGPU security troops. These forces of the agency formerly known as the Cheka used whatever measures were required to bring compliance with the policy.

The suppression and control tactics included military sweeps of resisting villages, systematic execution or Siberian exile for all presumed kulaks, and the mass murder of many other peasants. Stalin also purposely caused a horrible famine in the Ukraine (1931–1932) that killed an estimated 6,000,000. The total death toll from collectivization probably reached at least 10,000,000 and probably many more. Stalin meant to have his way.

Stalinist methods brought the collectivization of nearly two-thirds of the farms by the end of the first Plan. Virtually all agricultural land belonged to collectives by the end of the 1930s. From then until the collapse of the Soviet Union, the small private garden plots allowed by the government usually totaled only two or three percent of the farm area.

INDUSTRIALIZATION

Soviet Russia's economic masters intended under the first Plan to improve all old industries and establish many new ones to manufacture cars, trucks, airplanes, plastics, and other products typical of a modern society. The directors of this gigantic project encountered tremendous problems: the inevitable mismanagement caused by controlling a massive industrialization process from the center of the world's largest nation, the extremely small numbers of both skilled and unskilled factory workers, and the difficulty of industrial training and supervision in a mostly illiterate society.

The barriers to success ensured that the Soviet Union would not achieve the very high goals of the first Plan. Steel production, for example, fell about forty percent short of the projected 10,000,000 tons. Tractor output missed the mark even further with the manufacture of 51,000 of the planned 170,000. Similar shortfalls occurred in nearly all Plan categories. Stalin ignored the failure to achieve anticipated results and proclaimed that industry had met its goals in January 1933, nine months ahead of schedule.

Stalin's lie simply magnified an important truth. The Soviet Union had experienced fantastic industrial growth, even if the Plan had not been fulfilled. Iron production had nearly doubled, the generation of electricity almost tripled, and steel mills yielded about a thirty-seven percent increase in 1933 over 1928 numbers. Overall, the advance meant that the industrial revolution truly had begun.

The second Five-Year Plan (1933 to 1937) brought the economic transformation almost to completion. When the Second World War interrupted the third Plan in 1941, the Soviet Union had become a leading industrial nation. The USSR ranked third in manufacturing, behind the United States and Germany but ahead of Britain.

This remarkable achievement had required drastic measures. The government turned away from early Communist ideals about economic equality and used pay raises, medals, and other special benefits to promote high production. As an additional labor incentive, officials trumpeted the superhuman output of workers such as the coal miner Alexsei Stakhanov and then rewarded them with extra wages and other favors. They developed this practice into a continuing program of "Stakhanovism."

Threats as well as rewards influenced employee effort. Tardiness and other bad work habits brought penalties, usually financial but sometimes much more severe. Very persistent violation of rules could result in jail sentences or execution. Forced labor by millions of people imprisoned for economic and political offenses, in fact, became a prominent part of the Stalinist industrial system. Thus, although peasants suffered the most in this decade of industrial revolution, factory workers felt the pain of the effort too. Living standards for all working-class families also declined between 1928 and 1941.

Stalinist Terror

The chain of forced labor camps that helped build the roads, canals, dams, and factories of an industrial nation served another purpose for Stalin. Since anyone, even the wife of Stalin's closest associate, could disappear into this system with its literally deadly living and working conditions, the camps inspired universal fear. This dread immeasurably strengthened Stalin's dictatorial power. Before the end of the 1930s, he had many other instruments of terror to enforce his will.

STALIN'S ATTACK ON THE PARTY

Stalin had many admirers both in the Party and in the nation at large by the end of the first Plan in 1933, despite the pain of industrialization. A Party Congress early in 1934 gave Stalinists an opportunity to praise themselves warmly, but critics also took action, an indication of the growing discontent in the USSR. These Communist opponents of Stalin tried to elect Sergei Kirov as general secretary instead of Stalin. Their effort failed, but Stalin's enemies persisted. When the 1,200 delegates selected the 139 members of the Party Central Committee, Stalin received more negative votes than any other candidate. His favorable ballot count still enabled Stalin to join the Committee, but the outcome indicated a real threat to his power.

Stalin responded decisively and characteristically. In December 1934, he began his campaign to subdue the Party by having Kirov murdered. Then Stalin charged members of the secret police organization (renamed NKVD in the 1930s) with partial responsibility for this killing. After the secret trial and execution of thirteen of these men and nearly 100 other Communists, Stalin blamed and imprisoned several top Party officials. Eventually, more than 30,000 citizens of Leningrad, where Kirov had lived and had a large following, were sent to forced labor camps.

THE GREAT PURGE

Most of the people purged in 1934 belonged to the Party. Soon the organization faced a much greater wave of terror. Stalinists began a siege of treason charges, trials, executions, and imprisonment that struck down tens of thousands of Communists between 1936 and 1938. These victims included Bukharin, Zinoviev, Kamenev, and virtually all other founders and early leaders of the Party.

Stalin concentrated his assault on the Party, but his terror reached far beyond it. The arrest and punishment of someone usually led to similar treatment for his or her family, friends, and other associates. Before it ended, this Great Purge also swept members of the artistic elite and most Red Army officers into NKVD execution chambers or labor camps. Finally, Stalin accused the NKVD chief of going to extremes in the suppression campaign and had him killed. The public trials then stopped. Mass murder continued, leaving hidden "killing fields" around many major cities. Graves in a killing field near Minsk in Byelorussia contained the remains of more than 100,000 people by 1941.

THE REIGN OF A TERRORIST

Stalin's practice of ruthless terror and the governing structure that he built in the 1930s gave him more power than any modern state leader had ever possessed. Industrialization under the Five-Year Plans and the events of the Great Purge revealed the exceptional authority that Stalin had over economic and political institutions. But he extended his control far beyond these typical areas of government concern. Stalin's strong influence in education, science, and other areas of life, in fact, indicates the truly totalitarian nature of his reign. Large numbers of university professors who seemed insufficiently devoted to the ruler's doctrines were sentenced to the work camps. Scientific theory, especially in biology, had to agree with

Stalin's uninformed views. His desire for social control was almost boundless.

Socialist Realism. Stalin intended to dominate the arts as well as the academic world. Creative works in every field had to measure up to the ruler's vague standards of "socialist realism." In practice this policy meant that written and visual works had to convey Communist propaganda messages and that music had to have tunes that Stalin liked. Failure to satisfy Stalin's artistic tastes meant loss of career and income, imprisonment, or even death.

The Stalin Constitution. As Stalin built his structure of total dictatorship, he also presented a new Soviet constitution that promised the citizenry very extensive personal freedoms and the provision of every material need. Officials explained that the conversion of the USSR to a fully socialist economy necessitated the replacement of the constitution adopted during the NEP era. The "Stalin Constitution," released in 1936, actually gave the Soviets none of the liberty and little of the welfare program it described. But it contained at least one meaningful section, the article that specified the supremacy of the Party in the USSR.

The New Communist State and the Capitalist Powers

Stalin claimed that the extreme danger of a capitalist invasion made his policies necessary. He argued that bourgeois leaders would not long tolerate the existence of a Communist state. Therefore, the USSR had to have a modern industrial economy at once. In no other way could the Red Army have the power to defend the nation. This swift economic and military build-up, moreover, could occur only if the ruler kept the nation under iron discipline and dealt ruthlessly with anyone who hindered the transformation.

SOVIET DIPLOMATIC RELATIONS

Stalin broke from NEP practices and turned to his new policies of forced industrialization and military development to make Soviet Russia safe in a capitalist-dominated world. In his quest for security through diplomacy, however, Stalin continued the approach of the NEP era. Foreign Ministry officials through the 1920s and 1930s used mostly traditional methods for dealing with other countries. For example, they pursued and finally secured formal diplomatic recognition from the same capitalist nations that Communist doctrine identified as enemies.

Diplomats of the young Communist state achieved other successes in addition to this official international acceptance. They arranged a special relationship with Germany (the Treaty of Rapallo) in 1922 and a nonaggression agreement with Estonia, Latvia, Poland, and Romania in 1929. By 1935, the Foreign Ministry completed an even more important negotiation and signed a mutual security pact with France.

Soviet officials combined these diplomatic steps toward security with a strong drive for disarmament and international cooperation for peace. The latter policy effort led finally to Soviet membership in the League of Nations in 1934. As recently as the late 1920s, Soviets had shunned the League as a bourgeois club and capitalist states had barred their admission. The USSR in many respects had lost its image as a renegade state by the mid-1930s.

THE COMINTERN

Although the USSR depended mostly on economic development, the Red Army, and diplomacy for its security, Soviet leaders took another, more unorthodox approach to the promotion of its interests abroad. In 1919, they founded the Comintern, a new Communist international organization that attempted to get Communists everywhere to weaken capitalist states and back Soviet policies. This self-proclaimed subversive purpose conflicted with the Foreign Ministry's traditional diplomacy and sometimes hindered the development of good relations with capitalist nations.

THE COMMON FRONT

When Fascist governments in Germany and Italy began to appear extremely threatening to the Soviet Union in the mid-1930s, the Comintern became less openly hostile to capitalism. The organization then proclaimed a "Common Front" policy, urging all political forces opposed to fascism to fight together against this new menace. In practice, Comintern activity in both its subversive and Common Front phases was of little importance to the global standing of the USSR. When the Communists and Fascists finally clashed in 1941, Soviet industry and the modern Red Army stood between the Soviet state and disaster.

When the whirlwind of the Great War struck Europe, it delivered the Russian old order a fatal pounding. The already strained institutions could not withstand the extreme pressures of this long siege. As the tsarist system finally collapsed early in 1917, few Russians mourned its fall. A provisional government took charge and promised democracy soon. But the leaders kept the nation at war, a grave mistake.

In November 1917, a second revolution brought to power a Communist government led by Vladimir Lenin. Competing forces resisted, and a devastating civil war exploded across Russia, lasting until 1920. Victorious Communists thereafter began to transform life in the vast region they had taken. The new government established a "proletarian dictatorship" and carried out a program of extensive but not complete economic socialization during the 1920s. The nation began to recover from the material destruction of war and revolution.

The leaders of the new Communist state struggled through a difficult power transition after Lenin's death in 1924. Joseph Stalin finally emerged triumphant by the end of the 1920s. He immediately accelerated the economic revolution, forcing peasants into a collectivized system of farms and ending all vestiges of private enterprise. Farmers died in the millions as they resisted the change.

Despite stiff opposition, the economic transformation came quickly. The nation went through its industrial revolution in a single decade, from the late 1920s to the late 1930s. At the same time, Stalin drastically tightened his personal control over the state, a feat accomplished in part by the execution of nearly all the leaders of the Communist revolution and the officers of his army.

The emergence of this Communist state and the simultaneous strengthening of similar movements in other European countries stimulated the growth of the extremely violent counterforce of fascism. This and other repercussions of the rise of Communism profoundly influenced the course of world history for the rest of the century.

Selected Readings

Carr, Edward H. *The Bolshevik Revolution.* 3 vols. New York: Macmillan, 1951

Conquest, Robert. *The Great Terror.* New York: Collier Books, 1973.

Filtzer, Donald. *Soviet Workers and Stalinist Industrialization.* Armonk, NY: M. E. Sharp, 1986.

Fitzpatrick, Sheila. *The Russian Revolution, 1917–1932.* New York: Oxford University Press, 1982.

Hindus, Maurice. *Red Bread: Collectivization in a Russian Village.* Bloomington: Indiana University Press, 1988.

Kennan, George F. *Russia and the West Under Lenin and Stalin.* Boston: Little, Brown, 1961.

Lewin, Moshe. *The Making of the Soviet System.* New York: Pantheon, 1985.

Medvedev, Roy. *Let History Judge: The Origins and Consequences of Stalinism.* New York: Columbia University Press, 1990.

Schapiro, Leonard, and Peter Reddaway, eds. *Lenin.* Boulder, CO: Westview Press, 1987.

Tucker, Robert C. *Stalin as Revolutionary, 1879–1929.* New York: W. W. Norton, 1974.

14

Fascist Europe, 1918–1939

January 1919	Nationalist forces crush the Spartacist attempt to establish communism in Germany
March 1919	Mussolini organizes his first Fascist combat group in Italy
July 1919	The Weimar (German) Republic completes its constitution
March 1920	Militarists attempt to seize control in Germany (The Kapp *Putsch*)
July 1921	Hitler assumes command of the German Nazi Party
November 1921	The Fascists emerge as a political party in Italy
October 1922	The Fascist "March on Rome" brings Mussolini's selection as Premier of Italy
January 1923	French and Belgian troops occupy Germany's Ruhr valley
November 1923	Hitler attempts to overthrow the German Republic (beer-hall *Putsch*)
April 1924	The Acerbo Bill gives the Fascists control of the Italian parliament
June 1924	Italian Fascists murder Giacomo Matteotti, one of their leading parliamentary opponents
February 1929	Italian Fascists and the Catholic Church reach an understanding expressed in the Lateran Treaty
Autumn 1929	The Great Depression begins
January 1933	Hitler becomes Chancellor of Germany
1932	Antonio Salazar becomes dictator of Portugal
March 1933	The Enabling Act establishes the Nazi dictatorship in Germany

June 30, 1934   "Night of the Long Knives"—Hitler purges his rivals, including leading Nazis

September 1935   Nazi Germany establishes the anti-Semitic Nuremberg Laws

1936–1939   The Spanish Civil War brings a Fascist regime to power under Francisco Franco

In the late 1700s, the Left emerged in Europe as a movement that demanded equality for all people in wealth, social standing, and political power. Advocates of this creed thus stood for a complete reversal of ancien values. Communism arose a century later as the most extreme leftist movement, at least in theory.

When Lenin and Stalin subsequently founded the first Communist state, they violated the principle of political equality and secured absolute authority for the ruler. Yet Soviet Communism remained leftist in the socioeconomic leveling accomplished by state ownership of all farm, industrial, and commercial property. This Left dictatorship also at least promised that all citizens would enjoy equality in every sense when the new proletarian system matured.

The triumph of the Left in Russia inspired working class militants across Europe to hope for and sometimes openly fight for a socialist or communist victory. But most Europeans to the west of the Soviet Union were enraged or terrified by the rising leftist forces. In their mood of wrath and fear, many welcomed a new extremism of the Right—fascism. The founders of this right-wing movement proclaimed the inherent inequality of humanity. They vowed to crush the Left and thereby end the class war that supposedly threatened to make everyone proletarians.

Somewhat surprisingly the Fascists' right-wing doctrine of inequality had a very broad appeal. Many ordinary people thought that they could rise to the top in a Fascist society. Others simply adored the leaders of these rightist movements and expected them to bring security, power, and glory for citizens of all classes. Above all, Fascists lured devoted followers with their pledge to defend private property and stand up for the nation against the socialist and internationalist campaign of the Left. With such messages, Fascists gained enough support to dominated the continent by 1939.

THE BIRTH OF FASCISM IN ITALY

Italy's young and often shaky liberal democratic system remained intact under the strains of the Great War. Italian democracy proved too weak, however, to withstand the burdens left by that conflict. Within four years after the First World War ended, Italy gave birth to Europe's first Fascist dictatorship.

Repercussions of the Great War

Italy deserted the Triple Alliance in 1915 and entered the war on the side of the Allied Powers. This diplomatic change enabled Italian Premier Vittorio Orlando to join the leaders of Britain, France, and the United States as one of the "Big Four" executives in the peace negotiations in 1918. Military victory and great-power status, however, did not lead to progress for Italy after the war. The nation, on the contrary, sank into despair and became torn by the worst strife since its violent struggle for unity had ended in 1871.

THE PEACE OF PARIS AS AN ITALIAN DEFEAT

The urge to expand had driven Italy into the war in 1915. The Adriatic Sea that separated the Italian and Balkan peninsulas had territory along its northern and eastern shores that strongly tempted Italians. Expansion into these areas could increase the nation's security and add to its wealth. Italians, moreover, populated part of the region. When the Allied Powers promised this Austrian land as a reward for joining the war against the Central Powers, Italy accepted the offer.

In the Paris negotiations, the Allied leaders denied Orlando this territory. They argued that the unexpected fragmentation of the Hapsburg Empire removed the Austrian threat to Italian security. Allied diplomats also decided that the region contained too many Slavs to permit Italian rule. Italy had sacrificed 500,000 soldiers and spent itself into a crippling debt for this territory. Despite these costs of victory in the war, the government had no choice but to accept this "defeat" at Paris.

D'ANNUNZIO AND THE CONQUEST OF FIUME

Gabriele D'Annunzio, a militant Italian nationalist poet, believed that he had a choice about the lands on the Adriatic. In September 1919, he marched his private nationalist army into the Adriatic port of Fiume and declared it his kingdom. Many Italians less inclined to dramatic action adored D'Annunzio for his patriotic feat and felt a killing rage toward their own leaders for their cowardice at Paris.

A FALTERING GOVERNMENT

Italian parliamentary institutions rested on shaky foundations even before the shock of the Paris settlement. Since unification in 1871, national leaders had not solved the problem of economic backwardness in the south. They also had not overcome regional loyalties that hindered effective government. As a result, support for the national political system weakened over the years.

THE WORKING CLASSES IN REBELLION

The government tried to increase its following during the war with promises of land redistribution to help poor peasants. When national leaders did not carry out the reform soon after victory, their inaction dashed the hopes of Italy's large farm population. The peasants tried their own solution. They began to take the land away from its aristocratic owners.

Industrialists and urban workers found little more to please them in government policies than did the peasants. Business owners and laborers had made drastic changes in the manufacturing system to meet the needs of a nation at war. At the end of the struggle, they expected government assistance to ensure continued business profitability and employment during the transition to peace. Legislators again proved incapable of satisfying their constituents. Direct action suited urban laborers as well as it did the farmers. Workers in northern centers took over their factories. Industrialists and the owners of farm estates now had another bitter complaint, the loss of their property.

PARTISAN DEADLOCK IN PARLIAMENT

Changes in the party system hindered the ability of the government to respond to citizen needs. New Socialist and Catholic parties had emerged and gained great strength in the parliament. Both parties wanted reform. Divisions within these organizations, however, reduced their power to take action in the legislature. Furthermore, the four leading parties—Liberals, Democrats, Catholics, Socialists—would not cooperate with one another.

With the parliament so divided, it could not form a strong executive cabinet. Italian leaders, therefore, hardly led at all. Their reaction to illegal land and factory seizures was typical: They approved the peasants' theft and ignored the urban labor action.

A MOUNTING CRISIS

Italy's worsening crisis reached dangerous proportions in 1919 and 1920. In June 1919, Italian diplomats signed the Paris treaty giving up their territorial claims. A wave of strikes and property seizures crested in 1920. Industrialists and aristocrats faced these horrors and also expected the hated Socialists in the parliament to enact many unwanted reforms. Inflation struck all segments of society, but especially the middle classes, harder and harder after the war. By 1920, Italian money had lost eighty percent of its buying power compared to 1914. To make economic matters worse, large numbers of returning veterans could find no jobs. The crisis climaxed in December when the government shelled Fiume to drive out D'Annunzio, the hero of Italian patriots. In this state of misery, the nation longed for a savior.

**The Response
of the Political
Right to Chaos**

The two-year crisis after the Great War prompted many rabid nationalists to arise with claims that they could save Italy and lead it to greatness.
They organized bands of tough street fighters and prepared to enact their
programs by force if necessary. The figure of Benito Mussolini overshadowed all other nationalist militants.

BENITO MUSSOLINI (1883–1945) AND FASCISM

Mussolini began his political career as a Socialist before the First World
War. His writing and speaking skills soon earned him a leadership position
in the party, and he became the editor of its journal. Despite his success on
the Left, Mussolini broke with the Socialists. They continued to oppose all
nationalist combat after the Great War began in 1914, but Mussolini wanted
Italy to fight against the Central Powers. When Italy entered the war, he
acted on this belief and volunteered for duty.

By the end of the war in 1918, Mussolini had moved to the far Right.
Soon he was ready to fight for his new principles. In 1919, Mussolini
organized his *Fasci di Combattimento* (Combat Groups) for street war with
leftists, the force he now considered Italy's great enemy. *Fasci,* the particular
Italian word chosen to emphasize that these were solid units of political
fighters, gave the movement its name—fascism.

FASCIST IDEOLOGY

Most scholars deny that Fascists had an ideology. But even if many
theorists recognize no structure of political doctrine, Mussolini and his
followers vividly expressed the beliefs and attitudes for which they fought.
Fascists depicted their most important principle with the movement's symbol, the *fasces*. They borrowed this image from the ancient Roman imperial
design of an ax protruding from a bundle of tightly bound rods. Originally,
this symbol represented the unity, power, and glory of the state at a time
when ancient Italians ruled the world. Without words, the Fascists thus
promised dedication to Italian tradition and a repetition of the Roman
achievement. The speeches and actions of the Fascists constantly reinforced
this ultranationalist spirit.

In keeping with their determination to make Italy supreme, Fascists
appeared to be viciously intolerant of anyone who pursued individual or
class interests. Such divisiveness in their view weakened Italy. Fascists
denounced liberalism and democracy as ideologies that glorified personal
rights above national duty. They expressed even greater contempt for the
socialist and communist left. The Marxist campaign for international working-class revolution posed the ultimate threat to a triumphant nation.

Fascist tirades against liberal democratic institutions focused especially
on the evils of the parliamentary system of government. Mussolini's forces

charged that legislators debated but did nothing to achieve the greatness Italy deserved. Fascists would end the talk and drive the nation forward.

In this frantic advance, however, the Fascists promised never to destroy the true Italian legacy. The Fascists would preserve a hierarchy of classes rather than grind everyone into the proletariat. They would defend private enterprise and profits for industrious Italians. They would not nationalize property. The street war on Marxists reflected the movement's commitment to these principles.

Fascists declared that success in their crusade required the total submission of all Italians to them. They believed that they deserved this unquestioning obedience because of their exceptionally pure national spirit. Then everyone, party members and ordinary citizens alike, had to look to the Fascist leader as their ultimate authority. No one else so completely embodied the traits of an Italian—courage, forcefulness, discipline, and a spirit of self-sacrifice.

THE APPEAL OF FASCISM

The Fascists' ideology quickly made them the favorites of aristocrats and the lower middle classes. Fascism also attracted some industrialists. These segments of society shared the Fascist spirit of superpatriotism and hatred for socialists and communists. Fascists also provided useful and sometimes brutal services to factory owners and aristocrats. Mussolini's *Fasci* (also called the "Black Shirts") attacked strikers and protected property from seizure. These tactics caused most Italians to view the Fascists, rather than the government, as the leading force for law and order in an increasingly chaotic society.

The Fascist Struggle for Power

Mussolini's right-wing warriors continued their combat against strikers and land-grabbers in 1921. They also intensified their struggle to gain political power. In May, the *Fasci* used threats and violence to influence elections to the legislature. The Black Shirts assaulted Left politicians. Beating opponents and force-feeding them huge quantities of castor oil became common practices. The police and courts approved and did nothing about the brutality.

THE FASCIST PARTY ON THE ATTACK

After months of street warfare to prepare them for government responsibilities, Mussolini organized his followers into a political party in November 1921. This new Fascist party already had about 300,000 people in its ranks and thirty-five representatives in the legislature. As Fascist power spread from public squares to the halls of government, the party's Socialist enemies tried to counter the Right by increased labor militancy. The

Socialists ordered a general strike for August 1922 but it failed. Too few workers had responded to the call.

Fascists ignored these signs of weakness on the Left, raised the alarm of impending Communist revolution, and went on a rampage against the Left. The Black Shirts wrecked Socialist and Communist presses. They destroyed opposition-party buildings. In several cities, Fascists took even bolder steps. They threw out duly elected Socialist leaders and took charge themselves. This violent right-wing campaign against an exaggerated threat succeeded remarkably well. The Fascists' power and popularity expanded rapidly.

THE MARCH ON ROME

As defenders of private enterprise, public order, and the Italian flag, Fascists appealed to an ever larger public. Responses to the Fascist struggle for power revealed that by mid-1922 the party's following included more than aristocrats, the lower middle class, and a few industrialists. Fascists had by then become the heroes also of military leaders, the Catholic Church hierarchy, and the Italian king, Victor Emmanuel III (r. 1900–1946).

Mussolini knew his moment had arrived. In September 1922, he began talks with royal officials and others to arrange his accession to government power. The Black Shirts strengthened their leader's bid for control by a mass march on Rome on October 28, 1922. Government leaders wanted to stop the Fascist action by force. The king refused to sign a martial law decree, then offered to make Mussolini Premier of Italy. When these developments made the way to Rome completely clear and safe, Mussolini followed his Black Shirts into the capital and took charge of Italy.

GERMANY IN TRANSITION

Until the last days of the First World War, most Germans expected to win. Word of their country's military defeat and impending surrender plunged Germany into despair and chaos in October and November 1918. Revolts broke out and quickly spread. Emperor William II abdicated on November 9, 1918, and the Moderate Socialists in Berlin declared Germany to be a republic. Despite the declaration, the nation had only begun its difficult transition to self-government.

The New Republic

The Moderate Socialists who led the new government did not plan to enact radical Left reforms. They stood for democracy and the gradual development of an improved life for the masses. Before they could launch any programs, however, the republican leaders had to fend off rebels and at the same time organize their machinery of government.

THE SPARTACIST REVOLT

Beyond the circle of Socialists who supported the new republic stood others who wanted to follow the path of the Russian Bolsheviks. One of these revolutionary Marxist forces, the Spartacist Union led by Rosa Luxemburg and Karl Liebknecht, prepared to overthrow the new government even before it was fully formed. The Spartacists struck their blow for proletarian revolution on January 5, 1919, but suffered immediate and crushing defeat. German troops smashed the rebellion, arrested its two leaders, and murdered them on January 15.

THE WEIMAR CONSTITUTION

German military leaders had used their army to stop the Spartacists because they hated the Left. These militarists cared little for the idea of a republic. Supporters of representative government needed to construct effective political institutions if they were to have any chance of success in Germany. They met in a constituent assembly at Weimar from February to July 1919 and completed the fundamental laws of the German Republic.

The Weimar Constitution provided for an elected president empowered to appoint a chancellor. A cabinet of ministers under the chancellor formed the government's executive office. The Weimar document also established a legislative house (*Reichsrat*) comprising representatives from the nation's eighteen states. Another legislative body, the *Reichstag*, had members elected for the nation as a whole rather than as representatives of districts. The constitution of this "Weimar Republic" gave Germany its first truly democratic government.

FLAWS IN THE NEW SYSTEM

Although the new system permitted real citizen influence, it also made it very difficult for a chancellor and cabinet to govern. If the executives could not pass laws, they had to overcome the stalemate in one of two ways. They could resign, then the president would appoint a new chancellor who would try to win votes in the Reichstag. Or a chancellor unable to pass bills could dissolve the Reichstag and hope that the subsequent election provided a working majority.

The multitude of political divisions in Weimar Germany meant that chancellors could get a working majority only by arranging the support of a group of parties. These coalitions seldom lasted long. On the average, cabinets fell apart every eight months. Under these conditions, successful self-government was very difficult to achieve.

THE VERSAILLES TREATY CRISIS

Passionate German militarists despised the Weimar Republic especially for its acceptance of the Versailles Treaty. The article specifying Germany's responsibility for the war and requiring reparations disgraced the nation, in their view. Above all, restrictions on the troop strength and armaments of the German military enraged the officer corps. Military leaders did not intend to accept these provisions that would so weaken the nation's forces. They attempted to nullify the treaty's restrictions by financing private armies to sustain the military strength and heroic spirit of Germany.

THE KAPP *PUTSCH*

In March 1920, the republic began to carry out the military limitation clauses of the Versailles Treaty. Troop units that the government ordered to disband refused to obey, however, and took over Berlin. They elevated Wolfgang Kapp to leadership of their newly declared German state. The legal government then fled the capital. This Kapp *Putsch* (coup) collapsed when labor forces countered with a general strike that shut down Berlin. The Left took heart from this success against right-wing militarists and rebelled in other cities. German army units suppressed these new working-class outbreaks as they had the Spartacists. The Weimar Republic remained in power, but it survived again because its enemies on the Right defeated the Left opposition.

THE BATTLE OVER REPARATIONS

Military clauses in the Versailles Treaty had maddened German officers and inspired the Kapp *Putsch*. Reparations provisions of the peace settlement also endangered the government. Paris negotiators left the size of Germany's penalty payments unspecified. After an extended dispute, Germany and the Allies decided that the total owed was 132 billion marks (about thirty-two billion dollars). Compliance presented staggering economic problems for the republic, but Weimar leaders adopted a "fulfillment" policy. They would pay as much as they could, another sin against the nation from the Right's point of view.

The steps taken to meet reparations obligations produced a devastating inflationary trend. The value of German money (the mark) plunged to historic lows and continued downward. When declining economic conditions made it impossible to meet the reparations schedule, France and Belgium decided to punish nonpayment. In January 1923, French and Belgian troops occupied an important German mining and industrial region, the Ruhr valley. Laborers in the Ruhr stopped work to protest the foreign takeover, and the government pumped in funds to support the workers. As a result, inflation reached cataclysmic proportions. In 1914, 4.2 marks equaled a dollar. The Ruhr crisis caused German currency values to plunge so low that a single dollar equaled 4.2 trillion marks by 1923. The German economy was wrecked, and everyone suffered.

As this crisis developed through the early 1920s, the growing right-wing opposition forces blamed all the nation's woes on the Weimar government. Militant nationalist organizations targeted the republic's leaders for assassination. Matthias Erzberger had signed the armistice ending the First World War. Assassins felled him in August 1921. Walther Rathenau, a brilliant Weimar leader associated with the policy of fulfillment, died at the hands of fanatic nationalists the following June. Then the crisis worsened.

Adolf Hitler (1889–1945)

During the early 1920s, the south German state of Bavaria became a stronghold of belligerent nationalist movements committed to the destruction of the Weimar Republic. By 1923, the reparations and inflation crisis so weakened the government that nationalist leaders in Bavaria assumed they could easily overthrow the Weimar Republic. They planned to march to victory in the same way that Mussolini had the previous autumn. The German conspirator with the strongest attack force was Adolf Hitler.

AN IMMIGRANT SUPERPATRIOT

In 1923, when Hitler was twenty-four, he moved from his native Austria to Munich in the Bavarian region of Germany. As an ethnic German who believed passionately that everyone of that nationality should live in a unified state, he felt ecstatic and at home. Hitler viewed the outbreak of the Great War the next year as a blessing. He could fight for Germany. In heroic service as a message carrier at the front, Corporal Hitler suffered wounds and earned a very prestigious medal. The end of the war confronted Hitler with dull civilian life in the horrible atmosphere of a nation that had surrendered.

HITLER'S IDEOLOGY

The beliefs that Hitler held dear made acceptance of Germany's fate very difficult. He claimed that his experiences as a young ethnic German living in Vienna (1908 to 1913) gave him a rocklike structure of principles that never changed. These convictions included not simply nationalism but a racist form of the ideology. Hitler preached that true Germans belonged to the Aryan superrace, a group destined by their superior genetic traits to rule the world. With such ideas, Hitler found much to despise about Weimar Germany.

Hitler's belief that Jewish influence predominated in Weimar intensified his hatred of the existing order. A supremely vicious anti-Semitic (anti-Jewish) ideology, in fact, formed an inseparable part of Hitler's racist nationalism. He described Jews as a parasitic race with the potential to pollute pure Aryan blood and weaken the superior Germans. In his view,

Jews destroyed culture; Germans created it. Hitler always bluntly offered a solution—the extermination of all Jews. He would be able to make good use of this racist nationalist creed in Munich; such ideas were widely popular there.

FORMATION OF THE NAZI PARTY

When Hitler returned from the war, he entered the ranks of the militant nationalists committed to destruction of the Weimar Republic. He joined the German Workers Party, a small right-wing group, and rose quickly in the organization. His racist nationalist message and hypnotic speaking ability helped to swell party membership. In July 1921, Hitler's party made him its all-powerful leader (*Fuehrer*). The organization now used the title National Socialist German Workers Party. Although Hitler rejected true socialism, this Right party hoped the title would win laborers away from the Left.

Hitler's Nazis (from the German words for "National Socialist") magnified their influence by political violence. As Fuehrer, Hitler commanded a brown-shirted political combat troop with two regular responsibilities—to shut down the meetings of opponents and protect members of the party. These Storm Troopers (*Sturmabteilung* or SA) also stood ready for the special duty of a revolutionary assault on the government. Hitler, other Bavarian nationalists, and right-wing political officials in that region thought that they could take over the country with such forces behind them.

THE MUNICH BEER-HALL *PUTSCH*

When concessions by Weimar leaders caused the conservative officials in the Bavarian government to change their minds about revolt against the republic, Hitler took the initiative. On November 8, 1923, as his formerly rebellious associates held a meeting in a Munich beer hall, Hitler burst in, shot the ceiling with his pistol, and forced the Bavarian officials to support his seizure of power in Germany. They agreed, but their compliance meant nothing. They were ready to stop the Nazis at the first opportunity.

When Hitler and the Storm Troopers paraded into a central Munich square on November 9, they encountered police officers, soldiers, a hail of bullets, and immediate defeat. Fourteen Storm Troopers died in the gunfire. Hitler flattened himself on the street, avoided injury, and fled. After his arrest several days later, the Fuehrer was tried for treason and received a five-year sentence.

In certain respects, victory lay hidden behind this Munich defeat. The Nazi dead became useful martyrs in subsequent propaganda campaigns. The Fuehrer's very light sentence for treason also revealed the favor this racist nationalist found among many officials, including those in the judiciary. Court sympathies permitted Hitler to enter a relatively comfortable prison environment, write a book (*Mein Kampf*), and enjoy release after less than two years. The *Putsch* and prison experience made Hitler recognize the steps he needed to take to seize Germany. *Mein Kampf* also became an important Nazi propaganda tool that helped Hitler in his struggle for power. Mussolini's surprising success and Hitler's qualified victory at Munich had brought fascism to vigorous life in Europe by 1923.

FASCIST ITALY

During their struggle to achieve power, Fascists asserted that they came as nationalist revolutionaries to end the established system of parliamentary liberalism and crush the Communists who threatened to take Italy for the Left. Mussolini assured the nation with his first words as premier that Fascists could have destroyed the parliamentary system but did not want to, "for the present."

The Transition to Dictatorship

In the beginning, members of the other parties joined the Fascists in the parliament and in the executive cabinet. Mussolini and his party seemed tamed by the responsibilities of office. Non-Fascists in the government thus agreed to give the new premier extraordinary executive authority for one year.

Mussolini began at once to transform the system by putting Fascists in charge of the government bureaucracy and the upper legislative house (the Senate). He also brought the police under party control and converted the Black Shirts into an official force on the public payroll. Despite these advances in power, the party still did not fully rule the important lower house of the parliament (the Chamber of Deputies) and faced serious opposition there.

THE ACERBO BILL

Before the legislative elections took place in April 1924, the Fascists secured passage of the Acerbo Bill, an electoral law that doomed parliamentary government. The act provided for the party with the most votes above a minimum of twenty-five percent to take two-thirds of the Chamber seats. The Acerbo Law and the Black Shirts' talent for voter intimidation ensured the Fascists a two-thirds majority in the Chamber after the spring elections. Their next step was to silence the minority.

THE MATTEOTTI MURDER

Giacomo Matteotti, a Moderate Socialist deputy, boldly fought fascism with words. In the parliament, he vehemently condemned Mussolini and demanded that non-Fascist deputies stop cooperating with the Fascist leader.

Matteotti also reached out to a larger audience with explosive information. He published a book that documented many cases of Fascist violence and lawlessness. On June 10, 1924, Fascists abducted Matteotti and murdered him.

Public outrage over the assassination kept Mussolini's government on the brink of collapse for the rest of 1924. Opposition deputies tried to hasten the fall by boycotting parliamentary sessions. Unwittingly, they had given up their last lever of power. Mussolini reasserted himself in January 1925. He publicly accepted responsibility for the murder and released his Black Shirts to attack anti-Fascists. Soon Mussolini purged the government of non-Fascists, outlawed all parties except his own, and brought the press fully under party control. With these actions, the Fascists approached totalitarianism.

The Fascist State

The trend of Mussolini's government toward absolute dictatorship weakened in the latter 1920s. The Italian Fascist state, in fact, never became fully totalitarian, even though Mussolini kept his powerful dictatorial grip on the nation. The ruler's failure to exercise more complete control resulted in part from the ability of traditional authoritarian institutions, such as the government bureaucracy, the military, and the Roman Catholic Church, to remain somewhat independent within the state.

THE RULING PARTY

Despite Fascism's less than totalitarian power, Italy still operated under a one-party dictatorship. The ruling Fascists structured their party in a hierarchy much like the Communists' in the USSR. Instead of local cells, the Italian party had *Fasci*. The organizational pyramid above the *Fasci* extended to a Fascist Grand Council at the top.

True to the Fascists' right-wing belief that authority should be concentrated in the hands of a few leaders, Mussolini exercised dictatorial power over the Grand Council and the rest of the 1,000,000 lesser party members. As Il Duce's chief agents, the Fascists, in turn, reigned supreme over all non-party agencies and people.

FASCIST GOVERNMENT

Formal government structures remained unchanged under the Fascists. The king kept his position as technical head of state. Daily executive functions of government continued to be carried out by a premier and his cabinet. The two-house legislature still met. Citizens, moreover, retained the right to vote for Chamber deputies. But this system was largely a sham.

Under fascism, the king became a figurehead until Mussolini's government began to collapse during the Second World War. Mussolini served as permanent ruling premier, and the members of a single docile party sat in his parliament. Italians who voted had the meaningless choice of accepting or rejecting a candidate list presented by the Fascists.

The Fascist Socioeconomic Order

Fascist Party and government mechanisms denied political control to Italy's 30 million citizens, who, nevertheless, stayed loyal. The party found it relatively easy to keep the support of most segments of society. Fascist policies, for example, ensured the continued social and material well-being of the traditional privileged classes. The lower middle-class did not get such concrete rewards but remained devoted to the Fascists as a bulwark against communism.

PROPAGANDA AND SOCIAL CONTROL

Fascist propaganda techniques also excited and attracted the masses. From his balcony and in other settings, Mussolini spoke to huge crowds and swayed them with his oratory. His generally dramatic flair enhanced this effect in public addresses and appearances. Il Duce's words and images reached a nationwide audience through the press, radio, and the cinema. The mass media, in fact, constantly bombarded Italians with propaganda designed to bend the citizenry to the party's will.

CORPORATIVISM

The actions that drew large segments of society to fascism left many industrialists less than enthusiastic about the party through the early 1920s. Fascist leaders pursued the support of this important group in a special way once the party achieved power. In 1925, Mussolini's government recognized a combination of industrialists as a "corporation" and granted it extensive economic power. Subsequently, the party also set up corporations for large-scale employers in trade and agriculture. The party then arranged similar organizations for labor and the professions, but without giving them economic influence.

By the 1930s, the Fascists began merging these corporations with government institutions, claiming to have created a new "corporative state" in which socioeconomic classes lived and ruled themselves in harmony. The government promised that this system would yield prosperity for all classes. In reality, corporativism was a myth covering state-approved economic supremacy for propertied interests. It guaranteed a material advance for the upper classes only.

THE LATERAN TREATY

By 1929, the Fascists decided to court the church as they had business. This action too would benefit their cause. The party arranged the Lateran Treaty (February 11, 1929) ending the state of non-recognition that had existed between the popes and the government since the completion of Italian unification. This agreement accepted the pope as the ruler of his own territory, Vatican City in Rome. He, in turn, gave up church claims to other territories in central Italy. Thereafter, the Fascist state could operate without risk of conflict with the papacy.

THE TRIUMPH OF NAZISM IN GERMANY

Enormous problems associated with the Versailles Treaty threatened to destroy the Weimar Republic during its first five years (1918–1923). This time of danger for the new government climaxed with the foreign occupation of the Ruhr valley that began in January 1923 and Hitler's beer-hall *Putsch* the following November.

The Recovery of the Weimar Republic

Gustav Stresemann held office as chancellor during most of 1923 and thereafter was foreign minister until his death in 1929. In these positions, Stresemann implemented policies that gave the German republic its most secure and prosperous years.

THE DAWES AND YOUNG PLANS

Stresemann led Germany from its ruinous inflation to economic recovery and greater political stability by a series of well-conceived actions. He quickly started to bring Germany's rampant inflation under control by drastically cutting the money supply and ending the costly Ruhr work stoppage. With the cessation of resistance in the Ruhr, Stresemann also signaled the Allied Powers that he wanted to cooperate to end the reparations conflict, the underlying cause of many of Weimar's problems.

Negotiations with the Allies then produced the Dawes Plan in early 1924. This agreement reduced reparations payments for the next five years and had a very beneficial effect on the German economy. When the Dawes Plan expired, Stresemann secured even better payment terms in the Young Plan. He also won an Allied promise to withdraw troops from the German Rhineland which they had occupied since the end of the Great War.

When Stresemann died in October 1929, he had brought a remarkable political, economic, and diplomatic renewal for Germany. Through all Stresemann's struggles to restore Weimar, Hitler and other militant nationalists had fought against the republic with a vengeance. Every agreement Stresemann reached with the Allies simply strengthened the nationalists' view of him as a traitor.

THE GREAT DEPRESSION

In the month of Stresemann's death, the New York stock market crashed. Business shares plunged to half their original value within a few weeks.

Soon many enterprises and banks failed. Numerous other financial institutions stood on the brink of collapse. They began to demand repayment of huge loans contracted by European nations in the wake of the Great War. As a result of the especially heavy debts of Germany and Austria, these countries quickly followed the United States into a deep economic slump.

By 1932, this "Great Depression" had spread to virtually every European nation. It created masses of jobless people, many of whom were ready for extreme measures to end the crisis. The especially severe shock of the depression in Germany made the nation highly susceptible to the Nazi idea of a dictatorial nationalist savior.

HITLER'S RESURGENCE

Hitler left prison in late 1924 convinced that the Nazis should never again attempt a coup. He had had enough of facing bullets and sitting in cells. Legal victory over the republic became the new party watchword. Hitler at once began to convert the Nazis into a party designed to win Reichstag elections.

Soon, Hitler had an effectively organized movement with a national structure similar to the Italian Fascist party's. After slow growth for several years, the depression hit in 1929 and party membership surged. It soon became the strongest party in Germany. Hitler's brown-shirted warriors multiplied also. Desperate jobless men flocked into the Storm Troopers for action and wages. The depression drove voters to Hitler too. In the July 1932 Reichstag elections, the Nazis took 230 seats, 100 more than the second-place Socialists.

The Destruction of Weimar

Industrialists, aristocrats, and officers in the military comprised the moderate Right leadership in Weimar Germany. The crisis produced by the depression made these conservatives fear a surge in strength for the Left. From 1929 to 1933, Defense Minister Wilhelm Groener and his adviser, General Kurt von Schleicher, spearheaded the battle of the moderate Right to gain control over the government and completely nullify Socialist influence.

HITLER'S LEGAL ENTRY

Groener and Schleicher pursued their goal at first by getting President Hindenburg to appoint moderate Right chancellors who then tried to obtain a majority in the Reichstag. They selected Heinrich Bruening as chancellor in March 1930, but after fourteen months his government failed. When Franz von Papen, their second choice, lasted only six months, Schleicher himself became chancellor (December 2, 1932). His Cabinet collapsed in less than two months.

Schleicher and his moderate Right supporters thought they had only two choices at this point—Papen or Hitler. Schleicher considered Papen too willing to cooperate with Socialists. Hitler would never befriend Marxists, but he presented problems too. Many people of the moderate Right disliked the outrageous display and bullying tactics of radical Right groups such as the Nazis. This behavior made the Nazis unpleasant associates. It did not make them unacceptable.

Schleicher felt confident of the course to take. Since the Nazis had more Reichstag deputies than any other party, Hitler could control the necessary votes. The moderate Right political professionals thought that they in turn could control him. The Schleicher faction pressured Hindenburg, and he appointed Hitler chancellor on January 30, 1933.

THE REICHSTAG FIRE

Hitler built his dictatorship with lightning speed once he took office. A fire that destroyed the Reichstag building in late February 1933 provided the Nazis with an occasion to act. They blamed Communists and began a vigorous campaign to suppress them. During the attack on communism, the Nazis outlawed the Marxist party. The Nazis also arranged to suspend the rights of individual expression in order to silence all opponents of their actions.

THE ENABLING ACT

In Reichstag elections the month after the fire, Storm Troopers unleashed the most extreme siege of threatening behavior ever. Even though the Nazis won only forty-four percent of the votes with these tactics, Hitler easily dominated the new assembly. He made deals that secured the support of all parties except the Socialists. Then on March 23, 1933, Hitler presented the Enabling Act, a law granting him dictatorial power until April 1, 1937. Socialists cast the only negative votes, too few to matter.

THE NIGHT OF THE LONG KNIVES

Legal opposition to Hitler had ceased to exist but resistant factions remained. Influential moderate rightists such as Schleicher worried the Fuehrer. They might not support him strongly enough. Members of the radical Right who wanted to use political violence in their own way bothered Hitler even more. These troublesome militants on the far Right included Storm Trooper (SA) chief Ernst Roehm and many other well known SA leaders. Hitler was determined to end the possibility of independent Storm Trooper action.

The Fuehrer struck on June 30, 1934. A wave of assassinations on this "Night of the Long Knives" snuffed out the lives of Roehm, Schleicher, and other potential opponents. This purge increased the prominence of Hitler's personal guards, the *Schutzstaffel* (SS). The SS was the killer force that carried out the murders. This special agency thereafter became one of the chief instruments to implement Hitler's every wish.

The Nazi State

In the process of smashing Weimar institutions and sources of possible resistance to nazism, the party forged its new state. Nazi actions in May and June 1933 closed all independent trade unions and replaced them with a single Labor Front under party control. In July, all opposition parties were outlawed. These measures against parties and unions removed two important nongovernmental structures that could have limited Nazi authority.

GOVERNMENT REORGANIZATION

At first, much of the upper structure of government remained unchanged under the Nazis. Germany still had a president (Hindenburg), chancellor (Hitler), Cabinet, and two-house legislature. Hitler, however, wielded all the authority in this system. As one indication of the Nazi leader's supremacy, when Hindenburg died (August 1934), Hitler became president as well as chancellor.

The Nazis made more obvious changes in governmental institutions at other levels. The Fuehrer issued a decree in April 1933 requiring the removal of all civil-service personnel not absolutely loyal to the Nazis. This action to tighten control over central government bureaucrats coincided with steps to subdue officials in territorial subdivisions such as Bavaria and Saxony. These and other states making up the *Reich* (empire) had kept significant power over local affairs since the unification of Germany. Laws passed in April 1933 and January 1934 gave the central government dominance over bureaucrats at lower levels.

The Nazis also seized supreme authority over law enforcement. Hitler empowered himself and other Nazis to interfere at will in the operation of the courts. In April 1933 the party organized the Gestapo (secret police) under Heinrich Himmler. This covert force and a special security division of the SS had unlimited power to arrest and punish citizens. Hitler and his party were the law in the Nazi state.

A WAR ECONOMY

The Storm Troopers who were slaughtered on the Night of the Long Knives died in part for their sin of believing in the literal meaning of "National *Socialism*." The SA rejected international working-class ideals but longed to take the property of the rich and use it to benefit other social classes within the nation. Hitler spilled their blood freely in a dramatic expression of his rejection of socialism in any real sense of the word.

The Fuehrer would not take the money, goods, or enterprises of the wealthy. His economic obsession was to give the Nazi state the ultimate war machine. Financiers, industrialists, merchants, and farmers could own and profit handsomely from their businesses or land, as long as they served this singular purpose. Hitler governed, not the capitalists. But the business classes grew rich.

A SUBSERVIENT SOCIETY

In their effort to possess the souls of all Germans, the Nazis established the Ministry of Popular Enlightenment. Joseph Goebbels (1897–1945) directed this agency as it removed the spirit of enlightenment from all publications, radio broadcasts, films, and plays. The Nazi mind entered all literature and art. These works became empty shells.

Although some people resisted or fled the country, almost the entire cultural and scientific elite readily cooperated in Goebbels's campaign to present a thoroughly racist-nationalist view of life. Schools at every level slanted education to serve Nazi purposes. They taught absolute obedience to the leader. They urged faith in his Aryan and anti-Semitic myths. Indoctrination continued beyond school hours in the Hitler Youth, the nation's only legal organization for young people. (Everyone ten to eighteen years old belonged.) The party staged massive rallies, especially at Nuremberg, to deepen the nationalist trance of young and old alike.

Religion Under Nazism

From the perspective of the Nazis, their attack on jews was a "racial" rather than a religious matter. Despite this myth, the Nazi attempt to remove all jews from Europe and erase the influence of Judaism constituted an attempt to destroy both an entire ethnic group and a religion fundamental to European civilization. Nazi leaders showed more tolerance toward Christianity, as long as Christians displayed absolute loyalty to Nazi dogmas. Christians did not have to die, if Hitler could possess their souls.

THE NUREMBERG LAWS

Immediately after taking power, the Nazis unleashed their assault on Jews. The party began to seize their property and excluded them from businesses and professions. Much of the early anti-Semitic legislation was incorporated as "race law" clauses in codes affecting the press and other aspects of life. The Nuremberg Laws in September 1935 contained a more sweeping attack. They ended Jewish citizenship in Germany, outlawed marriage between Germans and Jews, and made sexual intercourse between members of these "races" a crime.

CRYSTAL NIGHT

Another anti-Semitic surge occurred in late 1938. A Jewish youth embittered by the deportation of his parents from Germany to Poland killed a German Embassy official in Paris on November 7. A wave of anti-Semitic destruction broke out across Germany. Mobs smashed through Jewish districts, destroying their shops, torching their homes and synagogues, and killing several people.

The trail of broken windows left by this attack inspired the description of this time of violence as "Crystal Night." After a government review of the event, officials fined the Jews one billion marks for the damage done by the rioters who had attacked them. An intensification of the campaign to herd Jews into concentration camps also followed Crystal Night.

THE CHRISTIAN RESPONSE TO NAZISM

Many Christian leaders offered no objections to the actions of the Nazis. Their silence induced Hitler to allow the churches to stay open. His spirit of compromise toward a faith that he personally rejected even included a formal agreement with the Catholic Church (July 20, 1933) to tolerate its operation of schools and other organizations. Thereafter, the Nazis gradually escalated their program to diminish the influence of Christianity. Their struggle against this religion and other actions by the party led Pope Pius XI (1922–1939) to issue sharp official criticisms of the Nazis. His successor, Pius XII (1939–1958), proved more tolerant of Nazism.

Protestant leaders also exhibited diverse attitudes toward Nazism. In late 1933, a group of 8,000 pastors split over whether they should support or oppose Hitler. Three-fourths of them formed a movement against Nazism. Many of these resistant ministers eventually suffered greatly for their stand. The other Protestant leaders kept their faith in the Fuehrer, as did most of the members of the German Christian churches. Many German Christians responded to Hitler as though they had found God on earth.

THE BORDERLANDS OF FASCIST EUROPE

The First World War and the Peace of Paris left the former Austrian territories and the Balkan States with very ineffective governments, gigantic economic problems, and severe social conflicts. These conditions in East Europe ideally suited the growth of extremist movements. In several of these societies of the region, socialists and communists soon attempted to seize power on behalf of the downtrodden working classes. Then the rising force of fascist and other similar Right movements pushed the Left extremists aside and by the 1930s ruled every East European state except Czechoslovakia. Events followed a somewhat similar pattern in Spain and Portugal, thus completing a wide band of fascist nations around the great Italian and German dictatorships.

Fascism in East Europe

New, restored, or restructured nations covered the map of East Europe because of the collapse of the Russian and Austrian Empires at the end of the Great War. Authoritarian political traditions were strong throughout the region except in Czechoslovakia. All the formerly autocratic countries had new self-governing systems that they had to learn to use. At the same time, they had to solve the serious problems left by the war.

A RESTORED POLAND

Poland provides a good example of the political difficulties of the region. The Poles won independence from Russia as the Great War drew to a close. Allied peacemakers then arranged a very favorable territorial settlement for the restored nation. Poland proceeded to establish a parliamentary democracy, turning away from monarchy for the first time in the nation's long history. The legislature, in fact, had such power that it could virtually ignore the president.

Despite such seemingly favorable political circumstances, the Polish government proved completely incapable of solving economic and national-minority problems that threatened to destroy the new system. The all-powerful Sejm (lower legislative house) debated endlessly and did nothing. One critic said that the flies in the chamber died of boredom during the meaningless discussions.

Poles gave up on their democratic experiment by 1926 and accepted a military dictator as ruler. Centuries of authoritarian government had not equipped legislators for their difficult tasks, but they had prepared the nation to yield to an autocrat.

THE VICTORY OF THE RIGHT IN EAST EUROPE

Although the specific circumstances varied in the other countries of East Europe, almost all of them had political traditions and problems that encouraged the failure of young self-governing institutions. The experience of Estonia, Latvia, and Lithuania (the Baltic States) very closely paralleled Poland's. Events in Austria took a similar course, up to a point. This small remnant of the Hapsburg Empire also made the transition from democracy in the 1920s to a Right dictatorship by 1934. Then in the late 1930s, the new Austrian rulers developed a system with much more strongly Fascist traits than in Poland.

Hungary turned to a rigid authoritarian government more quickly than the other states of the region. Hungarian Communists led by Béla Kun attempted a revolution at the end of the Great War. After the Communist failure in late 1919, Hungary began a decade under a very authoritarian government that attempted to restore *ancien* traditions. By 1931, more modern authoritarians won control. Hungarian Fascists established a regime

CENTRAL EUROPE
AFTER WORLD WAR I

Pre-war Boundaries
Post-war Boundaries
German Losses
Russian Losses
Bulgarian Losses
The Former Austria-Hungary

Fig. 14.1   Central Europe After World War I

much like Hitler's. Right-wing dictatorships also supplanted feeble parliamentary systems in Bulgaria, Albania, and Greece by the end of the 1930s.

Iberian Fascism   Neither Portugal nor Spain, the two states on the Iberian Peninsula, had strong modern political and economic institutions in the 1920s. In both nations, the aristocracy, the Catholic Church, and the military leadership clung tightly to *ancien* traditions. These sectors of society remained a powerful force.

SALAZAR IN PORTUGAL

The parliamentary government that Portugal had established in 1910 fell to an army rebellion in 1926. General António Carmona ruled until 1932 when António Salazar (1889–1970) began his long dictatorial reign. Salazar brought to Portugal a variety of fascism similar to Mussolini's, except less flamboyant and more truly committed to old traditions. Salazar devoted himself to the promotion of Catholic tradition in particular.

FRANCO IN SPAIN

King Alfonso XIII (r. 1886–1931) helped to establish Primo de Rivera as a Fascist dictator in Spain in 1923. Despite the strength of traditional forces in this country, liberals and leftists mounted an opposition movement that led to Rivera's departure in 1930 and the king's abdication in 1931. Alfonso's opponents then established a republic and proceeded to enact a liberal and socialist reform program.

Spain's extremely deep-seated social and economic problems presented almost insurmountable barriers to the success of these efforts to create a "workers' republic." The very hostile reaction of the Right to this venture completely doomed it. The landed aristocracy, the Catholic Church, and the military had sufficient influence in political and other institutions to block most reforms. A more dangerous threat appeared with the emergence of a new Fascist movement, the Falange. In 1936, General Francisco Franco (1892–1975) commanded these forces of the Right as they challenged the republic on the field of battle. The Spanish Civil War raged until 1939 when Franco finally destroyed the republic. By the time of Franco's triumph, three-fifths of the European states had Fascist governments. In many respects Modern Europe had become Fascist Europe.

When the First World War ended in November 1918, almost all European states had democratic governments. Italians rejected democracy four years later and willingly submitted to the right-wing dictatorship of Benito Mussolini and the Fascists. By 1939, similar authoritarian regimes had taken charge in Germany, Portugal, Spain, and every East European country except Czechoslovakia. This political conversion was generally welcomed by the citizens of these Fascist states.

The Fascist and other Right dictatorships maintained their broad popular support in a variety of ways. They protected the privileges and property interests of the rural and urban upper classes and thus encouraged the loyalty of these elites. The lower middle and working classes did not do so well economically, but the Fascists offered much more that kept these groups devoted—huge military buildups that provided jobs and a sense of power, emotionally satisfying fanatic nationalism, and a leader with a god-like image.

The enticements offered by Right dictatorships to crisis-ridden societies with strong authoritarian traditions made the victory of fascism over democracy relatively easy in most of Europe. But in a small circle of nations of the European north and northwest, the institutions of self-government survived through the 1920s and 1930s. None of these democratic states, however, exhibited the vibrancy of the Fascist regimes.

Selected Readings

Bullock, Alan C. *Hitler: A Study in Tyranny*. New York: Harper & Row, 1964.

Dawidowicz, Lucy S. *The War Against the Jews, 1933–1945*. New York: Holt, Rinehart, and Winston, 1975.

Eyck, Erich. *A History of the Weimar Republic*. New York: Atheneum, 1970.

Fest, Joachim C. *Hitler*. New York: Harcourt, Brace, and Jovanovich, 1974.

Finer, Herman. *Mussolini's Italy*. Hamden, CT: Archon, 1964.

Hitler, Adolf. *Mein Kampf*. Boston: Houghton Mifflin, 1962.

Mack Smith, Denis. *Mussolini*. New York: Viking, 1982.

Rogger, Hans, and Eugene Weber, eds. *The European Right: A Historical Profile*. Berkeley: The University of California Press, 1965.

Seton-Watson, Hugh. *Eastern Europe Between the Wars, 1918–1941*. 3rd ed. Hamden, CT: Archon, 1962.

Spielvogel, Jackson J. *Hitler and Nazi Germany: A History*. Englewood Cliffs, NJ: Prentice-Hall, 1988.

Tannenbaum, Edward R. *The Fascist Experience: Italian Society and Culture, 1922–1945*. New York: Basic Books, 1972.

Trythall, John W. D. *Franco: A Biography*. London: Hart-Davis, 1970.

15

The Diminished Circle of Democracy, 1918–1939

April 1916	Irish nationalists struggling for independence from Britain launch the Easter Rebellion
1918	The Dadaist movement in art and literature begins
April 1919	British troops attack independence demonstrators in Amritsar, India
1922	T. S. Eliot publishes "The Waste Land"
	Oswald Spengler completes *The Decline of the West*
1923	The British Labour Party wins control of the government for the first time
1924	Thomas Mann publishes *The Magic Mountain*
May 1926	A twelve-day strike breaks out in Britain
1928	All adult women in Britain gain the right to vote
1930	Freud publishes *Civilization and Its Discontents*
1931	The Statute of Westminster grants freedom to the British dominions and organizes the British Commonwealth
1932	Aldous Huxley publishes *Brave New World*
February 1934	A right-wing attack on the French government leads to the Stavisky riots
May 1936	The Popular Front, a French Left coalition, wins control of the government
1937	Picasso paints *Guernica* as a war protest
1938	Ireland gains full independence from Britain
1939	European physicists split an atom for the first time

In East Europe, democracy endured through the 1920s and 1930s only in Czechoslovakia. Sixteen nations in that region and in South Europe turned from self-government to Right dictatorship in these two decades. Societies elsewhere in Europe resisted this transition to fascism. A northern tier of states comprising Finland, Sweden, Norway, Denmark, and Britain preserved their democratic institutions throughout this period. France, Belgium, Holland, Luxemburg, and Switzerland formed another block of democracies directly south of Britain.

Among the North European democracies, the states other than Britain displayed striking vitality throughout these two decades as they developed and utilized the institutions of popular government. Four of the five democracies south of Britain recovered from the war and coped with economic depression in the 1930s without serious difficulty, although they enjoyed somewhat less dramatic political success than the northern democracies. The political record of France, the fifth country in this southern group, varied markedly as the years passed.

French leaders responded in a truly impressive way to the destructive effects of the Great War, and the country was thriving by the end of the 1920s. When the depression struck in the next decade, however, the government faltered seriously. By 1939, France was a dangerously weakened nation. Britain, the country with the most deeply rooted parliamentary tradition and a century of experience in successful reform, easily kept its democratic government intact through these two troubled decades. But the British accomplished little else. From the early 1920s onward, the leaders of Britain seemed at a loss as they faced the problems of the era.

THE STRONGHOLDS OF EUROPEAN DEMOCRACY

Most of the smaller or less populous democracies governed themselves with remarkable success in the twenty years after the First World War. They demonstrated that social crises such as the Great Depression did not require the surrender of political authority to dictators. In several of these strongholds of democracy, political trends in fact ran counter to the authoritarian currents of the time as constitutional changes allowed increased popular influence over government.

The Nordic Democracies   The most impressive advances for democracy during the fascist era occurred in the Nordic countries—Denmark, Norway, Sweden, and Finland.

Fig. 15.1   Europe, 1924–1937

THE SCANDINAVIAN NATIONS

Denmark, Norway, and Sweden have many linguistic and cultural similarities, and historians often refer to the three nations as Scandinavia. The industrial revolution began in these countries in the closing decades of the 1800s, later than in most of Europe. Such a delayed transition to a modern socioeconomic system tended to retard the development of popular influence in government in other regions of Europe. This pattern did not occur in Scandinavia.

Democracy in Scandinavia. By the 1870s, all the Scandinavian nations had assemblies with a degree of influence over public affairs. Thereafter, these societies managed a very orderly transition to mature parliamentary systems. Norway completed this change to representative government in 1884, Denmark in 1901, and Sweden in 1917. Full political democratization came to Scandinavia almost as quickly as representative practices. Norway granted the vote to all adults in 1913, Denmark in 1915, and Sweden in 1921.

Socialism. The Scandinavians proceeded from the achievement of political democracy by 1921 to the development of socialism in the 1920s and 1930s. This movement toward the equalization of wealth took place in an atmosphere of constructive compromise, as had the earlier process of democratization. Instead of demands for the nationalization of enterprises, Scandinavian socialists cooperated with other political factions to organize and control the economy in a way that ensured the welfare of the masses without destroying private enterprise.

The Response to Depression. As a result of Scandinavia's transition to socialism, the wave of depression that swept over Europe in the 1930s caused minimal suffering in these three Nordic countries. Businesses failed and the number of unemployed people grew, but Scandinavian governments carried out extensive reform programs to prevent economic misery. Political leaders increased the coverage of previously established welfare programs and thereby took care of virtually all sick, disabled, and elderly citizens. These Nordic states also devised insurance systems to ease the plight of the unemployed. Sweden went even further and organized government work projects to provide jobs for displaced laborers. No other European governments equaled the success of these three states in their response to the depression.

FINLAND

The progress of democracy in Finland came under very different circumstances. Sweden began to annex parts of Finland in the 1100s and continued this process until the country became a dependent province. It remained subordinated to Sweden through the 1700s. In 1808, Russian autocrats supplanted Finland's Swedish overlords. The tsars continued as the Finns' masters until 1917. The people of Finland, however, persistently resisted this foreign domination. Their struggle brought them increased control over their own affairs in the latter 1800s and early 1900s.

As the Finns advanced by degrees toward independence, they also became pioneers of democracy. In 1906, they won the right to have a one-chamber parliament and gave the vote to all adults. No other European nation allowed women to vote on parliamentary deputies at that time.

Finland achieved complete independence during the Russian revolutions in 1917. Finnish Communists and their opponents struggled for supremacy for months thereafter. Following the defeat of the Communists, the Finns continued the process of democratization. They approved a constitution in 1919 that institutionalized the self-governing systems they had begun to build even before independence. Finland's democratic leaders then began a program of socioeconomic reform. A law passed in October 1922 took land from large aristocratic estates and divided it among poorer farmers. One-third of Finnish peasants became landowners as a result.

With its moderate leftist approach to government, Finnish democracy remained strong and the nation thrived throughout Europe's fascist era. But Finland did face serious threats from the Right during the depression. The government resisted fascism by outlawing militaristic political organizations and the display of party uniforms and symbols.

The Smaller West European Democracies

Although their social reform programs did not equal Scandinavia's, four small democracies in West Europe took important steps after the Great War to strengthen their institutions of self-government and enhance the lives of their citizens.

THE BENELUX COUNTRIES

Belgium, the Netherlands (Holland), and Luxemburg form a triangle of countries with frequently linked histories. Because of the often close relationship among these states, they have become known (from the merger of portions of their names) as the "Benelux Countries." These nations developed strong traditions of representative government in the 1800s. In 1919, all three countries altered their constitutions to increase the political authority of the citizenry. Belgium established universal male suffrage and gave the vote to portions of the female population. Luxemburg and Holland extended electoral rights to all adults.

During the depression, the governments of Belgium and Holland intervened actively in the economy to ease the effects of the depression. Even so, the crisis conditions of the 1930s became serious enough to encourage the rise of Fascist movements in both these nations. The two governments responded with anti-Fascist legislation similar to Finland's. By the late 1930s, parliamentary election results in Belgium and Holland revealed that the appeal of fascism had dropped to insignificant levels. Democracy held firm in the Benelux countries.

SWITZERLAND

A simple and practical form of democracy evolved in Switzerland as the country emerged in the late Middle Ages and Early Modern era. By the mid-1800s, the Swiss had developed a system of government that embodied the modern democratic principles of the High Enlightenment. Defenders of *ancien* tradition in the 1800s considered Switzerland to be a center of radical democracy that threatened to infect all of Europe.

The Swiss maintained these strong traditions and institutions of self-government during the fascist era. Radical Right movements, however, gained enough adherents in the depression years to concern Swiss leaders. They countered fascism with laws against militarist political organizations. The government also reduced the appeal of Right extremists with a program of socialist legislation similar to Scandinavia's.

Czechoslo-vakia—a Democratic Outpost in East Europe

The sociocultural region in which the Czech state emerged after the First World War had a well-established tradition of religious and artistic individualism. Democracy thus found a very favorable environment for growth there.

THE FOUNDERS OF THE NEW STATE

Czechoslovakia's founders, President Thomas Masaryk and Foreign Minister Eduard Beneš, were highly capable leaders strongly committed to popular sovereignty. They took full advantage of Czech traditions and built a vigorous democratic system in the nation's early years. Their policies also encouraged a surge of prosperity in the 1920s and early 1930s. The government achieved this success by enacting a rural land redistribution plan similar to Finland's and supporting the further development of the nation's already strong industrial economy.

THE STRUGGLE AGAINST DEPRESSION AND FASCISM

The Great Depression threatened to undermine Czech democracy and drive the nation toward Right authoritarianism as it had so many other European states. As conditions worsened in the 1930s, a large German minority within Czechoslovakia's western borders (in a region called the Sudetenland) grew increasingly restless. Pro-Nazi movements formed there and began to work for the merger of the Sudetenland with Germany.

Militant nationalist sentiments soon began to affect other ethnic minorities, such as the Slovaks. These nationalist groups began to court the support of Hitler for their cause. The government fought back with both anti-Fascist legislation and police attacks on Right extremists. These tactics succeeded until international forces beyond Czechoslovakia's control led to the absorption of the nation by Nazi Germany in 1939. By then, only France and Britain had the potential to defend European democracy against the forces of fascism.

FRANCE, 1918–1939

The French Third Republic left the Great War as a grievously damaged victor. The nearly 1,500,000 dead from the conflict included especially heavy losses among young men. Over half the males from age 20 to 32 in 1914 were dead by 1918. Two million seven hundred thousand soldiers suffered non-lethal injuries, but more than 100,000 of them lived with permanent disabilities.

France's enormous material losses included 300,000 totally destroyed homes in the region of heaviest fighting. Thousands of workshops, public buildings, bridges, farms, and other facilities also lay in ruins. Destruction on a smaller scale than France experienced left many European democracies too weak to survive.

A Decade of French Ascendancy

The ravages of war did not bring the collapse of democracy in France as it had in Italy. Instead, France rebounded quickly and became the strongest power on the continent in the 1920s.

THE QUEST FOR EFFECTIVE GOVERNMENT

French leaders had to master a monstrously complex political apparatus at the same time that they confronted the staggering economic problems left by the war. The governing executive (the Premier) had to secure a majority in the lower house (Chamber of Deputies) in order to pass legislation. The Chamber's 600 members, however, were divided into so many political factions that premiers could seldom be sure of winning a vote. A defeat on an important issue left a premier no choice but to resign—the law prohibited dissolving the Chamber and arranging an election to try to gain a majority.

A government leader who wanted to carry out constructive policies had to find a way to stay in office for an extended period in a system in which premiers on average remained in power for nine months. Political longevity, in turn, required the management of very delicate coalitions. At times in the 1920s, leaders failed miserably at this task. For example, during a single year beginning in June 1925, France had six executive cabinets.

A few exceptional people overcame this tendency toward government instability. Raymond Poincaré accomplished the unusual feat of holding the premiership from January 1922 to June 1924 and from July 1926 to July 1929. He and two other premiers with somewhat shorter terms provided France capable democratic leadership. Their political achievement contributed greatly to the nation's remarkable economic recovery during the 1920s.

THE ECONOMIC RESTORATION

The government assumed that German reparations payments would enable France to retire its huge war debt and cover the cost of rebuilding the structures destroyed by the military conflict. French leaders thus decided to borrow heavily and proceed with the reconstruction of facilities and the improvement of the industrial system. The modernization of industry helped to bring prosperity within a few years. In the short run, however, this policy caused a financial crisis.

Germany's failure to pay reparations as the government had anticipated left France with a dangerously large and growing public debt. Financial institutions began to refuse to lend money to the French government, thus threatening its recovery program.

Premier Poincaré attempted to solve the problem by forcing reparations payments. He applied pressure by sending troops into Germany's Ruhr valley in 1923. The expense of military occupation, however, depleted public funds. As a result, investors lost confidence in French currency (the franc), and its value plunged. The greatly diminished buying power of the franc caused almost all the French to suffer from the crisis.

The failure of Poincaré's Ruhr occupation plan led him to retire in 1924. After two more years of worsening economic conditions, he agreed to serve as premier again. Poincaré's careful management of French economic policies from 1926 to 1929 produced a surge of prosperity. The strength of this recovery enabled France to avoid the effects of the Great Depression until about two years after the collapse in other industrial nations.

Economic Depression and Political Decline

The depression swept misery into the lives of multitudes of people in every nation that it struck. In France as elsewhere, businesses and banks failed, the jobless rate soared upward, and vast numbers of people could not acquire even the most critical necessities. Thus, even though the French suffered less than the citizens of most other nations affected by the crisis, there was a great need for swift and effective government action.

GOVERNMENT DEADLOCK

Although the depression necessitated a dynamic response, the machinery of French democracy almost ground to a halt. Parliamentary elections in May 1932 appeared to give controlling power to two parties of the Left. But their philosophies differed too sharply for them to work together. One of these parties, the United Socialists led by Léon Blum, wanted to nationalize large industrial and financial institutions and enact programs to create jobs. The other group, Édouard Herriot and his Radical Socialists, demanded a very different policy. Despite their name, the Radicals opposed the socialization of enterprises and insisted on strict control of government spending. The split resulted in a deadlock and the collapse of a series of executive cabinets (five within thirteen months).

THE GROWTH OF FRENCH FASCISM

Discontent over the government's inaction provided an environment for the strength of the radical Right to grow. Older authoritarian groups increased in militancy, and several new ones sprang to life. These fascistic organizations included *Action Française* (French Action), the *Croix de Feu* (the Cross of Fire), and the *Jeunesses Patriotes* (the Young Patriots). Banking and industrial leaders provided funds for such Fascist groups and for radical Right newspapers that launched a sharp attack on the government. French democracy was under siege.

THE STAVISKY RIOTS

The climactic attack on the faltering government was sparked by a financial scandal. In 1933, French officials arrested Serge Stavisky for fraudulent activities as a dealer in stocks and bonds. He escaped, and either killed himself or was murdered. The right-wing press charged that the police assassinated Stavisky to cover up his ties to government leaders. These newspapers also urged opponents of the republic to force its transformation. Fascist organizations added their support to the campaign against the French Republic.

The enemies of the republic continued their efforts until they got the kind of response from the public that they wanted, a march on the legislature on February 6, 1934. The struggle to invade the Chamber's meeting place became a night of riots that left twenty-one dead and hundreds injured. In the wake of this attack, another premier and his cabinet resigned.

Governments Right and Left

The parliamentary invaders during the Stavisky crisis included Communists, but most of the opposition came from the extreme Right. For two years after the riots, the premiers and their cabinets somewhat reflected the mood of this antidemocratic Right instead of the attitude of voters in the last parliamentary elections (1932). Two of the premiers during this period shared the Fascist hostility toward representative government even though these men were executives in such a system.

THE POPULAR FRONT

The right-wing attitudes of government leaders in the mid-1930s drove French leftists together. By the end of 1935, the Radical Socialists, United Socialists, and Communists had formed an official association which they called the Popular Front. This Left coalition won the parliamentary elections in May 1936. Léon Blum took office as the Popular Front premier during a heightened economic crisis accentuated by strikes involving 300,000 workers.

Blum immediately implemented extensive reforms. For distressed laborers, the Popular Front granted a workweek shortened to forty hours, provided paid vacations, and arranged other benefits. In an effort to control the economy better, the government also nationalized the Bank of France and the war ammunition industry.

RED-SCARE TACTICS

This program of the Left government shocked the Right. The enemies of the Popular Front fought back by raising dire warnings that Blum was leading France to communism. The militant Right also insisted that the premier's supposedly pro-Communist spirit ensured hostile relations with Germany. Critics of the Popular Front projected that a war with the Nazi state could result from Blum's policies. In the view of the premier's detractors, such a fight spelled disaster since it would seriously weaken France and Germany, leaving Soviet Russia dominant in Europe. The French Right's slogan became "Better Hitler than Blum."

A NATION DIVIDED

In a battle over domestic policies, Blum lost the parliament's support after a year in office. He resigned in June 1937. Blum returned in 1938 in an attempt to unify France on foreign policy questions, but in a few months he accepted defeat and quit again. The unity of the Popular Front parties had weakened greatly by 1938, and this Left coalition collapsed before the end of the year. A Right-oriented government took power once more, but it too lacked solid support in the parliament and among the citizenry. Irreconcilable political conflicts had split the nation by 1939. A powerful and united Nazi Germany began its conquest of Europe that year.

BRITAIN, 1918–1939

The First World War took about half as many British lives (600,000) as French. Moreover, since Britain had no battles on its own soil, the island kingdom entered the peace with all its homes and factories intact. Yet the war still struck Britain hard. The nation had lost many men in the prime of life, with an especially heavy toll among the upper classes that provided most of the society's leaders. The war also hastened the disintegration of the British Empire and the decline of Britain's economy.

The Fragmentation of the Empire

Surges of empire building over a 400-year period brought about one-fourth of the earth into Britain's realm by the 1920s. The empire contained about 500,000,000 people, over 300,000,000 in the single colony of India.

THE DOMINIONS

Most of the nearly 70,000,000 imperial citizens of European origin lived in Ireland (the Irish Free State after 1921), Canada, Newfoundland, Australia, New Zealand, and South Africa. These territories, known as "dominions," had controlled their own domestic affairs since the 1870s. Britain still had the technical authority but not the power to take the entire empire to war in 1914. The dominions voluntarily supported Britain with troops and resources, but their sacrifices and the national spirit inspired by the war convinced them to complete the process of independence.

Under growing pressure from the dominions after the war, Parliament passed the Statute of Westminster (December 1931) granting freedom to the dominions. They accepted a new status as members of the British Commonwealth of Nations. Thereafter, economic interests, cultural and emotional ties, and a pledge of loyalty to the monarchs ensured a close relationship between the former dominions and Britain. But these independent states no longer belonged to the empire.

INDIA

India's struggle for independence strengthened rapidly in the late 1800s and early 1900s. Then, in India as in the dominions, the Great War intensified national feeling and the urge for liberation. Indian leaders sent troops to fight for Britain in the European war in part to win more freedom as a reward for the support. The British offered small compensation. Official recommendations in 1918 indicated plans to extend only extremely limited political rights to a very small minority of Indians.

The Indian Congress Party, led by Mahatma Gandhi (1869–1948), stepped up its nonviolent campaign of protest against British control. Brutal repression followed, especially at Amritsar. Imperial troops killed almost 400 and wounded 1,200 unarmed demonstrators in the "Amritsar Massacre," April 1919. Most British leaders condemned this action, but Imperial control remained tight.

Gandhi continued his nonviolent struggle, and masses of people joined the effort. Other Indian nationalists answered British force with assassination and terror. Parliament tried to weaken the resistance by extending a few more rights to Indians in 1935. The opposition to imperial control did not diminish. Britain was losing the struggle by the end of the 1930s but would not yet surrender.

THE MIDDLE EAST AND EGYPT

British imperial control also met fierce resistance in the Middle East (territories east and south of the Mediterranean) and Egypt during the 1920s and 1930s. The British had subdued Egypt before 1914. The First World War settlements ended the authority of Turkey over several states (such as Iraq) east of the Mediterranean and left Britain in charge of them. Nationalist attitudes bred among these subject peoples by the Great War ensured that they would fight for independence. By the late 1930s, Britain had almost completely yielded to nationalists in the region. The more rigorously controlled people in Britain's African colonies had no chance for a similar victory until the 1950s and after.

IRELAND

Nearer the center of imperial power, a revolutionary battle raged against the British even before the Great War ended. In April 1916, an Irish nationalist party, the Sinn Fein ("ourselves alone"), led an uprising meant to gain full independence from the empire. The British government crushed this "Easter Rebellion" and executed fifteen of its leaders. This bloody encounter intensified Irish hostility toward Britain so much that the partial liberty offered in Parliament's 1914 Home Rule plan (see chapter 11) was no longer acceptable.

In the 1918 parliamentary elections, the Irish districts selected mostly Sinn Fein candidates. These new legislators refused to attend Parliament in Britain. They established the Dail Eireann (Parliament of Ireland) and chose Eamon De Valera, a militant nationalist, as president of their newly declared Irish Republic. Britain considered all of these steps to be illegal and continued the repression.

In Ulster, a small northern section of Ireland, the mostly Protestant population also bitterly opposed the movement for Irish independence. Separation from Protestant Britain would leave Ulster Protestants as a minority within Catholic Ireland. This circumstance stiffened British resistance to liberation.

In 1921, after three violent years, Britain and moderate Irish nationalists arranged a compromise. The treaty they signed left Ulster united with Britain but gave southern Ireland dominion status and control of domestic affairs. Militant Irish nationalists ignored this settlement and fought on until 1938 when they won complete freedom for all of Ireland south of Ulster. With Ulster still attached to Britain, very hostile relationships existed between the Protestant majority and Catholic minority in that region. Later in the century, a virtual civil war erupted between them.

The Decline of the British Economy

The disintegration of the empire weakened Britain economically. As territories pulled away from Britain, they accelerated the development of their own industries. Markets for British goods thus shrank. Many other changes within Britain and abroad added to the economic woes of the nation.

AN AGING INDUSTRIAL SYSTEM

As the first nation to industrialize, Britain enjoyed many economic advantages until the latter 1800s. Then Germany and the United States began to forge ahead. These nations had more abundant resources and newer manufacturing systems that gave them a competitive edge. British industrialists made matters worse for themselves by clinging to old ways in management and production.

A WAR-DAMAGED ECONOMY

The Great War sharpened the decline for Britain. The country had to concentrate so completely on the manufacture of war matériel that its customers in the global market turned to the United States. After the war, the still declining British industrial system could not win back these consumers. Even the peace settlement hurt Britain. German reparations to France included payments in coal. When former British customers bought this coal from France, one of Britain's most important industries was seriously crippled.

British workers felt the effects of these historic and global trends in a very personal way by the early 1920s. Almost 700,000 had to sign up for unemployment benefits in 1920. Six months later, three times that number were out of work. The jobless population stayed above 1,000,000 for the rest of the decade. Then the Great Depression came.

Muddling Politicians

In popular mythology, the British government has a reputation for "muddling through." This image suggests that when leaders confront problems, they simply struggle along at their usual pace with few if any clear ideas about solutions. Britain's record of highly effective reform throughout most of the Modern era contradicts this view of the system. But the governments of the 1920s and 1930s did "muddle," and they barely made it through the difficulties of the era.

PARTIES IN TROUBLE AND TRANSITION

A coalition of parties had formed an executive cabinet to conduct the war. This mixed cabinet under Liberal Prime Minister David Lloyd George continued in office after the war until 1922. In these years, the economy needed serious attention; Lloyd George knew little about such matters and devoted most of his time to foreign affairs.

A fully Conservative cabinet replaced the coalition government in 1922. Stanley Baldwin, the new prime minister, had a talent for presenting mediocre ideas in impressive speeches. His flawed plan for economic improvement—quick payment of war debts to the United States—made bad conditions worse. Britain's economy needed stimulation. His program further burdened an already sluggish system.

The Rise of the Labour Party. The moderate socialist program of Britain's Labour Party gained steadily in appeal throughout the early 1900s. By the 1920s, Labour and the Conservatives dominated British politics. The Liberals took a third-party position and continued to weaken. When the 1923 elections gave Labour control of the government for the first time, Prime Minister Ramsay MacDonald showed no interest in a socialist economic program. He preferred to continue Baldwin's conservative financial plan.

Labour charted a course in foreign policy, however, that led to a conflict with the Conservatives.

Recognition of the Soviet Government. Labor leaders wanted no socialism at home, but they sympathized with the struggling Communists in the USSR. The MacDonald government thus arranged a diplomatic recognition treaty with Soviet Russia. Labor lacked the votes to pass the treaty. This failure of support in the House of Commons forced MacDonald to schedule elections.

The Zinoviev Letter. As the campaigns for House seats drew to a close in October 1924, foreign ministry officials reported discovery of a message from a Soviet leader urging British Communists to undermine their government. This "Zinoviev letter," a forgery prepared by anti-Communists in Britain, made MacDonald's Soviet recognition plan seem dangerous. It weakened Labour's already slim chance of victory in the elections. Baldwin and the Conservatives won and immediately blocked the recognition treaty.

SLIPPING INTO DEPRESSION

In his second term, Baldwin tried to strengthen the economy by raising the value of the nation's currency (the pound). As the worth of the pound climbed, so did the cost of British products. As a result, business leaders cut their laborers' wages in an effort to reduce prices and stay competitive in world markets. The muddling British leadership left workers with no hope of a reversal of their fortunes. The slide into depression continued.

THE GENERAL STRIKE

British coal mine operators reacted to the faltering economy with a plan to cut wages and reduce workers' hours. Mine unions threatened a massive strike. The Baldwin administration tried to arrange a compromise settlement. It failed. The miners struck (May 1, 1926), and other worker organizations joined them, taking forty percent of all unionized laborers off the job.

With almost twenty percent of the total work force (union and nonunion) idled, the government still managed to defeat the general strike. Volunteers kept transportation and communication systems in operation and distributed critical supplies such as milk. Sympathy strikers yielded and resumed work on May 12, 1926. Coal miners refused to surrender until the end of the year. The outcome left labor more passive and the government complacent about the economy.

The Great Depression in Britain

After a decade of gradual decline, the Great Depression took the British economy into a breathtaking plunge. The sale of British goods abroad dropped fifty percent between 1929 and 1932. In the same period, the painfully high 1929 unemployment rate of ten percent more than doubled.

Seven million of Britain's 45,000,000 people had no income but government welfare by 1932.

THE STYMIED SOCIALISTS

In June 1929, the Labour Party and Prime Minister MacDonald resumed control of the government. These socialist leaders decided to ease the fall into depression by a reduction of government spending, including cuts in benefits to the jobless. Most of the Labour Party flatly rejected this conservative plan from its own leaders. Since MacDonald could not deliver socialist votes in Parliament, he had to resign his position as prime minister (August 1931).

A TIMID COALITION

The day after his resignation, MacDonald returned to office and organized a coalition cabinet with Conservative, Labour, and Liberal members. The Labour Party expelled MacDonald and the other cabinet socialists from its ranks. This "National Coalition Government" remained in power through the rest of the 1930s. Even though MacDonald kept his position as prime minister until 1935, Conservatives such as Baldwin and Neville Chamberlain increasingly controlled government policies. Finally, they took charge officially—Baldwin became prime minister in 1935, Chamberlain in 1937.

Under the influence of these Conservatives, the government tried somewhat more active measures to improve the economy. Coalition leaders began by a reversal of the currency policies Baldwin had established in the mid-1920s. This change expanded the money supply, lowered currency values, and made it easier for struggling citizens to pay debts. Then the cabinet arranged a more drastic shift in economic practices. In an attempt to protect British farmers and manufacturers, the government abandoned its ninety-year-old doctrine of free trade and established a tax on foreign wheat and certain industrial imports.

Through additional anti-depression legislation, the government provided aid to the extremely depressed shipping industry and assisted in the movement of jobless workers to locales with better opportunities. The economy eventually began a slow climb, but these cautious programs had far too little effect to lift Britain from the depths of depression.

BRITISH DEMOCRACY UNDER CRISIS CONDITIONS

Emergency circumstances during the Great War encouraged the growth of government controls and the centralization of political authority. This experience did not weaken the British commitment to democracy, however. One month after the end of the war, the government extended the right to vote to more people. Older laws allowed all males over twenty to vote. The new law included women (those over thirty) in the electorate for the first time. A further change in 1928 provided for women over twenty to vote. Persistent economic troubles in the 1920s and the crisis conditions of the Great Depression did not undermine these still growing democratic institutions in Britain.

Britain thus stood as a firmly democratic state at the end of the 1930s. Yet the nation had declined sharply in economic and military strength since 1918. The British were at war with the Fascist states by September 1939. Within months, Britain was the only European democracy left to carry on the fight.

THE ARTS AND IDEAS IN AN ERA OF CRISIS

Europe entered a long siege of military and socioeconomic crises in 1914. The shock of these events wrecked many democratic governments and seriously strained others. This era of crisis, and especially the horrible slaughter of the Great War, also deeply affected European art and thought.

Artistic Visions of Despair

Picasso, Kandinsky, and other abstract painters who began important creative trends before 1914 became Europe's leading artists during the 1920s and 1930s. The movement they inspired dominated the visual arts through the rest of the century. In the crisis decades after the Great War, these artists expressed reactions to events of the era in certain of their paintings. Picasso's *Guernica* (1937) earned especially great fame as an artistic condemnation of air attacks that killed civilians during the Spanish Civil War.

DADAISM

The general mood of despair as well as specific events affected the arts in this period. In 1918, a group of artists and authors began a campaign to express their view that everything in life was meaningless. They even gave their movement a meaningless name, Dada, to emphasize this attitude.

The Dadaists gave speeches and produced works of literature and art that were intentionally incomprehensible. Paradoxically, Dadaism did convey a very clear message—these members of the artistic elite despised the inhumanity of their era.

SURREALISM

The spirit of intense social criticism evident in Dadaism also was reflected in surrealism, another literary and artistic movement of the post–World War I period. Surrealist works owed much to the inspiration of

Freudian psychology. The artists and writers in this movement presented distorted visions that suggested a dreamlike or nightmarish state of mind. They depicted the near madness that personal traits or social conditions could bring into anyone's life.

The Spanish painter Salvador Dalí (1904–1989), produced highly acclaimed surrealist works such as *Persistence of Memory*. In this painting, Dalí scattered a mystifying collection of items, including three melted watches, around an eerie landscape. It suggested a bleak and strange world.

Literature—the Inspiration of Tragedy

The tragic conditions of war and severe economic distress destroyed European governments but at the same time encouraged outstanding achievements in writing as well as art. Many of the greatest literary works of the twentieth century appeared in the 1920s and 1930s as authors responded to the traumas of the era.

STORIES OF RUIN AND MADNESS

T. S. Eliot (1888–1965), an American who emigrated to Britain, suggested in his works that humanity faced nothing less than doomsday. In "The Waste Land" (1922), Eliot expressed in complex poetry his vision of teeming barbaric invaders devastating the civilized world. Thomas Mann (1875–1955) experienced the painful years of war and social crisis in Germany, but his novels presented a slightly more hopeful view of the future than Eliot's poetry. *The Magic Mountain* (1924) indicated that even though Mann equated Europe with an insane asylum, sensitive and intuitive people had the potential to bring about a social recovery.

Although the First World War strongly influenced these works, many authors wrote little or nothing about the four-year struggle. Others, however, directly confronted their readers with the raging battles. In the German novel *All Quiet on the Western Front,* Erich Maria Remarque (1898–1970) provided one of the most vivid portrayals of the horrors of life and death in the trenches.

REACTIONS TO SOCIAL OPPRESSION

Leading authors had condemned the increasing social dominance of industrial machines and bureaucracies in the late 1800s and early 1900s. The world war and subsequent crises intensified these trends so despised by the literary elite.

In Britain, D. H. Lawrence (1885–1930) expressed his demand for greater freedom from social restraints with a sexually explicit novel, *Lady Chatterley's Lover* (1928). Franz Kafka (1883–1924), an ethnic German living in Czechoslovakia, wrote works that described a world with no opportunity for greater liberty. The societies that Kafka imagined in *The*

Trial and *The Castle* made freedom virtually impossible through the operation of absolutely powerful bureaucracies that no one could understand.

Oppressive trends in Soviet Russia in the 1920s caused Yevgeni Zamyatin (1884–1937) to anticipate living in the kind of society that Kafka depicted. Zamyatin's novel *We* (1929) used a futuristic story to describe and condemn the totalitarian system that he saw emerging. Aldous Huxley's *Brave New World* (1932) and novels by others after the 1930s also denounced the new dictatorships with fictional predictions of the future.

Doomsday Scholarship

Several important scholarly publications that appeared in the two decades after the First World War reflected the same mood of despair found in much of the art and fiction. In *The Decline of the West* (1918–1922), Oswald Spengler argued that cultures have life cycles and that his civilization was already in the grip of certain death.

Freud's reflections on the implications of the Great War led him to conclusions that differed little from Spengler's. In *Civilization and Its Discontents* (1930), Freud indicated that the inherent traits of humanity would forever jeopardize the social order. Carl Jung (1875–1961), a former disciple of Freud's who became an intellectual opponent, expressed very similar doubts about the future of humanity. Many other leading European scholars displayed the same anticipation of doom.

In 1934, American scientists arranged a conference to review expert opinion on the possibility of making nuclear bombs. European physicists unraveled enough of the mysteries of the structure of matter to split an atom by December 1939. This experiment proved that scientists could produce nuclear weapons. Almost six years later, the United States brought the Second World War to a close by dropping atomic bombs on two Japanese cities. Europeans and Americans thus had gained the knowledge to carry out the destruction of civilization feared by so many artists and intellectuals during the 1920s and 1930s.

The remembrance of war and the experience of economic crisis and collapsing democracy in the 1920s and 1930s left many European artists, writers, and scholars feeling hopeless. They communicated their sense of impending doom in strangely new varieties of painting or in works of fiction and scholarship. When government leaders in France and Britain confronted severe economic problems in these years, they often appeared to struggle on with as little optimism as the intellectuals and artists displayed.

The failure of democratic governments in France and Britain to cope with the Great Depression left many citizens in misery and gave the masses every reason to share the despair of their leaders. French society seemed especially torn and weakened by the end of the 1930s, even though the nation had shown great vitality only a decade earlier.

Despite the apparent problems in the two nations usually viewed as the most powerful democratic states, both France and Britain remained firmly committed to representative government after suffering through the decade of the Great Depression. Many smaller and less populous democracies, moreover, achieved remarkable political and economic successes during the 1920s and 1930s.

European democracy had hardly thrived in these decades, but many self-governing states had proved their power to endure. In 1939, the Europeans in both the dictatorships and the democracies faced a six-year war that would test their capacity to survive as it had never been tested in modern history. The Fascist states began this struggle at a moment when the other European nations could not match their military strength.

Selected Readings

Aldcroft, Derek H. *The European Economy, 1914–1970*. New York: St. Martin's Press, 1978.

Carroll, Donald, and Edward Lucie-Smith. *Movements in Modern Art*. New York: Horizon Press, 1973.

Childs, Marquis W. *Sweden, the Middle Way*. New Haven, CT: Yale University Press, 1961.

Dangerfield, George. *The Damnable Question: A Study in Anglo-Irish Relations*. Boston: Little, Brown, 1976.

Graves, Robert, and Alan Hodge. *The Long Weekend: A Social History of Great Britain, 1918–1939*. New York: Norton, 1963.

Greene, Nathanael. *From Versailles to Vichy: The Third French Republic, 1919–1940*. New York: Crowell, 1970.

Hamilton, George H. *Painting and Sculpture in Europe, 1880–1940*. Baltimore: Penguin Books, 1972.

Kemp, Tom. *The French Economy, 1913–1939: The History of a Decline*. London: Longman, 1972.

Kindleberger, Charles P. *The World in Depression, 1929–1939*. London: Allen Lane, 1973.

Mowat, Charles L. *Britain Between the Wars, 1918–1940*. Chicago: University of Chicago Press, 1955.

Pawel, Ernst. *The Nightmare of Reason: The Life of Franz Kafka*. New York: Farrar, Straus & Giroux, 1984.

Sontag, Raymond J. *A Broken World, 1919–1939*. New York: Harper & Row, 1972.

Taylor, Alan J. P. *English History, 1914–1945*. New York: Oxford University Press, 1965.

16

A Greater War, 1939–1945

November 1921	In the Washington Conference, eight leading naval powers pledge to limit the size of their fleets
1928	Nations of the world begin to sign the Kellogg-Briand Pact vowing to give up war in the pursuit of state interests
March 1936	Hitler orders German troops into the Rhineland in violation of the Versailles Treaty
November 1937	Germany, Italy, and Japan organize the Anti-Comintern Pact
March 1938	Germany annexes Austria (the *Anschluss*)
August 1939	Germany and the Soviet Union complete the Nazi-Soviet Pact, an agreement that they will each take Polish territory but will not fight each other
September 1, 1939	Nazi Germany invades Poland and sparks the Second World War
June 1940	France surrenders to Germany
August 1940	Germany begins the ten-month air attack known as "the Battle of Britain"
June 22, 1941	Germany launches Operation Barbarossa, the invasion of the USSR
December 7, 1941	A Japanese aerial attack on Pearl Harbor, Hawaii, brings the United States into the Second World War
January 1942	Nazi leaders implement the plan to kill all Jews in Europe
September 3, 1943	Fascist Italy surrenders to the Western Allies
June 6, 1944	The Western Allies invade northern France on "D day"

February 1945   Churchill, Roosevelt, and Stalin meet at Yalta to plan the final steps to victory and the post-war control of conquered territories

April 1945   Mussolini is executed by Italian anti-Fascists, and Hitler commits suicide

May 7-8, 1945   Germany surrenders to the Allies

August 1945   Japan surrenders after the United States drops atomic bombs on Hiroshima and Nagasaki

The Great War left all the European states desperate for security. Despite this common desire, serious international conflicts persisted throughout the early 1920s. The struggle between France and Germany over reparations payments even led the French to send troops into the German Ruhr region.

After a compromise on reparations in 1924, the European states entered a period of improved relations that lasted nearly a decade. They settled border disputes, arranged better trading relationships, and established limits on naval armaments. During this era of harmony, France and the United States proposed that the nations of the world swear not to start wars of aggression. More than twenty states quickly signed such an agreement (September 1928). Almost three times that number eventually took this peace pledge.

Eleven years after the French and Americans completed their visionary treaty, Europe plunged into a war of much greater destruction and horror than the First World War. Nazi Germany had steadily led the European states on a six-year march to the abyss that they reached in September 1939. France and Britain believed almost until the last moment that they could help Hitler realize his goals for Germany and stop the rush to war. They were wrong. The Fuehrer's goal was the conquest of Europe.

TOWARD SECURITY AND PEACE

During the peace negotiations at the end of the Great War, French representatives worked diligently to arrange buffer zones and military restrictions that would make their country safe from further German aggression. Geography protected Britain quite well, but the British usually agreed that security on the continent required the customary defensive measures preferred by France.

The United States accepted most of France's protective plan, but President Wilson doubted the value of such traditional security arrangements. Wilson struggled vigorously to incorporate into the Paris treaties the peacemaking ideals he had expressed in the Fourteen Points. (See chapter 12.) In the decade after the Paris negotiations ended, the Europeans tried both France's time-honored approach to security and Wilson's visionary peacemaking strategies.

The Implementation of the Paris Treaties

The Allied Powers concluded the Peace of Paris in June 1919. During the following year, they implemented its provisions for an international peace and security agency.

THE ESTABLISHMENT OF THE LEAGUE OF NATIONS

The League of Nations assembled for the first time at its headquarters in Geneva, Switzerland, in November 1920. It met, however, without representatives from the United States. None would ever attend. The American Senate had objected to the internationalist character of the League and rejected the treaties that Wilson signed at Paris.

The American decision against participation left the League under British and French domination. These two nations soon developed conflicting views of the proper role of the agency in world affairs. French leaders urged the League to stand ready for swift intervention to stop aggressor states. The British stubbornly objected. They insisted that the League should encourage international communication and avoid action. During most crises, the League usually did little or nothing, as Britain wished.

THE ATTEMPT TO WEAKEN POTENTIAL AGGRESSORS

The Paris treaties set strict limits on the military power of the defeated nations. (See chapter 12.) After the war, the victors began the enforcement of these treaty articles. The imposition of these military limits somewhat reduced the war-making potential of Germany, Austria, Hungary, and Turkey. Their desires for aggressive action never disappeared, however, and soon they were secretly rebuilding their military forces.

New Arrangements for Security and Cooperation

The formation of the League of Nations did not drastically alter the conduct of international relations. Most countries continued to have direct interaction with other states as they always had.

DEFENSE ALLIANCES

At the time of the Paris peace negotiations, the United States and Britain concluded a separate agreement with France. They pledged to aid the French if Germany ever attacked. Several months later, the Americans and British withdrew their promise of assistance. France quickly built a new system to restrain Germany by arranging defense treaties with Belgium (1920) and Poland (1921).

THE QUEST FOR IMPROVED RELATIONS

French and British leaders convened a general economic conference at Genoa, Italy, in April 1922. They hoped to stimulate European economic recovery by getting the Soviet government to pay foreign debts left by imperial Russia. The positions taken by the negotiators made a resolution of their economic conflict impossible.

The Rapallo Treaty. Before the Genoa conference ended, the Germans and Soviets revealed that they had recently met in Rapallo, Germany, to sign a treaty of friendship and economic cooperation. A common status as outcast nations had drawn Germany and the Soviet Union together, but their closer association worried the other European states.

The Locarno Agreements. In 1925, European leaders held extended negotiations in Locarno, Switzerland, that produced much better results than had the Genoa meeting. These Locarno conferences led to a series of treaties that ended disagreements about the location of German, Belgian, and French borders. These three nations decided to accept existing boundaries. They also promised to settle all future disputes among themselves by peaceful means. The Locarno agreements left many international problems unresolved, but they increased European harmony sufficiently to inspire a widespread belief that an era of peace had dawned.

The Campaign Against Weapons and War

Even though the confidence in forceful means of protection remained very strong after the First World War, disarmament and antiwar movements made unusual progress in the 1920s.

THE DISARMAMENT DRIVE

In November 1921, the United States opened the Washington Conference for a consideration of naval armaments and Asian issues. The representatives of six European and two Asian states joined the Americans for three months of negotiations. They concluded two agreements on Asian affairs and one on naval armaments. The United States, Britain, Japan, France, and Italy signed the naval arms treaty. They accepted limits on the size of their heavy warship fleets and pledged not to build any of these large vessels for ten years. These same five nations met for the London Naval Conference in 1930 and agreed to limits on smaller vessels, including submarines.

The League of Nations established a commission in 1926 to prepare for a conference that would bring a much larger group of nations together to arrange limits on the full range of military forces. This effort led to a series of Geneva Disarmament Conferences that began in February 1932, with sixty states in attendance. Negotiations continued without success until Hitler's withdrawal of Germany from the Conference effectively stopped this drive for disarmament in October 1933.

THE KELLOGG-BRIAND PEACE PACT

After the completion of the Locarno agreements and the organization of the League's disarmament preparatory commission, optimism about the possibility of establishing truly peaceful international relations became unusually strong. An agreement arranged by Frank Kellogg, the American secretary of state, and Aristide Briand, the French foreign minister, reflected the spirit of the times in an especially vivid way.

The pact presented to the world by Kellogg and Briand in 1928 proposed that nations pledge to stop using war to achieve their goals. Virtually every state with the power to wage war on a significant scale signed this Kellogg-Briand Pact (formally known as the Pact of Paris). Even though this promise of peaceful behavior had no discernible effect on international relations, the pact symbolized the very significant advancements toward peace that took place in the decade after the Great War.

TOWARD WAR

The hopes for tranquility fostered by developments in the 1920s faded rapidly in the early 1930s. Gustav Stresemann had set Germany on a course toward peace in 1924, but Hitler's triumph succeded in reversing his country's direction in foreign affairs, a change that soon transformed the entire environment of European international relations.

The Resurgence of the German Threat

Hitler intended to have a vastly more powerful German military force and an expanded empire *within* Europe. The implementation of these policies immediately heightened the threat to peace in Europe. Hitler quickly made his country's aggressiveness apparent. In October 1933, nine months after Hitler became German chancellor, he withdrew his country from the Geneva arms talks and the League of Nations.

GERMANY'S NULLIFICATION OF THE VERSAILLES MILITARY LIMITS

Hitler considered the military limitations placed on Germany by the Versailles Treaty to be even more insufferable than League membership. In March 1935, he openly proclaimed that Germany no longer recognized the validity of the Versailles arms limitations clauses. Officials from France, Italy, and Britain met to consider possible responses to Germany's violation of the treaty. They did nothing, however, largely because the British had decided years earlier that the Versailles restrictions were unrealistic and overly harsh.

THE REMILITARIZATION OF THE RHINELAND

A year after the easy rearmament triumph, Hitler won another and more striking victory. The Versailles Treaty required the demilitarization of German territory on the Rhine River. Hitler ordered troops to return to the Rhineland in March 1936. The Fuehrer's generals opposed this move because they feared a French attack that Germany was too weak to resist.

Hitler's forces again met no opposition. French and British leaders had long assumed that this remilitarization would occur and did not strongly object. British and French officials certainly had no interest in waging war as a means of resisting such an action. Hitler's success in the Rhineland made it much more difficult for German officials and European leaders to resist Nazi aggressiveness in the future.

The Emergence of the Rome-Berlin Axis

Despite the similarities between Italian fascism and German Nazism, Mussolini viewed Hitler as a threat to Italian interests until 1935. Hitler's reaction to an Italian imperial war that began that year changed Mussolini's attitudes and opened the way for the fascist states to build a much closer relationship.

THE ITALIAN CONQUEST OF ETHIOPIA

Italy tried to conquer Ethiopia during Europe's imperial campaigns in Africa in the late 1800s. The Ethiopian triumph over Italy's troops in 1896 stopped this venture and humiliated the Italians. Mussolini longed to take revenge for this defeat. He also claimed that a Mediterranean-African empire was Italy's destiny. These incentives led to an Italian attack on Ethiopia in October 1935.

Hitler supported this aggressive act, to Mussolini's great pleasure. The members of the League of Nations, however, condemned Italy and voted to impose economic sanctions. The League decision meant that member states were to stop trading with Italy so that resource shortages would force an end to aggression. The sanctions failed to have this effect because of the League's inability to prevent the shipping of petroleum to Italy. Ethiopia fell in May 1936. Mussolini's victory under these circumstances marked the virtual death of the League of Nations. Since Italy and Germany had stood together against the world during the assault on Ethiopia, the Fascist states were virtual allies by 1936.

FASCIST SUPREMACY IN INTERNATIONAL AFFAIRS

Neither the League nor the democracies dominated relations among the European states after the mid-1930s. The two leading Fascist powers had taken charge of events. In 1936, when Franco and the forces of the extreme Right began their war to destroy the Spanish Republic, Mussolini and Hitler jointly supplied military aid to the Fascist rebels. This assistance made it possible for Franco to win by 1939. In contrast to the action of the Fascist states, the democracies declared their neutrality and denied help to the Spanish Republic. Soviet Russia sent advisers to assist the Spanish government; the presence of these few Communists, however, had no significant influence on the outcome of the civil war in Spain.

Even in the early months of the Spanish conflict, the ability of the Italians and Germans to cooperate gave them a new sense of power. Negotiations between Italy and Germany conducted in October 1936 resulted in a strengthened Fascist relationship that Mussolini called "the Rome-Berlin axis." The Italian leader announced this association on November 1 1936, and boasted that the new power alignment would subsequently control the turn of events in Europe. In November 1937, Fascist Japan joined with Italy and Germany to form the Anti-Comintern (anti-Communist) Pact, an indication that these three nations dreamed of world domination.

To the Brink of War

By the time the Fascists organized the Anti-Comintern Pact, the strength of the Right dictatorships and the weakness of the democracies made it relatively easy for Hitler to begin a vigorous campaign to build his empire in Europe. The Fuehrer's drive to expand also pushed Europe toward war.

THE *ANSCHLUSS*—HITLER'S ANNEXATION OF AUSTRIA

Hitler's doctrines emphasized the Nazi plan to build a new German *Reich* (empire), the third in history. This Third *Reich* would rule the world and endure for one thousand years, according to the Fuehrer. The realization of this destiny required that the great German people have *Lebensraum* (living space). The nation had to expand. Since the early 1920s, the Fuehrer had proclaimed in shouts and publications that this enlarged Germany had to include Austria, his homeland.

After the Austrian Nazis tried to overthrow their moderate Right government in 1934, their party was declared illegal. Hitler began his annexation campaign in February 1938 by ordering Austrian Chancellor Kurt von Schuschnigg to allow the revival of the party and add Nazis to the Austrian cabinet or face a German invasion.

Schuschnigg submitted to these demands but announced plans for a plebiscite in which Austrians would vote on whether to remain free and independent. A furious Hitler prepared to invade and told Schuschnigg to turn the government over to Arthur von Seyss-Inquart, an Austrian Nazi. When Britain and France refused to assist Schuschnigg, he resigned and Seyss-Inquart became chancellor. The new Austrian leader invited German forces to enter his country and establish order. Hitler's troops marched in, and Austria merged with Germany on March 13, 1938.

THE CZECHOSLOVAKIAN CRISIS

The Sudetenland, a well-fortified highland region in Czechoslovakia, stretched in a narrow semicircle around the border next to Germany. Most of the Sudetenland's population was ethnically German. In March 1938, Hitler induced these Sudeten Germans to begin a campaign for complete control over government within their part of Czechoslovakia. Since compliance with this demand would nullify Czech power in an area critical to national defense, a Sudeten German victory on this issue would make Czechoslovakia more vulnerable to a Nazi attack. Hitler expected a Czech refusal, which he meant to use as an excuse to invade.

As the Czech government tried to resolve the conflict with the Sudeten Germans, Hitler gathered his forces for an attack. The Czechs had two defense treaties that promised them protection. One required France to aid Czechoslovakia if any aggressor invaded. The other obligated the Soviets to assist in Czech defense whenever the French did. British leaders feared that these agreements would lead to a general European war that Britain was not at all prepared to fight. Pressure from Britain convinced France not to aid Czechoslovakia, regardless of treaty obligations. Without French support, the Czechs could expect none from the Soviets. Czechoslovakia thus was alone in the struggle. In early September 1938, the Czech government surrendered authority over the Sudetenland to its German inhabitants.

Even though the Czechs had yielded, the crisis did not end. Hitler responded to every Czech concession with a more extreme demand. This process continued until late September 1938, when the Fuehrer insisted on the annexation of the Sudetenland to Germany and the surrender of all fortifications in the region to his armies. Czechoslovakia refused to comply. An intense war scare gripped Europe.

Appeasement. Neville Chamberlain (1869–1940), the British prime minister beginning in 1937, had encouraged repeated Czech surrenders to Germany during the Sudetenland crisis. The British leader believed that Europe could avoid war by a policy of appeasement—calming Hitler by submitting to most of his demands. In Chamberlain's opinion, the Fuehrer would insist on nothing more, once all German regions were added to the Nazi state. Édouard Daladier (1884–1970), the French premier, agreed with Chamberlain and joined the chorus for appeasement. When Czechs would concede no more to Hitler, the British and French leaders surrendered for them.

The Munich Agreement. On September 29, 1938, Chamberlain, Daladier, Mussolini, and Hitler met in Munich, Germany, to discuss the conflict over the Sudetenland. They did not invite Czech and Soviet representatives to the conference even though the crisis threatened the existence of Czechoslovakia and involved vital Soviet security interests. In the discussions at Munich, the four leaders quickly arrived at a simple solution.

They offered Hitler everything he wanted. He accepted the gift of the Sudetenland and its forts.

The German Annexation of Czechoslovakia. Chamberlain and Daladier went home to tell their relieved citizens that the Munich agreement guaranteed "peace in our time." They believed that the settlement fully satisfied Hitler since it gave him the last European territory with a German-majority population. In mid-March 1939, less than six months after the Munich conference, Germany took control of all Czech territory under the pretense of stopping political disorder.

THE DECISION TO FIGHT AGGRESSION

The cynical demonstration that Hitler intended to rule more than German populations ended the policy of appeasement. Since territorial disputes clearly indicated that Hitler soon might threaten Poland, Britain and France now tried to ensure peace by vowing to defend the Poles if they came under attack. If these West European states could convince the Soviets to threaten Germany from the east, Hitler would face extreme risks in any further attempts to expand.

THE NAZI-SOVIET PACT

Moderate Right West European leaders, including Chamberlain, exhibited a certain fondness for fascism. Fascists, after all, supported capitalism and fought communism with a vengeance. This tendency of both fascist and democratic governments in West Europe to have an extremely hostile attitude toward communism made it difficult for British and French leaders to cooperate with the Soviets even when the fate of Czechoslovakia hung in the balance. Stalin was aware of these sentiments among Western leaders and somewhat justifiably suspected that they appeased Hitler in order to turn Nazi aggression toward the USSR.

Britain and France became much more hostile toward Germany after the fall of Czechoslovakia, but the democracies made only a halfhearted effort to entice the USSR into an anti-Nazi alliance. Hitler, however, temporarily suspended his campaign of hatred against communism and energetically pursued an agreement with Stalin. The Soviet leader was surprisingly receptive to these Nazi advances.

The German and Soviet dictators both realized that they could benefit by temporarily ignoring their opposing ideologies and striking a deal. Germany and the Soviet Union wanted to regain territory lost to Poland at the end of the Great War. They could take this land by combined action. If they opposed each other, they risked a costly war and reduced their chances of making territorial gains. Stalin saw an additional advantage in reaching an understanding with Hitler. The Soviet leader expected Germany eventually to attack the Soviet Union, but he wanted to delay this invasion as long as possible in order to prepare defenses.

With fascist and communist passions somewhat subdued by the spirit of *Realpolitik,* Hitler and Stalin accepted a pact arranged by their top diplomats. On August 24, 1939, German foreign minister Joachim von Ribbentrop and Soviet foreign minister Vyacheslav Molotov announced the signing of a ten-year Treaty of Non-Aggression.

This Nazi-Soviet Pact contained public pledges that Germany and the USSR would neither attack each other nor join any group of nations hostile to the cosignatories of this agreement. Secretly, Stalin and Hitler arranged for the Soviets to annex Latvia, Lithuania, Bessarabia (part of Romania), and a section of Poland and for the Nazis to take the Polish territory they wanted. This agreement removed the last barrier to Hitler's attack on Poland and left Europe poised on the brink of war.

ON THE ATTACK

In the Great War, armies slaughtered each other along almost immobile lines. The greater war that began in 1939 moved like a swift storm across vast stretches of land, causing death and destruction on a much more horrible scale than in the First World War. The Soviet Union alone lost more people in the Second World War than did all the nations involved in the First World War. On September 1, 1939, a stunning attack by Germany on Poland began a plague of warfare that lasted six years and spread around the globe.

The Nazi and Soviet Campaigns in Northeast Europe

The German invasion of Poland brought French and British declarations of war on the Nazi state within two days. Italy did not enter the war at this time. Overwhelming German military power quickly decided Poland's fate.

BLITZKRIEG IN POLAND

Nearly 2,000,000 Nazi troops divided into massive columns behind powerful mobile armored forces drove into Poland from three directions. Waves of attack planes supported the invaders on the ground. Within less than two weeks, these *Blitzkrieg* (lightning war) tactics subdued most of Poland. Alarmed by this formidable military display, the Soviets rushed into their assault on eastern Poland in mid-September. The Polish government surrendered and the state disappeared before the end of the month. The Soviet Union and Germany each took about half of the conquered territory.

"THE WINTER WAR"—A SOVIET CAMPAIGN AGAINST FINLAND

Soon after the Soviets secured their holdings in Poland, they forcibly annexed the Baltic States (Estonia, Latvia, and Lithuania) to provide an expanded security zone in the northwest. The USSR attempted to make its borders north of Leningrad more secure also by taking Finnish territory north of Leningrad. The Finns refused to allow this annexation and prepared for war. From late November 1939, until early March 1940, Finland won the admiration of the anti-Communist world by fighting the USSR to a standstill. Then the Soviet army broke through, and Finland sued for peace. After this difficult "Winter War," Stalin got his strip of Finnish territory.

Germany's Triumph over Western Europe

As Stalin struggled to seize security zones around the Baltic coast, Hitler prepared to take all of West Europe. The Nazi leader gathered his forces and waited for spring.

THE "PHONY WAR"

Britain and France were at war with Germany beginning in September 1939. But for six months, these nations did not fight. During this "sitzkrieg" or "phony war," Britain engaged in a modest strengthening of its military forces. After the Great War, France had built the Maginot Line, a series of forts facing Germany. The French rested behind Maginot from September 1939, until April 1940, and did nothing to increase the nation's military power. With armaments and armies about equal to Germany's, France had little incentive for a frantic multiplication of troops and weapons.

THE FALL OF FRANCE

Neither the Maginot Line nor a numerical balance of forces promised France security against a *Blitzkrieg* from the east. When the Nazi forces launched their westward assault on April 9, 1940, they seized Denmark on the first day and conquered Norway within three weeks. Several days after the victory in Norway, German armies simultaneously invaded the Netherlands and Belgium. The Dutch surrendered within four days (May 14), and Belgium fell ten days later.

The "Miracle of Dunkirk." During the attack on Belgium, the German army crashed through the Ardennes Forest, penetrated French border defenses, and rushed across northern France to the shores of the English Channel. This German thrust through Belgium and across northern France trapped the Belgian army along with hundreds of thousands of British and French troops sent in to help the Belgians. A British armada of military and private vessels had to evacuate nearly 400,000 soldiers from the beaches of Dunkirk. This "miracle of Dunkirk" saved a vast corps of military professionals that Britain desperately needed.

The French Surrender. The fall of Belgium opened France to the crushing blows of extremely well organized invading armies. After this entry in the north in mid-May 1940, the Germans swung south *behind* the Maginot Line. As Hitler's armies approached Paris, Mussolini decided to declare war on France and Britain. The Germans needed no help in France. They took Paris by mid-June and continued south against disorganized and demoralized defense forces. France surrendered on June 22.

Vichy France. Although the Germans occupied and directly controlled most of France, they left a southwestern quadrant of the country under a puppet government led by Henri Pétain and Pierre Laval. Since Pétain and Laval established headquarters in Vichy, this fascist remnant of the state became known as Vichy France. Many French citizens who opposed surrender to the Nazis joined underground resistance groups or fled to Britain. The anti-Fascist French in Britain organized the Free French movement under the command of General Charles de Gaulle (1890–1970).

IN A BATTLE FOR SURVIVAL

The fall of France in June 1940 left Hitler supreme on the continent. In swiftly moving battles, his armies had conquered six nations. Finland, Sweden, and Switzerland remained neutral and posed no threat to Germany. All other continental states were fascist, except Soviet Russia. Only Britain and the USSR stood between Hitler and the complete conquest of Europe.

German onslaughts against the British and Soviets in 1940 and 1941 forced these enemies of Nazism into a fight to survive. When the Nazis invaded the Soviet Union, they quickly conquered most of the highly populated part of the country. Hitler's armies then occupied territories that contained nearly all the Jews of Europe. The Nazis immediately began to implement their plans to exterminate Jews. Hitler had repeatedly sworn that every one of these "subhumans" would die. During the rest of the war, the Jewish people faced a more brutal struggle than any other group in Europe.

The Battle of Britain

With France subdued by June 1940 and the Soviets still honoring their nonaggression pact with Germany, the Nazis could concentrate on the defeat of Britain. A *Blitzkrieg* across the English Channel, however, posed special problems. The *Luftwaffe* (German air force) had to drive Britain's Royal Air Force (RAF) from the skies before German armored units and armies could move onshore to conquer the island nation. Hitler's previous campaigns, especially in the Netherlands, indicated that a lightning war from the skies could defeat the RAF and leave Britain exposed.

WINSTON CHURCHILL (1874–1965) IN COMMAND

Chamberlain resigned and Winston Churchill became the British prime minister in May 1940. This new leader gave the nation masterful and inspiring direction throughout the war. As soon as Churchill took charge, he challenged the citizenry to prepare for the sacrifices necessary to ensure victory.

HITLER'S FIRST DEFEAT

The RAF and *Luftwaffe* fought the Battle of Britain with increasing fury from August until November 1940. Attacks diminished during the winter months, but other hard strikes came in May and June 1941. Thereafter, the air raids subsided as Germany gave up the plan to invade Britain and turned its forces against the Soviet Union.

By the end of the war, German air raids had killed 60,000 British civilians and left 4,000,000 of the nation's 13,000,000 homes severely damaged. An additional 500,000 houses were destroyed or wrecked beyond use. The Battle of Britain caused most of these losses. But the air war in the autumn of 1940 also cost the Nazis dearly. They lost almost half of their 1,291 bombers. This loss seriously weakened the German air force for the duration of the war. More important, Britain was not only unsubdued but aroused to the cause of war against Germany. A Nazi blitz had failed for the first time.

The Balkan and North African Campaigns

Soon after the Battle of Britain began, Mussolini decided to expand his empire. He provoked wars with the British in North Africa (August 1940) and with the Yugoslavs and Greeks in the Balkan Peninsula (October 1940). By December the Italians were losing badly on all these southern fronts.

Since a Fascist Italian collapse would expose Germany to a British attack from the south, Hitler had to send forces into the Balkans and North Africa. The Germans quickly conquered Yugoslavia and Greece. In North Africa, General Erwin Rommel, the "Desert Fox," led his forces to victory over the British in Libya. Then Rommel threatened British positions in Egypt.

By June 1941, these operations in the Balkans and Africa gave Hitler the security he needed in the south. But the Battle of Britain and the wars started by Mussolini had reduced Germany's military resources and forced Hitler to delay the invasion of the Soviet Union. The schedule alterations especially worried Nazi leaders since seasonal weather patterns could determine the success or failure of military operations.

"The Great Patriotic War"—A Soviet Triumph

For more than fifteen years before the Second World War, Hitler emphatically publicized his conviction that the German race could realize its destiny as world rulers only by having the grain, petroleum, and other resources of the Soviet southwest. The Nazi-Soviet nonaggression pact

(1939) in no way reduced Hitler's commitment to this vision of an Aryan empire. Germany had to fight Soviet Russia.

PREPARATION FOR THE ULTIMATE *BLITZKRIEG*

In late June 1941, a Nazi strike force of about 3,000 tanks, 5,000 planes, and 3,000,000 soldiers stood ready for Operation Barbarossa, the invasion of the Soviet Union. Since February, British, American, and Soviet intelligence services had warned Stalin of an impending attack. He refused to believe the reports and ordered his commanders to do nothing to strengthen border defenses. Stalin declared that a Soviet army buildup would provoke Hitler to invade.

THE SOVIET COLLAPSE

On June 22, 1941, the Nazi invasion began along a 2,000-mile front. Numerically, the Soviet forces were not badly outmatched, and they fought with courage. But the quality of their equipment and military leadership in no way compared with Germany's at this stage of the war. During the first ten days, the Nazis advanced more than 100 miles inside Soviet borders, took 150,000 prisoners, and destroyed 75 percent of the Soviet air force. Stalin disappeared for eleven days, possibly an escape into drunkenness. He had left his people alone to fight the struggle they called "The Great Patriotic War."

The invaders continued their incredibly rapid advance throughout the summer. In September 1941, Nazi forces reached the outskirts of Leningrad and Moscow. They thus threatened to seize the two largest and most highly industrialized cities in the nation. German troops took Kiev, the third largest city, on September 19 and within ten days began to exterminate Jews. Nearly 35,000 died in the first two days of killing. The slaughter did not end in Kiev until the Nazis left over two years later. Almost no Kievan Jews were left alive.

RESISTANCE

The Soviet public almost never saw or heard Stalin during the 1930s. On July 3, 1941, he emerged from his eleven days in hiding and spoke to the nation by radio. Startled Soviet citizens heard their all-powerful leader appeal to his "brothers and sisters." Stalin urged them with a warmly personal and deeply patriotic message to rise and destroy the invaders. The Soviets responded. Their stiff resistance stopped the Nazi line of advance in the north and central regions by the autumn of 1941.

In late 1941 and throughout 1942, the nation rallied to the cause of resistance. Partisans (underground fighters) battled the Nazis in occupied territory. The Soviets relocated factories and work forces beyond German

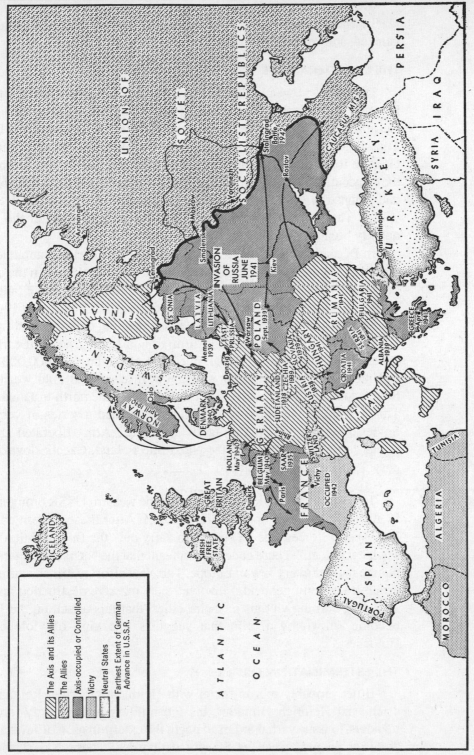

Fig. 16.1   Axis Expansion in Europe to 1942

reach. War production rapidly increased. The Red Army expanded, reorganized, and went on the attack.

THE COUNTERATTACK

Distance and weather in the Soviet Union somewhat blunted the Nazi invasion drive during the last two months of 1941. The great length of German supply lines and axle-deep mud slowed the pace of the *Blitzkrieg*. Then bitter cold began to take its toll on Nazi troops and equipment. The German forces had not come prepared for the extremely low temperatures they encountered (sometimes forty below zero Fahrenheit) because Hitler had planned to start Barbarossa early enough to defeat the Soviets before winter. The price of the delay to attack Britain and conquer the Balkans quickly became evident.

In December 1941, the Red Army mounted its first counterattack along the entire front. This winter offensive pushed the Nazi lines in the center of the nation westward away from Moscow. The Red Army drive failed in the south. The Germans continued to advance there until September 1942. Then the Soviets stopped them and inflicted a punishing defeat at Stalingrad.

In the north, Nazi lines held firm around Leningrad until early 1944. When this 900-day siege ended, one-third of the city's 3,000,000 citizens had died, most of them from starvation, disease, and cold weather. The Soviet counterattack finally began to succeed in the north in January 1944. This assault on the Nazis near Leningrad opened a series of very strong Soviet offensive drives. During 1944, the Red Army liberated almost all Soviet territory and pursued the Nazis into Poland, Czechoslovakia, Hungary, Romania, and Bulgaria.

The Holocaust

The Nazis' occupation of Poland and the western USSR brought virtually all European Jews under Hitler's power. After these eastern conquests, Nazi special forces (the SS) began to carry out "the final solution" of "the Jewish problem." These code words meant that the Nazis implemented their plan to murder every Jew in Europe. The Nazi effort to kill an entire genetic group (to commit genocide) involved such massive destruction and death, including burning victims or their bodies, that this attack on the Jews has become known by a term that suggests this kind of violence—"the Holocaust."

THE EXTERMINATION ORDER

Hitler probably met in secret with Hermann Goering, Reinhard Heydrich, and Heinrich Himmler, his top military and security-force commanders, to issue verbal orders to begin the extermination of Jews and other "inferior people," such as Slavs and Gypsies. These Nazi leaders then implemented the command through a chain of subordinates. In later war-crime trials, a typical response of the actual executioners was that they felt nothing as they watched victims suffer and die since they were only obeying superiors.

TERROR AND SLAVE LABOR

Nazi terror in Poland began immediately after the occupation of conquered territory in 1939. The invaders seized academic and religious leaders and imprisoned or killed them. When action by the Poles or other conquered peoples led to a Nazi death, German officials typically ordered the execution of 100 of these jailed civilians for each Nazi casualty.

In January 1942, Heydrich met fifteen security-force commanders to tell them the plan for Jews in Poland and other eastern territories. Most were to be worked to death. Extermination would await the strong ones who managed to survive these slave-labor conditions. Occupying forces in Poland began to carry out the plan by herding all Jews into walled or fenced-off sectors of their cities—the Jewish ghettos.

On starvation diets, ghetto residents were forced to work at a cruel pace in war production plants. Jews tolerated these conditions too well to suit their captors, however. The Nazis thus decided to begin shipping them to death camps. The ghetto in Warsaw had a population of 400,000 people in mid-1940. Slave labor and deportation for extermination took all but 70,000 by April 1943.

When heavily armed SS units entered the Warsaw ghetto on April 19, 1943, to slaughter these remaining captives, the Jews rebelled. Squads of Jewish men and women used gasoline bombs and light weapons they had smuggled in to fight the SS troops. It took a month to crush the rebellion. Almost all the Jews died fighting or were shipped to death camps.

DEATH SQUADS

Einsatzgruppen (special task groups) followed the German army into the Soviet Union during Operation Barbarossa. The special assignment of these units was the mass murder of Jews. These death squads used gunfire to slaughter hundreds of thousands of people, mostly but not exclusively Jewish, in villages and cities all over the western USSR. At times, the *Einsatz* troops in cities such as Kiev killed people more rapidly than the special death camps.

THE CONCENTRATION CAMPS

Nazi occupying forces in every conquered territory from France to Soviet Russia deported huge numbers of Jews to concentration camps. The Germans sent Jews to several compounds built before the war but most went to new prison centers in East Europe. Almost thirty camps, including Dachau and Buchenwald, were organized to provide slave labor. The horrible conditions in these institutions ensured that inmates would live in great misery and die rapidly.

The Nazis constructed several camps that had no purpose but the swift mass murder of Jews and other "subhumans." They built the five largest extermination centers in Poland and equipped them with gas chambers for the mass murders. The Nazis also constructed huge furnaces to burn the bodies. Auschwitz, the largest of all the death camps, destroyed 6,000 people a day when in full operation. Victims went naked into concrete rooms expecting "baths." With people of both sexes and all ages crowded close together, SS executioners dropped in pellets from above that released suffocating gases. The victims died excruciating deaths, tearing at the walls and ceiling with their bare hands.

THE FINAL VICTORY

The Nazi final solution took the lives of about 6,000,000 of Europe's 10,000,000 Jews. Only ten percent of the Jewish children living in German-occupied territory survived the Holocaust. The ninety percent who died numbered 1,500,000. Information about these mass murders began to reach the outside world early in the war, but most leaders doubted the stories at first.

By the summer of 1944, however, Britain, the United States, and the Soviet Union knew about the large extermination camps but did nothing. Jewish leaders urged the Western Allies to bomb the gas chambers and the railroads leading to the camps. British and American leaders rejected these pleas. They said such attacks were impractical and might make conditions worse for the Jews.

Several European nations saved the Jews within their borders by refusing to deliver victims as ordered by the Nazis. The Danes and Finns rescued virtually every one of their Jewish citizens. Even Fascist Italy protected most Italian Jews from deportation to the death camps. Millions of other Jews saved themselves through their own struggles, concealment, or flight. In these ways, about 4,000,000 Jews lived through the Holocaust and won an agonizing victory over their greatest enemy in history.

IN A FIGHT TO THE FINISH

In mid-summer 1943, the Nazis and fascists still ruled most of the continent. This position of power over so much of Europe enabled Hitler to threaten the existence of Britain, Soviet Russia, and the Jewish people until that time. During July and August 1943, the three greatest military powers in the world other than Germany mounted attacks and began to reconquer

Europe from the fascists. Hitler now faced enemies committed to the total defeat of the Nazis and their allies.

The Anti-Fascist Coalition

From the beginning of the Second World War in Europe, the United States provided support to Britain. America's Lend-Lease Act formally established and expanded this assistance program in March 1941. Soon after the Nazis invaded the USSR in June 1941, Britain and the Soviets signed a mutual aid agreement. Then the United States began lend-lease assistance to the Soviet Union the following November. In response to Hitler's escalating war in Europe, an anti-Fascist coalition had begun to emerge.

THE ATLANTIC CHARTER

During the early months of the war, Churchill and U.S. President Franklin Roosevelt discussed broad peace aims as well as the practical matter of military aid. These leaders held a conference at sea in August 1941 that produced the Atlantic Charter. This declaration contained a pledge to stop aggressors and ensure the right of all nations to choose their form of government. Britain and the United States also promised to advance the welfare of societies without exploiting them in any way. As British and American leaders pursued peace during the next four years, the firm alliance indicated by the Charter never weakened, despite the conflicts that sometimes developed between those two nations.

THE UNITED STATES AT WAR

The United States provided aid to Britain and the USSR early in the war. At the beginning of December 1941, however, more than two years after the Second World War erupted in Europe, the United States was not fighting. Then events in Asia transformed the European conflict into a truly global war with the United States as a main participant on both sides of the world.

Leaders with attitudes similar to those of the European Fascists rose to supremacy in Japan during the 1930s. Under militant nationalist influence, Japan conquered territory in China in 1931 and 1937. The outbreak of the Second World War in 1939 weakened the grip of European imperialists in Asia and gave Japan new opportunities for expansion. Japanese leaders expected to make gains in British India, French Indochina, and the Dutch East Indies (Indonesia).

For almost a century before the Second World War, commercial interests had led the United States to become increasingly involved in Asian affairs. An extremely powerful navy made the Americans intimidating competitors for any nation that wanted influence in Asia. In 1898, for example, the United States fought and defeated Spain, then seized the Philippines.

The United States remained a formidable influence in Asia in the 1930s. Japanese imperial ambitions thus placed them on a collision course with the

Americans. With an air attack on the U.S. Pacific fleet at Pearl Harbor in the Hawaiian Islands on December 7, 1941, Japan intended to end the power of this rival in Asia. Since Japan's Italian and German allies declared war on the United States on December 11, the immediate effect of the aerial strike was that America entered the war in Asia and became a fighting ally of Britain and the USSR in Europe.

The Allied Campaigns in North Africa and Italy

American strategists decided early in the war to devote most of their resources to the European military struggle until the Allies (The United States, Britain, and the USSR) defeated the Fascists in that region. In 1942, as the Soviets pounded against Hitler's forces in East Europe, the British and Americans opened their combined West European campaign with a year-long air war against Nazi military and industrial centers on the continent.

The Americans also joined the British war against Rommel in North Africa in November 1942. Two weeks before the United States entered this desert conflict, British forces under General Bernard Montgomery had turned the tide at El Alamein. The Western Allies completed the victory in North Africa by May 1943.

THE CASABLANCA CONFERENCE

Stalin had insisted throughout 1942 that the Western Allies open a second front in West Europe so that the Soviets would not have to fight the ground war on the continent alone. As British and American troops battled toward victory in North Africa, Roosevelt and Churchill met at Casablanca, Morocco, to consider war plans, including the possibility of invading West Europe.

When their ten-day conference ended on January 24, 1943, the Western Allies had publicly proclaimed their decision to fight Italy, Germany, and Japan until these enemies surrendered unconditionally. Roosevelt and Churchill also secretly agreed to invade southern Europe through Sicily very soon.

Critical military circumstances in the Soviet Union had prevented Stalin from accepting the invitation to attend the Casablanca conference, but Soviet representatives attended and informed their leader of the outcome. The plan to open a second front in the west pleased Stalin, but he strongly preferred an attack across the English Channel into northern France.

THE DEFEAT OF FASCIST ITALY

The Western Allies developed a new military technique during 1942, the amphibious assault. These attacks over water and onto enemy shores quickly became an American and British specialty. On July 10, 1943, only weeks after the Allied victory in North Africa, the United States and Britain launched massive amphibious invasions of Sicily and began intensive bombing in Italy. The Fascist Grand Council, which had always passively obeyed Mussolini, met in mid-July and ordered their leader to surrender command of the army. King Victor Emmanuel III reasserted his authority and dismissed Mussolini as premier.

Pietro Badoglio, the new premier, took action at once to avoid an Allied invasion and a land war in Italy. He ordered the Fascist Party to disband and opened peace talks with the Western Allies. Negotiations continued until September 3, 1943, when the Badoglio government agreed to unconditional surrender. On the previous day, the first Allied troops had invaded southern Italy.

The collapse of the Fascist state and Italy's surrender did not end the battle for control of the peninsula. Hitler had anticipated the collapse of his Italian ally and rushed troops in to hold central and northern Italy. The Fuehrer also sent a special-forces group to rescue Mussolini, who had been under arrest since his dismissal as Italian premier. The Nazis then reestablished Mussolini as the head of a German puppet state in northern Italy. Bitter fighting between the Western Allies and the Nazis in northern Italy continued until the end of April 1945. As the Nazi defeat in Italy neared, Mussolini tried to escape to Switzerland. Members of the Italian anti-Fascist resistance forces captured and executed Mussolini and his mistress on April 28, 1945.

The Liberation of West Europe

Allied war production capacities expanded rapidly during 1942 and 1943. The anti-Fascist coalition also advanced steadily on battlefields in Italy and the Soviet Union throughout 1943. Allied leaders thus began to consider war and victory plans in more detail.

THE TEHERAN CONFERENCE

In October 1943, American, British, and Soviet diplomats held a conference in Moscow. They agreed to continue to cooperate to defeat the Nazis. The Allies also pledged to nullify the power of Germany to wage war and punish Germans who committed war crimes. Churchill, Roosevelt, and Stalin then met in Teheran, Iran, for their first "Big Three" conference, November 28, 1943, to January 12, 1944. They reaffirmed the agreements made in Moscow in October, decided the timing of a cross-Channel invasion, and promised to form a new world organization after the war.

D DAY AND BEYOND

By late spring 1944, 5,000 vessels waited in British ports to carry over 2,000,000 Allied troops across the English Channel for a landing on the Normandy shores in France. Success required that the Allies' 12,000 planes establish control of the skies over northern France.

Strategists selected June 6, 1944, for the invasion date (code-named "D day"). The location and timing of the attack surprised the Nazis, but they mounted a fierce resistance. Despite the stubborn defensive battle, the Allies secured a sixty-mile-wide section of beach within a week and brought the more than 2,000,000 troops into northern France during the next three months.

AN ALLIED FRONT IN SOUTHERN FRANCE

The Allies intensified their growing threat to the Nazi position in West Europe by opening still another front. On August 15, 1944, French and American troops invaded the southern coast of France. As the Allied armies in the north and south battled their way toward the heart of France, resistance fighters escalated the struggle behind Nazi lines. Parisian citizens also joined the fight and won control of their city during a rebellion in late August 1944.

THE BATTLE OF THE BULGE

In northwestern Europe, Allied gains continued during the autumn and winter after D day. They drove the Nazis from Brussels, Belgium, on September 2, 1944, and crossed the German border ten days later. Then the advance halted. In December, after three months with static fronts, Hitler ordered a counterattack toward Belgium.

The Nazis' offensive in December 1944 almost broke through and divided the Allied forces in northwestern Europe. Inexperienced American soldiers finally stopped the German offensive during the ten-day Battle of the Bulge that ended December 25, 1944. American, British, and French forces then resumed their massive drive toward Germany and completed the liberation of West Europe by early 1945.

The Soviet Conquest of East Europe

Eighteen months of slow and deadly combat brought Soviet troops into a small northeastern pocket in Bulgaria by June of 1944. From that position north to the Baltic Sea, Germany still held a border strip of the USSR Soon after the Western Allies landed at Normandy (June 6), Soviet forces charged into Nazi lines in the east. For a month the front moved rapidly westward, toward Poland and Romania.

THE ANTI-NAZI UPRISING IN WARSAW

On August 1, underground forces in Warsaw, Poland, revolted against the German occupiers as the Red Army neared the city. The Nazis waged war on the desperate rebels for two months. The Soviets were forty miles away but immobile. German troops crushed the rebellion, killed 200,000 Poles, and completed the destruction of Warsaw by early October 1944.

THE DRIVE TO THE BORDERS OF GERMANY

The Soviet army took Warsaw three months after the Nazis completed their brutal war against the city. Poles charged the Soviets with allowing the extermination of the Warsaw underground in order to weaken their nation. Red Army leaders insisted that after a long offensive, their forces lacked the strength to attack between August 1944 and January 1945. Once the Soviets resumed their attack, they continued the hard fight westward, reaching the borders of Germany within weeks.

The Yalta Conference

On February 7, 1945, Churchill, Roosevelt, and Stalin met at Yalta on the Soviet Crimean peninsula in the Black Sea. The anti-Fascist coalition urgently needed to make decisions about the restoration of the states that the Allies had recently liberated in East and West Europe. Furthermore, since the conference opened with Allied armies converging on the last stronghold of Nazism, the three leaders wanted to plan the final steps to victory, decide the postwar fate of Germany, and consider global peace-building methods.

THE AGREEMENTS ON EAST EUROPE

Stalin came to Yalta with the Red Army in control of most of East Europe. With this powerful advantage, he proceeded to make several demands. Stalin insisted that the Soviets must keep the territory acquired from Poland in 1939, that the Poles should be compensated with the annexation of eastern German lands, and that Poland must have a government friendly to the USSR. Since Poland and Russia had a long history of extremely hostile relations, the insistence on a pro-Soviet Polish government meant that Stalin did not want to allow this country to choose its leaders freely. The Soviets thought their need for protection from invaders from the west justified this demand.

The Western Allies won only minor modifications of Stalin's plan for Poland. Roosevelt and Churchill accepted the Polish border changes in principle but left the precise boundaries between Poland and Germany unspecified. The three leaders agreed to establish a government in Poland led by the Lublin Poles (a pro-Soviet group). Stalin, in turn, yielded slightly and accepted the inclusion of a few members of a pro-Western Polish faction in the government.

In keeping with American demands, the three allies also pledged to provide for the free election of democratic governments in nations liberated from the Fascists. The position of Soviet forces in East Europe made it possible for Stalin to ignore his promise for free elections. If the Western Allies wanted strict compliance with this agreement, they would have to be prepared to go to war with the Soviets.

WAR PLANS

Although the Yalta agreements included understandings about victory strategies in Germany, the most significant war plans pertained to the struggle in Asia. The United States expected an extended battle with Japan and believed that it was critically important to have Soviet help against this enemy. The Japanese and Soviets were still at peace in February 1945, but the USSR promised to declare war on Japan within three months after the defeat of Germany. In return for this important concession to the Americans, Roosevelt agreed to Soviet territorial gains in Asia, including the acquisition of the Japanese Kuril Islands.

THE FATE OF GERMANY

Stalin believed that the future security of the USSR and the peace of Europe required that Germany be demilitarized, divided into smaller states, and stripped of its industries. Although the United States had previously proposed a very similar plan, by February 1945 Roosevelt favored much milder treatment of Germany. Churchill took an even more lenient position toward Germany than Roosevelt. The British leader also argued forcefully for French participation in the postwar control of Germany. Churchill's aim was to give the Germans and French sufficient strength and influence to counter Soviet power on the continent.

In the negotiations on German issues, Churchill and Stalin fought to achieve their aims. Roosevelt considered the maintenance of Allied solidarity so important that he was willing to yield more to Stalin than the British thought wise. Despite the American president's attitude, Churchill more nearly achieved his goals than did Stalin.

The Allies decided to divide Germany into four zones of occupation. Churchill and Roosevelt had ignored Stalin's objections and given France an area to control. Although Berlin was sixty miles inside the Soviet zone, the negotiators also arranged for each of the four occupying nations to take charge of a section of the capital. The four allies pledged that once they took charge in Germany, they would nullify Nazism and militarism in that nation.

In punishing Germany, the Western Allies would not go beyond occupation, denazification, and demilitarization. They refused to accept the Soviet plan to strip Germany of its industry and split the nation into separate states. Germany would remain much stronger than Stalin had intended to allow. Churchill and Roosevelt also rejected Stalin's demand that the Germans pay a large reparations sum to the Soviet Union. The Western leaders agreed only to discuss that issue in the future.

THE COMMITMENT TO FORM THE UNITED NATIONS

Before the Yalta discussions ended on February 12, the Big Three expressed their support for the plan to establish a new global association to replace the League of Nations. The Allies promised to participate in a United Nations organizational conference scheduled for late April 1945 in San Francisco.

The Conquest of Germany

Allied armies arrayed along broad fronts in both East and West Europe had advanced steadily toward Germany during the last six months of 1944. The final stage of the Second World War in Europe began the month after the Yalta Conference as U.S. troops poured across the Rhine River into the heart of Germany and the Soviets gathered for an assault on Berlin. Despite the inevitability of defeat, Hitler would not allow his nation to surrender. Germany would fight until the Third *Reich* and its founder were destroyed.

THE AIR WAR AGAINST GERMANY

The destruction of German cities began during the earliest days of the war as the British RAF flew night bombing raids over the *Reich*. As soon as the United States entered the conflict, American bombers began to carry out daylight attacks that concentrated on the ruin of German industry and transportation.

These aerial assaults intensified throughout the war. By mid-1944, the Western Allies had so completely overwhelmed the German air force that they could attack repeatedly anywhere in the nation. Most German cities, including many with no important military or industrial targets, were struck time after time until they lay in ruins. An especially devastating series of attacks directed at Dresden during the Yalta Conference killed an estimated 150,000 to 200,000 people, almost all of them civilians.

THE ALLIED BREAKTHROUGH IN WEST GERMANY

The western portion of Germany extends about 500 miles from north to south and almost 300 miles from east to west. The Elbe River separates this western region from a smaller eastern sector with Berlin at its center. The Rhine River flows northward along the nation's western border near France. In early March 1945, the armies of the Western Allies under the command of U.S. General Dwight Eisenhower attacked east out of France toward the Rhine.

As the Allied offensive began, Nazi armies in west central Germany withdrew after destroying all the Rhine bridges except one. This single structure enabled Eisenhower's forces to cross the river with exceptional speed and drive through the heart of West Germany. They reached the Elbe River, sixty miles from Berlin, by April 11.

On April 12, Roosevelt died. Eisenhower had to decide his next moves in Germany before Harry Truman, the new U.S. president, had time to become involved in war strategies. Churchill wanted to keep the Soviets out of East Germany. He urged Eisenhower to cross the Elbe and continue on to the German capital. The American general refused. In Eisenhower's judgment, the best course to military victory was for the Western Allies to swing into southwestern Germany while the Soviets conquered eastern Germany.

THE DESTRUCTION OF THE NAZI *REICH*

As Eisenhower completed the campaign in West Germany, the Soviets advanced through the rest of East Europe and into East Germany. Vienna, the Austrian capital, fell to the Soviets on April 13. The Red Army forces under Marshal Georgi Zhukov then began their offensive sixty miles east of Berlin on April 16, 1945.

A few Soviet units entered the outskirts of Berlin on April 20. Other Red Army contingents fought on westward and met the Americans at Torgau on the Elbe on April 25. Hitler remained hidden in a bunker in Berlin, as Allied forces swarmed over Germany. With the Red Army fighting the last Nazi defenders of Berlin in the streets above the Fuehrer's stronghold, Hitler killed himself on April 30.

The delivery of messages of submission by several Nazi commanders on May 7 inspired Truman and Churchill to declare victory in Europe on May 8. Since the Nazi high command surrendered on May 9, Stalin designated that date as the day of triumph. The Fascist era in Europe had finally drawn to a disastrous close.

The Asian Holocaust

After the attack on Pearl Harbor, Hawaii, in December 1941, the Japanese and Americans fought each other with special ferocity. Japan conquered the Philippines and advanced toward Australia until March 1942. The Americans then devastated the Japanese navy the following May in the Battle of the Coral Sea and in early June at Midway Island.

The United States conducted a relentless offensive after Midway, taking island after island in extremely deadly combat. American forces suffered very heavy casualties as they attacked well-entrenched and determined Japanese defenders. But intense U.S. naval bombardments, aerial assaults, and ground attacks with flame-throwers, tanks, and massive infantry forces almost totally exterminated the Japanese troops on islands such as Tarawa and Peleliu.

By June 1944, the U.S. Army Air Force opened its war on Japan. The bombing continued with mounting fury for over a year. Naval vessels also joined the attack on Japanese cities. Thousands of tons of bombs and heavy artillery shells rained down on the island nation, incinerating heavily populated urban centers.

A very different kind of aerial attack then occurred on August 6, 1945. Residents of Hiroshima watched as a small flight of U.S. planes passed over their city. Since they saw no mass of bombers, they assumed the aircraft were on a reconnaissance mission. Instead, a B-29 had dropped a single 9,000-pound atomic bomb that drifted down by parachute. When it exploded above ground, 80,000 to 100,000 people died instantly. The number of deaths from this bomb doubled during the next five years.

Stalin acted on his Yalta pledge on August 8, 1945, and declared war on Japan. On the following day, the United States dropped an atomic bomb on Nagasaki, Japan, killing about 60,000 people. Japanese leaders indicated within two days that they wanted to surrender. They officially yielded on August 14 and signed the surrender documents on September 2.

President Truman told the world that he had ordered the use of atomic bombs to hasten the end of the war and save the lives of the estimated 500,000 troops that an invasion of Japan was expected to take. Critics of his decision charged that Japan would have surrendered soon even without an invasion. They believed the nuclear attacks on these cities were unnecessary. A few scholars later argued that Truman ordered the nuclear attacks in order to demonstrate American power to Stalin or to stop the war before the Soviets could advance very far into Asia.

In the 1920s, Europeans joined people from every quarter of the globe in a concerted effort to prevent a second plunge into world war. They pursued security and harmony by establishing the League of Nations, negotiating arms limitations, and arranging protective treaties. The hope for peace strengthened throughout the 1920s, but the dreams faded in the next decade as Fascist aggression increased in spite of all the peacemaking efforts.

British and French leaders had a great dread of the war that seemed to be approaching. In a vain effort to maintain peace, they made concessions to Hitler, the most militant Fascist dictator. These attempts to appease the Fuehrer did not end Nazi aggression, however. Only war could give Hitler what he desired—the annexation of East Europe and a chance to deport or murder every Jew on the continent.

In September 1939, German armies struck into Poland with lightning speed and ignited the Second World War. The Nazi military storm then raged across Europe during the next two years, overwhelming all opposition from western France to the Soviet Ural mountains. These conquests gave Hitler and his Fascist allies control of almost the entire continent by late 1941. As soon as the Nazis took East Europe, they began to exterminate Jews and other "subhumans." The slaughter did not stop until British, Soviet, and American forces blasted their way into the heart of Europe and crushed the Italian Fascist state and the Nazis.

After the Allied victory in Europe in May 1945, the war continued against Japan, the Asian member of the Fascist alliance. The defeat of the Japanese required a deadly war of island invasion and aerial bombardment that climaxed in the atomic infernos at Hiroshima and Nagasaki in August

1945. *Even before these last battles of the Second World War, a cold war had begun between the Western Allies and the Soviets. This conflict soon created a threat of nuclear holocaust that haunted the world until the last decade of the century.*

Selected Readings

Calvocoressi, Peter, and Guy Wint. *Total War: The Story of World War II*. London: Allen Lane, 1972.

Churchill, Winston S. *The Second World War*. 6 vols. Boston: Houghton and Mifflin, 1948–1953.

Davidowicz, Lucy. *The War Against the Jews, 1933–1945*. New York: Holt, Rinehart, and Winston, 1975.

Delzell, Charles F. *Mussolini's Enemies: The Italian Anti-Fascist Resistance*. Princeton, NJ: Princeton University Press, 1961.

Feis, Herbert. *Churchill, Roosevelt, and Stalin: The War They Waged and the Peace They Sought*. 2nd ed. Princeton, NJ: Princeton University Press, 1967.

Hastings, Max. *Overlord: D Day and the Battle of Normandy*. New York: Simon and Schuster, 1984.

Krakowski, Shmuel. *The War of the Doomed: Jewish Armed Resistance in Poland, 1942–1944*. New York: Holmes and Meier, 1984.

Sherwin, Martin J. *A World Destroyed: The Atomic Bomb and the Grand Alliance*. New York: Vintage Books, 1977.

Weinberg, Gerald L. *World in the Balance: Behind the Scenes in World War II*. Hanover, NH: University Press of New England, 1981.

Wright, Gordon. *The Ordeal of Total War, 1939–1945*. New York: Harper & Row, 1968.

17

The Superpower Spheres in Europe, 1945–1968

April 1945	A meeting at San Francisco founds the United Nations
July 1945	The Allied leaders meet at Potsdam for their final war conference
March 1947	The "Truman doctrine" promises aid to nations fighting communism
June 1947	The United States begins Marshall Plan aid to rebuild Europe
February 1948	The fall of Czechoslovakia completes the Soviet seizure of East Europe
June 1948	The Soviets begin an eleven-month blockade of Berlin
April 1949	Western nations form the North Atlantic Treaty Organization
June 1950	The Korean War begins
November 1952	The United States explodes the first hydrogen bomb
March 1953	Stalin dies
1956	Khrushchev assumes control of the Soviet Union
	A Soviet invasion ends the Hungarian revolt against communism
	The British and French invade Egypt but fail to retake the Suez Canal
1957	Six West European states organize the Common Market
	The Soviets conduct the first successful test of an intercontinental ballistic missile
August 1961	The East Germans construct the Berlin Wall
October 1962	The Cuban missile crisis takes the world to the nuclear brink

1963 Britain, the United States, and the Soviet Union sign the Limited Test Ban
Treaty ending nuclear bomb tests except underground

1964 Soviet leaders force Khrushchev into retirement

From 1815 to 1945, Central and West Europeans exercised mastery over their continent and much of the rest of the world as well. For more than two decades after the Second World War ended in 1945, the Central and West Europeans not only lost their supremacy but found themselves under the domination of the Soviet Union and the United States.

The Soviets truly ruled in East Europe. They transformed the governmental and economic systems of almost all the states of this region with little consideration for the wishes of the East Europeans. In West Europe, the United States dominated foreign and military policies but largely left the states in this area in control of their own internal affairs.

The division of the continent into these superpower spheres strongly affected European and world affairs until the 1970s, and did so to a lesser extent until the last decade of the century. This influence resulted in part simply from the ability of the Soviets and Americans to hold sway over these regions. But the change in the international power structure after 1945 shaped the course of events in Europe and the larger world even more because each of the superpowers struggled in every way except open war to dominate the other. One of the particularly important effects of this "cold war" was to place Europe and perhaps the rest of the world under the threat of a nuclear holocaust from the 1950s onward.

THE AFTERMATH OF EUROPE'S GREATEST WAR

The Americans, British, and Soviets coordinated their assault on the European fascists effectively enough to deliver a crushing defeat to their enemies. At the end of the war, however, the political conflicts between the Western Allies and the Soviets made it impossible for the victors to gather for a peace conference. Eventually, the foreign ministers of the conquering nations negotiated treaties with all the defeated states except one. They never arranged a formal settlement with Germany.

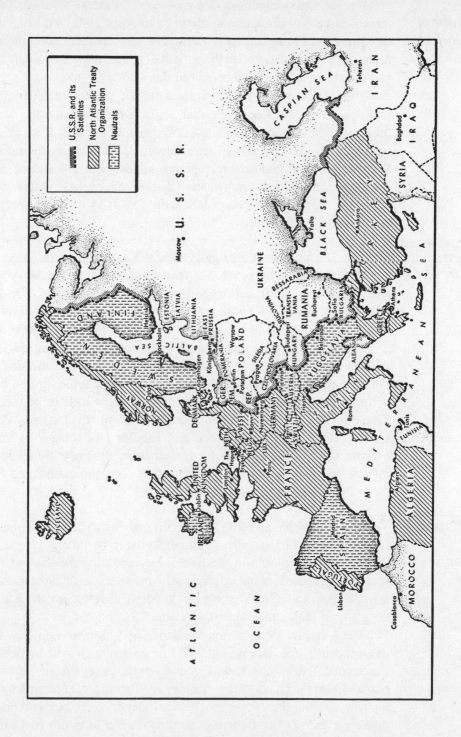

Fig. 17.1   Divided Europe

The Establishment of the United Nations

Despite the antagonism within the anti-Fascist alliance, the Soviets joined in the San Francisco conference in April 1945. This meeting led to the formation of the United Nations. The UN founders committed the new international organization to the pursuit of peace, improved living standards, and equal rights for all the people of the world.

The idealism of the UN organizers did not blind them to certain political realities. Churchill, Roosevelt, and Stalin had agreed that the successor to the League of Nations could make critical decisions only if the great powers remained united. The UN Charter, therefore, gave supreme authority to a Security Council comprising representatives from the United States, the Soviet Union, Britain, France, and China. Each of these states could block any request for extraordinary UN action, such as military intervention in conflicts between nations.

War-Torn Europe in 1945

The Second World War gave the nations of the world good reason to attempt to organize for peace. Six years of searing warfare between the Axis and Allied Powers left Europe with truly incredible losses. The dead numbered about 45,000,000 with approximately equal numbers of military and civilian casualties. (The war in Asia killed an additional 20,000,000.)

This massive violence caused great suffering among the survivors. Almost every Soviet and Polish family "had someone missing from the table" at the end of the war. Thirty-five million people injured by the war suffered not only the wounds but the prospects of little or no medical care. The war also destroyed about one-fourth of all dwellings in Poland, the USSR, Yugoslavia, and Greece and smaller percentages in many other nations. Critical shortages of food, clothes, medicine, and fuel added to the misery. Damage to industry, transportation, communication, and agriculture made the prospects of rapid recovery bleak.

The Collapse of the European Empires

Asian, African, and Middle Eastern peoples struggled to liberate themselves from European control throughout the imperial era. Japanese success in taking Asian colonies from the Europeans during the Second World War weakened the western imperialists' grip on that region. The war also inspired a worldwide anticolonial spirit that made it difficult for the Europeans to keep any of their subject territories after 1945.

These trends led to a rapid collapse of European empires. India won independence from Britain in 1947. France lost control of Indochina during the Second World War, began a deadly fight to regain the region in 1946, but in 1954 surrendered the territory to liberation forces led by the Vietnamese. During the 1950s and 1960s, independence movements in Africa drove the Europeans from that continent. The long era of European imperialism was over.

The end of European empire left a changed global political structure in the 1960s. The capitalist states of North America and West Europe (the "First World") no longer possessed global empires but dominated world affairs because of their military and economic power. The "Second World" of Communist nations, though in conflict with one another, challenged the capitalists for world supremacy. The nations of Asia, Africa, and Central and South America that refused to align with either side in the cold war formed a "Third World" bloc of mostly poor but increasingly important states. Europe had experienced great losses in the Second World War and its aftermath. The Third World, however, gained its freedom.

The Superpower Spheres and Soviet-American Rivalry

Among the nations that suffered the most in the Second World War, none was in a better position to guarantee against a recurrence of these horrors than the Soviet Union. Stalin's drive to defeat the Nazis brought a Red Army of 11,000,000 into East Europe. This military force gave the Soviet leader power over a band of states that covered the entire western border of the USSR. He intended to protect this boundary by converting these nations into a pro-Soviet buffer zone. Nothing but an all-out attack by the Americans and West Europeans could prevent the implementation of this plan.

Since Stalin's troops also held other territory farther to the west, including eastern Germany, he hoped to take the ultimate step toward Soviet security—the nullification of German military power. The occupation of German territory west of the Elbe by the Americans, British, and French left Stalin with no chance of success in this venture against Germany unless the Western Allies cooperated.

The United States held a position of strength in West Europe similar to that of the Soviets in the east. The Americans not only occupied much territory in West Europe but also had armed forces of 12,000,000, exclusive possession of atomic weapons, and the world's most highly developed industrial economy. The United States certainly had the power to prevent Stalin from carrying out his intentions in Germany or to prevent Soviet expansion westward, if the Communist leader had such aggressive ambitions. The Americans also had the potential to influence the fortunes of West Europe in many other ways.

THE ORIGINS OF SOVIET-AMERICAN HOSTILITY

Although a cooperative effort against the fascists drew the superpowers into their adjacent European spheres, the two nations had a history of antagonistic relations. They had begun to clash in the latter 1800s as Tsarist Russia extended its empire toward North China and the United States sought to capture markets in the same region. Relationships worsened after the Bolshevik victory in 1917 and subsequent U.S. intervention in the Russian Civil War.

The threat of fascism brought a Soviet-American reconciliation from the mid-1930s to the mid-1940s. An atmosphere of hostility then began to form once more as the defeat of the common enemy drew near. Most of the issues that brought about this renewal of conflict pertained to East Europe.

THE MOVEMENT TOWARD SOVIET CONTROL IN EAST EUROPE

Soviet forces drove the Nazis out of Poland during January 1945. As the Red Army continued the battle against German troops elsewhere in East Europe during the spring, the Soviets took steps to give the pro-Communist Lublin group (see chapter 16) supremacy over the coalition government in Poland. Stalin forced similar conversions of the coalitions in Romania and Bulgaria during 1945. Before the end of the year, Hungarian Communists also took the first steps toward control of their nation's government.

President Truman angrily condemned these actions and told the Soviets to keep their Yalta pledge of free elections in liberated nations. Stalin had assumed that Western leaders viewed the election promise as he did, as a public relations device. Furthermore, Britain and the United States had rejected his insistence on having influence in Italy when they reconquered that nation in 1943. Stalin thus ignored Truman's demand for a voice in East European affairs. With the Soviet military fully in charge of most nations in the region, little could be done to change Stalin's policy.

The Potsdam Conference

On July 17, 1945, Churchill, Stalin, and Truman met for the final Big Three conference at Potsdam, a suburb of Berlin. The results of the negotiations gave little evidence of the developing split between the Soviets and the Western Allies.

POLICIES TOWARD JAPAN AND GERMANY

Stalin quickly reaffirmed that the Soviet Union would declare war on Japan as promised at Yalta. The three leaders also announced continued support for the Yalta plan to demilitarize and denazify Germany. The Allies agreed, furthermore, that they would promote democracy in Germany, accept the Soviet proposal to annex part of East Germany to Poland, and punish fascist war criminals. In 1946, twenty-one Nazi officials stood trial at Nuremberg. The Allies convicted eighteen and executed ten of these people.

THE ZONES OF OCCUPATION IN GERMANY

The Big Three nations had agreed at Yalta that each of them would occupy a zone in Germany. Stalin also accepted the proposal to allow France a sector to control. The three Western Allies occupied zones west of the Elbe River. The Soviets took charge in the smaller eastern region. Berlin, in the heart of the Soviet zone, was divided among the four powers in the same way. At Potsdam, the Allies decided that they would keep the four zones economically unified.

REPARATIONS PLANS

Several of these agreements suggested greater harmony than actually existed. The decisions on reparations indicated the tendency toward conflict. The Western Allies rejected the Soviet plan to take farm products and dismantled industrial facilities from all the occupation zones in Germany. Western leaders would only affirm that the Soviets could take ten percent of West Germany's industry. Since the Americans and British could not control Soviet actions in East Germany anyway, they agreed that the USSR could decide how much to take from the eastern zone.

THE REPLACEMENT OF CHURCHILL

Churchill's party lost an election after he left for Potsdam. Clement Attlee, the Labour Party leader, then became prime minister and represented Britain from July 28 until the meetings ended on August 2. This change in leadership had little effect on the results of the conference.

ALLIED RELATIONSHIPS

Neither the conflicts evident at Potsdam nor the willingness of the Allies to resort to power politics had made East-West cooperation impossible after the conference. The Big Three still expected to work together in Europe. They arranged for a joint Allied Control Commission to supervise the occupation of Germany. The leaders also agreed that their foreign ministers would negotiate treaties with the defeated fascist states. The Soviet-American rivalry had not yet become a struggle for supremacy.

THE BEGINNING OF THE COLD WAR

In the latter months of 1945, Western leaders became increasingly concerned about the trend toward Soviet control over East Europe. By January 1946, Truman gave up on cooperation with Stalin. Churchill expressed extreme alarm about the Soviets a few months later. He traveled to the United States in March 1946 and issued an ominous warning in a speech at Westminster College in Fulton, Missouri. The British statesman depicted the Soviets as enclosing East Europe behind an "iron curtain."

Superpower rivalry intensified throughout 1946 and 1947. Leaders in the United States decided that force alone could prevent the Soviets from expanding their sphere in Europe and perhaps beyond. The Truman administration began to pursue a military buildup so that the United States could ensure the "containment" of communism. In a book titled *The Cold War,* Walter Lippmann, an American journalist, criticized this emerging anti-Soviet policy.

The conflict continued to escalate, however. By early 1948, the Soviets and Americans were locked in a struggle for dominance that involved almost every tactic other than armed combat. Lippmann's book gave this relationship its name. Although the main battleground of this "cold war" was Europe, the first encounters occurred in a tier of states at the northeastern end of the Mediterranean.

Superpower Conflict in the Eastern Mediterranean

In order to secure the main supply route for American aid to the Soviet Union, Red Army troops occupied northern Iran during the Second World War. Soviet forces ignored their scheduled departure date in early 1946 and briefly supported a local rebel group. After a few threats from the United States and Iranian offers of very favorable oil trading rights, the Soviets left. Then Iran canceled the oil deal.

THE GREEK CRISIS

Events in Greece that climaxed in 1947 agitated the United States even more than the Iranian crisis had. The oppressive policies of a Right authoritarian government in Greece provoked a strong Left revolutionary movement that seemed near victory by February 1947. In March, the British decided that economic problems at home required an end to their decades of involvement in Greek affairs. They informed the United States that American aid would have to replace British support for the right-wing Greek government.

FOREIGN INTRUDERS IN GREECE

The Truman administration was ready for drastic action. American leaders considered the entire region north of the Black Sea to be threatened by Soviet aggression. Stalin appeared to have tried and failed to expand into Iran. Then the USSR began to pressure Turkey to allow the passage of Soviet ships between the Black Sea and the Mediterranean through Turkish waters. By March 1947, both Turkey and Greece appeared to be at risk.

American officials had an exaggerated sense of the danger. They assumed Soviet involvement in the Greek revolution and worked feverishly to get Congress to approve funds for the defense of the Greek government. In reality, Communist Yugoslavia supported the Greek rebels, but the Soviet Union did not. Furthermore, the revolution in Greece had no connection to Soviet policy toward Turkey. The already dense atmosphere of the cold war prevented most Western leaders from seeing the possibility that these Eastern Mediterranean problems were not the result of an interconnected plot controlled from Moscow.

THE TRUMAN DOCTRINE

On March 12, 1947, Truman proclaimed to an emergency session of Congress his doctrine that the United States had to support any free nation threatened by "armed minorities" or "outside pressures." More immediately, Truman called for $400 million to save Greece and Turkey from the imminent danger of totalitarian revolution or conquest. Administration officials asserted during congressional hearings that if these Eastern Mediterranean states fell, the revolution would spread into Europe, perhaps even as far as France. Within two months, heavy majorities in both houses voted to grant the money.

Early East-West Conflicts in Europe's Heartland

The presence of the Red Army enabled the pro-Soviet minorities in Poland, Romania, Bulgaria, and Hungary to begin their climb toward power in 1945. These East European Stalinists advanced steadily in strength thereafter. In Poland, Romania, and Bulgaria, the pro-Soviets surpassed all their opponents in strength by 1947. Communists in Hungary made gains during 1946 and 1947, but their competitors remained a serious challenge. Later, the Soviet-supported factions would achieve exclusive control in these four states and Czechoslovakia as well.

AN AMERICAN ECONOMIC BARRAGE

Beginning in early 1945, the Americans communicated increasingly strong objections to the Soviets about the transformation of East European governments. The Truman administration also demanded that Stalin open the region to world trade. American leaders used economic weapons in an attempt to force Stalin's compliance with these demands.

In January 1945, the Soviets requested a loan of $6 billion to begin rebuilding their country. The United States replied that when they treated the East Europeans properly, the possibility of aid would be discussed. Stalin's course of action remained unchanged.

The Americans increased the economic pressure. In May 1946, they violated a Potsdam pledge and blocked the Soviets from taking industrial hardware from the American zone in Germany. During 1947, both the Soviets and the Western Allies continued this struggle by converting their German occupation zones into separate economic units, again in violation of the Potsdam agreements.

THE MARSHALL PLAN

The United States fought the cold war with diplomatic and economic weapons in the Eastern Mediterranean, East Europe, and Germany from 1946 to 1948. George Marshall, the U.S. Secretary of State beginning in 1947, introduced the ultimate weapon in the economic cold war in June 1947. Marshall feared that Stalin might soon be able to seize more Central and West European states as ruined economies caused governments to fall. He proposed that the United States establish a large-scale aid program to promote the rapid economic reconstruction of Europe.

The United States invited all European states, including the Soviet Union, to apply for aid under the Marshall Plan. Stalin discovered, however, that provisions in the plan would enable the United States to gain detailed information about the Soviet Union. He would never allow any foreign nation to learn how severely the war had damaged the Soviet industrial system. Stalin also concluded that the program would make East European countries subordinate to the United States. Neither the Soviet Union nor any East European state would ever accept this assistance. West European leaders welcomed the aid offer and began to plan an administrative system to manage the use of funds.

COMINFORM AND COMECON

For a year before Marshall proposed his plan, Stalin had slowed his consolidation of power over East Europe. His view of the dangers of the American aid program led the Soviets to accelerate the takeover. In July 1947, they organized the Communist Information Bureau (Cominform), a fourth revival of the Communist international. The Soviets intended to use Cominform to strengthen control over Communists in all European countries, especially in the eastern sphere. Another step toward increased power came in 1949 with the establishment of the Council for Mutual Economic Assistance (COMECON) as an agency of economic control in East Europe.

THE FALL OF CZECHOSLOVAKIA

In early 1948, Poland, Hungary, Romania, and Bulgaria were already ruled by Soviet-controlled dictatorships. The Czechs still had a coalition government that included prominent non-Communists such as Foreign Minister Jan Masaryk. But Czech independence had been doomed since July 1947, when the government indicated its interest in accepting Western aid under the Marshall Plan. On February 25, 1948, the Czech Communist premier, Klement Gottwald, acted on Stalin's orders and created a one-party dictatorship. In mid-March, Masaryk was found dead after jumping or being thrown from an upper-floor window.

These events in Czechoslovakia occurred as the U.S. Congress considered legislation to implement the Marshall Plan. Masaryk's death made passage of the act more certain. In late March of 1948, Congress approved the establishment of the European Recovery Program (the formal title of the Marshall Plan). West Europeans received almost $75 billion in Marshall Plan aid before the end of the 1950s. These funds enabled the participating states to use their own vast resources effectively in a program of rapid economic reconstruction. The Marshall Plan also tied West Europe more closely to the United States and completed the division of the region into Communist and anti-Communist spheres. For more than forty years, there would be two Europes.

The Militarization of the Cold War

As the Marshall Plan went into effect, the character of the cold war changed. The Truman administration continued to employ diplomatic and economic weapons against the Soviets, but in 1948 the United States began to depend on military power as the main instrument for the containment of communism in Europe.

THE FIRST BERLIN CRISIS

American opposition to Stalin's control over East Europe resulted in the Truman administration's economic warfare against the Soviets. This campaign included the beginning of efforts to restore the industrial strength of West Germany and to unify the economic systems of the three western occupation zones.

The Berlin Blockade. In June 1948, Stalin attempted to force a reversal of U.S. policies in Germany by closing all ground routes from the west into Berlin. Since the city was isolated 100 miles inside the Soviet zone, this action threatened the control of the Western Allies over their sectors of this important administrative center. A surrender of control or a reversal of U.S. policy in West Germany would give Stalin an important cold war victory.

The Berlin Airlift. The Western powers neither yielded to Stalin nor launched a military attack. Instead, they decided to fly in all the food, fuel, and other supplies needed by the more than two million residents of Berlin. As the massive airlift continued through 1948 and early 1949, the Soviets harassed the flights with blinding searchlights, but they fired no weapons. Truman left little doubt that any Soviet military assault would lead to war. He had ordered B-29s with atomic bombs to bases in Britain to wait out the Berlin crisis. In May 1949, Stalin ended the blockade.

THE COLD WAR ALLIANCES

Stalin's forceful closing off of Berlin and Truman's atomic threat to the Soviet Union dramatically revealed the militarization of the cold war. The transformation to an armed confrontation had begun earlier, however. In early 1946, Soviet leaders had begun to proclaim their intention to use science and technology to vastly increase their nation's military power. Furthermore, as a result of uneven postwar force reductions, the Red Army seemed more threatening in 1947 than it had in 1945. The Soviets had over 3,000,000 troops in East Europe two years after the war, and the United States had reduced its forces to less than 2,000,000.

The Western European Union. The imposing military strength of the Soviet Union and a lingering fear of Germany caused West European leaders to be concerned about their security. The fall of Czechoslovakia prodded them into action. In March 1948, Britain, France, and the Benelux countries (Belgium, the Netherlands, and Luxemburg) signed the Brussels Treaty, a mutual defense pact that established the Western European Union (WEU).

NATO. In April 1949, Italy, Denmark, Norway, Portugal, Iceland, the United States, and Canada joined the nations of the WEU to form an enlarged western military alliance. The twelve nations in this North Atlantic Treaty Organization (NATO) pledged that if any one of them were attacked they all would join the fight against the aggressor. This anti-Soviet alliance indicated the completion of the Western powers' shift to a policy of Communist containment by military threat rather than political and economic pressure.

The Warsaw Pact. The Soviet Union's subjugation of East Europe ended the independence of the armies of Poland, Hungary, Czechoslovakia, Romania, Bulgaria, and East Germany. Stalin allowed the armed forces of these states to exist only as part of a larger military structure that he commanded. Soviet leaders formally established this involuntary alliance system as the Warsaw Treaty Organization ("Warsaw Pact") in 1955.

The Formal Establishment of Two German States

Once Europe was frozen into superpower spheres with two groups of states in hostile confrontation, the reunification of Germany became impossible. The occupying forces in practice had converted the defeated nation into two states by 1948. In the following year, the cold war competitors took the final steps in the division of Germany. The Western Allies founded the Federal Republic of Germany ("West Germany") on May 23, 1949. Soviet Russia then hastened to establish the German Democratic Republic ("East Germany"), on October 7, 1949.

THE WEST GERMAN CONSTITUTION

An assembly of German leaders drafted the constitution of the new Federal Republic. After the Western Allies and local governments in West Germany approved this document, it went into effect. At first, American, British, and French military commanders kept partial authority over armaments, foreign relations, and several other aspects of West German public affairs. The Federal Republic became fully independent in 1955.

West Germany's constitution established a parliamentary democracy. The founding law gave the chancellor broad powers over the central political system, but it also left local governments enough authority to restrain the federal executive. The new state structure made it unlikely that either the immobility of the Weimar government or the dictatorship of the Third Reich could recur.

WEST GERMANY UNDER KONRAD ADENAUER

After the West Germans held their first legislative elections, the representatives chose Konrad Adenauer (1876–1967) as chancellor. Adenauer, an elder statesman famed for his stand against Hitler, needed above all to convince other nations that West Germany had left its Nazi past behind. The chancellor at once began to work for firm and friendly relations with the western democracies, including France. At the same time, Adenauer tried to maintain a diplomatic association with the Soviets. These policies soon made the Federal Republic highly respected in the West without completely alienating the USSR.

Adenauer achieved equally impressive results in domestic affairs. His party, the Christian Democratic Union, advocated an extensive welfare program and government economic intervention. But the Christian Democrats opposed the nationalization of economic enterprises. This combination of policies worked well. When Adenauer left office in 1963, West Germany was a very prosperous welfare state. Despite criticism of Adenauer's authoritarian methods, this success helped to keep his party in power to the end of the 1960s.

A STALINIST LEADER FOR EAST GERMANY

Europe's strongest socialist and communist movements emerged in Germany in the late 1800s. After the Nazi era, Marxist ideals still appealed to many Germans. But when East Germany became a state in 1949, the citizens would not have elected a Stalinist to lead their "Democratic Republic." German preferences mattered little. Walter Ulbricht, a devoted Stalinist, led the German Communist Party when the new government emerged in the eastern zone. Although others held the titles of president and premier, Ulbricht wielded supreme power in East Germany.

The Superpower Arms Race

At the end of the Second World War, the United States and the Soviet Union ranked far above every other nation in industrial capacities and military power. Both nations sharply reduced the size of their armies until the late 1940s. The superpowers then began to expand their military forces again, although the number under arms remained low compared to the war years.

Throughout the cold war, the Soviet Union maintained larger ground and air forces than did the United States. The combined armies of NATO, however, more nearly matched those of the Warsaw Pact by the time both alliances reached full strength. Despite this rough balance in troops, the United States held an unchallenged lead in overall military power at least until the late 1970s. Superiority in armaments, especially nuclear weapons, gave the Americans this advantage, an edge they intended to keep. Soviet

Russia, however, entered the cold war fully committed to achieving armament superiority. A long and costly arms race had begun.

ATOMIC BOMBS AFTER HIROSHIMA

When the Second World War ended, the United States continued to manufacture atomic bombs. The stockpile probably numbered more than 100 by the late 1940s. Because of the power of these bombs, even this small arsenal posed an awesome threat to the Soviets. The softball-size uranium mass in the Hiroshima bomb exploded with a force equal to 12,000 tons of TNT. At Nagasaki, the blast equaled 20,000 tons. Although most U.S. weapons specialists expected the American atomic monopoly to last a decade or more, Stalin's determination to counter the special threat of atomic weapons led to a successful Soviet test in September 1949.

"THE SUPER"

During the late 1940s, U.S. officials and scientists had secretly debated whether to develop a hydrogen bomb. This weapon, which they called "the super," had many times the power of an atomic bomb. A few scientists thought that the H-bomb might start a nuclear chain reaction that would burn away the earth's atmosphere.

Despite disagreements and concerns, the Soviet A-bomb test convinced Truman to proceed at once with the hydrogen bomb. He called a news conference in January 1950 to announce that he had ordered the production of the super. On November 1, 1952, the United States exploded its first H-bomb. The Soviets tested theirs the following year.

THE FIRST NUCLEAR STRIKE FORCES

For many years, the typical hydrogen weapons had the power of 1,000,000 tons of TNT. The United States deployed its first jet bombers (B-47s) in 1950. The B-47 could carry four of these "one-megaton" bombs to the USSR. In the early 1950s, the Soviets had a few propeller-driven bombers that could reach the United States. The planes lacked the range to return to the USSR, however.

The Opening of the Asian Cold War Front

Although the superpowers confronted each other most directly in Europe, their rivalry affected events far from that continent. The arms race generated by the cold war also heightened the danger of many non-European conflicts. The first serious cold war crisis outside Europe developed in Korea.

THE OUTBREAK OF THE KOREAN WAR

When the defeat of Japan brought the liberation of Korea in 1945, the Soviets occupied the half of the peninsula north of the thirty-eighth parallel, and U.S. forces took control in the south. Both nations withdrew their troops by the end of the 1940s. They left behind, however, a Communist dictatorship in the north and an anti-Communist dictatorship in the south. In June 1950, the North Koreans invaded South Korea and quickly conquered most of the peninsula.

U.S. INTERVENTION IN KOREA

President Truman ordered U.S. forces to join the fight against North Korea. He also asked the United Nations to condemn the aggression of North Korea and support the South Koreans. As a protest demonstration, the Soviet representative had temporarily stopped attending Security Council sessions. The Soviets thus missed their chance to veto UN involvement, and the Council agreed to back South Korea. This decision changed the military character of the war very little. Most of the anti-Communist troops were American and South Korean.

The United States turned the tide and conquered almost the entire Korean peninsula by the autumn of 1950. A year earlier, Communists had won control of China. They allowed North Korean military units to cross the border for refuge. President Truman declared that he would allow neither the use of atomic weapons nor any attacks on the People's Republic of China. He asserted that such actions would provoke a nuclear war with the Soviets. General Douglas MacArthur, the U.S. commander in Korea, opposed Truman's policies and threatened action against China. Truman dismissed him.

CHINESE INTERVENTION IN KOREA

China assumed the possibility of an American attack and launched an offensive into Korea. The Chinese reconquered North Korea, and the war settled into a stalemate at the thirty-eighth parallel. An armistice ended the war in 1953.

WEST EUROPE'S MIRACLE RECOVERY

The West European nations tended to rely on military force for their security after the Second World War. Events in Korea heightened the Western Allies' fear of a Soviet surprise attack in Europe and resulted in an accelerated NATO buildup. Many Western leaders on both sides of the Atlantic, however, also urged European unification as a vital part of the effort to encourage peace and prosperity on the continent.

The First Steps Toward European Unification

The advocates of unity included several of Europe's best known public figures—Robert Schuman (France), Konrad Adenauer (the Federal Republic of Germany), Alcide De Gasperi (Italy), Paul-Henri Spaak (Belgium), and Winston Churchill (Britain). Despite such strong support, progress toward political union was very slow. Significant steps toward economic integration occurred by the 1950s, however.

THE EUROPEAN COAL AND STEEL COMMUNITY (ECSC)

Two French officials, foreign minister Robert Schuman and finance minister Jean Monnet, shared the conviction that peace on the continent depended especially on the relationship between France and Germany. In the 1950s, they led an effort to arrange a form of economic unification that they believed would make war between the French and Germans virtually impossible. They supported a plan to end the ability of these two countries to have independent control over resources critical to the conduct of war.

In 1951, six nations negotiated an agreement based on this principle. France, the Federal Republic of Germany, Italy, Belgium, Luxemburg, and the Netherlands agreed to merge their coal, iron, and steel economies in a structure called the European Coal and Steel Community (ECSC). This first important step toward European unity greatly improved the prospects for peace among the members of the ECSC.

THE COMMON MARKET AND EFTA

The six nations in the ECSC quickly realized that this organization yielded remarkable economic benefits. This awareness led them to begin work on a more comprehensive system of integration. In 1957, the countries in the ECSC signed the Treaty of Rome establishing the European Economic Community (EEC or the "Common Market").

The EEC members agreed that by 1967, they would stop charging customs duties on goods that they traded among themselves. In addition to the establishment of this customs union, the EEC nations promised to advance toward greater economic unity and raise living standards within their territories. The treaty also expressed a commitment to work for global harmony and prosperity. In a separate agreement, the six Common Market members established Euratom, a joint organization responsible for the unification of their atomic energy development programs.

Britain led the way to the establishment of the European Free Trade Association (EFTA) in 1960. Denmark, Norway, Sweden, Austria, Switzerland, and Portugal joined Britain in this organization committed to the removal of trade barriers among the member states. EFTA did not project the realization of the more complete economic union planned by the EEC.

Socialization of the West European Economy

West Europe's progress toward economic unity helped to bring about such rapid economic recovery that western observers soon described the change as a "miracle." Governmental alterations at the national level also contributed to this remarkable economic surge.

ECONOMIC CONTROL AND PLANNING

The Great Depression and home-front experiences during the Second World War convinced most West Europeans that nations had to control economic development in order to ensure the well-being of their citizens. This outlook caused postwar political and business leaders to devise varied systems of national economic management.

Most West European nations attempted to direct their economies by greatly increasing state intervention. Governments that took this approach typically nationalized the largest banks and other big enterprises such as coal mines, utilities, and mass transit systems. Several states established economic control through the close cooperation of public and private agencies without a drastic increase in government ownership of or power over enterprises. As these states heightened economic control, the governments in almost all of them also began long-range planning to guide economic development.

THE WELFARE STATE

After the war, a vast expansion of public welfare programs became typical for West European governments. They established reforms intended to give virtually all citizens housing, education, and health care, regardless of their level of income. The welfare state pioneered in Scandinavia during the Great Depression soon emerged in almost every West European nation.

RECOVERY AND PROSPERITY

Central management of state economies in West Europe brought a quick recovery from the war and decades of phenomenal growth. In order to replace the homes lost during the war and provide residences for an expanding population, governments funded massive programs of home construction. In the more populous states such as Britain, builders erected several hundred thousand homes each year. West Germany provided 10,000,000 new dwellings between 1948 and 1958. This building boom helped to spur overall economic expansion.

A few West European countries returned to prewar industrial and agricultural production levels by the late 1940s. Most others achieved this recovery by the mid-1950s. Annual production rates then continued to climb at an unusually fast pace into the late 1960s. This expanding economy made jobs available for almost everyone, and incomes soared upward. By the 1960s, West Europe had moved through postwar restoration to prosperity.

The Democratic States of West Europe

Most of the governments that guided West Europe's miraculous recovery were constitutional democracies. Dictators ruled in only two countries, Spain and Portugal. Political factions in the democracies extended from communist and socialist parties on the Left to anti-Marxist authoritarian groups on the Right. Usually, only the center and moderate socialist parties had the power to govern.

In several states, Christian democratic movements developed into the strongest centrist parties after the Second World War. Christian democrats typically supported economic planning and government welfare programs. They favored the interests of the business community, however, and wanted to avoid extensive nationalization of enterprises. The communists and socialists gradually dropped their revolutionary programs and became simply reformist parties. These Left factions then differed from the Center mostly in the extent of nationalization and welfare they favored.

THE SMALLER DEMOCRACIES

The eight small or less populous democracies of North and West Europe that exhibited such exceptional political and economic strength during the depression years continued to thrive after the Second World War. The governments of Denmark, Norway, Sweden, Finland, the Benelux countries, and Switzerland provided effective leadership as they confronted the demands of the postwar era. Rapid economic development brought these societies to new levels of prosperity. In the Scandinavian states, socialist economic policies, including extensive welfare programs, distributed the benefits of economic progress to all citizens. Developments in Sweden illustrate circumstances in Scandinavia, with Sweden also exemplifying the generally remarkable success of the smaller democratic states.

SOCIAL DEMOCRACY IN SWEDEN

Sweden's Social Democrats (socialists) led the nation in the expansion of democracy and the construction of a socialist economy before the Second World War. They continued to extend both democratic rights and socialism after 1945. The voters indicated their strong approval of this policy by keeping the Social Democrats in power until 1970. From 1946 to 1969, the party and the nation continued to back the same leader, Prime Minister Tage Etlander. His party ordinarily held about half the seats in the Riksdag (parliament) and usually kept the support of the Center Party as well. Several other parties divided the remainder of the seats.

Private and State Enterprises. Private enterprise thrived under Sweden's socialist government. Ninety percent of all businesses remained privately owned and vigorously active in both domestic and international trade. The state planned and directed the economy but owned less than three percent of the nation's enterprises. Members of the Cooperative Union, a nongovernment organization, jointly owned the rest of Sweden's enterprises.

The Welfare Program. Sweden's very extensive public care system reflected the socialist spirit of the nation in a more obvious way than did business ownership practices. The Riksdag expanded Sweden's welfare program in 1946 with the provision of health insurance for all citizens. Legislation in the 1950s and 1960s guaranteed an adequate income for the elderly and families with dependent children. Social democracy brought the Swedes complete and lifelong care but also heavy tax payments. Still, they had incomes sufficient to buy more cars and television sets per person than in any other European state.

THE LARGER DEMOCRACIES

From 1945 to the late 1960s, the socialists in Britain, France, West Germany, and Italy did not dominate government as they did in Sweden. Christian democrats usually led the governments on the continent. From 1951 to 1964, the Conservative Party held power in Britain and followed moderate reformist policies similar to those favored by continental Christian democrats.

Despite their minority status, Socialists still exercised an important influence in the larger democracies. The Labour Party governed Britain from 1945 to 1951 and again in the latter 1960s. Both the communist and socialist parties were very strong in Italy and France for a few years after the Second World War. During the 1950s and 1960s, Italian, French, and West German socialists significantly influenced political developments, sometimes as members of governing coalitions led by Christian democrats.

These Center and Left parties joined forces after 1945 to develop socioeconomic institutions that were moderate versions of Scandinavian socialist democracy. Britain, for example, nationalized the Bank of England, coal mines, railroads, and the steel industry. France and Italy followed similar policies of partial socialization. West Germany avoided such direct government control, but political, business, and labor leaders cooperated to manage the economy very effectively. Welfare systems in all four states provided a full range of social services for all segments of their societies.

THE SOVIET UNION AND THE TRANSFORMATION OF EAST EUROPE

During the 1930s, Stalin had condemned many Russian traditions, especially the historic Russian Orthodox faith. In his guise as a revolutionary Marxist, Stalin would not tolerate these old ways. Hitler's conquest of the Western USSR brought a drastic change in Stalin's attitudes.

Stalin, as war leader, rallied the Soviet people with patriotic appeals, urging citizens to remember the heroes of Russia's past and use them as models. The government even eased the suppression of the Russian Orthodox Church, an important indication that an era of greater personal liberty had arrived. When the war ended, many Soviets expected the new tolerance to continue.

The Soviets made great sacrifices to complete their industrial revolution before 1940. After the hardships of the 1930s, they experienced the destruction of *Blitzkrieg* and occupation. The war destroyed 70,000 villages, almost 2,000 towns, and large sections of many major cities. The Soviet people anticipated that peace would bring an end to the painful deprivations as well as greater liberty.

The Renewal of Stalinist Repression, 1945–1953

Contrary to the citizens' expectations, no relaxation of dictatorship and economic hardship came with the triumph over Nazism. Stalin kept absolute power and used it to force a further expansion of heavy industry. When Stalin sensed a challenge to his authority in the early 1950s, he began to prepare for a new terror purge. Stalinism had not changed.

AN ECONOMY FOR "STEEL EATERS"

After the war, central control of the economy continued under new Five Year Plans. The promotion of heavy industry remained the overriding concern of the leadership. Stalin indicated in the first postwar plan that he intended to have a fifty percent increase in industrial production within five years. Consumer goods would not become more plentiful.

The Soviet people had no choice but to accept this policy dictated by the "steel eaters," as they called the advocates of heavy industry. But even Stalin could not stop the spread of popular expressions that reflected the discontent he caused. People complained that under communism their country had learned to cook steel but not cabbage.

THE *ZHDANOVSHCHINA*

Any dissent more daring than jokes among close friends remained as difficult after 1945 as during the purges of the 1930s. From early 1946 to mid-1948, Stalin entrusted many duties, including the strict regimentation of political and artistic expression, to Andrei Zhdanov.

During the two-year *Zhdanovshchina* (era of Zhdanov), leading scholars, writers, artists, and composers suffered vicious public condemnation whenever they produced works that did not agree with extremely vague official standards. People attacked in this way usually lost all opportunities for income-producing activity. In an apparently random way, Stalin also at times ordered imprisonment or execution for "offenders." Although this new time of repression became associated with Zhdanov's name, the policy was Stalin's.

THE PERSECUTION OF MINORITIES

Stalin suspected many of the Soviet Union's ethnic minorities of insufficient loyalty to him. As a result, his most cruelly repressive blows in the 1940s and 1950s struck these groups. A few Crimean Tatars supported the Nazis during the German occupation. In 1944, Stalin forced almost the entire population of 250,000 Tatars to move from their homeland near the Black Sea to Soviet Central Asia. Large numbers of these people died from the extreme hardships of careless resettlement. Other ethnic groups suffered similar deportations.

In the late 1940s and early 1950s, Stalin decided that Soviet Jews were beginning to love the new state of Israel more than the USSR. He ordered long Siberian exile or execution for more than two dozen of the most brilliant Jewish intellectuals and cultural leaders. Then Stalin turned on Jewish members of the medical profession.

THE "DOCTORS' PLOT"

In 1952, the Soviet government falsely charged that a group of doctors, most of them Jewish, had conspired to assassinate Stalin and other top officials. These innocent medical specialists and their spouses disappeared into Stalin's prison system. The spreading circle of persecution suggested that a new purge was about to strike, perhaps taking people at the pinnacle of the party.

STALIN'S DEATH

By the early 1950s, several of the younger Communist leaders began to advocate moderation of Stalin's harsh system. They also started to position themselves for an opportunity to succeed the aging leader. Stalin probably intended to exterminate these upstarts, along with the "treasonous" Jews. This purge never occurred. Stalin died on March 5, 1953, before he could carry out a new wave of murder.

Stalin's East European Empire, Late 1940s to 1953

By the end of the 1940s, most East European states had become dependent Soviet territories under Stalinist dictators. Soviet officials, local Communist parties, and the Red Army served as Stalin's imperial staff and enforcement agents. They imposed Soviet-style governments on Poland, East Germany, Czechoslovakia, Hungary, Romania, and Bulgaria. Austria remained jointly occupied by the Soviets and the Western Allies.

THE EMERGENCE OF COMMUNIST SOCIOECONOMIC SYSTEMS

In the late 1940s, aristocratic social structures and agricultural economic institutions still had significant strength in East Europe. Communist governments could not destroy these remnants of the *ancien* system as quickly as they had removed the old government machinery.

The long social reign of a wealthy and propertied upper class soon ended, however. East European governments also proceeded with the rapid development of state-owned industrial economies and collectivized farm systems. When Stalin died in 1953, the reshaping of six East European societies according to his design was well advanced. In one Balkan state, however, the ruling Communists by then had purposely erected a system with hardly a trace of Stalinism.

YUGOSLAVIA UNDER TITO

The Red Army drove the Nazis from most of East Europe but not from Yugoslavia. Anti-fascist resistance forces within Yugoslavia fought the Nazis throughout the war and liberated the country in 1945. Josip Broz Tito (1892–1980), a Communist, led the strongest of these guerrilla forces (the Partisans). When the Second World War ended, the Partisans used their military power to defeat rival Yugoslav groups. This forceful action enabled Tito to seize control of the country and establish a Communist government in November 1945.

The Strength to Resist Soviet Imperialism. Stalin tried to force Yugoslavia into his East European empire but failed. With the Partisans rather than the Red Army in control of Yugoslavia, Stalin could apply little force. Tito had the further advantages of popular support and geographic separation from the Soviet Union. Under these circumstances, Yugoslav Communists could follow an independent course.

The Yugoslav-Soviet Split. Stalin insisted that Yugoslavia remain an agricultural country and supply farm products to the Soviet Union; in contrast, Tito ordered the industrialization of Yugoslavia. The Soviet leader demanded that Tito not support Communist rebels in Greece in 1946; Yugoslavia backed the revolt anyway. In 1948, Stalin expelled Yugoslavia from the Communist international (Cominform). The barriers between Tito and Stalin had become insurmountable.

Yugoslav Communism. In 1947, Tito's first actions as Yugoslav president hinted of Stalinism. He began to organize a highly centralized communist system with collectivized farms and state-controlled social-ized industry. But when it became apparent that such changes were ill-suited to Yugoslav society, Tito made drastic adjustments. By the mid-1950s, Yugoslavia had a moderately decentralized government, state-aided private agriculture, and a nationalized industrial system that allowed limited worker control in the factories. Yugoslav Communists permitted no rival parties to exist, but in other respects their system had little resemblance to Stalin's.

An Era of Reform Under Nikita Khrushchev, 1956–1964

During the years that Tito developed his divergent form of communism, Georgi Malenkov and other Soviet leaders also indicated their desire for a "new course" for the USSR. After Stalin's death, policy debates among the contenders for leadership revealed that the new-course advocates wanted less repression, more emphasis on consumer goods production, and a less hostile relationship with the West. Even Lavrenti Beria, the head of the feared secret police, argued for these changes.

Despite the appeal of these proposals, both Malenkov and Beria quickly lost their bids for power. Beria's leadership of the secret police made him seem too dangerous to his associates. In December 1953, they had him shot. Malenkov lacked sufficient support in the upper Party bureaucracy. In 1953, his opponents forced him to surrender Party leadership (the office of First Secretary) to Nikita Khrushchev (1894–1971). Malenkov remained in the less important post of government premier, but he lost that job too in 1955.

KHRUSHCHEV'S EMERGENCE TO POWER

The struggle to succeed Stalin ended with the triumph of Khrushchev in 1956. The new leader, who had earned a reputation as a typical Stalinist steel eater, continued the emphasis on heavy industry. Yet Khrushchev was no Stalinist. He first revealed his drastically different attitudes with a shocking attack on the record of Joseph Stalin.

DE-STALINIZATION

Khrushchev opened his "de-Stalinization" campaign at the Twentieth Party Congress, a gathering of more than 1,000 Party members in February 1956. In a four-hour speech, the new Soviet leader poured out descriptions of Stalin's brutal deeds. Khrushchev's indictment concentrated on the bloody purges of the 1930s, the persecution of minorities such as the Crimean Tatars, and Stalin's costly mistakes in the conduct of the Second World War. Khrushchev's speech and later policies indicated that he had adopted a moderate version of the new-course policy and tied it to a battle against the Stalinists and the Stalin legend. For the rest of the Soviet era, Communist leaders tended to divide into Stalinists who wanted to keep most of the old system and reformers who fought for a less rigid dictatorship. Under Khrushchev, the reformers had their day.

THE END OF THE TERROR

Stalin's government charged millions of innocent people with political offenses and sent them to Siberian work camps. Death rapidly emptied the prisons; new arrests constantly refilled them. More than 8,000,000 lived in this "gulag archipelago" (chain of prison "islands") at the time of Stalin's death. Khrushchev's attack on Stalin inspired great public pressure to empty the gulag. Less than two years after his anti-Stalin speech, the Siberian camps were practically empty. Strict controls on political activity continued, but the terror had ended.

KHRUSHCHEV'S EARLY REFORMS

Before Khrushchev took supreme power in the Soviet Union, he was the Party's top agricultural official. He attempted to raise farm productivity by opening grasslands to cropping (the Virgin Lands project) and by pushing for the consolidation of collectives into huge agricultural cities.

Khrushchev's most widely known revisionist tendency began to affect Soviet life soon after the attack on Stalin in 1956. At that time, Khrushchev began to allow creative writers to express themselves more freely, especially about the era of Stalin. Throughout the rest of his years in power, Khrushchev periodically permitted these "thaws" for all the Soviet arts.

ADMINISTRATIVE DECENTRALIZATION

Khrushchev inherited a government organized to give the ruler in Moscow the maximum power over every aspect of life in the nation. In the late 1950s, he reduced the authority of this highly centralized system in several important ways. First, Khrushchev shifted judicial control to lower administrative levels by abolishing the national bureau that had supervised the court system. A similar reform of economic institutions followed as Khrushchev ordered the decentralization of industrial management and agricultural administration. These changes modified the dictatorship but left it very powerful. After the economic reforms, for example, Moscow still had complete power over agricultural and industrial goals. Khrushchev also later restored much of the central government's control over economic administration.

REDUCED PRIVILEGES FOR THE PARTY ELITE

The cultural thaw and the reduction of central authority disturbed many Party leaders, but Khrushchev caused still greater agitation with other reforms. He dictated changes in Communist Party election procedures that would force the periodic replacement of one-fourth or more of the officers. Since only the four percent of the citizens who were Communists voted in Party elections, this reform promised no more than a slight shift toward democratization *within* the elite organization and none beyond it.

Party officers who faced the prospect of losing their high-level jobs and privileges despised even this small step toward popular authority. Khrushchev added to their rage by making the children of the Communist elite compete equally with others for access to higher education. These and other reforms made powerful enemies for Khrushchev in the Party hierarchy.

The Struggle for Liberation in East Europe, 1953–1968

East Europeans resisted Soviet domination from the beginning of occupation until the collapse of the system in 1989. Stalin stopped prominent political leaders in the region from openly opposing him, but the hidden forces of dissent grew stronger. Within three months after Stalin's death, the rage exploded as Czechs and East Germans rioted (June 1953). The Soviet army quickly suppressed these outbreaks, but the forces of two larger rebellions were already gathering elsewhere in East Europe. Khrushchev's moderation of the Stalinist system in early 1956 encouraged these East European dissenters to act more boldly.

THE POZNAN RIOTS

For three years after the Czech and East German riots, discontent increased among Polish artists and intellectuals. They approved of Marxist principles but despised the Stalinist variety of communism established by their government. Polish Communist leaders faced a still greater threat when de-Stalinization and hard times combined to provoke a violent labor protest. On June 28, 1956, workers in Poznan rose in a revolt so massive that the government brought in the army to stop it. The crisis then worsened because the soldiers refused to shoot the strikers. Large contingents of security police finally ended the riots.

FROM PROTEST TO AUTONOMY IN POLAND

The Poznan riots drove Poland's Communist leaders to consider changes that would reduce the discontent. By October 1956, the deliberations of the party politburo (executive committee) began to reflect the influence of Wladyslaw Gomulka, a Communist who preferred independence from Moscow.

Khrushchev and several other Soviet leaders arrived unexpectedly, joined the policy discussions, and raised objections to Polish reform plans. Rumors of a Red Army invasion began to spread but had little effect on Gomulka and his associates. The preparation of Polish workers and security forces to resist the Soviet troops probably did influence the Soviet leader's attitudes, however.

Khrushchev grudgingly accepted Gomulka as first secretary (leader) of the Polish Communist Party and yielded control over Poland's internal affairs to him. In return for this grant of autonomy, Poland had to remain a Communist state and a member of the Warsaw Pact. Under Gomulka's leadership (1956–1970), the government of Poland kept industry fully socialized but emphasized consumer goods production and ended forced collectivization of farms. Gomulka also permitted the Catholic Church to take a more active role in national affairs.

AN ANTI-SOVIET REBELLION IN HUNGARY

In his position as Hungary's Communist premier (1953–1956), Imre Nagy was a vigorous anti-Stalinist reformer. In February 1955, the Soviets arranged Nagy's dismissal. Erno Gero, a more repressive ruler, replaced him as premier. The Petofi Circle, an organization of Hungarian cultural leaders, led a campaign of militant opposition to the Gero government. In 1956, Khrushchev's attacks on Stalinism and the movement toward autonomy in Poland inspired a great intensification of the Hungarian movement for reform.

On October 23, 1956, dissenters poured into the streets of Budapest, Hungary's capital, to express their support for Communist reformers in Poland. The demonstration quickly changed to a protest against Hungary's Stalinist government. Gero answered with a threatening radio address and a police attack on the protesters. The antigovernment forces then rioted. Gero countered with a request for Soviet troops to suppress the revolt. His action transformed the riots into an anti-Soviet rebellion backed by units of the Hungarian army.

SOVIET REPRESSION IN HUNGARY

Khrushchev attempted to restore peace by a series of steps. He withdrew Soviet forces, accepted Imre Nagy's return as premier, and placed János Kádár in charge of the Hungarian Communist Party. Khrushchev intended for Kádár to control Nagy's reform impulses, permitting only enough change to pacify the Hungarians. Khrushchev's plan failed. Recent events left the citizenry unwilling to accept Communist dictatorship or Soviet domination. Nagy reestablished a multi-party political system, pledged to allow elections, and on October 31 announced Hungary's withdrawal from the Warsaw Pact.

Soviet troops returned to Hungary on November 4 and launched a furious attack on the rebels. Thousands of Hungarians died in a week-long fight against the Soviets. Hungary could not win against the Red Army. After the defeat of the rebels, the Soviets placed Kádár in full control, arrested Nagy, and executed him in 1958.

Kádár perpetuated Communist dictatorship in Hungary and kept his country in the Warsaw Pact. But he also reduced government repression and implemented economic reforms. The government promoted a more consumer-oriented commercial economy and developed an agricultural system of mixed private and cooperatively owned farms. These reforms gave Hungary the most prosperous East European economy by the late 1960s.

THE VARIETIES OF EAST EUROPEAN COMMUNISM

The suppression of Hungary violently demonstrated Soviet opposition to the dismantling of Communist governments or to the weakening of the Soviet security system in East Europe. But Soviet leaders accepted the necessity of nationalist variations in communism. Gomulka and Kádár deviated from the Soviet pattern of communism, especially in economic practices, without interference. Poland and Hungary used their limited autonomy to develop somewhat more moderate Communist systems than that of Soviet Russia.

In Romania, Gheorghe Gheorghiu-Dej followed a course of moderate reform similar to Hungary's until the latter 1950s. Then he reverted to more Stalinist policies. Gheorghiu-Dej's successor, Nicolae Ceausescu, perpetuated this more rigid communism after 1965. Czechoslovakia took the Polish-Hungarian path away from Stalinism and, unlike Romania, continued on the new course. By the late 1960s, Czechoslovak Communists began to implement policies very similar to Nagy's in 1956. The Soviets watched with growing concern.

THE CLIMAX OF THE COLD WAR

Stalin's successors had conflicting opinions about cold war policies. Beginning in the early 1950s, several insisted that the hostility toward the United States and its allies had to end. They argued for a policy of "peaceful coexistence." Other Party officials demanded a continuation of Stalin's "hard-line" practices. They thought that the American threat required a counterthreat.

Khrushchev shifted between the Stalinist and anti-Stalinist positions, partly in an effort to keep the support he needed from different factions in the Party presidium. (The Party executive committee, usually with a membership of about a dozen, was called the politburo until Stalin changed the name to "presidium" in 1952. It became the politburo again in 1966.) This split in the presidium and the efforts to keep the support of equally divided Communists in other nations caused the Soviets to shift unpredictably from peacemaking actions to threats.

Until 1962, the United States more consistently followed a hard-line policy toward Soviet Russia. The Eisenhower administration (1953–1960) multiplied its hydrogen bomber fleet and promised "massive retaliation" for any Soviet aggression. A force of 1,600 long-range airplanes with over 7,000 nuclear bombs backed up this threat by 1962.

During John Kennedy's presidency (1961–1963), the United States began an expansion of the intercontinental nuclear rocket force; it increased from 156 in 1962 to 1,054 by 1967. Although this buildup triggered an arms race of unprecedented proportions, a close brush with nuclear war in 1962 led Kennedy and his successor, Lyndon Johnson, to practice their own version of peaceful coexistence. This change caused the United States to mix war threats and peacemaking efforts as the Soviets had since the mid-1950s.

Since the Soviet Union and the United States continued to dominate European international relations until the late 1960s, the interactions between the superpowers often dramatically affected circumstances and events within their spheres on the continent. The East Europeans discovered through Hungary's bitter experience that they could do little to increase their influence at the international level.

The West Europeans always had a significant degree of control in foreign affairs. During the 1960s, the nations of West Europe began to act with even greater independence. This increased influence still left the states in the American sphere with almost no power to control the risk of a nuclear war that could incinerate the continent.

Coexistence and Competition

Soviet leaders who wanted to break away from Stalinism began to affect events in Europe by 1955. Moscow informed the Western Allies that the Soviet Union wanted to cooperate in the arrangement of a peace settlement with Austria. Since 1945, this former Nazi-dependent state had remained divided into zones occupied by Britain, France, the United States, and Soviet Russia. Cold war attitudes had made all previous negotiations concerning Austria futile. Soviet Russia now offered to withdraw its troops, if the other powers would remove theirs and leave Austria neutral. The West agreed. On May 15, 1955, the four Second World War Allies signed a peace treaty with Austria.

THE GENEVA SUMMIT

Soviet Russia intended for the Austrian settlement to encourage other peacemaking steps. Another cooperative effort quickly followed but without concrete results. For the first time since the meeting at Potsdam in 1945, the leaders of Britain, France, the Soviet Union, and the United States met for a summit conference. They convened at Geneva, Switzerland, in July 1955 to discuss the arms race and the future of Germany. Progress on policies toward Germany was impossible. The Soviets insisted that their security required a disarmed Germany that belonged to neither superpower sphere. The Americans demanded a reunified Germany, armed and tied to NATO.

Near the close of the summit, Eisenhower presented an "open skies" plan that he claimed would reduce the threat of nuclear war. He proposed that each superpower allow the other to fly over and photograph its military bases in order to watch for war preparations. The American public media already provided Soviet Russia with most of the information they could gain from overflights, so Eisenhower had offered his adversaries very little.

The Soviets considered secrecy a fundamental security instrument and refused even to publish accurate maps of city streets. Open skies would give the United States much new data. Soviet Russia rejected Eisenhower's proposal. The cold warriors had negotiated in a friendly atmosphere at the summit, but they left with this "spirit of Geneva" as their only accomplishment.

THE SUEZ CRISIS

From 1919 until 1945, Britain and France dominated the Arab states in the eastern Mediterranean region. Arab nationalism and the weakened condition of France and Britain at the end of the Second World War forced the West Europeans to surrender this part of their empire. The final withdrawal occurred in 1955 when the British left the Suez Canal zone. Britain and France still owned most of the Suez, however. Furthermore, Europe needed more and more oil, most of which had to pass through the canal. Such interests ensured a reaction by the Europeans when Egypt nationalized the Suez in July 1956. In November, Britain and France invaded Egypt in an attempt to seize the waterway.

Virtually every nation in the world, including both superpowers, condemned British and French aggression. Before the invasion, the Eisenhower administration had led the effort in the United Nations to get international condemnation of the developing Soviet repression in Hungary. The United States also was actively pursuing better relations with the Arab nations. The European attack on Egypt threatened these policy efforts and prompted American opposition to the assault on the Suez. From the Soviet viewpoint, France and Britain had committed an act of capitalist imperialism. Before the crisis ended, a message from Moscow warned British and French officials that they risked a "rocket attack" if they did not withdraw.

France and Britain called their troops home. The Soviet missile threat meant little at the time since no nation had yet demonstrated a nuclear rocket potential. Furthermore, the West Europeans probably assumed that the Soviets would not risk a Third World War to drive them from the Suez. France and Britain had to withdraw because of their economic dependence on the United States, the superpower that dominated their sphere.

HARD-LINE PRESSURES IN THE COMMUNIST WORLD

In August 1957, the Soviets successfully tested an intercontinental ballistic missile (ICBM). They demonstrated missile superiority more dramatically two months later by orbiting Sputnik, the first artificial earth satellite. The rocket threat during the Suez crisis had been more than bluster.

These grand achievements left Khrushchev still dissatisfied with cold war circumstances. Soviet Russia had serious problems with China. Chinese Communist leaders considered the Soviet challenge to western capitalism to be too weak and demanded a more militant cold war policy. Soviet Stalinists agreed with China. Khrushchev needed a more impressive cold war victory.

THE FINAL BERLIN CRISES

During the 1950s, growing numbers of East Germans fled the poverty of their Communist state for the prosperous world of West Germany. The Western Allies' control of West Berlin made these escapes easy to accomplish. East German leaders desperately wanted to close this avenue to the west. The emigration robbed them of much-needed talent and gave their state a very negative image.

Khrushchev attempted to solve this problem and secure a cold war triumph by forcing the Western Allies to withdraw from Berlin. The Soviet leader succeeded only in driving the superpowers closer to the nuclear brink when he pushed this issue in 1958 and 1961. The era of Berlin crises ended in August 1961 with the erection of the infamous wall that sealed in the East Germans.

Confrontation— the Cuban Missile Crisis

John Kennedy's first year in office (1961) brought a cold war escalation from the American side. His administration arranged an invasion of Cuba in an attempt to overthrow Fidel Castro's new Communist government. The American-backed Cubans who attacked at the Bay of Pigs failed miserably.

The Bay of Pigs fiasco enhanced Castro's image and tarnished the Kennedy administration's. Both factors encouraged Khrushchev to boldness in Cuban affairs. His threats about Berlin had brought no cold war victories for the Soviets. While the western nations somewhat fearfully awaited Khrushchev's next move in Germany, he turned his efforts toward the Caribbean. In early 1962, the Soviets began to place nuclear-armed rockets in Cuba. The missiles they first installed had a range of 1,175 miles. Others aboard ships on the way to Cuba could travel more than 2,500 miles.

Khrushchev probably intended for this dangerous step in the arms race to reduce the great gap between Soviet and American nuclear military power. He also might have expected this new threat to force U.S. concessions in Germany. The Soviets always claimed that the leading motive for missile placement was the defense of Cuba.

NUCLEAR WEAPONS AND A "QUARANTINE" FOR CUBA

On October 22, 1962, President Kennedy shocked the world with a dramatic television broadcast that revealed the presence of Soviet rockets in Cuba. He also proclaimed a naval "quarantine" of the island. This policy meant that the U.S. navy would blockade Cuba and prevent the arrival of military supplies. (Kennedy described the action as a quarantine because a blockade is an act of war.)

THE MOST DANGEROUS COLD WAR MOMENT

The Cuban showdown presented the Soviets with the risk of attack by jet bombers loaded with almost 6,500 hydrogen bombs. One hundred fifty-six ICBMs based in midwestern states, 144 additional missiles on submarines, and still more rockets in Italy and Turkey could deliver another 1,000 nuclear warheads to Soviet targets within minutes after launch.

Before the missile placement in Cuba, war-ready Soviet nuclear forces included forty-four ICBMs, twenty submarine-based missiles, and airplanes that could carry about 250 hydrogen bombs. In late October 1962, the Soviets expanded their nuclear threat by placing thirty-six rockets in Cuba. Each could deliver its one-megaton warheads to targets almost anywhere in the eastern United States. Missiles with twice that range were scheduled to reach Cuba before the end of October.

Despite the relatively small size of the Soviet strike force, it could have blasted up to 400 American sites with weapons more than fifty times as powerful as the atomic bombs used on Japan. The U.S. threat to the USSR was sixteen times as great as the Soviet threat to America. At the height of the crisis, President Kennedy confided that he thought the chances of total nuclear war were fifty-fifty.

THE RESOLUTION OF THE CRISIS

Two frightening days followed Kennedy's quarantine speech. Then, on October 24, Soviet ships steaming toward the blockade stopped. Anastas Mikoyan, one of Khrushchev's most trusted associates, ordered the halt without the prior approval of the Soviet leader. Several more very tense days followed as U.S. and Soviet leaders struggled toward agreement. Finally, Khrushchev secured a public pledge from the Kennedy administration that the United States would not invade Cuba. Kennedy also communicated to the Soviets an unpublicized agreement to remove missiles from Turkey. In return, the Soviets promised to take all the missiles out of Cuba.

A POSTCRISIS COLD WAR THAW

The mutual retreat from the threat of nuclear disaster provided momentum for improvement in Soviet-American relations. Superpower leaders became much less inclined to use threats to influence the course of the cold war. Formal agreements also helped to reduce tensions further. Within less than a year, Britain, Soviet Russia, and the United States arranged the Limited Test Ban Treaty banning all nuclear tests except underground. The superpowers also set up a "Hot Line," a special teletype system, to speed communication between Soviet and American leaders during crises.

THE ARMS RACE IN THE LATE 1960s

The thaw after 1962 did not bring a warm relationship between the superpowers, nor even a reduction in the intimidating nuclear arms. Soviet leaders accelerated their rocket development program. They never again wanted to be caught in such relative weakness as in the Cuban crisis. By 1968, the Soviets had increased their ICBM fleet from forty to 850.

This Soviet expansion still left the United States far ahead. The Americans had 200 more ICBMs than the Soviets. In other categories of long-range nuclear weapons, the United States had an even greater lead, providing a total American bomb and warhead arsenal five times as great as the Soviet stockpile. Whatever the superpowers had learned in the Cuban missile crisis, they had not discovered how to slow the nuclear arms race.

THE FALL OF KHRUSHCHEV

The Soviet Union desperately needed a conversion from the highly centralized Stalinist dictatorship to a system better suited to the changing needs of a diverse and increasingly educated population scattered over a vast land. Khrushchev successfully diminished the image of Stalin, but most of Khrushchev's reforms failed. They were not well-planned and thoughtfully implemented.

The Deposition

Both the progress in de-Stalinization and the attempted reforms infuriated the many Party leaders who wanted only to end Stalin's terror and keep the rest of his system. The dangerous and humiliating result of the Cuban venture strengthened the opposition to Khrushchev and probably sealed his fate. The Party presidium and most of the central committee (an executive group of about 200 Party leaders) decided to end Khrushchev's "harebrained schemes." They forced Khrushchev to retire in 1964.

The Collective Leadership and Leonid Brezhnev

The new rulers began as a "collective leadership" group—a dictatorial committee with Aleksei Kosygin (1904–1980) and Leonid Brezhnev (1906–1982) in the chief positions. By the early 1970s Brezhnev became dominant but remained more attentive to the wishes of his associates than Khrushchev had been. Under Brezhnev, life in the USSR became more stable or "stagnant," as the Soviets later described it. This success in preserving much of the old system doomed the Soviet Union.

*T*he outcome of the Second World War completed the process of weakening the once great powers of Central and West Europe and elevating the Soviets and Americans to supremacy. Germany's defeat and division especially contributed to this change in the balance of forces. Hitler's war destroyed the German state and severely damaged France and Britain. The collapse of Germany then brought the capitalist and communist superpowers into confrontation in the heart of Europe at a time when the states in the region could exercise but little influence on the Soviets and Americans.

These conditions created the cold war, an era of intense American and Soviet competition to dominate the world. In their quest for western border security and cold war victory, the Soviets kept six East European states subdued and forcibly converted them to Communist societies. The United States decided the main lines of West European foreign and military policy in the 1950s and 1960s, but left the nations in its sphere free to govern their own societies as long as they did not choose communism. The democracies elected to build welfare states with government-controlled economies. They prospered.

Until Stalin's death in 1953, the Soviet Union maintained its rigid dictatorial socialism and police-state terror. Khrushchev's crusade of de-Stalinization weakened old-style communism and freed almost all political prisoners. His reforms, however, failed to decentralize political and economic control sufficiently to draw on the talents and strength of the Soviet people, a change the society much needed in order to thrive.

Many Communist leaders opposed Khrushchev because his reforms took privileges away from Party officials. Stalinist hard-liners also feared that moderation of the dictatorship weakened the nation's ability to compete with world capitalism. These Communist opponents brought Khrushchev down. Brezhnev and his associates then reverted to a moderate form of Stalinist Communism.

Before Khrushchev's fall, he had attempted to change cold war policies as well as the Stalinist dictatorship. The Soviets began to pursue peaceful coexistence with the western powers. Too often, however, Khrushchev combined peacemaking gestures with belligerent ventures, especially in Berlin. The darkest cold war hour arrived during one of these threat attempts, as Khrushchev took his missiles beyond Europe to Cuba.

The cold war reached a terrifying climax during the Cuban missile crisis. A few leaders in the Soviet Union and the United States made the decisions that determined the outcome of that confrontation. More than 100 million Soviets and tens of millions of Americans probably would have died if nuclear war had occurred in October 1962. The nuclear holocaust also would have taken many millions of victims in the European states that stood between the two great powers. The nations of East and West Europe had no significant influence on the critical October decisions on which the fate of *the continent hung. Such was the condition of Europe during the decades when Europe was divided into the two spheres of the rival superpowers. After the 1960s, the Soviet and American grip on the continent loosened and an ultramodern Europe began to emerge.*

Selected Readings

Brzezinski, Zbigniew. *The Soviet Bloc, Unity and Conflict.* Rev. ed. Cambridge, MA: Harvard University Press, 1967.

De Porte, Anton W. *Europe Between the Superpowers: The Enduring Balance.* New Haven, CT: Yale University Press, 1979.

Ellwood, David W. *Rebuilding Europe: Western Europe, America and Postwar Reconstruction.* New York: Longman, 1992.

Jansen, Max. *History of European Integration, 1947–1975.* Amsterdam, The Netherlands: European Institute, 1975.

Levering, Ralph B. *The Cold War, 1945–1972.* Arlington Heights, IL: Harlan Davidson, Inc., 1982.

Medvedev, Roy A., and Zhores A. Medvedev. *Khrushchev: The Years in Power.* New York: Columbia University Press, 1976.

Milward, Alan S. *The Reconstruction of Western Europe, 1945–1951.* Berkeley: University of California Press, 1984.

Turner, Henry A., Jr. *The Two Germanies Since 1945: East and West.* New Haven, CT: Yale University Press, 1987.

Weisberger, Bernard A. *Cold War, Cold Peace: The United States and Russia Since 1945.* New York: American Heritage, 1984.

Yergin, Daniel. *Shattered Peace: The Origins of the Cold War and the National Security State.* New York: Penguin Books, 1990.

18

Toward an Ultramodern Europe, 1968–1993

1965	Italian students stage protests against conditions in their universities
1966	German students begin antigovernment demonstrations
July 1967	Soviet and American negotiations result in the completion of the Nuclear Non-Proliferation Treaty
1968	Rebellions by students, workers, and other dissenting groups flare across Europe
	Soviet forces invade Czechoslovakia to force an end to Dubček's liberal communist movement
Early 1970s	Brezhnev begins to promote *détente*, a reduction of East-West tension
1973	The Organization of Petroleum Exporting Countries (OPEC) cuts off oil supplies to much of West Europe and contributes to an economic slump in the region
	Britain, Ireland, and Denmark join the European Economic Community
December 1979	The Soviet Union invades Afghanistan
March 1985	Gorbachev becomes the leader of the Soviet Union
1986	A nuclear power plant disaster occurs in the Soviet Union at Chernobyl
	Spain, Portugal, and Greece enter the European Community
	The European Community adopts the Single Europe Act

April 1987	Soviet Russia establishes the Law on State Enterprises as part of Gorbachev's *perestroika* program
December 1987	The United States and the Soviet Union sign a treaty providing for the destruction of all intermediate range nuclear weapons
1989	The Soviet Union elects its first Congress of People's Deputies
	All East European nations formerly under Soviet control win independence
March 1990	The Communist Party of the Soviet Union votes to end one-party rule in the USSR
August 1991	An antireform coup attempt temporarily removes Gorbachev from power
December 1991	The USSR ceases to exist as a state
1992	Yugoslavia splits into separate states and civil war erupts
	The Czech Lands and Slovakia agree to separate
January 1993	The European Community's single market plan takes effect

After centuries of gradual and uneven social change, most of Europe became fully modern in the late 1800s. The most fundamental characteristic of modernity at that time was an industrial economy based on the production of coal, steel, energy, and machines, especially large-scale devices. This system of heavy industry still served a vital function in the 1990s. During the latter decades of this century, however, high-technology enterprises, particularly in electronics, became typical of the European economy. The relative importance of "smokestack" industries declined.

A trait associated with modernity almost as frequently as industry is a centralized state with a politically mobilized population. In modern Europe, such political institutions existed almost everywhere by the latter 1800s, usually in the form of the nation-state. Many European governments in that era drew their citizens into public affairs through democratic practices. Other governments depended on special institutions and programs to win or force broad support for authoritarian leaders. The modern states that took the form of popular dictatorships found ways to give citizens a false sense of self-government; a parliament with no real power was a typical device.

Modern Europe's popular authoritarian states actually were only partly modernized. As systems that gave power to a small minority, they resembled the ancien sociopolitical order more than they did the democracies. States with this modified authoritarian character lasted until the mid-1970s in the Iberian peninsula. Most East Europeans replaced such mass-supported authoritarian governments with democratic institutions only in the late 1980s. This expansion of democracy in the 1970s and after indicates that

European government became more truly modern at that time. In the last decades of this century, most other traits of modern European society changed with unusual rapidity along with the economic and political systems.

The emergence of Europe's more highly modern, or "ultramodern," institutions in the latter 1900s involved a less drastic transformation than the shift from ancien to modern ways in the 1500s and 1600s. Yet this late twentieth century transition radically altered many aspects of European life. As ultramodern Europe continues to develop, it will affect societies beyond the continent also. It will influence the world differently than in the modern era, but perhaps in an equally profound way.

1968—YEAR OF REBELLION

After the liberal and national revolts ended in the 1870s, popular uprisings occurred infrequently in Europe. Even in the social wreckage left by the Second World War, West Europeans showed little inclination toward rebellion. East European societies exhibited more discontent under the weight of Soviet oppression. Within the Soviet Russian sphere, however, the outbreaks before 1968 were relatively small, except in Hungary in 1956.

In 1968, a wave of rebellions suddenly swept across Europe. The surge of opposition to the established system in France had such force that it almost overwhelmed a powerful government established by Charles de Gaulle in 1958. These rebellions in 1968 resulted in part from the transition to an ultramodern way of life that had been developing since the end of the Second World War.

Student Rebellions

Ultramodern Europe educated more of its citizens than ever before. Both the welfare-state democracies and the socialist dictatorships shared this commitment to advanced learning, a change that brought many social benefits but also serious problems. Among the most obvious of these difficulties were the youth revolts that struck almost every West European state in the late 1960s. These outbreaks began as student rebellions in Italy.

THE ITALIAN UPRISINGS

Italy brought vast numbers of young people into its universities by the 1960s, but the educational institutions changed very little, except in size. The students found themselves dominated by authoritarian professors, submerged in studies that had little to do with important issues of the day, and crowded into huge classes (about ten times as many students for each teacher as in the United States).

The models of racial rights and student protest movements in the United States helped to inspire militant action to change conditions in Italian universities. In 1965, university students in Milan and Trent launched demonstrations demanding more control over their institutions and more opportunities to study subjects that they considered relevant. The struggle escalated thereafter. In 1967, more than 1,000 students seized the University of Turin's administration building and occupied it for a month. Outbreaks followed in several other major cities, including Florence and Rome. By 1968, the cry among students was not for educational change but for destruction of the existing social system.

POLITICAL REBELLION IN GERMANY

German youth uprisings began in 1966 as an attack on trends in government. Leftist student organizations struck first. They organized protests against the German Socialist Party for its plan to give up revolution and begin cooperation with the centrist Christian Democrats. In 1967, numerous protests broke out when the Shah of Iran, a right-wing dictator, visited Germany. The demonstrations became riots, resulting in the death of one student protester.

Anger over the killing during the anti-Shah demonstrations caused young rebels to fight still harder to wreck the established system. After the climax of these struggles brought violent protests to Berlin, Hamburg, Munich, and other major cities in 1968, the government showed few effects from the youth rebellion. German higher education did change, however. As a result of the disturbances, students gained a much stronger voice in university affairs, including a great deal of influence over curriculum and teaching methods.

A Revolutionary Strike in France

From 1946 to 1958, the legislature of the French Fourth Republic overshadowed the executive branch of government. In 1958, Charles de Gaulle won his twelve-year campaign for a new constitution providing for an extremely powerful executive. He then took office as the first president of the new Fifth Republic. De Gaulle gained his great authority democratically. Once elected, he governed as a "republican monarch."

THE STUDENTS AGAINST DE GAULLE

De Gaulle used his presidential supremacy to implement policies that ended America's dominance over French foreign policy and made his nation a more powerful force in European affairs. The Gaullist administration also tried to push France toward the more highly technical and large-scale form of industry that it believed the nation needed to produce greater prosperity and power.

By 1968, these and other trends in the Fifth Republic provoked a protest movement among university students. At first, they expressed opposition to de Gaulle's obsession with foreign policy and neglect of circumstances within France, including conditions in higher education. Student complaints about the universities focused on serious problems of governance and curriculum as well as seemingly insignificant matters such as a shortage of telephones and television sets.

Eventually, the dissent took on a much more serious tone and focused on the nature of French institutions themselves. The young critics demanded that the power of the masses replace the authoritarianism of the government and the universities. They rejected capitalism and called for socioeconomic leveling to accompany the change to complete popular democracy.

THE PEOPLE AGAINST THE GOVERNMENT

Demonstrations demanding student power at the University of Nanterre climaxed in the arrest of protest leaders on March 22, 1968. Students fought back by seizing university buildings. The government then closed the institution. This action incited revolt in other universities. In mid-May, police violence against the students created a wave of public sympathy for the rebels and hostility toward the government. Workers joined the revolt. On May 13, a general strike created an extreme crisis that appeared to endanger the existence of the Fifth Republic.

DE GAULLE AGAINST THE "COMMUNISTS"

De Gaulle kept the support of the military. A successful revolution would have been difficult to achieve. De Gaulle needed to win back his following among the citizens, however, in order to ensure the survival of the established system. On May 30, he appealed to the people in a television address that depicted the student and worker rebels as "communists." The president claimed that France could choose either communism or Gaullism. France chose de Gaulle.

Soon after the crisis, public attitudes changed. De Gaulle's authoritarian methods caused him to lose support both within his party and among the citizens. De Gaulle wanted maximum executive authority but not dictatorship; he resigned in 1969. French leaders responded to the revolt by granting moderately increased student influence in the universities and somewhat greater authority for workers in the factories.

A "Prague Spring"— Czechoslovakia's Liberation Movement

The early months of 1968 witnessed even more startling events in Prague, Czechoslovakia, than in France. During this "Prague Spring," the Communist leaders of Czechoslovakia started an anti-Stalinist "thaw" that soon became a reform movement with the power to destroy the Communist state.

DUBČEK'S LIBERAL THAW

Soviet Stalinists accepted the communist principle of economic equality and practiced it moderately well. They rejected the liberal ideal of individual rights. A society, however, could promote both equal wealth and personal liberty, in effect blending communist economic ideas with liberal political and cultural principles. Khrushchev's reforms liberalized Soviet political and cultural life to a very limited extent. In Czechoslovakia, Alexander Dubček (b. 1921) carried this process of liberalizing communism much further.

In the early 1960s, Dubček emerged as a reformist leader of the Slovak branch of the nation's Communist Party. He assumed control of the Czechoslovak organization in December 1967. In the following March, Ludvik Svoboda replaced Antonín Novotný as Czech president. Svoboda supported Dubček's liberal communist reform movement. These leaders ended government censorship, reduced the power of the security police, began to operate the Communist Party democratically, and offered the Czechs the right to form noncommunist political parties.

SOVIET INVASION—RETURN OF THE COMMUNIST WINTER

Soviet leaders watched Dubček and his sweeping reform effort very carefully. They assumed that this process of liberalization would lead to Czech withdrawal from the Warsaw Pact. Dubček pledged loyalty to the Soviet alliance but Soviet leaders refused to believe him.

On August 20, 1968, Soviet troops invaded Czechoslovakia in force. All the Communist states of East Europe except Romania supported this suppression of Dubček's "socialism with a human face." The Soviets removed Dubček as Czech party leader, but they did not execute him as they had Nagy in Hungary in 1956. For the next twenty years, the Czechs had to live without the liberal changes they had briefly enjoyed during the Prague Spring.

STAGNATION IN THE SOVIET UNION, 1968–1985

During the Czechoslovak crisis, Communist officials in Moscow publicly declared their intention to send troops to rescue any Warsaw Pact government whenever liberals such as Dubček threatened to establish capitalism. This policy, later known as the "Brezhnev Doctrine," meant that the moderate Stalinists who ruled Soviet Russia planned to preserve governments in East Europe that did not differ too much from their own.

This attempt to stop the liberalization of communism prevented all but minor changes in the governments of Soviet Russia and most East European states until the late 1980s. The sudden collapse of these systems between 1989 and 1991 indicated that the result of this conservative Soviet policy was stagnation rather than preservation.

Leonid Brezhnev's Ascendancy

From 1964 until 1971, a small group of Communist Party officials held executive authority in the Soviet Union. Leonid Brezhnev (1906–1982), Alexei Kosygin, and Mikhail Suslov emerged as the chief figures within the ruling group and appeared to share power equally. They emphatically proclaimed their commitment to this arrangement as a matter of principle, Lenin's idea of "collective leadership." At the Party Congress in 1971, it became evident that Brezhnev had risen to supremacy over the other "collective leaders." Like Khrushchev, however, Brezhnev could stay in power only if he kept the support of other top Communists.

THE STRUGGLE TO REFORM THE ECONOMY

The Brezhnev administration continued the effort to provide more consumer goods but without great success. The state also significantly increased spending on agriculture; yet in this area too little improvement in productivity followed. The attempt to reduce the emphasis on heavy industry was hampered by continued high spending on military and defense programs. Since the Soviet Union could not yet afford both "guns and butter," the consumer economy inevitably suffered. But the sacrifices gave the Soviet leaders what they apparently thought they had to have—military power approximately equal to that of the United States by the mid-1970s.

THE AUTHORITARIAN SYSTEM UNDER BREZHNEV

Khrushchev had attempted to drive the economy forward in part by moderately decreasing central authority over the productive system. Brezhnev indicated that he too wanted to modify the extremely centralized "command economy" developed by Stalin. His policies, however, gave the authorities in Moscow more economic control than they had when Khrushchev left office.

Brezhnev also gradually brought the ruling bureaucracies under his personal command. By the mid-1970s, he had developed a political machine of loyal followers that appeared to give him greater power in party, government, and military affairs than Khrushchev had possessed. Brezhnev maintained this position by giving his favorites, especially men from his home district, secure and highly rewarding positions in the bureaucracy. This method of rule made Brezhnev a personal dictator but without completely nullifying the spirit of collective leadership. It also perpetuated a very top-heavy bureaucratic system controlled by a virtually permanent and ever less effective elite.

Brezhnev and the Soviet Decline

Soviet leaders in the late 1980s viewed the Brezhnev years as a time of stagnation, especially economically. Industrial productivity and the quality of goods seriously declined. Even worse, a mismanaged farm system kept the nation always on the brink of an agricultural crisis. Crop failures forced the government to import huge quantities of grain in 1972 and 1975.

THE FAILURE OF LEADERSHIP

By the latter 1970s, Brezhnev's health was rapidly failing. This physical deterioration seriously diminished his ability to govern. Yet he clung to all his offices and powers. All the other aging bureaucrats that Brezhnev had raised to high positions followed his example. They kept their jobs and privileges and did almost nothing to solve the nation's potentially disastrous problems.

THE ANDROPOV INTERIM

Yuri Andropov led the USSR from Brezhnev's death in November 1982 until his own death in February 1984. He died after many months of ill health that hampered his struggles to reform the economy and end corruption.

THE LAST STALINIST RULER OF THE SOVIET UNION

A much less reform-minded figure, Konstantin Chernenko, became Soviet leader in February 1984. After just over a year of governance, in the moderate Stalinist style of Brezhnev, Chernenko died in March 1985.

STABILITY IN WEST EUROPE, 1968–1992

West Europeans encountered more social and economic problems after 1968 than they had in the previous two decades. Despite these increased difficulties, West Europeans continued to enjoy life in stable, progressive, and prosperous societies with effective democratic governments. Furthermore, in the mid-1970s, democracy finally emerged in Portugal and Spain.

The Struggle for Unity and Prosperity

The movement to unify the West European nations made notable progress in the economic sphere during the 1960s. From the early 1970s to the mid-1980s, this process of integration virtually stopped. Harder times encouraged governments to pursue policies of national self-interest rather than programs related to European unity.

OPEC AND THE EUROPEAN ECONOMIC SLUMP

Until the early 1970s, West European governments succeeded remarkably well in bringing prosperity through intervention in the economy and the establishment of extensive programs to promote employment and economic security. But during the early 1970s, the "economic miracle" stopped. Material progress slowed and became more difficult to achieve. This recession came in part as a result of action in 1973 by the Organization of Petroleum Exporting Countries (OPEC). This association of mostly Middle Eastern nations blocked oil exportation to some European countries. As a result of this petroleum embargo, the prices of goods in West Europe rose sharply. Despite this and other problems, the economic picture brightened a great deal by the 1980s.

THE EUROPEAN COMMUNITY

The economies of the countries in the European Economic Community (EEC) grew with unusual rapidity in the 1960s. This success attracted other European nations to this thriving group. Britain, Ireland, and Denmark entered the EEC in 1973, Greece gained admission in 1981, then Spain and Portugal became members in 1986. By this time, the organization had become known informally as the European Community (EC).

In the early years of the EC, its leaders established an administrative structure that they hoped would evolve into a European government. These institutions included the European Parliament, the Court of Europe, and two executive agencies—the Commission and the Council of Ministers. Despite the existence of this framework, by the mid-1980s, the EC had achieved only partial economic integration and almost no political unity.

THE SINGLE EUROPE ACT

During the thirty years after its founding in 1957, the twelve EC members had tied themselves more closely together economically by removing a major barrier to trade. They had arranged for producers in each member state to be able to transport goods to markets in the other eleven without paying entry taxes (customs duties). But hundreds of national regulations, such as differing product safety standards, still prevented the free flow of trade. The EC had become a customs union, but it remained divided into twelve national markets.

In 1985, the EC devised a concrete plan to remove all trade barriers and form a single market by January 1, 1993. Community members then signed the Single Europe Act (1986), an agreement that made it easier to change all the national regulations that blocked the movement of commerce within the EC.

Advancement toward both political and economic unity became surprisingly rapid by 1990. Whether realistic or not, a particularly grand vision of the possibilities for union was revealed at an EC summit in late April 1990. At this meeting, the twelve EC members declared their intention to achieve political as well as economic integration by January 1993.

West Germany—a Policy of Reconciliation

Willy Brandt (1913–1992) assumed office as the first Socialist chancellor of West Germany in 1969. His administration demonstrated that national leaders as well as international organizations can bring European states closer together, even when these nations are in opposing superpower spheres.

On a trip to Poland in December 1970, Brandt visited the memorial to the 400,000 Jews who died in the Warsaw Ghetto during the Second World War. In an apparently spontaneous action, the chancellor knelt on the wet stones in front of the monument and cried. Brandt's behavior in Warsaw reflected the attitudes that shaped his policies as chancellor.

As the leader of the nation that spawned Nazism and now stood at the center of the cold-war battle zone, Brandt felt a special obligation to help heal the wounds suffered by nations that Germany had attacked. The chancellor's diplomatic initiatives resulted in great progress toward harmony between West Germany and most East European states.

BRANDT'S *OSTPOLITIK*

Brandt devoted his strongest efforts in foreign affairs to the improvement of relations with the German Democratic Republic (East Germany), Poland, and Soviet Russia. In pursuit of this *Ostpolitik* (Eastern Policy), Brandt decided to reverse West Germany's previous stand and accept the boundaries of East Germany and Poland that the Soviets had established in 1945.

The chancellor signed treaties with the USSR (January 1970) and Poland (December 1970) formally expressing the new border policy. These agreements meant that West Germany for the first time accepted the Elbe as its eastern boundary and approved the loss of German territory to Poland. Brandt's *Ostpolitik* accomplished more than greater harmony between the Federal Republic and these two eastern neighbors. In the treaty with Poland, for example, German nationals left behind Polish borders by the 1945 boundary changes won the right to move to one of the Germanys.

In 1972, Brandt completed a treaty settling differences with East Germany. Again, the agreement not only reduced tensions between the states but also involved arrangements that helped ordinary German citizens. This treaty gave West Berliners at least limited opportunities to visit family members in East Berlin. All such movement had been stopped by the Berlin Wall in 1961. Before Brandt left office in 1974, he established better diplomatic relations with almost all East European countries as he had with Soviet Russia, Poland, and East Germany.

THE GERMAN SOCIALIST REFORM PROGRAM

German Socialists encouraged greater harmony within the Federal Republic as well as abroad. In 1959, Brandt's party made a public commitment toward achieving social justice through reform rather than revolution. This change in policy brought the Socialist Party closer to the position of the Christian Democrats and reduced the conflicts between these leading political groups.

Despite this adjustment in Socialist philosophy, Chancellor Brandt's extensive social reform plan encountered stiff resistance. He proposed an expansion of women's rights, fewer restrictions on abortion, and increased government spending on welfare and education. Brandt also called for labor to have as many representatives as management on corporate boards.

Conservative opposition and an economic slump that reduced government income prevented the implementation of the full reform program. Yet Brandt succeeded in building a stronger welfare state structure in Germany. Helmut Schmidt (b. 1918), Socialist chancellor from 1974 to 1982, eventually won passage of the Brandt measure that had provoked the strongest opposition, the law giving labor an equal voice in corporate policy-making. Schmidt had little interest in other social reforms. He concentrated instead on keeping West Germany economically stable during and after the recession of the early 1970s.

THE KOHL ERA

In 1982, the Christian Democrats returned to power under the leadership of chancellor Helmut Kohl (b. 1930). Schmidt had stopped the drive begun by Brandt to develop a more extensive welfare state system. Kohl implemented a moderate reduction of such government programs. The spending cut enabled the chancellor to reduce taxes.

In a decade when the West European economy remained sluggish, the Christian Democrats' conservative policies stimulated an expansion of private enterprise and strengthened the nation's financial condition. Asian competitors continued to cut into international markets previously dominated by West Germany, but Kohl's program enabled his nation to remain the largest exporter of goods in the world.

Laborers benefited also from the country's relatively great economic strength. They enjoyed a workweek under forty hours and more vacation time than the West European average of five weeks per year. West Germany did pay a price for this conservative method of dealing with the economic conditions of the 1980s—growing unemployment.

EXTREMISTS—LEFT, RIGHT, AND GREEN

From the late 1960s to the early 1990s, West Germany's stable political system and sound economy kept most of the nation unified and loyal to the government. Small opposition groups, however, continued their struggle for drastic change in the republic. The Baader-Meinhof gang, for example, expressed its radical leftist hostility to the established order by periodic acts of terror. Right-wing extremism also occasionally strengthened enough to increase support for parties or terrorist groups with Nazi tendencies.

The Green Party, the most important movement of dissent in West Germany, emerged as a formal organization in 1980 under the leadership of Petra Kelly (1948–1992). Kelly's group took a very strong stand for environmental action and against nuclear power plants and weapons. Although a faction in this new party considered the existing political system so corrupt that they would not participate in the West German government, others campaigned for office.

In 1983, the Greens won enough votes to send Kelly and twenty-six other members of her party to the parliament. The movement gained fifteen more seats in 1987. Three years later, however, the Greens failed to win the five percent minimum popular vote required for representation and lost all their seats in the legislature. The weakness of the antiestablishment Left, Right, and Green factions indicated the unity that had become typical of West German society by the end of the 1980s.

Sustaining Welfare-State Democracy

The West European democracies varied considerably in the extent to which they nationalized their economies after the Second World War. For example, governments in Sweden and the Federal Republic of Germany took over almost no enterprises at all, Italy and Britain nationalized many more, and France socialized more businesses than the other four (about twelve percent by the 1970s).

In 1981, France elected a Socialist president, François Mitterrand. He intended to socialize an additional five percent of the French economy, but he soon dropped this plan. As he governed the country during the 1980s, Mitterrand followed economic policies that differed little from those of European centrists such as the Christian Democrats. Mitterrand's shift to more conservative practices was typical of the Left in other democracies in the mid-1980s.

The democratic states of West Europe exhibited even more similarities in other economic policies. All of them except Britain engaged in long-term planning. Until the 1980s, the democracies other than Britain also intervened very actively in their own economies to maintain full employment and prosperity. Central control policies became less popular everywhere in the 1980s. All these states, including Britain, developed extensive welfare state programs after 1945. They continued these social aid systems thereafter, but several governments began to reduce welfare funding by the 1980s. The pattern of events in Italy after 1968 illustrates these general trends in most of the West European welfare states.

THE MODERATION AND POPULARITY OF THE ITALIAN LEFT

The political Left appealed strongly to Italian voters throughout the 1970s and 1980s. During the first of these decades, the Communist Party won control of many city governments and secured numerous seats in the parliament. The popularity of the Socialist Party then rose sharply in the 1980s, as the following of the Communists declined. Both these Left groups gained this wide support in part by rejecting their traditional commitment to revolution. By the early 1980s, the Socialists even declared their opposition to the nationalization of more enterprises. The Communists made an equally drastic transition and ended their opposition to Catholicism and NATO.

THE ITALIAN CENTER AND MODERATE LEFT IN CHARGE

Even though the Left parties learned to endear themselves to Italians, no Communist led the government during this period. Bettino Craxi was the only socialist premier (1983 to 1987). The inability of the Socialists and Communists to join forces enabled the centrist Christian Democrats to hold the chief executive position most of the time. Since all the premiers had to govern through a coalition of parties (usually five factions), these Center and moderate Left leaders found it difficult to carry out their responsibilities.

ITALY'S IMMOBILE GOVERNMENT AND SOCIAL PROBLEMS

The immobilizing effect of coalition politics caused the Italian government of the latter 1900s to earn a reputation for "muddling through" when problems developed, as they frequently did after 1968. In the early 1970s, recession struck. The social turmoil that began in the mid-1960s persisted throughout the following decade. These disruptions included terrorism by the Red Brigades, a leftist group that assassinated former premier Aldo Moro in 1978. The government also struggled during the 1970s and 1980s with the seemingly insoluble problems of Mafia violence and the economic backwardness of southern Italy.

THE CONTINUED SUCCESS OF THE ITALIAN WELFARE STATE

Through these sometimes troubled years, much also happened that pleased the great majority of Italians. The government reduced a few social assistance programs but largely maintained the welfare state system. Italian legislators also passed widely approved divorce and abortion rights laws, despite the opposition of the Catholic hierarchy.

Most impressive of all, the Italian economy grew at a record pace in the 1980s. By the early 1990s, Italy's industrial system produced more than Britain's and only slightly less than France's. Italy had joined the ranks of global economic leaders. This remarkable achievement resulted in part from the government's decision to turn somewhat more toward a market-oriented private enterprise system.

Attacking the Welfare State in Britain

From Italy to Scandinavia, the continental democracies had even more in common in 1992 than in 1968. They all had planned but not rigidly controlled economies, relatively few nationalized industries, and very complete but no longer expanding welfare programs. These states also appeared to have a gradually weakening commitment to their welfare state philosophies. In Britain, this shift away from government aid programs was much stronger than on the continent.

A LABOUR GOVERNMENT WITH CONSERVATIVE POLICIES

In the latter 1960s, Britain's aging industrial economy continued to lag behind the systems of the continental democracies. The Labour government of prime minister Harold Wilson (b. 1916) that took office in 1964 dealt with the nation's economic problems in a surprising way. Despite Labour's socialist philosophy, Wilson enacted measures usually viewed as favorable to the rich rather than the poor. The government reduced taxes, deflated the currency, and lowered spending on welfare. These actions brought a slight improvement in the economy by 1969. That same year, the Conservatives won the parliamentary elections.

CIVIL VIOLENCE IN NORTHERN IRELAND

Edward Heath (b. 1916), the new Conservative prime minister, faced a serious crisis during his first year in office. In 1969, violent battles erupted between Northern Ireland's Catholics and Protestants. Heath sent troops into Ulster, the portion of Ireland that remains united with Britain, but the civil conflict continued. At the end of 1992, it still had not ended.

A CONSERVATIVE GOVERNMENT AT WAR WITH THE UNIONS

Heath's effort to ease Britain's economic woes produced other social disruptions. His government attempted to restore economic health by a campaign against the higher wages and other concessions demanded by labor unions. The workers responded with a wave of strikes, some of which Heath settled by agreeing to sharp increases in wages. The inflation rate shot upward as a result of these developments.

In this atmosphere of worsening social and economic conditions, the Labour Party returned to power in 1974. Wilson resumed office as prime minister until 1976, when James Callaghan replaced him. Both these socialist leaders continued to follow conservative economic policies, as Wilson had in the late 1960s. Their methods failed. Prices went higher and more people lost jobs. In 1979, Labour lost control of Parliament.

Margaret Thatcher's Militant Conservatism

Margaret Thatcher (b. 1925) led the Conservatives to victory in 1979 with a campaign for fewer public enterprises, less government economic intervention, a smaller government bureaucracy, reduced welfare programs, and lower prices. During Thatcher's first years as prime minister, she concentrated on the problem of inflated prices.

THE BATTLE AGAINST INFLATION

The Conservative administration attempted to deflate the economy by raising interest rates and reducing government spending on health, education, and housing. Thatcher also cut taxes on the rich, began selling government enterprises to private investors, and encouraged business leaders to resist demands for higher pay. Prices began to drop, as the prime minister intended. But the policies also caused unemployment to rocket upward, from just over five percent in 1979 to more than twelve percent in 1982. Thatcher's popularity dropped sharply.

THE FALKLANDS WAR

One of the small remnants of the British Empire was a small group of islands, the Falklands, about 450 miles from the coast of Argentina. In April 1982, Argentine forces landed on the islands in an attempt to end the reign of Britain over this territory and its 2,000 inhabitants. Thatcher dispatched the British navy to prevent the loss of the Falklands. After a two-month war, Argentina accepted defeat. The British prime minister's support among her citizens increased dramatically. In 1983, Thatcher's party beat Labour decisively in the Parliamentary elections. Thereafter, the prime minister continued her war at home, on the welfare state.

THE WELFARE STATE UNDER SIEGE

For several years after the Falklands War, Thatcher kept strong voter support because her conservative policies seemed to bring economic progress. The prime minister's popularity gave her a long term in office that enabled her to continue to reduce the scope of government enterprise ownership and welfare assistance. The problem of inflation struck again, however, by the late 1980s. A high unemployment rate persisted also. As Britain's problems increased, Thatcher's public and party support slipped rapidly. In 1990, the Conservatives selected John Major (b. 1943) to replace the prime minister. The assault on the welfare state subsided with its structure diminished but intact.

GORBACHEV'S "REVOLUTION FROM THE TOP," 1985–1989

Mikhail Gorbachev took command of the USSR in March 1985. This vigorous and relatively young leader soon brought numerous associates who shared his commitment to reform into the administration. Gorbachev's approach to change was pragmatic—very flexible responses to developing conditions. As he set about these tasks, Gorbachev made clear his especially strong concern about the economy. He emphasized the problems of poor labor habits and bad management caused by the Stalinist command economy system. Gorbachev promised revolutionary change that would end the extreme centralization of economic power.

The Chernobyl Disaster

The monetary and human costs of poor management were underscored when procedural errors led to a nuclear power plant disaster at Chernobyl in April 1986. Less dramatic but still vivid evidence of such problems were the declining quantity and continued poor quality of many consumer goods.

Perestroika and Glasnost

Gorbachev addressed such problems by launching a program of *perestroika* or "restructuring" aimed at a drastic reshaping of the economy. In order to make the need for sweeping and possibly painful reform evident and acceptable, the new leader also established a policy of *glasnost* ("openness"). This governmental change meant that the public media and eventually the citizenry in general would be allowed much greater freedom to describe and criticize conditions and events in the USSR.

THE LAW ON STATE ENTERPRISES

One of the most important concrete steps of *perestroika* was passage of the Law on State Enterprises (April 1987). This act indicated that GOSPLAN, the state planning agency, would no longer rigidly control state industries and other corporations. The decentralization program did not bring much change to the economy, but more substantial change was to occur in the political system.

DEMOCRATIZATION

In early 1988, Gorbachev launched a vigorous campaign to give ordinary citizens an active role in local government and in the workplace. His administration also advanced plans for a new parliament that would enable the masses to have a voice at the national level. The citizens exercised a significant degree of free voting power as they elected the first Congress of People's Deputies in 1989.

This parliamentary reform brought a partial shift of ruling power away from the Communist Party, where it had centered most of the time since 1917. Then in March 1990, on the recommendation of the Communist Party, the Congress of People's Deputies voted to end the one-party system and allow multiple political parties to emerge. With this change, democratization began to have real meaning in the USSR.

THE MODERATION OF THE COLD WAR IN THE 1970s

In the late 1960s, the United States and Soviet Russia faced the possibility of the rapid destruction of their societies in a nuclear attack, a new prospect for America and an incomparably frightening danger for both nations. A new sense of urgency began to affect the policy of arms control in America and the Soviet Union.

The First Arms Control Agreement

By 1967, the United States knew that Soviet Russia was building an antiballistic missile system (ABM) to protect Moscow. The development of such weapons threatened to provoke a rapid escalation of the arms race. U.S. president Lyndon Johnson called for talks on ABM development. He also urged discussion of nuclear proliferation since the Americans and Soviets had begun to fear the spread of this military technology to nations with radically aggressive leaders.

THE GLASSBORO SUMMIT

A Soviet-American summit at Glassboro, New Jersey, in June 1967 resulted in improved personal relations between Johnson and Brezhnev. The meeting failed, however, to bring progress toward arms control. Soon after the summit, the United States began work on an ABM program of its own.

THE NON-PROLIFERATION TREATY

The drive to limit main-force nuclear weapons continued. In July 1967, the United States, Soviet Russia, and Britain adopted the Nuclear Non-Proliferation Treaty. Eventually, more than 100 nations signed this agreement to prevent the spread of nuclear weapons to nations that did not already have them. The completion of this treaty accelerated the movement toward negotiations on offensive and defensive weapons limitation.

Détente

In the late 1960s, the Brezhnev administration worked for improved relations with the United States and the other Western powers. Soviet leaders wanted to end the dangerously threatening cold war confrontation and begin an era of peaceful competition or *détente*. The near equality in nuclear strength that the Soviets had achieved by 1969 made them feel safe enough to pursue this policy of *détente*.

Soviet Russia needed *détente* in order to develop active trading relations with the West and thereby ease serious economic problems in the Communist state. The chances for a productive *détente* improved when the new U.S. president, Richard Nixon, took office in 1969. Prospects brightened because he wanted such relations. Furthermore, his reputation as a cold war hard-liner enabled Nixon to begin such a venture with little fear of political damage from his country's right-wing political forces. With both superpowers in favor of *détente,* the discussion of arms limitations that began during the Johnson administration became an official negotiating process.

THE STRATEGIC ARMS LIMITATION TALKS (SALT)

The Strategic Arms Limitation Talks (SALT) between the Soviets and Americans opened in 1969. After three years of difficult negotiation, the superpowers finally concluded their first limitation treaty, known as SALT I.

THE SALT AGREEMENTS

In 1972, SALT I established an upper limit on antiballistic missile systems and on the number of intercontinental nuclear rockets that each nation could have. It did not, however, establish controls on the number of warheads that could be placed on each ICBM. As a result of this loophole, during the 1970s both sides vastly multiplied the number of warheads that they could deliver to targets in the other country. The SALT II agreement, signed in 1979, corrected this problem but still allowed the arms race to continue at a slower rate.

THE HELSINKI ACCORDS

The cold war thaw of the 1970s brought the superpowers together for the first arms control agreements. This changed international atmosphere also inspired a grander peacemaking effort. In 1973, representatives from Canada, the United States, and every European state except Albania began to meet in Helsinki, Finland, to discuss a multitude of issues affecting Europe in the cold war era. This Conference on Security and Cooperation in Europe (CSCE) completed its work and signed a 30,000-word Final Act in August 1975.

The agreements in the Final Act, known informally as the Helsinki Accords, committed the thirty-five participating countries to acceptance of existing national borders in Europe. Since the only significant boundary disputes involved changes made by the Soviets during the Second World War, this accord was an important concession to them. This agreement on frontiers was especially significant since it approximated a Second World War peace treaty.

Several provisions of the Final Act pleased the Western nations almost as much as the boundary provisions did the Soviets. The accords included a pledge that CSCE members would not intervene in the affairs of other countries. This provision implied a condemnation of Soviet actions in Hungary and Czechoslovakia. An entire section of human rights accords similarly suggested criticism of the USSR. It affirmed individual freedoms that the Soviets regularly violated.

Western critics of the accords claimed that these idealistic statements about nonintervention and human rights meant nothing, since the CSCE had no way to enforce these standards. Dissenters in Communist nations, however, gave these human rights clauses substance by using them to judge the conduct of their governments. When Communist officials denied the personal freedoms they had sworn to allow, their critics ("dissidents") informed the world about these violations. Global public reactions to these exposures probably reduced the severity of life in the dictatorships.

The Continuing Arms Race

Although the Helsinki Accords indicated reduced East-West tensions and the SALT agreements moderated the arms race, the superpowers' stockpiles of weapons grew throughout the 1970s and 1980s. As a result of this arms race, in 1982 the U.S. had 2,032 bombers and missiles carrying 11,000 warheads. The Soviets had 2,490 rockets and long-range planes with the ability to deliver 8,000 warheads. Despite the differences in these arsenals, by the mid-1980s, the superpowers were in a state of "rough equivalency" in nuclear war fighting strength. The balance changed little after that time. This continuing arms race made *détente* difficult to maintain.

The End of Détente

An ever-present risk of nuclear holocaust kept the foundations of the Soviet-American *détente* weak. Brezhnev's actions in 1979 completely wrecked this fragile structure.

THE SOVIET INVASION OF AFGHANISTAN

In the late 1970s, conditions on the southern borders of the USSR confronted Soviet leaders with both grand opportunities and potentially serious problems. They gained an ally in the region when a Communist government took power in Afghanistan in 1978. This change gave the Soviets a chance to extend their influence toward the Persian Gulf, an oil-rich and strategically located region. Unfortunately for the USSR, anti-Communist rebels threatened to overthrow the pro-Soviet leaders in Afghanistan. When the Soviets sent in advisers to help the struggling Communist government, Afghans often violently attacked them.

The collapse of a strongly pro-Western dictatorship in Iran in early 1979 increased the prospects for the Soviets to gain a strategic advantage in the region near the Persian Gulf. Once more, however, a new problem also appeared. A revolutionary Islamic group had won control of Iran. This development heightened the possibility of independence movements among the millions of Islamic people in nearby Soviet republics. The combination of opportunities and dangers along the southwestern border perhaps encouraged the drastic action taken by the Brezhnev administration in late 1979.

When a rebel Communist faction overthrew the pro-Soviet leader of Afghanistan in December 1979, a Soviet army of more than 110,000 invaded. Soviet forces killed the new Afghan leader and replaced him with a more dependable Communist. Anti-Communist Afghans rose to challenge both the Soviet military and the government it established. Almost ten years of fierce guerrilla warfare ensued, a struggle that killed about 20,000 Soviet soldiers and ten percent of the people of Afghanistan.

The invaders left in early 1989 with the guerrillas in control of almost the entire country. A decade of death and destruction had benefited neither the Soviets nor the Afghans. Soviet intervention also brought the condemnation of a multitude of nations, from China to the United States, and drove the superpowers from *détente* to cold war crisis.

THE EUROMISSILE CRISIS

Another important step in the escalation of the cold war occurred in 1979. The Soviets deployed a deadly new intermediate-range mobile missile (the SS-20) in East Europe. The special threat the SS-20 posed to Western forces led NATO to decide to place even more lethal American weapons in Europe—the Pershing II and Cruise missiles. These "Euromissiles" that the United States began to deploy in December 1983 gave NATO the ability to strike with extreme accuracy and little warning almost anywhere in the western USSR.

The new Soviet and American intermediate-range missiles and the very belligerent attitudes of both superpower leaders after the election of President Ronald Reagan (1980) brought the cold war to its most dangerous level since the Cuban missile crisis. This crisis atmosphere lasted until Gorbachev began a drastic alteration of Soviet policies after he entered office in 1985.

Gorbachev's "New Thinking" in Foreign Affairs

Mikhail Gorbachev carried out sweeping changes in military and international affairs. Perhaps Gorbachev began this "new thinking," as he described it, because it was clear that to salvage the Soviet economic and political systems, the costs of military and foreign commitments had to be cut. Gorbachev made revolutionary policy changes. He ended the long-standing isolation of the USSR and the tradition of insisting that the Soviets alone had the correct idea of what constituted international relations. Gorbachev even dropped the Marxist notion of class conflict in global affairs and began to emphasize "common human interests."

Gorbachev's new thinking also led to other drastic changes. His administration lifted barriers that had prevented Jews from moving to other countries, ended the Soviet role in the Afghanistan war, and in December 1987 agreed with the U.S. to do away with all intermediate range nuclear weapons in Europe. Work continued on efforts to negotiate cuts in long-range nuclear missiles and to arrange reductions of conventional military forces in Europe. By 1991, these discussions produced agreements to reduce long-range weapons by thirty percent and to remove superpower armies from Central Europe.

ULTRAMODERN EUROPE'S FIRST YEARS

The traits of an ultramodern Europe emerged very gradually during the 1900s. These characteristics included a high-technology economy instead of a heavy industrial system, supranational organizations instead of nation-states, leadership in global economic networks instead of domination over world empires, and welfare-state democracies instead of bourgeois parliamentary or popular authoritarian governments. By the end of the 1980s, these characteristics became widespread enough to consider the recent past to be the first years of ultramodern European history.

1989—the Liberation of East Europe

By the time of the Czech revolt and its suppression in 1968, Brezhnev was firmly in control in the USSR. From that date onward, his policy toward East Europe was generally moderate. That attitude typified his overall foreign policy, in fact, with the important exception of his decision to invade Afghanistan. The Soviets continued to try to integrate the economies of the USSR and East Europe, but the effort generally failed. Increasingly, the East Europeans, especially Poland and Hungary, went their own way—toward more economic ties with the West and a less socialized economy.

SOLIDARITY'S LEADERSHIP IN THE POLISH INDEPENDENCE MOVEMENT

More dramatic sociopolitical action eventually followed quiet economic change, especially in Poland, where an independent labor movement (Solidarity) led the way with demonstrations and strikes. The Polish government fought back. It outlawed Solidarity, jailed leaders such as Lech Walesa, and declared martial law. Still, the Soviet-backed Polish government proved unable to rule effectively and in early 1989 yielded control to Solidarity and other opposition forces. A non-Communist government then took charge, the first such change in East Europe since the late 1940s.

NOVEMBER 9, 1989

An incredible sequence of events followed as one by one the Communist governments ended their monopoly of power in Hungary, East Germany, Bulgaria, Czechoslovakia, and Romania. In all these nations, non-Communist governments took over. Most of these states also moved toward genuine multiple-party democratic systems and some form of market economy. These five Communist systems all collapsed between early November and late December 1989. The beginning of this revolution came with breathtaking suddenness on November 9, 1989, with the opening of the Berlin Wall. The dancing on top of this structure, which a few months earlier would have brought instant death, proved to be a fitting symbol of the transformation that had come to East Europe, a change that would not have occurred this soon if the Soviets had not decided to release their grip on the region.

1991—the Collapse of the Soviet Union

Gorbachev's reform program indicated that he intended to guide the Soviet people through a gradual transition to democratic socialism. He failed to realize this dream of creating and preserving a democratic and socialist Soviet Union.

THE FAILURE OF ECONOMIC RESTRUCTURING

The policy of *perestroika* yielded greatly increased personal liberty for the Soviet people. From the spring of 1987 on, citizens enjoyed virtually complete freedom to express themselves informally, in the public media, and in the arts. Gorbachev also led in the establishment of a structure for democratic government. He found it impossible, however, to replace the dictatorial system of economic controls with a market-sensitive productive apparatus compatible with political democracy. Gorbachev could order freer expression and government practices; he could not order a Stalinist economy to operate differently. This economic failure virtually ensured that the national minorities would tear the union apart.

THE NATIONALITIES AT WAR WITH THE CENTER

The more than 100 national groups that formed the Soviet Union migrated and mixed throughout modern Russian and Soviet history. Even so, in the late 1900s, the USSR remained divided into territorial units, each of which contained a different dominant nationality. The Soviet state was organized into fifteen Union republics, one for each of the largest national groups. Smaller nationalities had territorial subdivisions within the fifteen republics.

In both the Tsarist and Soviet eras, the Great Russian nationality and the Russian Republic dominated all others. Russia before 1917, the Soviet Union after 1917, and East Europe after 1945 were really Russian empires. The Gorbachev administration decided to release the Soviet Russian imperial territories in East Europe. Many of the Soviet Union republics, especially Estonia, Latvia, and Lithuania, wanted independence as desperately as had the East Europeans. The liberation of East Europe inspired these republics to struggle harder for liberation from "the center," from Moscow and the Russians.

A thriving Soviet economy that benefited the national minorities might have encouraged loyalty to the union. Tsarist and Soviet governments alike, however, had not only controlled the economy from the center but also had applied policies that caused the national minorities to feel economically exploited. The miserable economic failure of the Brezhnev administration and the inability of the Gorbachev government to reform the system left the republics with the prospect of evolving from exploitation to ruin. They chose independence.

AUGUST 19, 1991—THE ANTIREFORM COUP

Gorbachev resisted the dissolution of the Union. He threatened military force against any republics that attempted secession except through very gradual procedures that he specified. Either Gorbachev or other more hard-line leaders used small-scale military actions to suppress nationalists in the Baltic republics and the Georgian republic. Liberation movements simply grew stronger. Finally, Gorbachev offered the republics a treaty that would allow them autonomy within a union held together mostly by economic interdependence.

On August 19, 1991, the day before the scheduled signing of the new union treaty, eight leading members of the Soviet government placed Gorbachev under arrest. These Communist officials intended to reverse the process of political and cultural liberalization and, above all, to stop the breakup of the union.

A DEMOCRATIC COUNTERCOUP

The borders of the Russian Republic encompassed about seventy-five percent of Soviet territory and more than fifty percent of the country's population in 1991. In the most democratic large-scale election in Russian or Soviet history, this republic had chosen Boris Yeltsin as its president in June 1991.

Yeltsin risked his life to lead the resistance to the antireform coup. The Russian Republic's parliament and thousands of Russians in Moscow, Leningrad, and other Russian cities joined in the opposition to the coup. The leaders of several other republics then publicly denounced the rebels who had seized Gorbachev. When important military and security police units refused to support the eight rebel leaders, their revolt collapsed. Gorbachev resumed control of the Soviet Union on August 21.

THE FINAL DAYS OF THE FIRST COMMUNIST STATE

The coup leaders intended to restore a more dictatorial form of communism and prevent the fragmentation of the union. Their attempted revolt and its failure made the survival of the Communist Party and the Soviet state impossible. The end came quickly.

Yeltsin had support among the 150,000,000 people in the Russian Republic before the coup. His success against the antidemocratic rebels strengthened his following among these people. Yeltsin used this increased power immediately. He decreed an end to Communist Party and secret police (KGB) activity in the Russian Republic. Soon, Yeltsin took control of the Soviet military forces, organizations, and offices within his republic. He also committed the Russian Republic to sweeping economic reforms that would lead to market systems similar to those in West Europe. In effect, these steps created a new Russian state comprising three-fourths of the territory and about one-half of the people of the former Soviet Union.

Gorbachev struggled to save the Communist Party by converting it to a fully democratic organization. It collapsed anyway, as Yeltsin and the leaders of other republics banned its activities. Gorbachev also tried to keep the Union intact, at least as a single economic system. This effort failed too. With the Soviet government tottering on the brink of bankruptcy and the state's production and supply apparatus rapidly failing, a centralized system could offer the republics virtually nothing economically except disaster.

Politically, the Soviet state had never appealed to many of the people in the fifteen Union republics. The three Baltic republics left the Union before and during the coup. By early December 1991, the other twelve republics informed Gorbachev that they would not sign a unification treaty. Within a few days thereafter, eleven of the twelve republics that had belonged to the USSR since the 1920s formed a new Commonwealth of Independent States. The republic of Georgia refused to join this association of sovereign states. On December 26, 1991, the Congress of People's Deputies dissolved the Union of Soviet Socialist Republics.

1993—Toward European Union or Disintegration?

The Single Europe Act passed by the European Community in 1986 brought rapid movement toward complete economic unity for the twelve EC nations. The act provided for the completion of this process of conversion of the twelve states into a "single market" by January 1, 1993.

THE MAASTRICHT TREATY

In 1990, several EC leaders began to promote an effort to achieve political as well as economic union by 1993. The advocates of fuller union met in the Netherlands in December 1991 to sign the Maastricht Treaty, an agreement providing for the EC to establish a common currency, a central banking system, and a unified foreign and security policy for its twelve member nations. As this movement toward very close integration of the EC states unfolded, other events suggested the chance for an even larger union of European nations.

THE EXPANSION OF THE EUROPEAN COMMUNITY

By late 1989, six Central European countries in practice became fully cooperative economic partners of the EC although they could not influence its decisions. Several other East European nations also had more limited special economic relationships with the EC at that point. The twelve EC nations alone have a population of 320 million people. Other countries now associated with the EC could expand the Community's economic population base to about 500 million.

Should all these ties become economically meaningful, Europe will emerge as a new economic superpower. Political unity might increase at the same time and advance these people toward a long-held dream of a "United States of Europe." But serious barriers to unity remain, the most important of which are deeply rooted national feelings and conflicts.

The continuing power of national divisions became apparent during the autumn of 1992 as the EC nations began to consider ratification of the Maastricht Treaty. Denmark rejected this agreement. France narrowly accepted it. The fate of the treaty remains uncertain in November 1992. Events in Yugoslavia in 1991 and 1992 revealed the still more destructive potential of national and ethnic differences.

A NEW BALKAN POWDER KEG

In mid-1991, the Balkan state of Yugoslavia began to disintegrate. The first serious crisis developed when Slovenia and Croatia, two of six ethnic provinces that made up Yugoslavia, declared independence. The Yugoslav government, under the influence of the ethnic Serbian province, then used military force in an attempt to prevent these secessions. This conflict subsided by 1992, but an even larger war erupted when Serb-led forces fought to keep the province of Bosnia-Herzegovina from leaving the federal state of Yugoslavia.

The members of the European Community and the United States formally recognized the independence of the provinces that separated from Yugoslavia. The EC and the United Nations also attempted to negotiate a settlement that would end the war in the Balkans. By November 1992 these peacemaking efforts had made no significant progress.

Circumstances in the 1990s seemed to pose no threat that these Balkan conflicts would explode into a general European war as they had in 1914. The apparent inability of the European Community to reestablish peace, however, raises doubts about the potential of an integrated continent to stop destructive crises.

The nature of the conflict in the Balkans also indicates the power of ethnic or national forces to pull apart states or larger associations of nations such as the EC. The decision of the Czech Lands and Slovakia to become separate nations, although reached by peaceful means in September 1992, provides another example of the disintegrating forces at work in Europe. Within the former Soviet Union, several other ethnic powder kegs threaten the peace and progress of Europe.

Events during ultramodern Europe's first years provide no clear indication of what to expect for the region as the second millennium ends and the third begins.

After three centuries of gradual development, modern institutions matured in portions of Europe by the late 1700s and early 1800s. The industrial economic order that emerged first in Britain in the latter 1700s had an especially strong influence on the formation of other modern European systems. The industrial economy also vitally affected the interaction of European states and the course of global affairs throughout the 1800s and 1900s.

Politically, modern Europe developed into a region consisting of nation-states that drew the masses into public affairs. These states gained citizen support through the operation of parliamentary democratic or popular authoritarian institutions. Bourgeois social classes or a combined middle class–aristocratic elite with bourgeois values dominated these states. The power provided by modern institutions and practices enabled the Europeans to conquer much of the world beyond their continent.

The European industrial nation-state system and its global imperial structure remained intact until the Second World War. When that conflict erupted, however, a transformation of modern Europe had already begun. The process of change accelerated during the war and continued still more rapidly after 1945, affecting most of West Europe and, in a somewhat hidden way, portions of East Europe. An especially important development was the shift toward a new form of industrial economy, one based on high-technology enterprises rather than heavy industries. Other changes, some even more profound, accompanied this economic transformation.

The nation-state endured as one of the strongest of modern European institutions throughout the latter 1900s. In one of the most drastic adjustments, however, Europeans began to strive for an integration of these states into new "supranational" structures. By the 1960s, the West Europeans made significant progress toward economic unification and took the first hesitant steps toward political union.

An important change also occurred within these nations as Europe became more united. Most states greatly increased government control over their economies and developed welfare systems that ensured the well-being of almost everyone. By the 1980s, European leaders began to reduce government economic authority and assistance programs, but this change did not alter the fundamental character of the postwar welfare state.

The loss of European empires after 1945 opened the way for this new, ultramodern Europe to develop a very different relationship with other regions of the world. Europe gave up its role as imperial master and became a leader in creating a new global financial and trading network that helped draw the world toward greater unity. By the 1990s, it appeared that at the end of an age of European domination of the globe, the societies of the continent had entered a new era of partnership with the people of other nations.

Selected Readings

Caute, David. *The Year of the Barricades*. New York: Harper & Row, 1988.

Colchester, Nicholas, and David Buchan. *Europower: The Essential Guide to Europe's Economic Transformation in 1992*. New York: Times Books, 1990.

Dahrendorf, Ralf. *The Modern Social Contract: An Essay on Politics of Liberty*. New York: Weidenfeld and Nicolson, 1988.

Doder, Dusko, and Louise Branson. *Gorbachev: Heretic in the Kremlin*. New York: Penguin Books, 1991.

Gwertzman, Bernard, and Michael T. Kaufman. *The Collapse of Communism*. New York: Times Books, 1991.

Index